RHETORIC AND THEOLOGY

Departing from the traditional focus on Erasmus as philologist and moralist, *Rhetoric and Theology* shows how Erasmus attempted to interpret Scripture by way of a rhetorical theology that focuses on the figurative, metaphorical quality of language, with a view to moral and theological reform.

Manfred Hoffmann concentrates on the theological sources of Erasmus' hermeneutic from 1518 to 1535, especially the *Ratio verae theologiae*, the *Ecclesiastes*, and the exegesis of Old and New Testament texts. He shows that Erasmus' hermeneutic is based on the concept of language as mediation. Words do not have the power to represent the truth unambiguously, but they appeal to our understanding in ways that draw us to the truth through the process of interpretation. For Erasmus it is through allegory that the divine Word carries out its mediation between letter and spirit.

Erasmus used the tools of rhetoric to read and understand Scripture, and thereby constructed a theological framework that has a direct relationship with his hermeneutic. Rhetorical theologians imitate the invention, disposition, inverbation, and delivery of divine speech by clarifying its composition, ordering its subject matter, internalizing its content, and communicating its transforming power of persuasion. Rhetoric provided Erasmus with the tools for finding theological loci in Scripture, drawing from it a repertoire for knowing and living, and translating it into sacred oratory.

MANFRED HOFFMANN was Professor of Church History and His-torical Theology, Candler School of Theology and Graduate Division of Religion, Emory University.

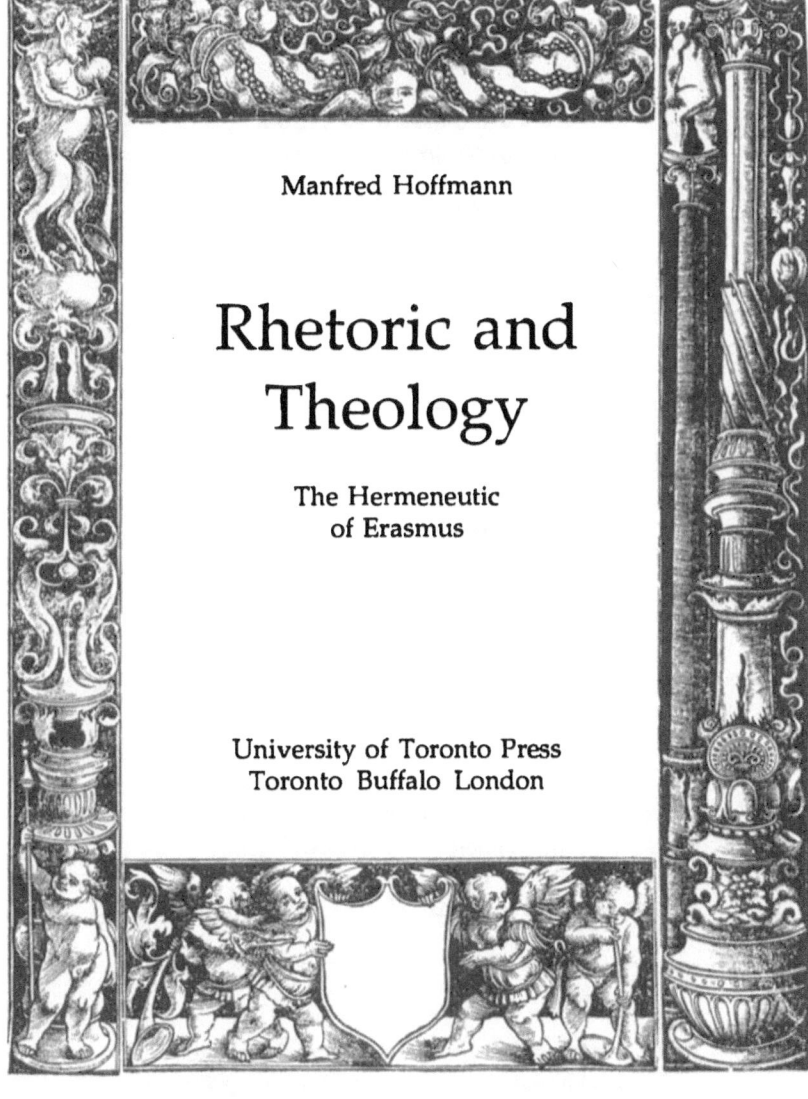

Manfred Hoffmann

Rhetoric and Theology

The Hermeneutic
of Erasmus

University of Toronto Press
Toronto Buffalo London

© University of Toronto Press Incorporated 1994
Toronto Buffalo London
Reprinted 2017

ISBN 978-0-8020-0579-3 (cloth)
ISBN 978-1-4875-8686-7 (paper)

Erasmus Studies 12

Printed on acid-free paper

Canadian Cataloguing in Publication Data

Hoffmann, Manfred, 1930-
Rhetoric and theology : the hermeneutic of Erasmus

(Erasmus studies ; 12)
Includes bibliographical references and index.
ISBN 978-0-8020-0579-3 (bound). – ISBN 978-1-4875-8686-7 (pbk.)
1. Erasmus, Desiderius, d. 1536
2. Bible – Criticism, interpretation, etc.
3. Erasmus, Desiderius, d. 1536 – Language.
4. Hermeneutics – History – 16th century.
5. Rhetoric – 1500–1800.
I. Title. II. Series.
B785.E64H6 1994   220.6'01   C93-095504-8

University of Toronto Press acknowledges the
financial assistance to its publishing program
of the Canada Council and the
Ontario Arts Council.

This book has been published with the help of
a grant from the University Research Committee
of Emory University.

TO BETSY

Contents

Acknowledgments / ix

Introduction / 3

ONE / ERASMUS, RHETORICAL THEOLOGIAN / 15

1 Images of Erasmus / 15
2 Humanism and Rhetorical Theology / 18
3 Point of Departure, Sources, and Procedure / 28
4 *Ratio verae theologiae* / 32
5 *Ecclesiastes sive De ratione concionandi* / 39
6 *Ratio* and *Ecclesiastes* Compared / 55

TWO / LANGUAGE, LITERATURE, AND SCRIPTURE / 61

1 Language, Nature, and Culture / 61
2 The Deterioration and Restoration of Language / 65
3 Words and Ideas / 71
4 *Bonae litterae* / 78
5 *Sacrae litterae* / 81
6 The Approach to Scripture / 89

THREE / THE ALLEGORICAL NATURE OF SCRIPTURE / 95

1 Letter and Spirit / 95
2 The Fourfold Sense of Scripture / 101
3 Allegory and Accommodation / 106
4 Allegory, Similitude, and Persuasion / 112
5 Openness and Hiddenness / 118
6 The Allegorical Method / 126

FOUR / SPEECH AND INTERPRETATION / 135

1 Invention / 135
2 Disposition / 142
3 The Harmony of Christ / 148
4 Theological *Loci* / 151
5 Law and Gospel / 156
6 The Variety of Persons, Times, and Things / 162

FIVE / THE VIRTUES OF SPEECH / 169

1 *Elocutio; puritas, perspicuitas* / 169
2 *Aptum; collatio, commoditas* / 176
3 *Ornatus; jucunditas, vehementia* / 184
4 *Prudentia; judicium, consilium* / 191
5 *Adfectus; ethos, pathos* / 200
6 *Virtus; honestum, utilitas* / 205

Conclusion / 211

Abbreviations / 229

Notes / 231

Bibliography / 289

Index of Technical Terms / 299

Acknowledgments

I have been occupied with work on this study for the better part of six years both in private research and in graduate seminars at Emory University. It is impossible to name all those who during that time have influenced my thinking in one way or another, students, colleagues, and friends alike. But I would be remiss if I failed specifically to mention the support of several persons and institutions.

I gladly acknowledge the financial aid for this project, particularly during a year's leave of absence from academic duties (1988–9), by grants from the Association of Theological Schools in the United States and Canada and from the University Research Committee of Emory University. I also appreciate the good offices of Ron Schoeffel as well as the guidance of the two readers of my manuscript, who made helpful suggestions for making it accessible to a wider audience. I thank Erika Rummel and James Tracy for reading with a critical eye an earlier version of the manuscript. I am above all grateful to my spouse, Elisabeth Lunz, whose labour of love in reading and rereading this manuscript exemplifies the many favours of our partnership. I dedicate this book to her.

RHETORIC AND THEOLOGY:

THE HERMENEUTIC OF ERASMUS

Introduction

After I had completed my book on Erasmus' theology, a theology informed by his theory of knowledge, his anthropology, and his ethics,¹ it became clear that the rhetorical matrix of his thought needed a more thorough treatment than I had been able to give at the time. That a coherent world view governed Erasmus' thinking had become fairly certain. Of course, his understanding of reality was neither derived from the metaphysical principles of the scholastic theologians nor arrived at, as theirs, by means of the cogent conclusions of a syllogistic, dialectical method. Even so, Erasmus saw all of reality, that is, nature, humanity, society, and history, ordered according to a univeral plan, the parts of which he thought were arranged in a harmonious whole. What can be called his ontology did not represent an abstract theory of being but sprang from a philosophy of the world and of human life that corresponded in large part to the Platonism of the church Fathers Origen, Jerome, and Augustine.

With the main characteristics of the Erasmian world view having come to light, it was necessary to examine the way in which this concept of reality is related to language. The daunting task that lay ahead consisted in finding out how the form of Erasmus' thought is informed by an equally comprehensive awareness of speech and interpretation. It seemed plausible to assume that an examination of his hermeneutic, especially his biblical interpretation, would reveal the way in which he combined ontology and rhetoric so as to construct a distinct theological framework. As if to complicate things further, a survey of the pertinent sources indicated that a study of his use of rhetoric could not confine itself to his introductory writings to the New

Testament, particularly the *Ratio verae theologiae*, but had to take account of his actual exegesis of Old Testament and New Testament texts. Finally, to delineate his hermeneutic as a whole, one had to include an analysis of his handbook on homiletics, the monumental *Ecclesiastes*.

Other specialists had meanwhile grappled with part of the problem. J.W. Aldridge claimed the promising title *The Hermeneutic of Erasmus* for what turned out to be a disappointing study. While Aldridge was correct in emphasizing Erasmus' return to the biblical sources as well as his recognition of their authority for the philosophy of Christ, he not only failed to see Erasmus within the rhetorical tradition but also came to the questionable conclusion that his exegetical method so relied on historical factuality and on human erudition that he became a forerunner of modern historical criticism, in contrast to Luther then and Barth now.[2] This approach was criticized by J.B. Payne, who for his part still did not touch on the rhetorical nature of Erasmus' theology, even though he moved in the right direction by concentrating on the distinction Erasmus made between letter and spirit and on his use of an allegorical and tropological exegesis.[3] T.F. Torrance more recently examined some of the sources that make up the basis of our study, yet without seeing Erasmus' hermeneutic within the context of his rhetoric, nor entering into a discussion with the current literature on the subject.[4]

Drawing lines from the rhetorical tradition of Italian humanism to Erasmus, C. Trinkaus was, to my knowledge, the first to suggest that Erasmus' theology is rhetorical in character.[5] Moreover, M. O'Rourke Boyle pushed research forcefully forward by analysing, though sometimes with overdrawn conclusions, some aspects of Erasmus' rhetoric with respect to their classical derivation, especially where his *De libero arbitrio* is concerned.[6] The most significant work, however, arrived on the scene with J. Chomarat's masterful study on Erasmus' use of grammar and rhetoric.[7] No one in Erasmus studies can bypass these two massive volumes. Yet since Chomarat examined the full sweep of Erasmus' work, he viewed his biblical exegesis as part and parcel of a general literary method rather than specifically from the perspective of his theology. Chomarat therefore missed the chance of providing a synthesis of Erasmus' theological hermeneutic. Finally, P. Walter published an insightful examination of Erasmus' rhetorical exegesis.[8] Even so, his reluctance to integrate

Erasmus' interpretation of Scripture into his overall system of thought as well as his neglect of the connection between hermeneutic and homiletics limited his view.

It is the intention of this study to show that Erasmus in fact espoused what can be called a *theologia rhetorica*. He committed himself to returning theology to its scriptural sources by means of the art of rhetoric, that is, by the knowledge of ancient languages and the humanist interpretation of literature. Purified in this way from textual corruption and liberated from misguided comments, Scripture would regain the original power of its divine authority. Its essential message, the philosophy of Christ, would engender the restitution of Christianity to its genuine ethos – much the same as it would restore nature to its original goodness. God's word would regenerate Christians to become believers who realize true religion in the world.

'In olden days,' Erasmus said, summarizing the history of theology, 'the Christian philosophy was a matter of faith, not of disputation; men's simple piety was satisfied with the oracles of Holy Scripture, and charity ... had no need of complicated rules ... Later, the management of theology was taken in hand by men nurtured in humane learning, but mainly in those fields of learning which today we commonly call rhetoric. Gradually philosophy came to be applied more and more, Platonic first and then Aristotelian, and questions began to be asked about many points which were thought to pertain either to morals or the field of speculation about heavenly things. At first this seemed almost fundamental, but it developed by stages until many men, neglecting the study of the ancient tongues and of polite literature and even of Holy Writ, grew old over questions meticulous, needless, and unreasonably minute ... By now theology began to be a form of skill, not wisdom; a show-piece, not a means toward true religion; and besides ambition and avarice it was spoilt by other pests, by flattery and strife and superstition.

'Thus at length it came about that the pure image of Christ was almost overlaid by human disputations; the crystal springs of the old gospel teaching were choked with sawdust by the Philistines, and the undeviating rule of Holy Scripture, bent this way and that, became the slave of our appetites rather than of the glory of Christ. At that point some men, whose intentions certainly were religious, tried to recall the world to the simpler studies of an earlier day and lead it from pools most of which are now sullied to those pure rills of living water. To achieve this object, they thought a knowledge of the tongues and liberal studies (as they call them) were of the first importance, for it was neglect of them, it seemed, that brought us down to where we are.'[9]

We shall argue that Erasmus intertwined his biblical scholarship with his overall understanding of language in such a way that rhetoric stood him in good stead for both interpreting the divine revelation in Scripture and construing from it a theological framework that raised his concept of reality to a higher level. In other words, he employed the art of rhetoric not only to read and understand Scripture but also to arrange theological *topoi* as highpoints of a comprehensive system that encompassed his ontology, anthropology, sociology, and ethics. For him the scope of theological language included the arenas of discourse concerning nature, human beings, society, history, and morality.

More precisely, we see Erasmus' hermeneutic as governed by the idea of language as mediation. Language, especially God's speech in Scripture, draws the reader into the truth through the process of interpretation. And it is the peculiar drawing power of allegory (the middle between the historical/literal and the spiritual/mystical sense of Scripture) that performs this metaphorical function. Here the divine word intercedes between heaven and earth as it translates the reader from the flesh into the spirit. This mediation through allegorical language engenders in the individual a harmonious consensus between word, truth, and understanding. It also generates true communication, love, and concord between human beings in society. The mediation of language therefore comes to fruition in individual and societal transformation. While Erasmus' dualistic view contrasted appearance with reality, letter with spirit, body with spirit, the visible world with the invisible world, and so on, the trichotomous framework he laid over this basic dualism introduced a process of mediation through which opposites are ultimately reconciled. The dynamics of mediation, central as it is in Erasmus' hermeneutic, informed all aspects of his world view.

Such a rhetorical theology had certainly to run afoul of what has been called dialectical theology. As soon as his edition of the New Testament had appeared (and especially when his *Annotations* and *Paraphrases* on the New Testament were published), Erasmus found himself entangled in a web of controversy with scholastic theologians of various stripes: 'They try to convince the ignorant and unlearned that the study of the ancient languages and of what men call the humanities is opposed to the pursuit of theology, while in truth theology can expect more distinction and more progress from them than from any other subject.'[10] Now the difference in general between the scholastic and humanist methodology was, according to E. Rummel, as follows: 'In their search for metaphysical truth, for a knowledge of God, and an understanding of the Bible, the scholastics used dialectical reasoning and in support of their arguments they cited most often the authority of medieval theologians, that is, their scholastic predecessors. The humanists, by contrast, used the philological approach and most often cited classical and patristic authorities.'[11]

To be sure, Erasmus did not reject the proper use of logical reasoning within the purview of rhetoric, as long as such dialectic avoided 'a violent desire for disagreement' and prevented problems 'thorny and intricate because of superfluous difficulties' as well as questions which served to 'parade one's cleverness' instead of enabling one to arrive at a 'correct judgment of true and false.'[12] And as far as philosophy is concerned, Erasmus wrote: 'Not that I think ... that the inquiry in the three divisions of philosophy [sc rational, natural, and moral] or that the investigation of phenomena beyond this world should be entirely condemned, provided that the inquirer is endowed with rich talent and is purged of rashness in defining, of obstinacy, and of the bane of harmony, the stubborn passion to get the upper hand.'[13] But he opposed 'academic theology, corrupted as it is by philosophic and scholastic quibbling'[14] and abhorred 'the corruptions of the logic and philosophy which are now so tediously and wastefully ground into the young at our universities ... I can see many gifted minds put off from learning subjects that would be really useful ... In fact, in many institutions such subjects, together with theology itself, are no longer taught; and at the same time the ancient tongues too and human studies in general are neglected. Their youth is wasted solely in quarrelsome disputations and in bitter polemical pamphlets. This is a great scandal ...'[15]

On the whole, then, it appears that dialectical theology constructed a dogmatic system from subtle distinctions, abstruse questions, and syllogistic conclusions. It applied the laws of strict logic to establish metaphysical principles once and for all. It erected an abstract structure of thought that, even as it was unrelated to the context of living language, was yet imposed on Scripture and reality. So Erasmus drew back from what passed for systematic theology, for its assertions precisely distorted the meaning of God's word in particular and the sense of language in general. Devoid of rhetorical prudence and failing to achieve harmony, dialectical theology was in effect as much useless for spiritual life as irrelevant to cultural progress. Erasmus turned instead to biblical interpretation in rhetorical terms. To put it simply, he abandoned the speculation on metaphysical problems in favour of understanding metaphorical language. Nevertheless, he did derive, as we shall see, rhetorical *loci* from his exegesis of Scripture and ordered them into a theological framework. This theological system, however, arranged as it was along the lines of divine speech, differed fundamentally from the dogmatic system of dialectical theology.

Erasmus made the aim of his life's work quite clear: 'My sole object has been my efforts should serve to some extent the public advancement of learning, and to arouse men's mind to embrace the pure teaching of Christ ... Heretofore, religious minds were chilled and sickened by a scholastic and argumentative theology, and they soon began to grow more cheerful when they tasted the gospel truth.'[16] 'In all my work my sole object has been to resuscitate the humanities, which lay almost dead and buried among my own people; secondly to arouse a world which allowed too much importance to Jewish ceremonial to a new zeal for the true religion of the Gospel; and finally to recall to its sources in Holy Scripture the academic theology in our universities too deeply sunk in the quibbling discussion of worthless minor problems.'[17] '[You] are well aware, I have no doubt, of the efforts I have hitherto expended, not only to advance the common good and the cause of the humanities, but in particular the knowledge of the gospel, to the benefit of all men and to no man's hurt.'[18]

The method of this study is primarily analytical where specific texts are concerned. But it aims also at a synthetic view of Erasmus' hermeneutic as it shaped, and in turn was shaped by, the structure of his theology. That is to say, although my interpretation rests on the exegesis of individual passages, it is not presented by juxtaposing, in a pedestrian way, a series of paraphrases on single texts in chronological sequence. Rather, I try to move beyond a merely historical, grammatical exposition in that I compare a variety of points from different sources in order to arrive at a synopsis. Seeing the whole, after all, is the goal of rhetoric. In my synthetic approach, I took the clue from Erasmus himself, who moved from *varietas* to *harmonia*, from individual meanings to a common sense, from *sensus* to *consensus*, in an effort to integrate the parts of speech into their overall arrangement, without violating, of course, the particularity of the parts. For Erasmus and for this study, interpretation can transcend literal meanings as long as it does not infringe on basic hermeneutical principles.[19]

When I deal with a specific text, then, documentation is always specific to that text. But conclusions drawn from the comparision of a wide range of statements are documented by a number of references which together support a point made. In other words, my method aims at deriving from a conglomerate of representative references a sense of Erasmus' understanding of the synthesis between rhetoric and theology. I have learned that in order to arrive at synthesis, the interpreter must accommodate himself or herself to the author, in order to think along the same lines.[20]

It must suffice at this point to sketch in broad strokes the outline of the present work to give the reader a first taste of its content.

Chapter one begins with a presentation of several images of Erasmus found in the scholarly literature since the nineteenth century. These portraits seem to have as a common feature an emphasis on the ambiguity of his person and work, and on the unsystematic nature of his thought, which is seen as limited primarily to ethical concerns. In search of a key to the heart of his thinking, we turn briefly to the history of rhetoric and humanism. Both the revival of Ciceronian rhetoric and the rediscovery of Plato by Italian humanists, along with the Platonism of church Fathers like Augustine, are seen as significant influences on the centre of Erasmus' thought. Ciceronian philological realism with its moral thrust coalesced with a concern for the metaphorical function of language. While Erasmus was convinced of the validity of the dichotomy of letter and spirit, he was also persuaded that allegory provided a metaphorical means to overcome this dualism.

For Erasmus, the theologian's true vocation arises from the

interpretation of the Bible. This conversation with Scripture aims at both personal transformation by the gospel truth and the ministry of teaching and preaching the word in such a way that it lends itself to the restitution of Christianity. The structure of Erasmus' theology will therefore become clear from the exegetical rules and principles of interpretation spelled out in the introductory writings to the New Testament, the *Ratio*, and in his handbook on preaching, the *Ecclesiastes*, and exemplified by his *Paraphrases* on the New Testament and his Old Testament *Commentaries* as well as other pertinent theological writings.

It was necessary in the first chapter to break the continuity of the argument in order to acquaint the readers with the overall structure and the essential statements of the two major sources, the *Ratio* and the *Ecclesiastes*. These rather lengthy analyses are supposed to give the readers an initial sense (in memory, as the rhetorical tradition suggests) of the topography of Erasmus' rhetorical theology. It is hoped that, drawing on the memory of this basic repertoire, the readers will find themselves more at home in the subsequent chapters, where particular points are taken up and integrated into the overall system of Erasmus' thought. Familiarizing the readers with this basic material at the beginning is all the more called for since these texts are unavailable in English.

What follows in chapter two is an overview of Erasmus' notion of language in general, his concept of literature and literacy, and his appreciation of the allegorical nature of Scripture. Language functions in his world of thought as a medium by which human beings become aware of themselves, of their place in nature, and of their role in culture. What is more, communication among human beings creates community, as the ideas and ideals expressed in language inform and shape their common life, whether in a positive or in a negative manner. Since language was debased in the past, it is the task of the humanist to restore its authenticity – a project that distinguished Erasmus' return to the sources from that of the Ciceronians and the scholastics alike. Looking then at the relationship of words and things enables us to become clearer about the type of ontology that supports Erasmus' rhetorical theology. A brief examination of the symbolic function of good literature leads finally to the focus on the incarnational nature and allegorical role of sacred letters, concentrated as they are in their *scopus*, Christ.

A detailed analysis of Erasmus' exegetical rules comes next in chapter three, with specific attention given to both his allegorical interpretation and his homiletical application of Scripture. Erasmus' rhetorical method concentrates on allegorical language for its ability to throw a bridge over the chasm between letter/flesh and spirit, the visible/material and the invisible/spiritual world, the law and the gospel. He modified the fourfold method of scriptural exegesis in such a way as to accommodate a humanist-rhetorical interpretation. While the historical sense remains the basis for any deeper meaning, it is the allegorical (Christological/ecclesiological) and the tropological (moral) sense of Scripture that is conducive to a metaphorical passage between history and mystery.

An examination of the relationship between allegory, accommodation, similarity, persuasion, and transformation widens the scope so as to clarify the Christological implications of Erasmus' emphasis on mediation. Scriptural language reveals the divine truth because in it Christ mediates between the letter and the spirit by accommodating himself to the human condition while remaining at the same time fully divine. As the supreme mediator, Christ is incarnate in the word. The expositor of God's mind, Christ persuades the reader to consensus, love, and concord, especially as truth is both hidden and revealed in Scripture.

The question of how rhetorical invention and disposition function in Erasmus' theology is the subject of chapter four. Here the general rules of grammar and rhetoric are applied to the interpretation of Scripture on its various levels corresponding to the historical, tropological, and allegorical methods of exegesis. Theological *topoi*, drawn from Scripture, are in turn instrumental for understanding the real meaning of the word. The theological implications of invention and imitation are explored, as is, especially, disposition since it arranges speech according to similarities and dissimilarities – an order of oppositions which is nevertheless brought into a whole by the introduction of a tripartite succession, with a middle link between beginning and end enabling a transition from start to finish. Thus the dynamics of a trichotomous sequence overcome a static dualism.

Since the true meaning of the biblical text derives from its reference to Christ (*harmonia Christi*), the theologian can extract from the story of Christ's accommodation of his teaching to various persons, times, and places (*varietas Christi*) the main *topoi* of Christian doctrine. Even more, the *Elenchus* of the fourth book of Erasmus' *Ecclesiastes* suggests a systematic blueprint of his theological thought as a whole. Here he lays out a dualistic framework that contrasts two dominions, God's and Satan's. But both are arranged, despite their opposition, in the order of rhetorical disposition from beginning to progress to consummation. While each dominion is different in origin, association, laws, modes of behaviour, and ends, they both follow a tripartite sequence in which the middle is central to the progress between origin and outcome, whether in positive or in negative terms.

The fifth chapter deals with elocution, the art of expressing thought with appropriate words and in a proper order. It includes a detailed examination of the rhetorical devices Erasmus found suitable for the task of biblical interpretation and preaching. Speech must be organized in accordance with both the equity of nature and the harmony of Christ. Moreover, speech must be aptly expressed for the delivery of its message to be effective. Therefore, it is essential for theologians to recognize the grammatical, elocutionary, and moral virtues expressed in Scripture so as to be able to employ them in the persuasive genre of sacred oratory.

Following Erasmus' own emphases, we pay particular attention to the virtue of clarity and the vice (or virtue) of obscurity; to the method of collation that renders interpretation and speech appropriate; to the appealing power of the figures of speech (*jucunditas*) and their power to move an audience toward moral transformation (*vehementia*); to the central role allegory and metaphor play as the figures of speech most suitable for theological discourse because they are most frequently found in Holy Scripture; to prudence as the discriminating judgment by which interpreters and preachers recognize, and accommodate themselves to, the variety of persons, times, and places; to the virtue of moderation that pervades Erasmus' hermeneutic as a whole; and to *affectus*, a rhetorical and human virtue that draws the hearer to the moral life (*honestum, utilitas*), the final goal of suasory oratory. Last but not least, Erasmus correlated the classical virtues with the Christian virtues of faith, love, and hope, whereby faith perfects the natural intellect and charity perfects the natural desire for piety.

The conclusion reviews the whole argument. One point made there may serve here as a conclusion to this introduction.

Erasmus interwove a dualistic and a trichotomous framework of understanding. Although contrasting letter with spirit, appearance with reality, the visible with the invisible, he nevertheless emphasized a process of mediation through which oppositions are ultimately reconciled. It seems that the rhetorical notions of *topoi* and *via* answered to these two frameworks. The *topoi* motif, governed by the similarity-dissimilarity principle, suggests the stability and coherence of the ideal truth centred on Christ as *scopus*. The *via* motive, on the other hand, with its tripartite movement of beginning, middle, and end reflects the story of Christ's life, the development of salvation history, and the Christian's spiritual transformation. A dualistic layout of topics is therefore animated by the notion of mediation as a progressive movement between up and down, inside and outside, heaven and earth, beginning and end. So two patterns characterize Erasmus' way of thinking. It is the coordination of form and dynamic, system and development, circle and story, teaching and life, that brings the characteristic manner of Erasmus' rhetorical theology to light.[21]

In order to make further research on Erasmus' rhetorical terms easier, I have translated the respective Latin words strictly by their English derivatives, because those who have to rely on secondary literature alone are often confused by the variety of expressions chosen to translate the same Latin word. So for instance I have consistently used 'prudence' for *prudentia* rather than 'wisdom' or another term that might have been more flowing in English. The same goes for *adfectus* (affection) and other technical terms. Even though these latinized words may at times render my English less felicitous and more 'academic,' it stays closer to the sources and ensures clarity as to Erasmus' original vocabulary. Moreover, I have made a conscious effort to use gender-inclusive language except when paraphrasing or translating the sources. Finally, I include in my discussion of secondary sources works in German and French, in order to facilitate an international dialogue, which is as yet not quite frequent on either side of the language divide. In all this I have tried to be faithful to Erasmus' principle of communication, which I find central to his rhetorical theology.

ONE

Erasmus, Rhetorical Theologian

1 IMAGES OF ERASMUS

The history of Erasmus interpretation has produced a puzzling variety of readings.[1] Despite repeated attempts at reducing his life and work to common denominators, the humanist has had a way of eluding his interpreters. For all the labels pinned on him, he remained an enigmatic figure. His personality cannot be clearly traced nor his place and role in history definitively fixed. If there is a basic theme running through most modern interpretations, it touches not on something certain but, ironically, stresses the ambiguity of his thinking and the ambivalence of his attitude.

Looking at Erasmus as both an unsystematic thinker and a 'man for all seasons'[2] could result in either positive or negative assessments. Those who came from a nineteenth-century liberal point of view tended to appreciate in him the broad-minded intellectual, impartial and adaptable, open to reason but critical of hypocrisy, fanaticism, and dogmatism. He was seen as a sceptic hiding behind the facade of the humanist. Modern liberalism had found its forerunner: a rationalist who espoused an undogmatic religion so general as to hold the ultimate truth in suspension, and a moralist who advocated so broad an unchurched fellowship of the spirit that he was willing to concede all sorts of personal convictions, if only they led to ethical improvement. Accordingly, he was heralded as a father of religious toleration and an early proponent of religious pluralism. No wonder, then, that his alleged relativizing of the truth and moralizing of religion squared readily with modern notions of historical contingency, social pluralism, religious individualism, and freedom of choice.

Liberal interpreters recognized in Erasmus their own ideas, ideals, and values. He appeared to them as a secularizer of the spirit and a prophet of positivism; a precursor of modern education and of research unhampered by dogmatic tutelage; a champion of freedom of thought and press; a rationalist like Montaigne or Voltaire, and a sceptic like Descartes; a scholar who preferred to be known for his philological work, a rhetorician and educator rather than a theologian; a moralist who, while prudently avoiding an open clash with the institutional church, doubted its doctrines as he advocated the restoration of Christianity along the lines of minimal beliefs and by means of the moral development of individuals.[3]

Like French, English, and American liberal interpreters, some German scholars aligned Erasmus with their world view and discovered in him the exponent of that type of undogmatic morality which they found in Jesus' teaching of the Sermon on the Mount.[4] Lutheran confessional theologians, however, would see him through their church father's eyes and thus from a dogmatic perspective: Erasmus was a *vir duplex*, a two-faced compromiser avoiding a stand; a *homo pro se*, an isolated individual who shunned the community of believers, missed the certainty of faith, and therefore lacked spiritual depth and moral strength.[5] Particularly in the controversy on the freedom of the will he was said to have been out of his depth as he exposed himself as a lightweight theologian.[6]

However, a new period in Erasmus interpretation, which according to some was even an 'Erasmus renaissance,' began during the first quarter of the twentieth century. It was ushered in by P.S. Allen's painstaking work on his letters and highlighted by the landmark biography of J. Huizinga.[7] The critical edition of *Erasmi epistolae* threw so much light on the historical background of his life that the priming colours were available for painting a truer picture of his character.

As a result, Erasmus was depicted as an equivocating but pious intellectual. Plumbing the complexity of his psychological make-up brought to light the conflicting features of a Protean personality: an egocentric in need of friendship; a man who hated lies and yet bent the truth when expedient; an individualist at once desiring personal freedom and bowing to authority; a hygiomaniac whose concern for his *corpusculum*[8] was symptomatic of his fear of death while he yet extolled the happy life. A sensitive idealist and a captious critic at the same time, a believer in the perfectibility of human nature and yet an elitist who did not think highly of the lower classes, Erasmus appeared as a tragic figure since he failed to carry his ideas into practice for lack of singleness of purpose. In short, he was a visionary, too advanced for his own time, too utopian for this world even now.

Following Huizinga's lead in one way or another, more and more scholars began to disassociate themselves from the older stereotypes by increasingly nuancing the Erasmus picture. In spite of all his unattractive traits, they tried to do him justice by understanding him on his own terms. In fact, his too human, vulnerable disposition made him the more sympathetic in a time of cultural uneasiness. His character revealed more favourable traits, as for instance his steadiness in adverse circumstances.[9] Moreover, his devotion to religious life came into view, particularly in terms of his Augustinian spirituality.[10] Still, the liberal interpretation persisted, as in A. Renaudet's stress on the humanist's so-called modernism and on his aspiration to a third church of the spirit that was to transcend all denominational boundaries by returning to the essentials of Jesus' message.[11]

It has been clear since the sixties that the newest phase of Erasmus studies was in the making, with the older picture being substantially revised. Just as the Amsterdam edition of his works[12] began to provide a critical text base for research in the sources, so the work of the Amsterdamer C. Augustijn not only helped to dispel inveterate clichés but also opened new insights, particularly into Erasmus' humanism and his relation to the Protestant reformation.[13] Other studies focused attention on his theology and biblical interpretation,[14] his relation to the classical and ecclesiastical traditions and to contemporary movements,[15] his ecclesiology and ecumenism,[16] his controversy with Luther,[17] and his political theory and pacifism[18] – to mention but the most important areas of research. Even though it takes time for the scholarly community to absorb and assess new findings, at least this much is now evident: A major shift is taking place at the cutting edge of Erasmus research.

Examinations into the humanist's philology and rhetoric, however, seem to have run on an independent track, with J. Chomarat's substantive work representing a milestone on this path.[19] While this line of research tended to minimize the contributions of studies on Erasmus' theological ideas, both sides came to similar conclusions in that they stressed that the ambiguity of his thought in reality represented an attempt to achieve consensus by discovering elements of truth on either side of an issue. But whereas those who worked on the linguistic aspects for the most part continued to see the sceptic and moralist, those who dealt with his religious thought found a generally orthodox believer who spared no effort to integrate reason and revelation, doctrine and life, faith and love.

2 HUMANISM AND RHETORICAL THEOLOGY

Even so, the question of whether Erasmus can be called a theologian has not yet been settled in the mind of everyone.[20] Was Erasmus a theologian at all, and if so, what kind of a theology did he teach? Certainly, he qualified for the title in that he was trained at Paris, acquired the degree of doctor of theology from Turin, was considered fit to receive invitations to teaching positions in divinity, was even offered the cardinal's purple, and was singled out by prominent patrons to take Luther to task in doctrinal controversy. Moreover, despite his caustic remarks on the unschooled, superstitious lot of the monks, he never renounced his vows as an Augustinian canon regular. And while he made a living as a freelance author, enjoying dispensation from priestly duties and dietary regulations, he remained true, in his mind at least, to his church and vocation. Still, did he consider himself a theologian?

Of course, he would not openly claim the title of theologian, partly out of modesty, partly for fear of being lumped with the scholastic crowd. He loathed the *neoterici* or *recentiores*, 'the modern class of theologians, who spend their lives in sheer hair-splitting and sophistical quibbling ...':

> It is not that I condemn their learned studies, I who have nothing but praise for learning of any sort, but these studies are isolated, and not seasoned with references to any well-written works of an older age, and so they seem to me likely to give a man a smattering of knowledge or a taste for arguing ... They exhaust the intelligence by a kind of sterile and thorny subtlety, in no way quickening it with

the vital sap or breathing into it the breath of life; and, worst of all, by their stammering, foul, and squalid style of writing, they render unattractive that great queen of all sciences, theology, enriched and adorned as she has been by the eloquence of antiquity. In this way they choke up, as it were with brambles, the way of a science that early thinkers had cleared and, attempting to settle all questions ... merely envelop all in darkness. Thus you can see her, once supremely revered and full of majesty, today all but silent, impoverished, and in rags; while we are seduced by the attractions of a perverted and insatiable passion for quibbling. One quarrel leads to another, and with extraordinary arrogance we quarrel over insignificant trifles.'[21]

Erasmus did not claim 'to be an expert in the rare science of theology, and yet I do not have so low an opinion of such brains or learning as I may possess as to think that I understand nothing that Augustine wrote ... In this affair my business is not with theological subtleties but with the correction of the text. I take upon myself a schoolmaster's part; questions of truth and falsehood I leave to those master-minds.'[22] With understatement he wished to be known as a grammarian, as one whose calling it is to provide by his philological work services ancillary to the queen of sciences: 'If anyone says I am no theologian my answer is: I am playing the part of the grammarian. If they disdain the grammarian, let them take note that the emperor does not disdain the services of the barber or secretary. If they cry out that no one except a theologian can provide this service, my answer is: I am the lowliest of theologians and have taken on the lowliest task in theology.'[23]

But then Erasmus could also turn the tables and say: 'There has been everywhere a lot of uneducated theologians, one like me you hardly find in many centuries.'[24] His conventional display of humility could not cover the fact that he did not mind others calling him a theologian and then some: 'Time was when hundreds of letters described me as the greatest of the great, prince of the world of literature, bright star of Germany, luminary of learning, champion of humane studies, bulwark of a more genuine theology.'[25] And Thomas More wrote to Dorp: 'He is not to be banished from the theologian's throne to the grammarian's footstool ... Erasmus is certainly not one of those grammarians who has mastered no more than mere words, nor is he one of those theologians who know nothing at all outside a tangled labyrinth of petty problems ... He has gained something vastly more useful, a general command of sound literature, which means sacred letters especially but not at the expense of the rest.'[26]

Indeed, whenever Erasmus insisted that he was concerned with the restoration of languages and humanist studies, he never failed to add that he was also committed to the renewal of genuine theology and the promotion of the gospels and piety: 'I support the humanities ... I recall theologians to the sources and point out to them where true religion has its roots.'[27] In his description of the true theologian he gave his readers to understand that he was also speaking of himself or at least of the ideal with which he wanted to be identified, a theologian who first of all interprets and communicates the word of God: 'The foremost goal of theologians is to interpret the divine Scriptures with wisdom, to speak seriously and effectively of faith and piety, not to reason about trifling questions, but to drive out tears, and to inflame the hearts to heavenly things.'[28] And as for his lifework, he expertly went about the business of an academic theologian, producing a corpus of theological literature that runs the gamut from the textual criticism, translation, and exegesis of Scripture, to theological treatises, editions of church Fathers, apologies, meditations, devotional writings, sermons, catechisms, prayers, and hymns.

Strictly speaking, Erasmus was certainly no denominational theologian. Siding with neither party, he steered a middle course between extremes. Although he blamed the Catholic authorities for enforcing the status quo of a tradition which from good beginnings had fallen into abuse, he shunned both the Reformation and its left-wing offspring because they upset the established order. All the same, he did espouse a reform program of comprehensive scope, the *restitutio christianismi* informed by the *philosophia christiana*. Yet he was far from presuming that this movement should take on its own form and run its course apart from the institutional church.[29]

Now the fact that Erasmus so strenuously resisted being identified with both Catholic scholasticism and Protestant confessionalism has led to the conclusion that even if he was a theologian he surely was not a systematician. His distaste for definitions, his dislike of assertions, and the built-in flexibility of his thinking were said to have kept him from organizing his thought into a coherent whole. It is true, he made statements such as this:

> The sum and substance of our religion is peace and concord. This can hardly remain the case unless we define as few matters as possible and leave each individual's judgment free on many questions. This is because there is great uncertainty about very many issues, and the mind of man suffers from this deeply ingrained weakness, that it does not know how to give way when a question has been made a subject of contention. And after the debate has warmed up each one thinks that the side he has undertaken rashly to defend is the absolute truth. In this regard certain men were so lacking in moderation that after defining everything in theology they contrived for those who are no more than men a new status of divinity, and this has aroused more questions and greater commotion in the world than the Arians in their foolishness once did. But certain pundits on some occasions are ashamed to have no rejoinder to make. On the contrary this is indeed the mark of theological learning: to define nothing beyond what is recorded in Holy Scripture, but to dispense in good faith what is there recorded.[30]

His thinking does contain a strain of Ciceronian scepticism, as prominently expressed in *De libero arbitro*, for instance: 'And I take so little pleasure in assertions that I will gladly seek refuge in Scepticism whenever this is allowed by the inviolable authority of Holy Scripture and the church's decrees.'[31] Even so, one must carefully assess the place and extent of his intellectual reserve before one consigns him to the camp of the doubters. Was the principle of suspended judgment (*epoché*), namely, that in certain cases 'it is more learned to be ambiguous and with the Academics to doubt than to make pronoucements,'[32] so fundamental as to prevent him from ordering intellectual insights into some kind of structure? Or did it serve primarily to oppose certain kinds of systematic thinking, such as the late scholastic theology in Paris or Louvain and the dogmatic assertions of Luther?

Erasmus' misgivings about scholastic and confessional assertions were no doubt caused by his aversion to absolute judgments: 'I assert nothing absolutely; I give the judgment of the church everywhere the reverence and authority which are its due; I am all for discussion, I decide nothing.'[33] He feared that because dogmatic statements claim certainty of truth for themselves, they exclude other options, pronounce differing insights to be false, and thus produce division instead of promoting unity. But unity and truth always belong together, for truth is not consistent unless it consists of harmony: 'No lie is so tightly put together that it is everywhere consistent with itself.'[34] In fact, unity and harmony rather than compelling proof or convincing argument are the evidence of the truth after all is said and done.

Erasmus' polemical scepticism is therefore symptomatic of a deeper 'hermeneutic of suspicion' that operated in his epistemology. This generic distrust had to do with his understanding of the relation between language and reality as it came to him through the tradition of Renaissance humanism, especially Valla.[35] The Italian humanists from Petrarch on had advocated Ciceronian rhetoric over against that application of Aristotelian dialectic which prevailed in the abstract conclusions of the philosophers, in the logico-semantic systems of the terminists and summulists, and in the speculative, metaphysical constructs of scholastic theologians.[36] While dialectical argumentation relied on cogent deductions from first principles to achieve certainty of truth, rhetoric followed an inductive process of persuasion toward verisimilitude.

This new style of speech, the 'New Learning,' was brought from Italy to the North by Rudolph Agricola, was propagated by Juan Luis Vives, and was cultivated by French, German, and English humanists alike.[37] Like the Italian humanists, Agricola replaced the formalist idiom of scholastic disputations with a humanist rhetoric of persuasion. But he took a different tack. While Valla had 'expanded the content of rhetoric to take in logic ... in Agricola's work, logic ... retained primacy over rhetoric ... Agricola had rhetoricized logic; but he had also devalued rhetoric, making it an appendage of logic.'[38] He redefined dialectic by associating it not only with the invention of *topoi* to determine probability but also with judgment which produces syllogistic reasons to establish certainty. Consequently, invention had become a matter of dialectic, and rhetoric was reduced to elocution.[39]

Erasmus, however, remained true to those Italian humanists who saw dialectic as a subordinate part of rhetoric.[40] To be sure, the Italian humanists, and Erasmus following them, did not abandon the dialectic method per se in the same way as they rejected the syllogistic conclusions of philosophical sophisms. Rather, they accommodated logical reasoning to the goal of rhetoric, which for them was an eminently practical art, an educational program that aimed at social utility and religious renewal. In the schooling of the *studia humanitatis*, students were instructed to read the ancient poets, orators, and historians rather than the philosophers.[41] Philosophy was considered useful only insofar as it supplied material for the moral dimension of discourse.

The controversy between rhetoricians and philosophers had, of course, a long history, one at least as old as the conflict between Socrates and the Sophist Protagoras. The story of these perennial disputes has been adequately told by specialists in the field.[42] What is significant as background for understanding Erasmus' concept of language is that Cicero's and Quintilian's rhetoric, a modification of the Greek art of speech to suit the needs of Roman public life, was passed on to him by the tradition of Italian humanism beginning with Petrarch.[43]

According to the rhetorical tradition as it was cultivated on the Ciceronian model, language gives expression to human life in concrete social conditions. Cicero, after all, had agreed with the Peripatetics, who like the ancient Sophists argued that oratory must comply with the usage of everyday language to be understood by ordinary folk in the marketplace.[44] It is this utilitarian focus on external circumstances and communal experiences that imparted a sense of philological realism in Ciceronian rhetoric. Speech is a means of interpersonal communication serving practical purposes rather than conveying definitive truth. Instead of addressing the intellect by compelling conclusions from first principles, oratory is to move an audience to action by stirring emotions and inspiring the will. While philosophers identified the *logos* primarily with *ratio* and therefore concentrated on the human intellect in such a way that exact knowledge was declared to be a virtue in itself, the rhetoricians understood *logos* foremost as *oratio*. 'What differentiates man from other animals, or brutes as they are called, is not reason, but speech.'[45] Yet speech applies foremost to public affairs and therefore makes human beings agents of social change. As a result, civic virtue serving the common good became the goal of public discourse.

This utilitarian concern engendered a strong sense of philosophical probabilism.[46] Rhetoricians believed that speech can advance human knowledge no farther than probable opinions. Suspicious of unilateral propositions cogently argued from unambiguous evidence, they looked for similarities on both sides of an issue with the intention of finding a solution as close as possible to the truth. After the process of comparison had reduced possibilities to viable options, one probability was expected to emerge as the most probable. If its truth was not absolutely certain, it certainly was persuasive, therefore plausible, credible, and acceptable, especially if it was morally useful. Thus verisimilitude came to represent the truth. The philological realism of Ciceronian rhetoric was balanced by a good measure of philosophical scepticism.

Moreover, audience approval replaced compelling proof on the part of the orator. Speakers were instructed to deliver their speech in such a persuasive way that, during its progress toward the most probable opinion, the hearer would be induced to recognize the truth. In other words, what went on in the audience was to be similar to what happened in oration. Consequently, the judgment of the matter was ultimately left to the audience: 'My case rests. Let others pass judgment.'[47] The orator expected an eventual agreement to emerge that expressed a consensus in the community. Also, since the true and the good always went hand in hand, it was hoped that this common sense would issue in social harmony. Free individuals would voluntarily agree among themselves rather than submit to a forced authoritarian judgment, and social harmony would be owing to democratic decision instead of enforced autocratic rule.

In spite of a good portion of Academic scepticism, however, rhetoric never completely severed its ties with philosophy – insofar as philosophy was practical. After all, Cicero had joined wisdom and eloquence: 'Wisdom without eloquence does too little for the good of states, but eloquence without wisdom is generally highly disadvantageous and is never helpful.'[48] Wisdom serves eloquence if it is conducive to virtue. But virtue was understood as a civic quality rather than an ideal to be sought for its own sake; virtue was a moral force in society rather than a formal category of perfection. Nevertheless, even as it constituted the practical goal of public discourse, virtue had to be placed within the context of moral philosophy. Certainly, Cicero's oratory followed the sophistic demand for popular *usus* and was therefore ecclectic in its use of philosophical commonplaces. But the content of his orations was yet informed for the most part by Stoic *topoi* concerning *vita et mores*, which indicated a certain philosophical structure and order.[49]

As well as ordering the philosophical content of speech, the rhetorical process itself was structured into a system.[50] Rhetorical invention was the gathering of *topoi* appropriate to the subject under discussion, disposition the arranging of the matter into the proper order, elocution the finding of the apt wording to be committed to memory and rendered in oration (pronunciation).[51] Thus the rhetoricians did systematize both the subject matter and the process of their speech, albeit in a rhetorical order for the purpose of public delivery in concrete situations rather than in a formal structure of ideas (*summa*) following the dictates of an abstract reason.

It is this rhetorical ordering in terms of collecting thought, arranging it in order, chosing appropriate diction for it, memorizing it, and delivering it in speech that provided the method of Erasmus' attempt at systematizing biblical theology. As we shall see, he established the scriptural source material by textual criticism, expounded the text by exegesis, compared its meaning to other contexts, and compiled theological *topoi* into a coherent whole – all of this for the practical purpose of persuading the hearer by the proclamation of the divine word. Rhetoric became sacred rhetoric as it supplied the method and structure for a theological hermeneutic. For Erasmus that hermeneutic began with interpreting the biblical texts and ended in communicating the gospel by means of the sermon. Erasmus' system was rhetorical in nature rather than rooted in the Aristotelian logic of classification and organization.[52]

There is yet another strand in the tradition of Renaissance humanism that affected Erasmus, namely, the use of allegory as a means of theological interpretation. As early as the *trecento*, classical poetry had become subject to an interpretation that took the myths of pagan deities as allegorical intimations of Christian meanings. This *theologia poetica* was in the fifteenth century increasingly coordinated with Ciceronian rhetoric. Thus poetical theology was transformed into what C. Trinkaus calls a *theologia rhetorica* that 'put all the language arts and sciences – the secular study of the world – at the service of the propagation of the divine Word.'[53] Brandolini and Valla were particularly instrumental in mustering ancient religion in the service of the Christian truth. While logic, they maintained, could only appeal to reason, rhetoric was able to persuade the hearer in matters of faith,[54] all the more so since allegory threw a bridge toward the transcendent world. But the added value of metaphorical language was seen as perfecting rather than destroying the literal meaning ascertained by textual analysis. The philological realism of Ciceronian rhetoric ministered now to Christian revelation, and the practical philosophy of civic virtues was fused with Christian ethics.

What is more, this *theologia poetica* enhanced by a *theologia rhetorica* exhibited a natural affinity with that *theologia platonica* which emerged in the middle of the *quattrocento* through the work of Ficino and Pico. With the introduction of a Platonizing philosophy into humanism, the allegorical interpretation of religious texts became even more prominent, broadening the avenue between humanism and Christian thought.[55] The moral elements of Ciceronian rhetoric, derived as they were for the most part from Stoic ethics, now merged with a Platonizing cosmology, anthropology, and epistemology to form a substructure which by allegory could be accommodated, without losing its classical form and content, to a Christian philosophy.[56] The humanist Platonists had achieved a synthesis between Platonism, rhetoric, and the Christian faith which was akin to the church Fathers', particularly Augustine's, attempt at enlisting classical antiquity in the service of ecclesiastical doctrine.

To what extent the Platonism of the Italian humanists influenced Erasmus is still an open question.[57] But there is no doubt that he was profoundly indebted to those church Fathers (particularly Origen, Jerome, and Augustine) who had baptized rhetoric to serve as handmaiden for their theology. Like his beloved Fathers of the third and fourth centuries, Erasmus used the wisdom of antiquity to broaden his theological view, yet without surrendering the specificity and finality of the Christian truth: 'Wherever the truth is discovered, it is Christ's.'[58] He oriented all learning toward Christ: 'This is the purpose of studying the basic disciplines, of studying philosophy, of studying eloquence, to know Christ, to celebrate the glory of Christ,'[59] for

'Christ is the author and originator of all branches of knowledge.'[60]

Just as the early apologists of the Christian tradition exploited the *spolia Aegyptiorum*,[61] so Erasmus was eclectic in accommodating not only Ciceronian rhetoric and Stoic moralism but also the cosmology, anthropology, and epistemology of Platonism to his philosophy of Christ.[62] He found the Platonist philosophers and the poets particularly useful because of their allegorical language, which in the case of the poets comes not so much from being inspired by the divine spirit (enthusiasm) as because their fables contain moral insights.[63] To be sure, ancient wisdom was not to be the determinative or decisive factor of theology, even if it was superior to much of what went on under the label of scholastic 'theology' or to an exclusively literal interpretation: 'As a matter of fact, if you read the poetic fable in an allegorical sense, it will be more profitable than the scriptural account if you do not penetrate the outer covering.'[64] Rather, philology and philosophy were means to an end. The theological end of the philosophy of Christ justified the philological and philosophical means.

No matter how much of Renaissance Platonism Erasmus absorbed as if by osmosis, his thought is clearly conditioned by the rhetoric of Ciceronian humanism and the theology of the Platonizing patristic tradition. Cicero's philological realism with its moral thrust coalesced with a concern for the metaphorical function of language. The closer connection between *verbum* and *res* produced by the emphasis on the social utility of language merged with a view that saw language reflecting ultimate reality, even divine revelation. This interest in the allegorical function of language, however, tended to relativize the letter as it entailed a basic distrust in the external word over against its recondite truth.

Augustine's stress on the dualism between body and spirit became decisive for Erasmus' *collatio visibilium ad invisibilia*:

> Let us imagine, therefore, two worlds, the one merely intelligible, the other visible. The intelligible, which may also be called the angelic, is the one in which God dwells with the blessed spirits, while the visible world comprises the celestial spheres and all that is contained therein. Then there is man, who constitutes, as it were, a third world, participating in the other two, in the visible world through the body,

and in the invisible through the soul. Since we are but pilgrims in the visible world, we should never make it our fixed abode, but should relate by a fitting comparison everything that occurs to the senses either to the angelic world or, in more practical terms, to morals and to the part of man that corresponds to the angelic. What the visible sun is here in the visible world the divine mind is in the intelligible world and in that part of you related to it, namely, the spirit.[65]

Analogically, then, allegory provides a hermeneutical transition between letter and spirit in the interpretation of texts. While the Platonic heritage of the church Fathers instilled in Erasmus a distrust in the letter (but not a rejection of it), he received from the rhetorical tradition a sense of literal realism. Consequently, Erasmus combined text-critical work on the sources with an allegorical interpretation of the divine word.

3 POINT OF DEPARTURE, SOURCES, AND PROCEDURE

Discovering Erasmus' relation to the rhetorical tradition in Renaissance humanism has already provided some significant clues to his theological thought. Nevertheless, this discovery is still preliminary to finding the specific coordinates that inform his theology. This is so because the search for truth by rhetorical means was for him propaedeutic to the theological task of interpreting the given, final truth in God's word, the Scripture. The starting point for approaching his theology, then, is his biblical hermeneutic, that is, his understanding of the sacred text. Erasmus saw the true vocation of theologians to be the exposition of the Bible: 'The foremost goal of theologians is to interpret the divine Scriptures with wisdom.'[66] His rhetorical method was therefore collateral to an exegetical procedure that was to elicit the meaning of the divine revelation from the Old and New Testament. Certainly, his emphasis on biblical primacy and rhetorical methods of interpretation was not entirely new,[67] but the way he intertwined biblical scholarship, rhetorical methodology, and theological construction made him distinct.

The philological and philosophical means Erasmus employed to arrive at an understanding of a text were taken into the service of an interpretation intended specifically to understand the word of God for the contemporary situation. Not that *bonae litterae* and *sacrae litterae* were so combined as to give each equal weight.[68] Rather, the quest of the ancients was to be preparatory to the philosophy of Christ as the lower to the higher wisdom, whereby the lower must neither be disdained for its servant role nor elevated to prominence.

Many scholars have come to agree that around the beginning of the sixteenth century Erasmus came to see his life's vocation in the philological treatment and theological interpretation of Scripture.[69] Actually, his interest in spirituality had predated his 'conversion' by more than ten years. The twenty-year-old religious at the Steyn monastery already had stressed that combination of good letters and personal piety which was to characterize his *philosophia Christi*, formulated as such only in his *Enchiridion* some fourteen years later. As early as 1488-89 he had regarded the study of the classics and the pursuit of a holy life as complementary. Erudition serves to enhance true religion.[70]

On the other hand, even after his decision to spend the rest of his life occupied with Scripture, he continued to engage in the *bonae litterae* and produced a wide-ranging corpus of secular writings. Just as he did not consider the difference between good and sacred literature to be absolute, so also his so-called conversion could not have meant a total break with secular scholarship. It was rather the culmination of an intellectual and spiritual process that reoriented his lifework. He was determined to concentrate on sacred literature as his proper project, even though he would continue with his work on good literature as his broader enterprise.

We are proceeding from the assumption that an understanding of the kind of theology Erasmus embraced, and of how its various elements were joined together in a system, will emerge from a careful study of the way in which he interpreted the sacred text. This method of understanding Erasmus' theology, I claim, is proper because it is similar to his own way of doing theology. For there is no doubt that scriptural exegesis was for him the supreme way of understanding the revealed truth of God. It is in his exegetical method, then, that we can discover not only the hermeneutical principles he espoused but also the structure he used to order his biblical theology. Furthermore, the content of this theology can be culled from the way Erasmus selected and interpreted points in the text; that is, how and why he either highlighted or ignored, joined or disconnected them by similarity and dissimilarity. In a word, his way of understanding God's word in Scripture indicates both the structure and the elements of his theology.

We shall see that Erasmus was not just a subjective thinker who ascertains the truth by the inductive method of an intellectual inquiry. Nor was he a rigid dogmatician who deduces the truth from formal philosophical and/or theological concepts. Rather, he was a man of the middle. He took the middle ground between the subjective search for truth and the objective authority of the truth. Erasmus was a master of an exegetical method that served a mediatorial purpose precisely in that it combined induction and deduction to arrive at the conviction of truth through both the act of convincing and the effect of being convinced. Neither a flexible rationalist nor a strict dogmatist, he wished to be known as a biblical theologian whose exegesis discloses the truth exactly by being open to its revelation.[71] The biblical text had for him a metaphorical quality of allegory, which makes interpreters strive for meaning while at the same time drawing them into the truth.[72] The freedom of the human search is both limited and perfected by the authority of the divine truth.

We maintain that the structure of Erasmus' theology will become clear from those exegetical rules and principles of interpretation which he spelled out in the 1516/18 introductory writings to his translation of the *New Testament* into Latin.[73] Moreover, in his *Paraphrases* on the New Testament and above all in his *Commentaries* on the Psalms, he repeatedly accounted for his exegetical approach and presented hints at his hermeneutic as well.[74] It is these hermeneutical reflections that offer the most significant clues to the structure of his theology. A careful analysis of the exegetical and hermeneutical references as found in his prefaces to the New Testament and in his *Paraphrases* and *Commentaries*[75] will help not only to clarify his method of interpretation but also to sketch his theology in broad strokes.

This approach will make it possible to assess how his rhetorical and theological means of interpretation converged; that is, to see what kind of connection there is between his use of rhetoric and his employment of theological categories.[76] The present bifurcation of philological and theological research could in this way perhaps be overcome and communication between the two sides be encouraged. This is all the more called for since Erasmus himself presented his synthesis of rhetoric and theology in the crowning culmination of his lifework, the *Ecclesiastes* of 1535.[77]

Earlier studies on Erasmus' theology have fixed the attention on his *Enchiridion* of 1503.[78] What this research generally achieved was to demonstrate that the liberal depiction of a rationalistic and moralistic humanist had produced a mere caricature. The *Handbook of a Christian Soldier* showed Erasmus as a spiritualist whose morality rested on a fundamentally religious attitude. However, this writing is in fact an ad hoc piece of devotional literature rather than a biblical commentary or theological treatise. Therefore, to describe his *philosophia Christi* in terms of personal piety reduces his theology to a narrow focus. Contrasting the spiritual moralist to the rational moralist is certainly a step in the right direction but hardly sufficient to comprehend the genius of his theology as a whole. The *philosophia Christiana* propounded in his biblical interpretation is characterized by a scope more comprehensively theological than the focus on the individual's spirituality and piety.[79] Erasmus' Christocentric understanding of scriptural revelation transcends that symbiosis of Platonic self-knowledge and *Devotio moderna* holiness which marks the imitation of Christ in the *Enchiridion*.

Consequently, if the turn to biblical literature was the decisive turning point in Erasmus' development, then the *Enchiridion* represents but the very beginnings of the new orientation and is thus less the touchstone of his theology than is his subsequent exegetical and theological work. An analysis of his theological thought must therefore proceed from his introductory writings to the New Testament some fifteen years later, particularly the *Ratio verae theologiae*. Moreover, it must include his actual exegesis of Old and New Testament texts, and enlarge the picture with material drawn from his other theological writings. Finally, just as the *Ratio* provides a convenient starting point for our inquiry, the *Ecclesiastes*, completed toward the end of his life, marks the end point.[80] This arrangement of sources not only reflects the succession of Erasmus' works over a twenty-year span but also includes his controversy with the reformers, which gave him the opportunity to amplify and qualify his theological thought in significant ways.

4 RATIO VERAE THEOLOGIAE

To familiarize the reader with the material that makes up the main body of our study, it seems useful to begin with an overview of the *Ratio*,[81] all the more since this is not available elsewhere. We do not intend a detailed analysis of the formal structure of the work.[82] Our survey must therefore remain sketchy, providing only a general outline, paraphrasing relevant passages, and quoting the most important statements. But we believe that presenting a synopsis of the whole piece at the beginning will make understanding the subsequent chapters of our study easier, and that is true for the *Ecclesiastes* as well. We shall come back to these surveys in the following chapters as we develop their hermeneutical implications.

The divisions of the *Ratio* appear to be as follows:

Introduction (H 177:1–178:19): Erasmus describes his task, defends his qualifications against possible objections, and refers to earlier literature, Augustine's *De doctrina christiana* and Dionysius the Areopagite's *De divinis nominibus* and *De mystica theologia*.

I. Preparation

1. (178:19–180:9): The fledgling theologian approaching Scripture must have a heart filled with the simplicity, innocence, and humility of faith, the singleness of love, and an eagerness to learn.

2. (180:9–186:34): Instruction in the secular disciplines is helpful unless it runs counter to Christ's teachings. The goal of education is 'to be changed, drawn into, inspired by, transformed into what you read.' True wisdom does not show itself in arrogance and stubborn disputes but in moral character and mildness. Studies in Greek, Latin, and Hebrew are required because Scripture is handed down in these languages. The student should be acquainted with the disciplines of grammar, dialectic, rhetoric, arithmetic, and music, including the natural sciences, geography, cultural history, and ethnography.

3. (187:1–191:30): Knowing the schemes and tropes of grammar and rhetoric is useful for the allegorical explanation of fables, especially those that pertain to good morals. As to rhetoric, the beginner should concentrate on *status*, *propositio*, *probatio*, and *amplificatio*, as well as on the twofold affects, *ethos* and *pathos*, because the theological profession rests more on affection than on

sophistic argumentation. Philosophy and dialectic are helpful as long as they do not degenerate into hair-splitting controversies. Should one dwell longer on profane literature, then let it be on that closest to sacred literature, poetry. For the prophets are replete with figures and tropes, and Christ clothed almost everything in parables. Also Plato, according to Augustine, was close to Christ's doctrine, and 'from the neighbouring and cognate the transition is easier.'

4. (191:31–193:23): 'The foremost goal of theologians is to interpret the divine Scriptures with wisdom (*sapienter*), to speak seriously (*graviter*) and effectively (*efficaciter*) of faith and piety, not to reason about trifling questions, but to drive out tears, and to inflame hearts to heavenly things.' The beginner must pursue this goal from the very first rather than grow old in the profane letters.

II. The doctrine of Christ

1. (193:24–195:1): A compendium of dogmas, drawn first from the gospels and then from the apostolic letters, will provide the novice with certain goals to which everything read can be referred: for instance, that Christ has founded on earth a new people wholly depending on heaven, disdaining the things of this world, living in simplicity, purity, concord, and mutual love as members of one body. Inspired by the Holy Spirit, they are a light to the world and a city on a hill. They desire immortality, fear neither tyranny, nor death, nor Satan, but live by trust in Christ's protection alone. 'This is the goal set by Christ, to which everything concerning Christians is to be referred ... These are the new dogmas of our author, which no philosophical school has handed down.'

2. (195:1–198:32): There is in these dogmas, however, a variety of things and persons. Certain things Christ clearly prohibits, others he clearly commands. Others he recommends by enticing with a reward those who are able to follow them, while not threatening with punishment those who cannot. Certain things he despises, others he dissembles. Therefore, to understand the meaning of Scripture, we must find out 'what is said, by whom, to whom, with what words, at what time, at what occasion, and what precedes and what follows.'

3. (198:33–201:33): The variety of times also sheds light on the obscurity of the arcane letters. First came the time preceding Christ. In the next period the gospel light rose, and the shadows

of the earlier law receded in preparation for Christ's proclamation. Then started the period when Christ's light shone into the world, and the nascent church received the Holy Spirit, even though the observation of the law continued. The fourth period was marked by the spread of Christ's religion over the whole earth and by secular authority no longer persecuting but protecting it; new laws were introduced which seem to contradict the decrees of Christ, unless we reconcile them, by the distinction of times, with the Scriptures. The fifth period is characterized by the church falling from the earlier vigour of the Christian spirit.

4. (202:1–208:37): Lest such a variety of times, persons, and things overwhelm the reader, it is useful to divide the universal people of Christ in three circles, with Christ being the one centre. The circle next to him is occupied by the clergy, the second by the secular princes, and the third by the common folk. Similarly, each natural element has its place in the lower world, where fire takes up the highest region and air, water, and earth hold their position in descending order. But fire, endowed with the supreme power of motion, gradually attracts everything to itself and transforms it into its nature. 'The boundaries do not serve for the transformation into the worse, but into the better.' In the same way, Christ accommodated himself to the weakness of human beings in order to draw them unto himself and transform them. Following that, Erasmus applies the notion of attraction, accommodation, and transformation to the function of popes, decrees, constitutions, human laws, and lawyers.

5. (209:1–211:27) The harmony of Christ: It is very useful to give careful attention to 'that admirable circle and consensus of the entire fable of Christ,' encompassing the types and oracles of the prophets, his incarnation, life, cross, and resurrection. He was the perfect example of poverty, humility, and innocence. 'Just as the whole circle of doctrine is in harmony with itself, so it is in agreement with his life, even with the discernment of nature itself.' Only in Christ do we find a circle and harmony that so renders all things congruous. It begins with the prophets and is rounded off by the life and teaching of the apostles and martyrs.

6. (211:28–223:31): 'But the variety of Christ does not confuse this harmony.' He became everything to everyone (*omnia omnibus*), sometimes revealing his divine nature, at other times acting as a human being. Also his miracles and his answers were varied in different circumstances, which on occasion gives offence

because it creates apparent contradictions. Still, we must not doubt the truthfulness of Scripture but take the circumstances into account and look for ways to explain the difficulty. Particularly problematic is the teaching of Christ's two natures; also the fact that the Jews rejected the gospel out of their own guilt, whereas the heathens were accepted in their stead.

7. (223:32-236:35): The apostles' lives and teachings were in harmony with the image of their teacher. Paul especially was a model of accommodation, becoming all things to all people. There follows an extensive *speculum pastorale* for the successors in the apostolic office, listing the vices to be avoided and the virtues to be pursued: innocence, charity, gentleness of heart, simple prudence, prudent simplicity, and a most certain faith. 'If those who followed in the office of the apostles excelled in this disposition, the church of Christ would be worthy to be called the kingdom of heaven.'

8. (236:36-259:31): Since the whole doctrine of Christ intends for our life to be pious and holy, it is proper to derive the example for our actions from the divine books, above all from the gospels. While Christ conducted himself variously to various people, he especially and continuously impressed on his disciples two things, faith and love. The life and teaching of all apostles accorded with the model Christ provided. But it was Paul who stressed love and peace as the basis for unity and concord in the face of divisions. As Ambrose had it: 'Peace is our religion.' The following section on the duties of the ecclesiastical office extends to 259:27. 259:28-31 summarizes the whole section.[83]

III. The interpretation of Scripture

1. (259:32-266:4): 'But a great deal of difficulty lies in the nature of the language in which the sacred Scriptures are handed down to us. For it is usually concealed and indirect in tropes and allegories and similes or parables, sometimes to the point of having the obscurity of an enigma.' Christ imitated the language of the prophets to exercise our sluggishness, so that the fruit of our labour would be the more pleasing. Moreover, it seemed right to hide and close the mysteries and conceal them from the profane and godless. Also, Christ used similitude because this kind of speech is above all pleasing, especially effective for persuasion, accessible and familiar to learned and unlearned alike, and to the highest degree in accordance with nature. 'In fact, the parable is not only effective for teaching and persuading

but also for moving the affections, for delighting, for transparency, and for impressing the same meaning deeply into the mind.' The eternal wisdom insinuates itself into pious minds, but it deceives the godless. Paul always imitated Christ by taking up the surface sense to the deeper meaning that is always the most true, the most sound, and most widely accessible.

2. (266:5–274:23): Certain tropes are owing to the idiomatic nature of Greek, Latin, and Hebrew. Other tropes, such as *synecdoche, hyperbaton,* and *hyperbole,* explain difficult passages. Even the trope of *irony* can be found in Scripture. 'There are several other figures of words and meanings that add to composition the weight (*gravitas*) or pleasantness (*jucunditas*) of speech. While the meaning of mystical Scripture indeed would be certain without them, they do flow more delightfully and effectively into our minds and are more fruitfully dealt with and passed on.' *Amphibologia* is a rhetorical vice that cannot always be avoided, even though Quintilian advised against it and Augustine preferred a clear solecism to ambiguous speech. The section ends with an annotation on the figure of *emphasis*.

3. (274:24–283:28): 'Allegories deserve special care since almost all of Holy Scripture is composed of them ... If taken on face value, the meaning of words is often patently false, sometimes even ridiculous and absurd.' Divine wisdom thus speaks to us in such a way that we have to look for concealed meanings. To be sure, we must not remove every historical sense, but sacred Scripture consists for the most part of a twofold meaning, literal and spiritual. Many passages exclude an ordinary sense, urging us to search by means of tropology for a meaning worthy of the Holy Spirit. However, the interpreter must observe moderation (*mediocritas*) in allegorizing. Attempting to accommodate all parts of a parable too scrupulously to an allegorical interpretation amounts to producing something like lifeless, contrived fiction. Conversely, without allegorical interpretation 'the meaning is frequently either absurd or destructive or good for nothing, trifling and lifeless.' The most familiar and efficacious kind of teaching comes from a comparison though similes. 'Christ takes the parables from the most common things, because he wished for his doctrine to be most popular.' But he wonderfully renews these *vulgata* in that he accommodates them to his philosophy.

4. (283:28–284:28): Sources for allegorical interpretation are found in Dionysius and in Augustine, who proposed the seven

rules of Tychonius. Yet 'it is not enough to consider how the eternal truth reflects itself variously in diverse things according to the simple and historical sense, according to the tropological sense that refers to morals and common life, according to the allegorical sense that deals with the mysteries of the head and of the whole mystical body, and according to the anagogical sense that touches on the heavenly hierarchy. One also will have to consider which degrees (*gradus*) there are in each of these, which differences, and which method of treatment (*ratio tractandi*).' For 'the type (*typus*) receives as it were another form (*figura*) in proportion to the variety of things to which it is accommodated, and according to the diversity of times.'

5. (284:28–285:35): The student of theology must above all learn appositely to quote Holy Scripture from its own sources. Moreover, to prevent twisting the words of eternal wisdom into an opposite sense, the meanings of both Testaments ought to be learned from the ancient interpreters. But 'the best reader of the divine books looks for the understanding of the words from what is said.' Interpretation draws the meaning from the text rather than imposing it on the text, or forcing the words to say what one presumes to know before reading.

6. (286:1–291:12): 'Also the rule is to be observed that the meaning which we draw forth from the obscure words corresponds with the circle of Christ's doctrine, conforms to his life, and finally is in accordance with natural equity.' In a lengthy section, Erasmus then gives examples of Scripture being estranged from its original meaning for various reasons. We, instead, must use the sacred words piously (*caste*) and fitly (*opportune*).

7. (291:13–293:13): It might be quite useful to collate 'theological *loci* in which you place everything you read as if in certain little nests. What you wish to express or conceal is thereby readier at hand ... Having arranged these topics in the order of the affinity or opposition of words and things ... everything notable in the Bible should be incorporated in proportion as it is concordant or dissonant. One could also register in this list anything of future use from the ancient interpreters of the Bible, at last even from the books of the heathens.' The best method of interpreting the divine letters is to clarify an obscure place by comparison (*collatio*) with other places. If most places agree, they are conducive to belief. But if they are at odds or even contrary,

they inspire us to a more determined examination. The collation of places is also of advantage for recognizing more certainly the idioms and tropes of the secret word.

8. (293:13–294:35): Instructed in these things, the novices in theology should meditate on Holy Scriptures day and night. What is thus impressed on their minds by constant practice (*usus*) goes over into their nature. The holy books must be committed to memory (*memoria*) and learned by heart, because it is from these sources that the true theology originates. 'Make your heart a library of Christ.'

9. (295:1–297:5): Can we understand Scripture without commentaries? While it is sufficient to be acquainted with the dogmas and to apply the comparison of places, the commentaries of the ancient interpreters relieve us of some of the work. But choose the best, like Origen, Basil, Nazianzen, Athanasius, Cyril, Chrysostom, Jerome, Ambrose, Hilary, and Augustine. Read them with discretion and reverence, for we ourselves assume the manner of the authors in whom we are continuously engaged. 'Not even the quality of food goes over into the nature of the body in the same way as reading translates into the reader's mind and morals.'

IV. True theology

(297:6–304:27): Theology has to do with life rather than with the syllogistic arguments of the scholastics, who quibble over contentious questions by means of dialectics and Aristotelian philosophy. 'Examining certain questions makes for little piety. Ignorance of other questions is possible without loss of salvation. There are those questions about which it is wiser to be uncertain and with the Academic philosophers to doubt than to make definitive statements.' So 'it is enough for us to believe, hold, and adore what is written.' The questions of the *neoterici*, marked as they are by curiosity rather than piety, adduce reasons that corrupt the strength of faith. For as long as we ask questions, we do not yet believe.

John admonishes: 'Search the Scriptures.' But Paul shows to what extent one should examine the secrets of Scripture and what the goal of theological knowledge is: 'charity out of a pure heart, and of a good conscience, and of faith unfeigned' rather than 'the novelty of vain babblings.' Not that Erasmus completely disapproves of the scholastic contentions (sometimes the truth lights up like fire sparking from stones colliding), but he calls for measure (*modus*) and discretion: 'Moderation will prevent us from questioning everything, discretion from questioning anything at will.' It is better to be a little less of a sophist than to be less versed in the evangelical and apostolic letters, better to be unfamiliar with certain of Aristotle's dogmas than to be ignorant of Christ's decrees. 'I'd rather be a pious theologian with Chrysostom than an undefeated one with Scotus.' 'In truth, we owe more to original manuscripts (*fascicula*) than to syllogisms.'

Conclusion (304:28–305:30): If you desire instruction in piety instead of disputation, be occupied with the sources and with those writers who have most nearly drawn from them. You will be an undefeated theologian if you do not yield to any vice. 'Great is the teacher who teaches Christ in purity.' Theologians derive their name from the divine prophecies, not from human opinions. And a good part of being a theologian is to be inspired, which does not happen other than through the purest of morals.

5 ECCLESIASTES SIVE DE RATIONE CONCIONANDI

As this treatise is quite lengthy, we must be content with sketching its broad outline and paraphrasing its content with regard to our theme.[84] The text is not readily analysable. Erasmus repeatedly interrupts his train of thought with digressions, more often than not caused by word associations within running commentaries on select biblical texts. One thing leads to another so that Erasmus time and again has to remind himself to return to the subject after lengthy disquisitions. Yet an overall structure emerges if we compare the layout of the first three books with the sequence of Quintilian's *Institutio oratoria*: *ars*, *artifex*, and *opus*.[85]

Erasmus begins in book I with *artifex*, the preacher, and then deals, in books II and III, with *opus*, that is, the *officia in dicendo* and the *partes operis*. However, he relinquishes 'the heading of art because those who have written about the precepts of eloquence themselves are uncertain whether rhetoric is an art, and because that supreme parent of eloquence acknowledged that it is the chief point of art to conceal art.'[86] In book IV he presents an index of theological *loci*. This sequence is indicated by Erasmus himself in the dedicatory letter: 'We divide the main argument into four books. In the first we point out the dignity of the office and the virtues that must be at the preacher's command. In the second and third we accommodate the precepts of the rhetoricians, dialecticians, and theologians to the use of preaching. The fourth is like a catalogue and shows which ideas (*sententiae*) the preacher ought to derive from which places (*loci*) in Scripture.'[87]

Book I. *On the dignity, purity, prudence, and the other virtues of the preacher* (ASD V-4 35:1; cf 246:160)

Introduction (35:6–36:47): The Greek word *ecclesia* means in Latin *concio*: an assembly of people called out to hear speeches on the affairs of the republic. Ἐκκλησιατής signifies the person who publicly speaks to the multitude. There are two republics, the profane and the sacred, with two *ecclesiastae*, performing different but not contrary functions, serving each other but aiming at the same goal: the tranquillity of both civic peace and Christian piety. In the sacred assembly the preacher explains sacred Scripture to the people.

I. The preacher

1. Word, heart, spirit, and speech (36:48–44:186): The preacher speaks the word of heavenly philosophy, Jesus Christ, the *verbum sive sermo Dei*. Flowing from the Father's heart, Christ is the most certain expositor of the divine mind; through him God speaks to us. The word of human beings, too, springs from their spirit: 'As is our word, so is our spirit.' Thus we cannot approach God other than through our spirit and language, for 'the mind is the source, the word is the image flowing forth from the source.' Just as Christ is the image of the Father so our speech mirrors what is conceived in the mind. Our words carry the power of their source, reproducing its useful or harmful affection. It makes all the difference, then, whether God or the devil rules the heart.

2. (44:187–54:388): In preparation for the ecclesiastical office, the student must acquire a profound knowledge of Scripture, practise literary composition, read diverse doctors, develop a sound judgment and uncommon prudence, nurture a sincere and strong mind, learn the precepts and practice of speaking, assemble *copia* of words and ideas, etc. The foremost source of ecclesiastical eloquence, however, is a clean heart. Renewed by the heavenly Spirit, it is able to understand Scripture, for the Bible was committed to writing by the same Spirit. 'The fountain of right speaking is wisdom.' Wisdom differs from knowledge in that a wise person, instead of knowing everything, is not only learned in the things that concern true happiness but also is transfigured by them. As often as we eat the food of evangelical

doctrine, it goes over into the inmost parts of our mind, becomes our nature, and strengthens our spirit.

3. (54:389–58:497): Part of the clean heart is the purity of life. From the preacher's heart the virtues of Christ's innocence, mildness, and benevolence must shine forth in word, life, and face, whereas vices, even the appearance of evil, are detrimental to ministerial authority.

4. (60:498–68:684): 'Faith pertains to dove-like simplicity, prudence to serpent-like caution.' Faithful are those who teach nothing but God's commandments and everywhere look to both the glory of God and the advantage of the sacred flock. It is the function of prudence, however, 'to discern from the circumstances of times, places, and persons what is to be applied to whom, when, and with what moderation.' Therefore, the ecclesiastic must learn how to accommodate to the variety of gender, age, conditions, natural dispositions, opinions, institutions of life, and customs. According to the rhetoricians, the precepts of art must yield to prudence, which they divide into *judicium* and *consilium*. While sacred orators receive prudence as a gift of the Holy Spirit, the Spirit yet accommodates to their natural disposition. 'The Holy Spirit does not remove the innate power of nature but perfects it.'

5. (68:685–76:875): The preacher's *scopus* is a heart clean and prudent to discern 'what is to be left unsaid, what to be said, before whom, at which time, and in what way speech should be moderated, knowing like Paul to change one's voice and to become all to all, whenever it seems expedient to the salvation of the hearer.' This faculty must be asked from God by prayer and sought by pious works. There are two kinds of good works: ceremonies (or corporeal exercises) and the spiritual works of piety. To exercise the body is useful only insofar as it enhances the spirit. Just as the pagan philosophers advised against *supercilium, superstitio, praeposterum judicium,* and *oblivio mediocritatis* in the body's training for endurance, so Christians should take the middle road by avoiding that immoderate severity to the body which is useless for spiritual growth.

II. The dignity of the teaching office

1. (76:876–77:937): Learned are all who believe the gospel, glean the heavenly philosophy from the Apostles' Creed, and keep the commandments of both laws, who are taught by Christ how to pray and in which way to pursue the goal of happiness. Still,

among the learned ones stand out the doctors who have received the special gifts of the Spirit to teach righteousness to many.

2. (77:938–84:50): The dignity of office is a gift of God. Preachers have received a tongue instructed in the words of the Lord, not in philosophical syllogisms or rhetorical flourishes. They hear the voice of the Spirit in the mind's ears – human ears, to be sure, but perfected by God and fortified through faith and obedience. While preparation in the human disciplines is helpful, the student must not grow old in them but early on advance to secret wisdom. The pastoral office serves to root out the depraved opinions and impious doctrines from the hearers' minds and to plant the good seed by means of a tongue that is instructed in the word of God, which is Scripture divinely inspired.

3. (84:51–114:661): To persuade effectively, one must love what one teaches. The heart itself provides the lover with the ardour of speech, and doctrine is the more efficacious the more teachers excel in what they teach others. Since burning comes before shining, the flame of the mind shines forth in the light of doctrine. True charity accompanies sincere faith.

The external characteristics of Old Testament priesthood (such as consecration, sacrifice, anointing, and vestments) reveal hidden meanings if interpreted spiritually. Purity signifies cleansing from human desires and adorning with the heroic virtues. 'From the (anointed) head comes the wisdom of sound doctrine, from the heart proceed voice and speech. It is not sufficient for the priest to know what is right and pious, unless there is the faculty of teaching others. It consists of a double word: the Old Testament hidden under the cover of figures and enigmas, and the New Testament revealing the mysteries and making known the manifest truth.' The same is true of the twofold sense of the entire Scripture, the lower and the allegorical or higher one. To explain these properly, truth ($ἀλήθεια$) must be present so that doctrine contains no error, but also clarification ($δήλωσις$) so that the hidden message of Scripture becomes perspicuous even to the unschooled.

One must not rush into office but spend much time preparing in one's heart the ability to teach. We cannot teach others what to believe and how to live unless our life and morals reflect what we are talking about. That Jesus acted before he taught tells us that the most efficacious kind of doctrine is that which declares piety in life. Two things guard the pastor's innocence of life: fear and love. Fear as the beginning of wisdom means to draw back from evil; love is to do good.

There is also a distinction between Old and New Testament doctrine. While Aaron instructed how to use God's law, the New Testament teaches that inerrant philosophy which the son of God has brought from the Father's heart to earth. Of course, it is difficult to explain the secret Scriptures, but the harder the task, the greater is the gift of the spirit. Although this gift is given freely, it does not eliminate our industry, prayers, and good works. Natural gifts (a healthy body) and the natural endowments for speaking (a good voice, articulate language, quick mind, and trustworthy memory) are faculties made ready by human industry. But just like the professional skills (expertise in dialectical arguments, proficiency in the rhetorical power of speech, and the knowledge of natural things), they are not destroyed by the Spirit but perfected. Furthermore, moral education through parents and educators, just as preparation in the best of the secular disciplines, enhances the faculty of teaching.

III. The authority of the teaching function

1. (114:662–180:924): The highest church office is that of bishop, and among the ecclesiastical functions the highest is teaching the heavenly philosophy, a mandate which the bishop delegates to presbyters. But to desire the vocation of preacher is not wrong, for 'to desire a good office is of charity.' In the following, Erasmus deals with the qualifications of clergy, their functions, jurisdiction, selection, and removal, and the abuses of the present time. Model bishops mentioned are Warham, Fisher, and Gregory I. This episcopal ideal is then set against the sorry state of contemporary Christian religion. The next section declares the bishop's office as superior to the prince's, and the work of parish priests as more difficult than monastic life.

2. (180:925–190:62): 'Next to God's authority comes the sublimity of the prophets, whom God endowed with a special dignity and through whom as interpreters he wished to disclose his inscrutable will to mortals.' Old Testament prophecies uncovered the past, foretold the future, or explained the divine secrets for the present without discriminating the times. But they yielded little by little to the evangelical light, becoming either lifeless or better when changed into a more sublime kind. The New Testament prophecy brings to light the mysteries of Scripture accord-

ing to the spiritual sense. It depends on the spiritual prophets, then, whether the church grows or diminishes. As the Spirit leads them into all truth, nothing remains hidden until the last day. Now the mystical Scripture provides the living food and water, to be dispensed according to the circumstances of the hearers.

3. (190:63–198:228): Evangelical prophets are even more excellent than John the Baptist, the prophet in the middle between the old and the new prophecy. For expressing the gospel with the tongue is more felicitous than pointing to it with the finger. Certainly, the Spirit remains the same, but it is differently dispensed according to the times. As the Spirit now perfects faith, it destroys the external signs which were earlier necessary because of infirmity and unbelief. The law served as a pedagogue to Christ. But when the sun of the gospel arose, the minor lights darkened; the interior overshadowed the exterior. The miracle of God calling from death to life surpasses the old miracles, and the resurrection in the forgiveness of sins supersedes the resurrection of the body.

4. (198:229–206:380): The five special duties of bishops/priests are administering the sacraments of the new law, praying for the people, judging, ordaining, and, the highest, teaching, which surpasses even the celebration of the Eucharist. Erasmus insists that he has nothing against monasticism or priesthood, but to put second things first is a perverted judgment (*praeposterum judicium*). Inverted choices are the fountain of all moral ruin. So also in ministry, the highest (teaching) must not be consigned to the lowest place, but the lowest must be raised to the highest. Consequently, humility rather than pride marks the excellent dignity of the minister.

5. (206:381–220:640): Since the church resides on the mountain of heroic virtues, teaching the gospel is like climbing up the mountain. As a lookout on the mountain top, the preacher is both the custodian of doctrinal harmony and the guardian against the enemies, the most dangerous of which are the capital vices. Sacred rhetoric not only heals those good if weak folk who have fallen, but also removes those who are incurable. Since the saving doctrine is not earthly but heavenly, preachers must proceed from the letter of Scripture to its mystical sense, from the carnal to the spiritual, comparing spiritual things with spiritual things. Human wisdom exhibits on the outside some quite great and admirable things but looked at more deeply they turn

out to be coal rather than gold. The evangelical philosophy, on the contrary, keeps its more splendid treasure in its inner recesses.

6. (222:641–240:27): Two things help teachers to render hearers teachable (*docilis*): Love makes them listen with pleasure rather than boredom; authority causes them to acknowledge the truth of what is taught. But both, love and authority, must be tempered by a prudence which so accommodates to the hearers' circumstances as to insure their advantage (*commodum*), their advancement toward piety. While preachers should strive in love to please all, they must nonetheless have Paul's word in mind: 'All is allowed, but not all is expedient.' Likewise, the preacher's authority must not offend the people's backwardness or customs. Rather, the prudent ecclesiastic will dissemble in order to temper the licence of the people. As to remuneration, the teacher's love gives freely and cheerfully; it earns well from everyone, benefits all, but does not ask benefaction from anyone in return. Nevertheless, heroic virtue does not reject the service of human gifts, whether innate or added by education and industry. Rather, natural dispositions are accommodated to the service of love. After all, perfect love makes all things common.

7. (240:28–246:159): Except for a brief admonition concerning faithful hearers, Erasmus' comments on the hearers are virtually all negative. Expecting histrionics from the preachers, the impious crowd (*vulgus*) behaves in the Christian assembly without decorum. Erasmus admonishes the people to listen to the preacher as if they hear Christ.

Conclusion (246:160-3): The subject of this volume was the dignity, difficulty, purity, fortitude, utility, and reward of the faithful ecclesiastic. The rest will be presented in the next volume.

Book II

Introduction (247:4–252:137): A heart created new by the generous God hardly needs copious rules for speaking. For it is the sincere disposition of the mind that prompts readiness of speech, an apposite delivery, and decent gestures. 'The chief point of (rhetorical) art is to conceal art.' Indeed, for certain ancient authors, 'rhetoric is nothing else than prudence of speaking.' Many of them were most eloquent without knowing art at all. Even so, the arts, taught early and moderately, develop the skilfulness of one's natural disposition. Rules and exercises aid our natural weakness. While practice translates art into experience, precepts enable a more certain and mature faculty of speaking. But precepts must 'through frequent use pass over into habit as if into nature.' To speak well, then, one must 'put little value on art, but only after the faculty of speaking has been developed by the use of art.'

I. Grammar

1. (252:138–260:302): Grammar, the foundation of all other disciplines, is 'the art of speaking correctly (*emendate*).' It is acquired by reading the most eloquent ancient authors and requires the knowledge of words, of the orderly arrangement of ideas, and of natural things in their variety of species. Moreover, grammar includes history, poetry, and the knowledge of antiquity. History is blind without cosmography and arithmetics.

2. (260:303–262:339): Four things are essential to the faculty of speaking: 'nature, art, imitation or example, and use or practice.' So powerful is nature that nothing is more important for poetry and rhetoric, for 'what is cognate is immediately apprehended.' Children are naturally teachable because of their willingness to imitate. But shyness or natural timidity render teaching useless, unless these impediments are overcome by zeal and practice.

3. (262:340–264:415): The three languages (Greek, Latin, and Hebrew) serve to unlock the books of the ancients. They also provide access to the sources of the divine books. Furthermore, expertise in the vernacular is necessary for preaching.

4. (264:416–268:483): Readings from profane authors include Demosthenes, Cicero, Aristotle, Plato, Livy, Virgil, the tragedians, Tacitus, Seneca, and Plutarch; from the ecclesiastical authors, Basil, Athanasius, Chrysostom, Gregory Nazianzen, and Origen; Tertullian, Hilary, Cyprian, Ambrose, Jerome, Augustine, Pope Gregory, Prudentius, Bernard, Pope Leo, Maximus, and Fulgentius. John Gerson is not very useful, Thomas Aquinas more so for philosophy and argumentation. Scotus and his kind are useful for the cognition of things but not for speaking. Add the more recent preachers. While no book is so bad that it will not yield some profit, the student should seek examples from the best.

II. Rhetoric

1. (268:484–274:594): Selecting some rhetorical precepts insofar as they are suitable for the preacher's office, Erasmus focuses his attention first on the triad of art, artist, and work. 'While we

admit that the eloquence of the preacher does not rest on art, we recognize that there must be some reason and prudence for speaking, which relies on judgment and counsel.' Enough has been said in the first volume about the artist, the preacher. Now it is in place to touch on the duties (*officia*) of speaking, then on the parts of the work (*partes operum*). The *materia* of rhetoric comes in three *genera*: the *genus forense*, which is remote from the preaching office; the *genus suasorium*, which for the preacher consists of teaching, persuading, exhorting, consoling, counselling, and admonishing; and the *genus encomiasticum*, which concerns doxology and thanksgiving.

2. (274:595–280:723): The *officia* of the preacher are *docere, delectare*, and *flectere*. Teaching is fundamental because it makes for understanding and persuasion. No one is delighted or moved by that which is neither understood nor believed. Delight comes from the *jucunditas* or rather *gratia* of speech. Eloquence is most powerful, however, if it changes (*flectere*), i.e., if it seizes (*rapere*) the affections of the hearers. The singular offices of the orator are *inventio, dispositio, elocutio, memoria*, and *pronuntiatio*.

3. (280:724 470:546): The *partes operis* are *exordium, narratio, divisio, confirmatio, confutatio*, and *conclusio*.

3.1 (280:727–304:362): *Exordium* (or the beginning of a speech) can arise, from Scripture; from history; from parables (narration in the *exordium*; *adfectus* in narration); from living nature; from present things; from similitude; from transition; from *sententia*; the material of introduction; invocation.

3.2 (304:365–310:524): *Divisio* either announces in a preliminary outline the order of things to come or, in a wider sense, shows the disposition of the work interspersed throughout the parts of speech.

3.2.1 (310:525–312:591): *Inventio partium principalium*. Partition must be distinct, clear, brief, and coherent. As the whole business of inventing the principal parts and arranging the inventory in a proper order is quite difficult, Erasmus touches here only on what the rhetoricians taught about the suasory and laudatory genre and adds what seems to be special about exhortation, consolation, and objurgation. The main point about the *genus suasorium* is to consider the subject matter and objective of persuasion, the audience, and the speaker. While preachers persuade to nothing but honest things, they persuade different people differently.

3.2.1.1 (312:592–316:719): The parts of the *genus suasorium* provide both the division and the propositions of the entire speech. While the Stoics contended that there is but one proposition, *honestum*, others separate utility from honesty. The concept *honestum* includes what in itself is right, beautiful, and decorous.

3.2.1.2 (316:720–328:20): The parts of the *genus laudatorium* (doxology; *bona externa: corpus, patria, parentes; bona animi: virtutes* and by comparison *vitia*) extol God and teach what is conducive to good living.

3.2.1.3 (328:21–332:138): *Exhortatio* is part of the *genus suasorium*, for persuasion teaches through arguments, exhortation stimulates the affections. The foremost parts of exhortation are *laus, expectatio publica, spes victoriae, spes gloriae* vs *metus ignominiae, magnitudo praemii* vs *horror poenae*, and *commemoratio illustrium*. Exhortation can also be derived from *miseratio, odium, amor, invidia*, and *aemulatio*.

3.2.1.4 (332:139–334:205): The parts of *consolatio* have to do with private and public suffering in persecution, war, pestilence, and famine.

3.2.1.5 (334:206–341:371): *Admonitio* must not be satisfied with arguing against vices but persuade that they are abominations, demonstrate the reasons for correcting evil deeds, and show how much more righteous and pleasant it is to walk in the way of virtue until perfection.

3.2.2 (341:372–344:451): *De statibus sive constitutionibus*. 'Status is the essential point of a case or a question on which the speaker focuses everything and to which the hearer especially looks.' Used foremost in legal cases, status a) as *status conjecturalis sive inficialis* seeks the truth by inference from a comparison of facts; b) as *status qualitatis sive jurisdicialis* inquires whether a fact was done lawfully; c) as *status finis sive definitivus* seeks by definition to name the fact. The preacher too should focus everything on a *scopus*, for anyone speaking in public must have an intentional goal.

3.2.3 (344:452–356:798): *Inventio partium sive propositionum* draws on the parts and circumstances of the total case. A proposition can serve either as the beginning of an argument, or after the argument as *conclusio* or *collectio* (*propositio probata*). To invent partition and arrange propositions in the order (*gradus*) of an argument, it is useful to know the *status, loci*, and *circumstantiae* of the case, plus the art of law, philosophy, and theology. The rest comes from natural talent and exercise.

3.3 (356:799–370:106): *Argumentatio sive probatio*. Aristotle found that three things give credence to the speaker: *prudentia*, *virtus*, and *benevolentia*. It is the task of proof to confirm the argument and to refute the opposite. Proofs are either *artificiales* (*praejudicia*, *rumores*, *tormenta*, *tabulae*, *jurisjurandum*, *testimonia*) or *inartificiales* (*signa*, *necessaria*, and *probabilia*). Before going into arguments, it must be mentioned that there are certain propositions confessed to such a degree that they do not need proof, such as the essentials of the Christian faith. The *nativa vis ingenii* is very useful for the invention of proof, because the faculty of reasoning comes before the art of dialectic.

3.3.1 (370:107–400:850): *Circumstantiae*. Arguments arise partly from natural disposition, partly from art. But we invent arguments more quickly and easily if we know the rhetorical places from which they are to be derived. Any proof is taken from the circumstances of persons and things. *Circumstantiae personae* include *genus*, *natio*, *patria*, *sexus*, *aetas*, *educatio sive disciplina*, *habitus corporis*, *fortuna*, *conditio*, *animi natura*, *studia*, *adfectatio*, *antedicta*, and *antefacta*, *commotio*, *consilium*, *nomen*. *Circumstantiae rei* are subdivided into *causa* (*efficiens*, *materialis*, *formalis*, and *finalis*); *locus*; *tempus*; *casus*; *facultas*; *instrumentum*; and *modus*.

3.3.2 (400:851–424:433): *Loci* (*topoi*). *Loci communes* serve to argue both ways, as for instance by amplifying virtues and exaggerating vices. Commonplaces are also used as a base for arguing single causes. Finally, *loci generales* make clear what happens generally to everything and how arguments, partly necessary and partly probable, are derived from single things. The general division of all questions is, 'Whether something is, what it is, and of what kind it is.' *Definitio* consists of *genus*, *species*, and *differentia*. *Divisio* and *partitio* include *exordium*, *incrementum*, and *summa*. *Similitudo* (with its subcategories: *fictio*, *analogia*, *exemplum*, and *imago*) is not only useful for proof but also lends much light and dignity to oratory. *Dissimilia* include *pugnantia*, *opposita*, *contraria*, *privativa*, *relativa*, *contradictoria*, *repugnantia*, *consequentia*. The next *loci* are *causae* and *effecta* with *generatio*, *corruptio*, and *comparatio*.

(424:434–427:489): *Catalogus* repeating the points of argumentation, the circumstances of persons and things, and the *loci*.

50 Rhetoric and Theology

(427:490–462:347): The observation of loci is not only valuable for proving by argument in order to persuade but also for teaching the complete knowledge of any subject of art so that the student understands. Erasmus turns now to the subject of teaching and shows how the *loci* from *definitio* to *comparatio* apply to theological subject matter.

(462:348–468:484): *Argumentatio* consists of *propositio, ratio, confirmatio, exornatio,* and *complexio,* or, in the shorter version, of *propositio, ratio,* and *complexio.*

3.4 (468:485–470:546): The *Epilogus* refreshes the hearer's memory, presents the entire cause, and adds more solid arguments. Another kind of peroration is the *conclusio* which appeals to the affections, that is, in the Christian congregation, to piety. The next volume will deal with *amplificatio, orationis jucunditas,* and *vehementia.*

Book III

I. The single offices

1. (LB V 951E–955B): So far Erasmus has covered only one of the orator's five offices, *inventio.* Now he returns to the broader subject and adds what seems to have been omitted. Next to *inventio* comes *elocutio. Dispositio sive ordo,* about which he began to speak when discussing *divisio,* functions in four ways: a) as symmetry and proportion of words (*commoditas*) providing speech not only with perspicuity and rhythmic measure (*modulatio*) but also with sharpness (*acrimonia*); b) as the order of the principal propositions of speech; c) as the order of the individual arguments; d) as the division of the whole speech into *exordium, incrementum,* and *summa.*

2. (955C–956B): If one learns by rote and anxiously depends on loci and images, *memoria* becomes artificial, that is, completely dependent on art, and thus hinders more than aids. The natural talent becomes dull, the ardour of speaking cools off, and the natural power of memory (which is most capable of many things, especially if intelligence, care, practice, and order enhance the felicitous nature of a human being) is stunted.

3. (956B–967A): *Actio sive pronuntiatio* has to do with the moderation of voice, of facial expression, and of the whole body, all of which are to be adapted to the respective subject matter. Also in this regard, reason and use perfect nature. Therefore, imitate the decorous, avoid the unbecoming, and above all observe what is decent.

II. *Virtutes orationis*

1. (967A-968E): Now Erasmus returns to those things which he had postponed and shows what makes speech powerful (*vehemens*), delightful (*jucunda*), and abundant (*copiosa*). *Loci communes* contribute to both the vehemence and the copiousness of speech. Commonplaces are those recurring meanings which, if amplified, help toward persuasion, whether through praise or blame. But more frequently they occur in the demonstrative genre. *Loci* are derived a) from *genera* and *partes* of virtues and vices; b) from meanings drawn from them and enforcing them; 3) from common life.

2. (968F-976D): *Amplificatio* increases or diminishes either things or words. Amplification of things makes for *adfectus*; amplification of words produces rhythm and measure (*modus*): amplification a) of words; b) through gradual increment; c) through comparison; d) through reasoning (*ratiocinatio*); e) from means (*instrumentum*); f) from occasion, circumstances, and places; g) through *emphasis*; h) through congeries; i) through augmentation and diminution.

3. (976D-987E): *Adfectus* are divided into two kinds, the milder (comic) and the more severe (tragic), with neutral affections residing in the middle. Both kinds of affections are derived from the circumstances of persons and things. The affections can be aroused in three ways: a) through imagination or fantasy, whereby the speaker reproduces the images of things; b) by evidence, whereby the total view of the thing is so presented to the hearer's mind that it seems to be displayed to the eyes rather than spoken; c) through prayerful reading of those scriptural passages that are most conducive to inflaming the heart.

4. (987F-1005E): The *schemata* (*figurae*) conducive to sharp, powerful, and serious speech (*acrimonia, vehementia, gravitas*) are enumerated along with the figures suitable to delightful, clear, brilliant, pleasant, and charming speech (*jucunditas, perspicuitas, splendor, festivitas, venustas*).

5. (1005E-1008B): *Sententiae* express in appropriate brevity either what one should do in life or what usually happens.

6. (1008B-1011D): Nothing persuades more effectively, presents the subject matter more evidently, moves more potently the affections, and makes speech more dignified, attractive, or pleasant than *metaphora*, if examples are drawn above all from Scripture, but also from nature. *Similitudo* or *collatio* is an explained

metaphor. *Imago* is a species of *similitudo*. *Similitudo* can also be useful for reasoning (*ratiocinatio*), as for instance to show the absurdity of a heretical position.

7. (1011D–1016F): The quality of similitude changes the *character orationis* (*jucundus, grandis, acris, mediocris, humilis*). But beyond the three traditional *genera elocutionis* (*humile, mediocre, grande*) there are others. A section is added here to exemplify the use of *schemata* in a biblical text (Matt 9; Luke 5) to effect *jucunditas, splendor, vehementia, adfectus*.

8. (1016F–1019A): There are other tropes in Scripture, like *hypallage, enallage, heterosis,* and *synecdoche*.

III. Allegory

1. (1019A–1025F): No trope causes more work than allegory. While the exegete must always be careful not to distort the genuine sense of Scripture, there are linguistic idioms that render the plain sense absurd. Therefore, the preacher must look at the interpretation of the Fathers, compare places (*collatio locorum*), consider times and persons, identify the context in Scripture or in various interpretations, and meditate at length in faithful prayer. To twist the text to human affections and impious meanings is to remove the authority of Scripture.

2. (1026A–1033F): To accommodate Scripture appropriately to the subject matter, it is not enough to cull opinions from modern anthologies. Rather, one must return *ad fontes* and elicit the genuine meaning from the scriptural context. The ancient interpreters should be read with discretion and judgment, their authority resting on their proximity to the origin (*vetustas*). Still, the authority of the patristic *consensus* can neither measure up to Scripture itself nor rival the apostles. Therefore, one must dissent from the Fathers if they overallegorize, for the letter is the basis upon which the superstructure of allegory is built.

3. (1033F–1037D): *De ratione allegoriarum*. Metaphor is the fountain of several tropes: *collatio, imago* and *abusio, aenigma, allegoria, proverbium,* and *apologus*. Metaphor is a brief similitude, while similitude or *collatio* is a metaphor unfolded and accommodated to the subject matter. The rhetoricians defined *allegory* simply as a continous metaphor, whereas in sacred literature and with the doctors of the church the term has received a wider meaning, sometimes standing for *tropus*, sometimes for *typus*. The modern theologians teach a fourfold sense of Scripture: *historicum sive grammaticum, tropologicum, allegoricum,* and *anagogicum*. The

ancient doctors knew only two senses: grammatical (or literal, or historical) and spiritual (which they variously called tropological, allegorical, or anagogical).

4. (1037D–1051D): Allegorical interpretation. One must neglect neither the literal nor the allegorical and tropological sense in Scripture. Nevertheless, necessity or utility compels us at times to draw back from the historical or literal sense. Even if the truth sometimes resides in the lowest sense and the words neither are absurd nor otherwise run counter to sound doctrine, the letter kills if we keep hanging on to it. The mysteries of celestial philosophy are hidden to impious folk but open to teachable people, whom they encourage, by attracting them pleasantly, to make a more avid effort. For the truth is more delightful if shining through allegories than revealed through simple narration, just as it is more powerfully imprinted in the mind.

5. (1051D–1058F): In explaining Scriptures, speech must be clear of obscurity. The obscurity of Scripture is due not only to the nature of tropes but also to other causes, such as incorrect translation; poor knowledge of antiquity; the use of words with different meanings but similar sounds; the use of the same noun to refer to different things; punctuation; pronunciations; contradiction, untruth, absurdity; and the difficulty of indicating the person in whose name a discourse proceeds.

6. (1058F–1062D): Rules of interpretation. Augustine related the seven rules of Tychonius concerning a) Christ and his mystical body, the church; b) the body of Christ divided in two parts, pious and impious; c) promises and law (letter and spirit; grace and commandment); d) genus and species, or the whole and the part; e) the quantity of time, or numbers; f) recapitulation; g) the devil and his body as one person. Augustine also said that Scripture can be interpreted in four ways: according to history, aetiology, analogy, and allegory. Instead of presenting more rules from ancient and modern authors, however, Erasmus advises, with Augustine, that the most efficacious rule of all is that 'we should love sacred letters before we learn, being truly persuaded that there is nothing written in them that is false, trifling, or human-minded, but everything replete with heavenly philosophy and worthy of the Holy Spirit in whatever form it appears, if it is properly understood. With this in mind, then, the whole corpus of Scripture should be attentively read and appropriated by long meditation.'

Conclusion (1062D–1072A): Erasmus returns to the question of *judicium* and *concilium*, which are applicable not only in invention but also in all offices of the orator. They adjust the address to the hearer's disposition, power of comprehension, and affections. Judgment determines what cause, person, time, place, and usage require, and sometimes, also, what is decent. Counsel makes the oratory persuasive. So preachers should be circumspect in accommodating to their audience in order to be beneficial to all.

Book IV

1. God and Satan (1071C–1074D): The following *elenchus* will aid those preachers who fail to develop an *index materiarum* for themselves. Two persons (God and Satan) are set up like columns of a building in which everything can be arranged in its proper place. The triune God who speaks to us in Scripture presides as the highest monarch over the celestial, ecclesiastical, and political hierarchies. Satan, by contrast, is the prince of darkness and author of evil whose malice God uses to tempt the elect and to punish the wicked. Turning the Trinity into its opposite, the devil corrupts what is created, incites humanity to sin, returns the redeemed to servitude, and heads a body of befouled members. His highest power is to hurt, his highest craft to destroy, and his highest malice to seduce and turn the order upside down. Where the Spirit binds and holds everything together, Satan breaks up and scatters everything.

2. Law (1074D–1078E): Although the law of God is always the same, it is variously revealed according to the variety of times and persons: the natural law for the created world, the law of Moses for fallen humankind, and the evangelical law for those who are restored and move on to perfection. Right in the beginning, Satan's law counteracted the divine law by the law of the flesh with its attendants, sin and death. Several *loci* arise from the law: on the difference between the old and new law; on the sacraments of both; on the consonance of both and how far the old is abrogated by the new; on the authority of canonical Scripture and how far it extends.

3. Virtues and vices (1078E–1083E): The law engenders the *locus* of the two kinds of sin and two kinds of death. Under the rubric of sin fall all kinds of vices. Opposed to vices are the virtues, the first among which are faith, hope, and love. As heroic virtues they are, respectively, correlated to the general virtues: prudence, fortitude, and justice, whereby temperance becomes a subspecies

of justice. The virtues in general are focused on piety as the natural affection toward God, country, parents, teachers, physicians and clergy. Next, the *officia caritatis* are arranged in stages, with respective *loci* and *contraria* listed in order. The *chorus temperantiae-intemperantiae* is followed by *loci* concerning Christian fortitude, and the entire section ends with the *clausula*: the extreme point of virtues and vices, the end of virtuous life in the glory of Christian death versus the end of vices in eternal despair.

4. In the following *Tituli* (1083E-1087F), Erasmus lists in outline the major headings and sections of the *elenchus*. In the *Sylva* (1087F-1100C), he makes an (eventually abortive) attempt at amplifying, specifying, and adding to that material. After an admonition to the theologians to excerpt their own commonplaces from Scripture as well as an exhortation to concord, the work comes to an abrupt and, as the author himself admits, incomplete end.

6 RATIO AND ECCLESIASTES COMPARED

Any attempt at comparing these two works with the traditional handbooks of rhetoric would go beyond our present compass. It would also lead us too far afield to try to identify their borrowings from classical and patristic authors. Suffice it to say that Erasmus mentions Augustine and Dionysius, the Pseudo-Areopagite, as sources for the *Ratio*; Augustine, Cicero, the *Rhetorica ad Herennium*, and Quintilian serve as background for the *Ecclesiastes*.[88] Still, neither the *Ratio* nor the *Ecclesiastes* is a mere compilation. As they bring together rhetorical, biblical, and theological subject matter, they are original in design and execution, even though they are certainly indebted to traditional models, especially to Augustine's *De doctrina christiana*, and draw on many sources. Besides tracing the numerous direct or indirect references to biblical passages and ancient writings, one would have to look for influences from the Italian humanists, especially Lorenzo Valla. Parallels to contemporary humanists, particularly Rudolph Agricola, Juan Luis Vives, and Philipp Melanchthon, must be drawn too. Erasmus had probably absorbed, consciously or as if by osmosis, a tremendous store of pertinent material.[89]

Comparing the outlines of the two treatises, however, does fall within the purview of our study. Even a cursory look gives us an idea as to how Erasmus connected the exposition of the sacred text with the composition of the sermon. Clearly, his rhetorico-theological hermeneutic guides both scriptural exegesis and sacred oratory. But the *Ratio* treats of hermeneutic more in terms of dogmatics, the *Ecclesiastes* more in terms of homiletics. The *Ratio*, an introductory writing to the New Testament, has more to do with interpreting biblical texts, whereas the *Ecclesiastes*, a textbook on preaching, puts the interpretation of Scripture to practical use in sacred rhetoric. Scriptural exposition becomes homiletical application in public discourse, using the deliberative or suasive genre.[90] The earlier work concentrates on understanding the theological content that informs God's accommodating language to humanity. The subject of the later work, in addition to repeating and amplifying the exegetical rules, covers the whole sweep of rhetorical items from the faculty, office, and function of the speaker (I), to the duties of speaking and the *inventio* and *dispositio* of the parts of speech (II), to memorizing and delivering oratory in an expression (*elocutio*) appropriate to both the text and the circumstances of the audience (III).[91] Book IV finally suggests a systematic framework of theological *loci*.

In the *Ratio*, then, Erasmus focused on clarifying the theological substance that informs the rhetorical form of the sacred text. Only by recognizing the divine wisdom in the tropes of Scripture can theologians explain the text appropriately. This is why they must be spiritually prepared as well as rhetorically trained before they can move from the letter to the spirit. For this reason also, a compendium of Christ's doctrine, drawn from the content of the New Testament, precedes the discussion of the allegorical nature of Scripture. Not until interpreters know the *scopus* of Scripture can they make sense of the variety of circumstances to which Christ accommodated himself by means of allegorical language. Yet the stress on the theological subject matter contained in Scripture does not keep Erasmus from alluding in the *Ratio* to practical implications, even if they are of a more ethical than homiletical kind.

The *Ecclesiastes* applies the scriptural exegesis to the rhetorical form of the sermon. This is not to say, however, that the rhetorical duties of the speaker and the devices of speech are absent from the *Ratio*. Since the biblical text is divine speech of persuasion,[92] it follows rhetorical rules. Therefore, the exegete must be able to recognize the linguistic clothing of the theological content. The biblical tropes are nothing less than the idiom by which the divine wisdom accommodated its word to human conditions. Still, the *Ratio* seems to be more theoretical in orientation, the *Ecclesiastes* more practical.

As a result, Erasmus does not expressly mention in his *Ecclesiastes* the doctrine of Christ's harmony (though it is implicitly present as *philosophia Christiana*). He emphasizes instead the rhetorical function of Christ, 'the most certain expositor of the divine mind,' as the linguistic medium between God and humanity.[93] Similarly, he stresses the preacher's prudence in accommodating the sermon to a variety of circumstances in the audience. He also greatly expands (after devoting the whole first book to the spiritual and moral qualifications for ecclesiastical office) the treatment of the theologian's training in rhetoric, and presents the offices of the speaker, the parts of speech, and the virtues of style in tedious, technical detail (books II and III). Moreover, he provides in the last book a system of *loci* which is to serve as a framework for integrating first biblical and then other material – not for the purpose of constructing an abstract theology but to have at hand a store of commonplaces for the invention and disposition of the parts of sacred oratory.

A case in point illustrating how Erasmus changes his orientation from the *Ratio* to the *Ecclesiastes* is his treatment of faith and love. In the *Ratio*, he points to simplicity, innocence, and humility as the attitudes that characterize Christ's conduct, and adds faith and love as the virtues which Christ teaches his disciples. Although Erasmus correlates here simplicity with prudence and connects this simple prudence (or prudent simplicity) with faith,[94] it is in the *Ecclesiastes* where he fully develops the rhetorical implication of the relation between faith and prudence: 'Faith pertains to dove-like simplicity, prudence to serpent-like caution.' Embracing *judicium* and *consilium*, prudence signifies the shrewd discernment of the variety of circumstances in the audience to which speakers lovingly accommmodate their language. A full explanation of the relation between simplicity, faith, and prudence occurs finally in book IV, where Erasmus parallels the philosophical virtues with the theological virtues: Faith belongs to prudence, hope to fortitude, and love to justice, with its subspecies temperance or moderation. Erasmus thus had extended the faith-prudence relation from a theological to a rhetorical dimension, yet without surrendering the primacy of faith as a theological virtue.[95]

Erasmus similarly extends his treatment of theological *loci* from one book to the other. The *Ratio*, after dealing with the allegorical nature of biblical language and inculcating the main rule of interpretation ('the meaning which we draw forth from the obscure words [must] correspond with the circle of Christ's doctrine, be in conformity with his life, and finally be in accordance with natural equity'), presents a seemingly arbitrary list of commonplaces including faith and love.[96] While these *loci* appear gathered here at random, they receive an ordered form in *Ecclesiastes* book IV, where Erasmus offers an inclusive system of theological *loci*, patterned in general it seems after the rules of Tychonius.[97] This system contraposes God and the devil, the laws and communities on each side, their behaviour patterns in terms of virtues and vices, and the respective ends of the Christian and vicious lives.[98] Erasmus' treatment of *loci* in the *Ratio* differs from that in the *Ecclesiastes* in that he moves from sporadic theological insights to a systematic pattern conducive to sacred rhetoric.

This leads us to a brief observation about the relation between exegetical and systematic theology. It is clear that Erasmus, like Calvin after him, understood theology as deriving from exegesis. Theological *loci* are extracted from the sacred text, even if corroborated at second hand by patristic interpretation and ancient wisdom. The resulting systematic work (in Calvin's case the *Institutio*, in Erasmus' case book IV of the *Ecclesiastes*) claims no independent standing but rather rests on biblical interpretation.[99] Calvin's compilation of *loci* in his *Institutes*, however, because it was taken apart from his commentaries, could lead subsequent readers to regard it as a systematic textbook of its own. Erasmus' collation of *loci*, on the other hand, remained in close connection with his homiletics and scriptural exposition. He was never seen as having produced an abstract systematic theology, so much less so since he disassociated himself from the scholastics.

For the humanist theologian Erasmus, systematic theology is ancillary to biblical interpretation. It draws theological conclusions from insights into the sacred text for the purpose of ordering the material so as to facilitate its homiletical and ethical use. Humanist theology does not construct from abstract first principles a metaphysical system that is an end in itself. But it does arrange theological *loci* in such a way that they form a repository from which the preacher draws the appropriate points for a sermon. In this sense, then, Erasmus was a systematic theologian. Foremost a philologist and a biblical interpreter, he derived his theologial conclusions from the sacred text and collated the material according to similarity or dissimilarity in order to provide a manual for the invention and disposition of sacred oratory. It was the art of rhetoric that guided the interpretation of the Bible by means of allegory, the systematic arrangement of theological *loci* by means of collation, and the homiletical application by means of the rules of speech, especially the observation of the variety of persons, times, and things.

To return to the comparison of the *Ratio* and *Ecclesiastes*: Despite their different orientation, the outline of the two treatises is basically the same, with the *Ecclesiastes* enlarging those sections that are significant for the office of preaching. Both treatises begin with the spiritual, moral, and educational qualifications of the theologian. Then they proceed to show how to interpret the tropes, figures, and allegories in the sacred text. There follows the advice to collate theological *loci*. Both treatises end with an appeal to concord.

Within this general outline, however, there are deviations. The section on spiritual, moral, and educational preparation is relatively short in the *Ratio*. In the *Ecclesiastes*, the subject of spiritual and moral qualification for ecclesiastical office occupies the whole first book, and the extensive presentation of rhetoric in all its ramifications fills books II and III. The lengthy chapter in the *Ratio* on Christ's teaching, including discussion of its harmony and variety, is missing in the *Ecclesiastes*. With the section on the linguistic nature of Scripture and on allegorical interpretation, the two writings are again parallel. Finally, a mere section in the *Ratio* becomes the subject of a whole, albeit short, book in the *Ecclesiastes* (IV): the collation of theological *loci*. The *Ratio*, in contrast to the *Ecclesiastes*, ends with a section on true theology. But both treatises append a passionate appeal to concord.

After presenting in this chapter various images of Erasmus in the scholarly literature from the nineteenth century to the present, we argued that Erasmus can be best understood from the perspective of his rhetorical theology. Not only the influence on him of certain Italian humanists but, above all, his agreement with the biblical interpretation of the Platonizing church Fathers makes it probable that a rhetorical theology indeed lies at the heart of his thinking. Several of his own statements confirm this assessment. Moreover, an overview of two key writings of our study, the *Ratio* and the *Ecclesiastes*, gave a first impression of the content of this rhetorical theology as it springs from his understanding of Scripture. We turn now to the question of how Erasmus understood language within his overall world view, moving from a general perspective on language in nature, culture, and good literature to the specific focus of sacred literature. It will become apparent that the mediatorial role of language is central to his concept of literature and literacy in general, and to his appreciation of the allegorical nature of Scripture in particular.

TWO

Language, Literature, and Scripture

ॐ

1 LANGUAGE, NATURE, AND CULTURE

Language plays a pivotal role in Erasmus' thinking. The fact that this point has been made so often does not render it a cliché. Language, literature, and literacy are central to his thought.[1] A humanist par excellence, Erasmus viewed everything through the lens of language. For him, it is speech that provides the means by which the human mind and heart, and with them human life as such, come to expression.[2] Even more, language is the very signature of all reality, encompassing nature, culture, and salvation – with the exception of the inner recesses of the divine mystery, of course, which lie beyond the reach of human speech and therefore demand wordless adoration.[3] The truth of both the sensible and the intelligible world, however, is so deeply embedded in the word that there is no other way to comprehend it than by reading and hearing, and no other way to communicate it than by writing and speaking.

Upon entering Erasmus' world of words and becoming familiar with his idiomatic use of language, it will be apparent that his way of speaking is motivated by two interacting powers: amplification and concision,[4] or more generally speaking, the enlarging effect of freedom and the concentrating focus on authority. This dynamic obtains paradigmatically, as we shall see, in his view on the relation between good and sacred literature, rhetoric and biblical exegesis, respectively. While Erasmus was no doubt a humanist with a high regard for the liberating effect of classical letters, he thought his primary calling was to be occupied with the authority of the Bible, the written word of God. Beyond the relation between *bonae litterae* and *sacrae litterae*, however, all of Erasmus' work, and therefore his thought in general, seems to have been conditioned by the same fundamental dialectic of movement and structure,[5] expansion and limits, widening and focusing, inclusion and containment.

Erasmus was one of the key figures in the cultural shift from the medieval prominence of visual images to the humanist preference for letters. More accurately, priority shifted from the visible image to the word in such a way that the symbolism of reality was seen as reflected primarily in literature. Language was not only a means of communication but also a mirror of the transcendent world. The most dramatic external evidence for this cultural change was, of course, the invention of the printing press and, as a result, the wide dissemination of literary knowledge. An emerging culture quite unlike that of the Middle Ages began to stress not only the need but also the right of all human beings to read and write. Every person was deemed capable of understanding, articulating, and communicating the truth. Everyone was thought to be able, upon proper education, to know, speak, and act for him/herself rather than to remain on the receiving end of dogmas passed down through the channels of an authoritarian system. Small wonder, then, that education became the common goal of a humanist culture which valued the literate person as representing humanity at its best: 'A man without education has no humanity at all.'[6]

In fact, a sense of human freedom was emerging. It expressed itself foremost in the humanist ideal of a 'liberal' education,[7] a formation process that opened for students a direct approach to original literature. Moreover, this unhampered access to the primary sources implied the freedom to make up one's own mind, to come to one's senses,[8] in an immediate response to the truth in the sources. Liberal education signified free learning in terms of the removal of pedagogical coercion, oppression, and dogmatism. Individuals were to be liberated from the constraints of those ruling establishments whose privileged representatives interfered in the natural learning process by telling folk what to think and how to behave. In the period of humanism, therefore, modern notions of freedom of conscience and freedom of thought began to stir.

Liberal studies, the *studia humanitatis*, were designed to give collegians the opportunity to find things out for themselves. The students were encouraged to become acquainted with both the language and content of classical texts, that is, with the substance and style of the word, in an unmediated, fresh encounter with the primary sources – a first-hand discovery of the truth, a one-to-one relation to what mattered in life. The excitement of finding the truth for oneself was to be superior to the acquisition by rote of a second-hand knowledge handed down by traditional authority. And the moral life issuing from this personal appropriation of the truth was to be much more spontaneous and genuine than the predetermined regulations of an authoritarian system had allowed.

However, it would be one-sided to regard Erasmus as only the representative of a paradigm shift toward freedom. He was at once innovative and imitative, original and traditional. While he broke with the late medieval ethos, he remained devoted to the patristic world of ideas and to classical, especially Platonic and Stoic, ideals. Moreover, he stood in a rhetorical tradition that claimed good literature as the source for instruction in moral and religious truths. Consequently, the learner was neither absolutely free to determine the source of knowledge nor at liberty to develop independent criteria for understanding the truth.[9] Rather, the truth is given by the author of language, the ultimate authority of any text. And for Erasmus that author is, in the final analysis, God,[10] who says the first word before all human speech and speaks the last word after all is said and done. The dynamic of freedom and authority in language is therefore not only a problem of the dialectic of good and sacred literature but, specifically, of the relation between rhetoric and theology.

Recent scholarship has been able to establish both the fundamental significance of language for Erasmus' thought and his place in the rhetorical tradition.[11] He was clearly one of the great rhetoricians in line with Cicero, Quintilian, and Valla. Now that linguistic studies have opened the way, it is time for us to turn to his theological language and draw attention to the systematic implications of its use.[12] This is possible because his general view of language provides a suitable entrance into his thought as a whole and specifically to his theology.

According to Erasmus, language supplies, for one thing, the means of communication among human beings. If used right, it mediates between persons and therefore builds community. Beyond the social nexus, however, language gives rise to humanity in that it is instrumental for human beings to live in the world at large according to their nature and end. Human speech is not only socially useful by encourging civility and honesty, but at its best it engenders *humanitas* as it evokes harmony with the order of nature. For it is the power of verbal expression that raises humankind to its proper place in the order of things, above animals and inanimate nature: 'What differentiates human beings from the other animals, or brutes as they are called, is not reason but speech.'[13]

Orderly human speech must correspond to the order of nature.[14] Vicious speech, on the contrary, calls forth at least disruption and disorder, if not the perversion of order that leads to chaos. True speech brings forth peace and unity; malicious speech is oriented toward violence and thus evokes dissension, discord, and destruction. Just as the proper use of language elevates human beings to the height of their station in the cosmos, so the misuse of language debases them to a subhuman, subversive region of brutality: 'A man who has never been instructed in philosophy or in any branch of learning is a creature quite inferior to the brute animals. Animals only follow their natural instincts; but man, unless he has experienced the influence of learning and philosophy, is at the mercy of impulses that are worse than those of the wild beast.'[15]

Language expresses not only the station of human beings in the realm of nature, but also reflects their ontological and ethical status in the higher realm of culture. To be sure, language provides the means of communication between human beings. But more important, language itself is the medium by which human beings orient themselves to the order of reality. By their capacity of speaking, they are capable of integrating themselves appropriately into the plan of the world. For it is the faculty of speech that gives them to understand both the meaning of their being and the purpose of their actions. Serving as a conduit for thought and deed, the human faculty of speaking is the agency for expressing and actualizing what is real and right.

In other words, language is the medium by which human beings become aware of themselves, of their place in nature and their part in culture. Speech not only characterizes human beings as such but also humanizes them and, in turn (since it is the mirror of the soul), shows up their humanity: 'Only God perceives what lurks in the heart of man. But the tongue was given to men so that by its agency as messenger one man might know the mind and intention of another. So it is fitting that the copy should match the original, as mirrors honestly reflect the image of the object before them ... It is most shameful for the tongue to be at variance with the heart.'[16] People are unable to make sense of themselves and the world except by virtue of their ability to turn ideas into words. In the same way, they fail to act appropriately until they conceptualize those ideals that shape moral opinions. Only by way of language can they recognize the world and realize their own humanity. Humanity is defined by speech: *Qualis vir, talis oratio.*[17] Even more, language not only defines human beings, it also forms them. What one speaks (and reads), one becomes, 'hence the famous saying of Socrates: "Speak, so that I may see you."'[18] This is why language is the foremost agency of education, the unique instrument for the formation of true humanity. Education in speech, that is, training in grammar and rhetoric, supplies the means to humanize human beings.

2 THE DETERIORATION AND RESTORATION OF LANGUAGE

Following Cicero, Erasmus believed that primitive humans were savages, speaking and living as barbarians without rules. Yet subsequent society became civilized when it developed laws that fixed the conventions of common life and thereby guaranteed cultural stability.[19] If therefore the human community needed to be ordered according to the order of nature, then knowledge had to reflect the harmony of nature. As Cicero had it: '... The great men of the past, having a wider mental grasp, had also a far deeper insight than our mind's eye can achieve, when they asserted that all this universe above us and below is one single whole, and is held together by a single force and harmony of nature; for there exists no class of things which can stand by itself, severed from the rest, or which the rest can dispense with and yet be able to preserve their own force and everlasting existence ... The whole of the content of the liberal and humane sciences is comprised within a single bond of union ... a marvelous agreement and harmony underlies all branches of knowledge.'[20]

Erasmus agrees: 'The conflicting forces of the elements are evenly balanced so as to preserve unbroken peace, and despite their fundamental opposition they maintain concord by mutual consent and communication.'[21] 'When I look a little more closely at the wonderful arrangement, the harmony as they call it, of things, it always seems to me ... that it was not without divine guidance that the business of discovering systems of knowledge was given to the pagans. For the great and eternal Disposer, who is wisdom itself, establishes all things with consummate skill, differentiates them with beautiful play of interchange, and orders them with perfect rightness, so that each balances another in a marvelous way; nor does he allow anything to move at random in all the immense variety of the world.'[22] 'Nature has always been most concerned to create harmony (*conciliare*) amongst all creatures, however they might seem opposed.'[23]

Consequently, there must be rules to regulate linguistic usage in accord with ordered knowledge that for its part reflects the harmony by which nature stabilizes itself. Just as the universe maintains its equilibrium against extremes by the law of symmetry and proportion, rhetorical principles serve to moderate language in such a way as to protect it from either excess or lack, from too much or too little. However, inasmuch as history tends spontaneously toward deterioration, language is endangered at least by capricious change, if not by the violence that threatens continuity, invites corruption, and leads to chaos. Even so, as degenerative as historical evolution may turn out to be, the restoration of language is possible, indeed mandatory. And it is the task of the rhetorician not only to guard but also to restore language.

Erasmus' reform program aimed at retrieving genuine culture by means of authentic language. Returning current language *ad fontes*, that is, to the pure sources of its golden age in antiquity, is the task of the humanist, who stands in the middle between the origin and goal of language, and in the presence of linguistic aberrations. What is more, the restoration of language in the cultural realm serves a higher purpose, the renewal of true religion, the spiritual rebirth of Christendom. It is therefore the theologian's mission to restore theology to its biblical sources and thus to reorient it to its pure origin. Only in this way will that true theology and sincere piety arise which makes for spiritual rebirth in the face of the present decline in the church: 'I have tried hard to recall a world too far sunk in sophistical quibbling to the sources of Antiquity, and to arouse a world that places too much trust in Jewish ceremonies to a pursuit of true religion.'[24] Grammatical *puritas* and rhetorical *aptum* in language correspond to *pietas* in religion, that is, purity of faith and life. On the whole, then, 'returning to the sources' is the motto linking the rhetorical obligation with the religious vocation of the biblical humanist. *Eruditio* and *pietas* are the distinguishing marks of the learned and pious intellectual.

Erasmus found himself confronted with three forms of language distortion: the vernacular, modist grammar (or scholastic dialectic), and Ciceronianism.

It was difficult for him to bear what he considered to be the barbarism of vernacular languages. The vulgar idiom of the masses tended in his view at least to revert to the inchoate, unregulated state of language before the law, if not to invite cultural disorder because of random usage. Uncouth speech was at best too particular, at worst too base to reflect the order of the universe. Elite humanist that he was, he judged the multitude on linguistic, aesthetic, and moral grounds.[25] Despite his occasional remarks that he wished everyone could read the Bible in their mother tongue,[26] he disdained the common folk for talking aimlessly, using vulgarities, naming things as they saw them, and failing to draw moral lessons. He was averse to an unruly and useless manner of speaking. Unlike earlier Italian Renaissance writers, notably Dante and Boccaccio, who lifted their vernacular to sublime heights, and unlike Luther, the man of the people, whose translation of the Bible inaugurated modern German, the pious intellectual Erasmus wished to see the classical languages prevail as the elegant *lingua franca* of 'second level' persuaders: 'If only the world limited itself to the use of two languages (Latin and Greek)!'[27]

However, his aspirations to make Latin the living language of civilization were thwarted by the formalism of the modist school. These medieval scholars had subjected grammar to dialectic by imposing those mechanistic laws which they had abstracted from *a priori* ontological and metaphysical principles. Following Valla's example, Erasmus charged them with choking the life out of Latin as they restrained it with the strait-jacket of their philosophical presuppositions. Such a confinement of language leads to its atrophy, if not to its death.[28]

Forcing grammar into the framework of modist dialectics was similar to subjecting the theological content of speech to dogmatic dialectics: 'To search out knowledge of the nature of God by human reasoning is recklessness; to speak of the things that cannot be set out in words is madness; to define them is sacrilege ... It is the mark of a dangerous recklessness to assert anything about the nature of God beyond what Christ himself or the Holy Spirit has disclosed to us.'[29] Whether one is concerned with the style or the substance of language, dialectic must be reined in by rhetoric, which requires *puritas* in grammar as well as *aptum* in elocution.[30]

Accordingly, Erasmus rejected the abstract formalism of the late-scholastic theologians who arrived at their cut and dried systems by strictly applying the rules of Aristotelian logic. Just as the modists, summulists, and terminists burdened language with grammatical dialectic, so the *neoterici* oppressed it by their syllogistic dogmatism, by airtight arguments drawing conclusions from exclusive definitions and barren premises. 'On what pretext will we ask pardon for ourselves, we who raise so many meddlesome, not to say irreverent, questions concerning matters very much removed from our nature, and who formulate so many definitions about matters which could have been either ignored without loss of salvation or left in doubt?'[31] These pseudotheologians violate language, even kill it, since their hairsplitting quibbles render it static in frozen formulas, and therefore deaden its vital power. At worst, they impose their suffocating structure on the mysteries of Scripture, preventing it from coming alive in the reader: 'This and much like it little by little was sapping the vigor of the gospel teaching; and the result would have been, with things slipping always from bad to worse, that the spark of Christian piety, from which alone the spent fire of charity could be rekindled, would finally be put out.'[32]

However, there was a hitch in the business of purifying Latin, for the Ciceronians had already attempted to restore the style of their model. Erasmus found himself confronted by Cicero's epigones, who, accusing him of barbarism, copied their master so obsequiously that they admitted no rules other than those drawn from their prototype: 'No one will be Ciceronian if even the tiniest word is found in his works which can't be pointed to in Cicero's *opus*.'[33] Yet for Erasmus this type of imitation amounted to art for art's sake and was liable to result in esoteric artificiality. The Ciceronian purists elevated one of the rhetorical principles, the esthetic *delectare*, over the other two and more important ones, the didactic *docere* and the ethical *movere*, and therefore abandoned the genuine purpose of rhetoric. Rather than being an end in itself, delighting readers is a means to an end, namely, teaching and moving them. So, as the Ciceronian purists[34] strained for effect on the exclusive pattern of their prototype, they enshrined Cicero in sterling silver and engraved his style in tablets of stone instead of reading the rules of language from living language itself.

For Erasmus language has a life of its own. It is the inner constitution and vitality of language that provide both its structure of content and pattern of style. Accordingly, the inherent order of language is to be read from the text itself, its texture and context, and in the light of the author's intention. Only then is the rhetorician able to draw up linguistic rules, which must not only be few and simple but above all serve ethical usefulness.[35] However elegant Cicero's style, no single author (except God in Holy Scripture) possesses a singular authority. To make the writing of one writer the pattern of all writing is to ignore the individuality of other authors, the design and purpose of each writing, and the historical setting of a particular text, that is, the specific coincidence of the persons, things, times, and circumstances described. Good authors become examples by virtue of their good use of language. Good style, however, must serve language rather than become its master. And its usage is good insofar as it is useful for moral progress.

So Erasmus saw himself standing between barbarians, on the one side, and medieval schoolmasters (or scholastic theologians) with their strange bedfellows, the Ciceronian purists, on the other. The common folk used language without rules and constraint, whereas the intellectuals forced heterogeneous rules on it from outside, whether the rigid laws of a philosophical system or the artificial principles of a mannered show-case rhetoric. At any rate, violence was done to language. It degenerated as it lost its vitality. It suffered either from too little or too much structure – and at that a structure not its own. It was either too free or too limited. Against the unlimited freedom of language, Erasmus advocated linguistic order in accordance with its own nature. Conversely, against the overstructuring of language, he pleaded for its inherent freedom. To restore language, then, the humanist must return language to itself. Only then will it reflect again its primordial authority as it becomes a means for human progress toward perfection.

We find the motif of freedom and authority occurring here again, now in the context of freedom and form. Against modist grammarians, scholastic theologians, and humanist Ciceronians alike, Erasmus sought to protect the freedom of language from the restrictions by form or style. Over against what can be called the libertinism of the vernacular, however, he insisted on the necessity of lingustic rules in accordance with nature. Finding himself between Scylla and Charybdis, Erasmus made a virtue of the middle: The proper balance between unrestrained freedom and limiting authority is to be found in *mediocritas*, the right measure that engenders moderation and thus prevents the excess of both libertinism and of authoritarianism.[36] And what is true of language applies also to education: Education is liberal as long as it is predicated on the right balance between freedom and authority.[37]

Therefore, in order to restore language, linguistic rules must be drawn (with the help of the best rhetoricians of antiquity) from language itself in accordance with the equity with which nature keeps its equilibrium. These rules must be few, simple, and useful. Language will not come into its own until moderation has brought about that balance of freedom and authority which reflects the original relation of spirit and structure in language itself. True humanists are alert to this condition. They let language come alive precisely by recovering its integrity, its pristine eloquence and goodness. Pedagogically sensitive restoration rather than radical change – this is one of the cardinal principles of Erasmus' reform: 'To restore what is corrupt is more virtuous than to beget what is unborn.'[38]

However, the historical deterioration of language is still less ominous than its destructive use, cutting as it does at its root. Error is one thing, malice another.[39] While good language is the medium for forming concepts in correspondence with reality and for framing opinions that inform responsible action, it can be so perverted as to turn into a medium of evil, with the devil using it for diabolical ends and the perversion of order, issuing in chaos. Language can become an agency for the unreal and wrong.

With this contrast of good language and evil language, Erasmus linked his hermeneutic with his theology and ethics. His overall view of reality reveals a basic dualism that affects his understanding of language as well, seeing it coming either from God or from Satan. Certainly, only God is the primordial source and ultimate goal of all that is said and done. But the devil causes evil as soon as language is used to pervert and destroy the good order of things. Consequently, language kills and makes alive, brings together (*conciliare*) and rends asunder. Through the word, truth came into the world, but also lies. 'Just as all evil started with language, so all salvation arose from language ... From language came sickness, but from language came also the medicine.'⁴⁰

Human language, then, can become the secondary cause of good and evil. Either as speaking good (in its ultimate form as blessing, *benedicere*, in correspondence with divine language, which implies *benefacere* and *bene mereri*) or as speaking evil (in its ultimate form as cursing, *maledicere*, in correspondence with diabolical language, which implies *malefacere* and *male mereri*), human speech reflects the service of human beings to God or to the devil.⁴¹ The faculty of speech places human beings ultimately between God and the devil, good and evil, and pulls them up or down depending on its positive or negative use. It belongs very much to Erasmus' view to say: By their word ye shall know them.

3 WORDS AND IDEAS

Although speech must be pure and easily understood where grammar is concerned, if one looks at vocables from the outside, there is hardly an essential connection between word and thought. To be sure, 'things are learnt only by the sound we attach to them.'⁴² There is still a resemblance between words and what they signify. But the thoroughgoing dualism in Erasmus' world view obtained also in his perception of the relation between word and reality (*verbum-res*).⁴³ In the juxtaposition of a linguistic realism and philosophical dualism, the latter with its sense of ambiguity ultimately prevailed. The naked word by itself appears at first sight as a compound of letters signifying things that belong to the visible, material world. But words are divorced from their true meaning not only because language in general has deteriorated over time but also because a fundamental duality pervades reality. The separation of letter and spirit is ultimately due to the human disobedience toward the divine word and, at worst, to the use of human language for diabolical purposes.

The gap between language and reality notwithstanding, words in a way still resemble the visible things they describe. The particular arrangement of letters and sounds even now can imitate the nature of things by appearance and resonance:

> But are words really created to sound like what they mean? I had always thought that their origin was accidental, or at best due to the whim of whoever inaugurated them. – No. Their constituent parts and the sounds they contain bear reference to their meaning, though there is no need for the meaning in its entirety to be phonetically represented. The presence of some similarity is enough. Even where none is apparent there must still be some reason why a particular word is allotted a particular meaning.[44]

Language remains to some extent intact as far as its external expression is concerned. In keeping with his understanding of the fall of humankind, Erasmus considered language as corrupt in an essential, though not absolute, way.[45] There are yet glimpses of original connections; words can still reflect natural things by similarity. But even on this level there is no univocity because one vocable can stand for several things,[46] several words (*voces*) can stand for the same thing, and one thing can bespeak multiple qualities as well. All the grammarian can do is to notice the plurality of words and clarify their resemblances to things on the literal, etymological level of language.

The essential dualism between letter and spirit, however, can be overcome only by the mediating function of words on the metaphorical level of language – a function which is not understood until one sees words as reflecting a meaning beyond their literal resemblance to natural things.[47] This higher relation between language and meaning is for Erasmus such that the reader must know the meaning before it can be found in words. This is why the intellectual and moral preparation must precede, or at least accompany, the approach to a text. On the level of theology, then, humility and faith are the only gateway to understanding the biblical word.[48]

There is for Erasmus neither a direct nor a definitive connection between words and the reality they signify. A fundamental ambiguity resists any attempt to formalize language into a mechanism of absolute certainty. Even so, the humanist sees an analogical correspondence between words and reality.[49] This coherence does not emerge, though, until one reads the *res-verbum* relationship in such a way as to hear its ontological overtones. In order to become aware of the real meaning of the words one must first recognize the priority of thought over words, of knowing and being over discourse, of the intelligent world over the sensible world. Conversely, the author must adjust the choice of words to the intellectual nature of the subject matter.[50] In either case, whether one is reading or composing a text, substance takes precedence over form, subject matter dictates style, reality governs its proper expression. One must participate, intellectually and ethically, in the reality expressed by words so as to be able to hear it in the words expressing it or to be able to express it in words that really reflect it.

This is why for Erasmus rhetorical *inventio* precedes *dispositio*.[51] In the classical tradition, invention did not primarily spring from the free, unschooled spontaneity of the orator's creativity. Rather, it was qualified by the characteristics of the chosen subject matter and its *topoi* within the overall view of reality.[52] Still, the fact that thought and structure are a priori does for Erasmus not exclude a certain originalty on the part of the speaker – an originality that rests in the speaker's nature as it reflects the order of nature as such. We take it, then, that also for Erasmus speech is shaped more by the expression of reality in nature and in rhetorical form than by the orator's arbitrary individuality.[53] Decorous and apt style expresses the author's linguistic adaptation to the reality of the subject matter. Style, as it were the bridge between *res* and *verbum*, is appropriate when the author's expression of reality corresponds as nearly as possible to reality itself.

We see that the rhetoricians' freedom of expression is limited by what is given in the subject matter and its classical treatment. Conversely, rhetoricians are free from set, confining rules so that they may absorb classical precedent in such a way that it becomes part of their own system: 'I welcome imitation with open arms – but imitation which assists nature and does not violate it, which turns its gifts in the right direction and does not destroy them. I approve of imitation – but imitation of a model that is in accord with, or at least not contrary to, your own native genius ... Again, I approve of imitation – but imitation not enslaved to one set of rules, from the guidelines of which it dare not depart, but imitation which gathers from all authors, or at least from the most outstanding, the thing which is the chief virtue of each and which suits your own cast of mind; imitation which does not immediately incorporate into its own speech any nice little feature it comes across, but transmits it to the mind for inward digestion, so that becoming part of your own system, it gives the impression ... of something that springs from your own mental processes, something that exudes the characteristics and force of your own mind and personality.'[54]

Form imitates substance and precedence, but in such a way that it corresponds also to the rhetorician's nature. So, knowing how to invent suitable subject matter, the rhetorician proposes a thesis, draws on the repertoire of *loci*, argues *pro* and *con*, corroborates propositions, collates adverse and supporting evidence, and above all persuades the audience through the three rhetorical offices: *docere, delectare*, and *movere*.[55] Once these guiding principles have conditioned the rhetorician to such an extent that they constitute a personal second nature, that is, a living culture of the mind, the use of rhetorical rules turns into a spontaneous imitation of nature and life, because the rhetorician is now free to take liberties with the rules. But this freedom arises from training, from memory and practice over the years.[56] And it must not exceed the bounds of rhetorical structure itself. Otherwise, art is liable to become both artificial and artful. Rhetorical freedom tends to turn into libertinism unless checked by moderation.

While the plasticity of language resists syllogistic conclusions from words to ideas as if from cause to effect, words nonetheless signal an underlying reality and thus communicate the metaphorical meaning of universal ideas and values. It is the middle function of rhetoric, between teaching and moving, to reconcile.[57] The word gives reality to understanding by mediating between the reader (or hearer) and its meaning, by creating community among human beings, and by reconciling God and humanity: 'In the end of all it should not be considered the fault of the gospel if someone makes a less than admirable use of something admirable in itself. It is called the gospel of peace, first as reconciling us to God and secondly as uniting us among ourselves in mutual concord.'[58] This is why words, though necessarily accommodated to the audience's varied comprehension, are to be in accord with reality itself, even if language becomes increasingly non-verbal when drawing near the ineffable source of all that is, the mystery of God.

What is true for the word-idea relation within the province of invention, applies also to the amplification of words and ideas where the disposition of speech is concerned (*copia verborum ac rerum*).[59] When amplified properly, pure, elegant, and apt words perform a mediating function as a bridge to ideas. Words become a mirror of thought in that they convey the meaning of what they say, metaphorically. And that meaning, in turn, can also be amplified by the right rhetorical methods. It is important to recognize, however, that the mediatorial function of words rests on their ability both to reveal meaning by reference and to conceal it at the same time by hindrance. As images of thought, words are at once open and closed.[60] If taken at face value only, they conceal the truth. If understood in their real meaning, they disclose the truth. It is in this way that words as images of thought lead to the truth.

Rather than expressing meaning in unequivocal terms, language is more attractive when it communicates through indirect speech, that is, through similitude, parable, and allusions: 'Can you imagine anything more appealing than the fables of the ancient authors? ... Consider pastoral poetry – is there anything more graceful?'[61] Indeed, 'all of human speech is crammed with tropes.'[62] For the letter is unessential in and by itself, even as it contains clues pointing beyond itself. This is why Erasmus preferred Platonic and poetic literature for preliminary training in biblical exegesis.[63] To be sure, he was aware that a certain objectification of the spirit in the letter cannot be avoided, or else the spirit could not be conceived. Despite his universal spiritualism, he did not devalue the external form. For this reason the student must learn languages, trace etymologies, and engage in philological text-criticism. The letter needs to be taken seriously. The truth cannot be not understood unless the word itself is first taken for what it is. Just as the humility of faith is the proper entrance into the divine text, so the humility of the letter is the proper access to the word in general.

Nevertheless, because the letter by itself is incapable of leading to the spirit, the letter must not be absolutized. This is the fundamental reason for Erasmus' relativism and scepticism. If one simply identifies language with meaning, words with ideas, the letter with the spirit, one will not be able to reach the truth. The move from the letter to the spirit is hindered by a dualistic separation. However, when the spirit has accommodated itself to the letter, this move from the spirit to the letter opens up an allegorical mediation. But even as the spirit assumes a literal form, the spirit transcends its form. Otherwise, people externalize religion by identifying the spirit with ceremonies and glorifying institutions, theologians grow old in fruitless school debates, and sovereigns misuse their office.

This characteristic relation between words and ideas, or form and spirit, helps to clarify the question of how far Erasmus was an idealist and spiritualist.[64] The spiritual, idealist tendencies in his thinking were certainly strong. Even so, he was not willing to surrender an actualist, pragmatic view. Accordingly, though the spirit does not need form, it becomes incarnate in form as it accommodates itself to the letter. While the word made flesh is distinct from the divine mind, the divine mind yet assumes the form of the *sermo*.[65] The word is unable to carry in its body a higher meaning unless the spirit enters into it and makes it its home. True knowledge, then, does stem from a spiritual understanding of the world. The realization of the truth in the world, however, becomes in the divine word an actual fact and for the Christian an actual task and accomplishment. In a word, for Erasmus the mediating relation between spiritualism and pragmatism is marked by the dynamic of separation and participation.

On the whole, then, the relation between the face value of words and their deeper meaning is symbolical because word and thing are not connected in a direct, linear way but rather are similar as with an image.[66] A word or a text reflects reality in a parabolic way. Erasmus was so firmly rooted in the Platonic way of thinking that he was unable to see the relation between word and thing as a unilateral, unambiguous connection. And yet, it was something like a first principle for him that word and reality indeed are related in a symbolical way. It is this hermeneutical orientation that accounts for both the dualism and symbolism in his thought. He tried to overcome a basic dichotomy by assuming a symbolical relation between *verba* and *res*.

The correspondence between word and reality admits of further analogies: Words are expressions of thought, language is the reflection of the soul.⁶⁷ Theologically expressed, Christ images God, the *philosophia Christi* mirrors Christ's teaching and life, and charity reflects faith. By the same token, the correspondence between words and reality obtains also on the negative side, namely, as far as the devil, lies, impiety, and heresy are concerned. It is this ontological place and epistemological function of language that determines its educational and ethical use. Language is the means by which humans, placed in the middle between God and animals, can move either up or down as they respond to the drawing power of the divine love or fall into the pull of brutish passions.

There is for Erasmus a correspondence between what one thinks, loves, and is, and what one says. The mind or heart, i.e., the images, opinions, and dispositions formed in the interiority of the human being, express themselves in language: 'As in sacred matters God the Father begets from himself his Son, so in us our mind is the source of our thoughts and speech; and as the Son proceeds from the Father, so in us speech proceeds from our mind.'⁶⁸ This is why a polished style is so important as an expression of both the clarity of thought and the purity of ethical and religious disposition. A sound and pious mind, or a refined and undivided heart, brings forth useful words that are beneficial to others, whereas impious opinions issue in invidious language detrimental to others. The soul breathed on by God and transformed by Scripture speaks the salutary word. Satan, by contrast, speaking through the serpent to seduce the human race, uses ungodly persons to propagate his law.⁶⁹ Therefore, both evil and salvation came by the word, both sickness and medicine.⁷⁰

Since only God knows what lies hidden in the inner recesses of the human heart, human beings are able to tell who others really are only by what they say and do. The insight 'as the human being so the speech' can be reversed into the evidence 'as the human speech so the human being.'⁷¹ But the relation between being and speaking seems to be for Erasmus stronger than that between being and doing. To be sure, an impious or pious mind will as a rule express itself not only in malicious or beneficial words but also in the production of good or bad deeds. But this is not a hard and fast rule. Erasmus is willing to make modifications and take exceptions into consideration. For it is possible that an impious person may produce a pious deed, and vice versa, a pious person may lapse into sin.⁷² Therefore, it is much more difficult to identify irreligious persons by their actions than by their word. Conversely, sinners, even though bad for the moment because of their moral conduct, can still belong to the Christian community if confessing the faith.[73] In general, however, the sequence is clear: Knowing precedes speaking, wisdom comes before style, ideas before expression, and what one says, one is and does.[74]

4 BONAE LITTERAE

Dealing with the ontological and ethical aspects of language (namely, with what one says, is, and does) has already led us to the verge of discovering what Erasmus considered to be its religious quality. But before we pass this threshold, we must tarry in the arena of cultural discourse and reflect on how he valued the aesthetic dimension of language. Moreover, before we study Erasmus' understanding of *sacrae litterae*, we must briefly look at his view of how language expresses itself in good literature.

According to the principles of rhetoric, good literature is characterized by the art of persuasion through the three oratorical offices: teaching, delighting, and moving.[75] *Docere, delectare, movere* are means whereby the orator offers insights into the truth, attracts by the elegance of speech, and moves to moral action. It would be mistaken, though, to relate each of these three functions to its respective domain alone, i.e., teaching to philosophy, delighting to aesthetics, and moving to ethics. Rather, each function (teaching, delighting, and moving) aims at reality as a whole, even as each has primarily to do with its cognate dimension (truth, beauty, and morality). That is to say, reality is ultimately not compartmentalized but marked by a harmony that unites the beautiful and good with what is true.

First a brief look at the aesthetic dimension of language. His dislike for the stylistic grandeur of the Ciceronians notwithstanding, Erasmus shared Cicero's view that genuine language is pleasing exactly in that it serves both goodness and truth: 'God has given us speech for this one purpose, to make the relations of men more pleasant.'[76] He considered style as a corrolary to substance, i.e., to the moral import and truth content of the word.[77] In fact, *delectare* is related to *movere* in that delight is seen as appealing to the milder *ethos* and therefore serving, in a preliminary way, the moving (*movere*) of the stronger *ethos*.[78] But more importantly, *delectare* had also to do with the teaching of truth (*docere*), which constitutes, after all, the basis for ethics by providing the knowledge for stirring both the milder and stronger affections.[79] The elegance and polish of form, the symmetry and proportion of expression, and the pleasant arrangement of material make language so attractive as to incline human beings toward the true and good.

This attractive feature of language serves a pedagogical purpose, that is, to draw the hearers into the word by opening them to the drawing power of its content of truth and moral import.[80] What is more, the beauty of the word corresponds also to the harmonious order of the universe: 'We can see that Nature has always been most concerned to create harmony amongst all creatures, however they might seem opposed. She has provided pleasure, like bait, to foster this harmony.'[81] Therefore, *voluptas* serves a transcendent purpose over and above the pedagogical function. As the principal attributes of reality, truth, goodness, and beauty belong together – and in this order of priority. For the greatest is knowing the truth.[82] Ethics follows from knowledge, and beauty attracts to knowledge. Goodness and pleasure are not as autonomous as truth. Enjoyment leads to, and doing follows from, knowing the truth.

While Erasmus followed the rhetorical tradition in assigning *delectare* a stylistic role and pedagogical function, he was also following the Platonic tradition when he pointed to beauty as a transcendent ideal expressing the harmony of the universe.[83] So it seems that in his thinking he combined rhetorical principles and their ethical orientation, on the one hand, with the ontology and cosmology of Platonism, on the other. The three *officia* of speech (teaching, delighting, moving) were correlated with the transcendent ideals of truth, beauty, and goodness.

Exactly as the medium for expressing reality, language itself becomes a symbolic reflection of what it expresses. Language itself comes to represent the true, beautiful, and good. The attributes of language come to symbolize the transcendent ideals to which they point. Or, turned around, the transcendent ideals become embodied in language.

Was spoken or written language more important for Erasmus? According to J. Chomarat, he gave the spoken word priority over the written word. And yet: 'Erasme est l'homme des livres, en tous les sens: bibliothèques, écritoire, atelier de l'imprimeur.'[84] The humanist could not have been unaffected by what Cicero had said: 'The pen is the best and most eminent author and teacher of eloquence, and rightly so.'[85] It is therefore plausible to assume that, despite his conventional appreciation for oration as such, Erasmus assigned to literature a higher value. He interpreted texts exclusively and showed no interest in delivering his work in public oratory. 'Renaissance' meant for him the restoration of original literature and, most of all, the rebirth of Christianity from its biblical sources. He did not develop a liking for the fine arts. None of the sights he saw during his frequent travels made as much of an impression on him as a good book. His main correspondents were fellow humanists, writers, and publishers rather than architects, artists, and musicians.[86] The foremost art of the liberal arts for him was the study of classical literature. A paragon of a humanist, he closely correlated language with letters.

He preferred literature in the original languages (especially Latin and Greek, but also Hebrew) to that in the 'modern' languages.[87] In fact, anything 'modern,' any innovation such as the theology of the *neoterici*, smacked to him of degeneration because he believed that over time words had become flat and dry, detached from their true meaning and discrepant from reality. It was in the ancient *bonae litterae* that he found an original correspondence between language and reality. Here he saw an author's knowledge, rhetoric, and honourable life so combined as to make a classical text a work of literature: 'Reverence is due to ancient authors, especially those authors who are recommended by the sanctity of their lives in addition to their learning and eloquence.'[88]

Consequently, the *bonae litterae* of classical antiquity represent the sources of the true, good, and beautiful.[89] The motto 'back to the sources' (*ad fontes*) is all the more important since the literature of antiquity is original. Close to its origin, language here corresponds with reality as nearly as possible. As a medium of knowing, good literature is an image of what is true. As a medium of doing, the goodness of literature is a metaphor of what ought to be done. And as a medium of attraction, the beauty of letters is a mirror of harmony. The readers' involvement in the text renders truth, goodness, and beauty so present as to change them into what they read.

Since the authentic texts of *bonae litterae* are authoritative, their language possesses the power of persuasion to transform the readers into what it says and to empower them to do what it intends. In other words, with the symbolic presence of reality in language comes the tranformative power of language. Its power of persuasion actually engenders in human beings what it symbolically says and is. The word not only draws them unto itself but also translates them into itself by making them over into the image of what it represents. One becomes what one reads; one is what one says. But also, one does what one is and reads: *Abeunt studia in mores*.[90] The word so draws human beings into a formation process that literate persons become true representatives of humanity. The word turns into a second nature of human beings empowering them to do what it says ought to be done. As a second nature, the word becomes a habit of action. This understanding of the drawing power of the word (*affectus*) was informed by both the rhetorical concept *persuasio* and by the Platonic idea *eros*.

5 SACRAE LITTERAE

Finally and most importantly, the symbolic representation of reality in language becomes a real presence.[91] Yet this happens only when God is pleased to speak: 'Now as God speaks most seldom and most briefly, so he speaks as truth both absolute and powerful. God the Father spoke once and gave birth to his eternal Word. He spoke again and with his almighty word created the entire fabric of the universe. And again he spoke through his prophets, by whom he entrusted to us his Holy Writ, concealing the immense treasure of divine wisdom beneath a few simple words.'[92] So God has revealed God's self on different occasions and in different circumstances, either through God's own words and acts or through various persons and events.

But all these divine interventions pale in comparison with the unique inverbation of Christ in Scripture: 'Finally he sent his Son, that is the Word clothed in flesh, and brought forth his concentrated word over this earth, compressing everything, as it were, into an epilogue. He combined the pledge of silence with brevity of speech, adding to both qualities the highest and most powerful truth. What manifests his pledge of silence? The fact that once the record of death is obliterated, there is then no mention of past offences. What proves his succinctness of speech? The fact that he encompassed the law and the prophets in two words: trust and love. The infinite talkativeness, so to speak, of forms and rituals has been eliminated, since the body and gospel light has shone forth. What shows his truth? The fact the whatever has been promised for so many centuries he fulfilled through his Son.'[93] Despite a succession of divine manifestations within a variety of contexts of the history of salvation, in *sacrae litterae* alone has the word assumed such a transcendent quality and universal dimension as to coincide fully with the reality it bespeaks.

Already the Old Testament foreshadowed the evangelical philosophy, and the pagan philosophers had an inkling of Christ's teaching because the evangelical philosophy is the restoration and perfection of nature.[94] However, it is in the New Testament, pre-eminently, where the divine has assumed the form of the letter. Here language and reality have at last come together in an unexcelled way: The written word is the incarnation of divinity, and the spirit of the word possesses the power of divine revelation. Christ's presence in the sacred word signifies that the word medium now actually embodies the divine mediator between God and humankind. With Christ's inverbation in Scripture, the mediating and transforming quality of language has reached its fulfillment by the power of the Holy Spirit. As a result, the human word is now so replete with the authority of God that the sacred text is alive with the presence of Christ, the *verbum dei*.[95]

The story (*fabula*) about Jesus of Nazareth is not only at one with the teaching and life of Christ, that is, with the philosophy and doctrine of Christ, but also with the divine person, Christ himself.[96] Indeed, Christ is almost more vividly present in Scripture than he was on his earthly sojourn. This is so because the written word renders him so clearly and truly that one would see less if one saw him with one's own eyes.[97] Just as in Erasmus' view of the relation between language and reality in general, so also here, in his understanding of Christ's word-presence in Scripture, the record seems to exceed verbal communication, the word to surpass sight, the intelligible to supersede the sensible, the spiritual to transcend the corporeal. This gradation is the reason why Erasmus' exegesis (as in fact that of all Platonizing interpreters of Scripture) is predicated on the premise that the spirit transcends the letter, even though it appears in the form of the letter.[98]

Because Christ is represented in the written word more completely than in his lifetime, Scripture has taken the place of Christ's earthly existence. Christ's presence was not fulfilled until Scripture revealed his power as God's final word to humankind. So the presence of Christ in Scripture seems for Erasmus to supersede Christ's historical presence. To be sure, the pre-existent Christ as the eternal word of God already possessed the fullness of the divine nature. Nevertheless, it is in the New Testament writings where Christ assumed the fullness of his stature in terms of God's final revelation to humankind.[99] For the New Testament has been written after the resurrection and therefore encompasses the complete circle symbolizing the perfect harmony of Christ's person, teaching, and life: 'Only after his death, resurrection, and ascension, only after the Holy Spirit had been sent from heaven, was it that the power of that mustard seed unfolded, that is, the power of evangelical teaching.'[100] Now that the *orbis Christi* has been rounded off by the proclamation and life of the apostles it returns to itself in perfect harmony.[101] God and text have become congruent in the living presence of Christ in the word.

God, though veiled in the ineffable mystery of God's being, is yet intelligible through language, most clearly and finally in the divine word-incarnation, Christ in Scripture, God's last word. This divine epilogue, however, perfects rather than destroys all good language in which human beings wrote their belles-lettres. Now that the holy has revealed the final criterion for the true, good, and beautiful, *bonae litterae* show themselves for what they are, auxiliary to the word of God: 'Although all learning can be referred to Christ, one type of learning leads to him more directly than others. It is from this point of view that you must measure the usefulness or lack of usefulness of all neutral matters. You love the study of letters. Good, if it is for the sake of Christ ... If you are interested in letters so that with their help you may more clearly discern Christ, hidden from our view in the mysteries of Scriptures, and then, having discerned him, may love him, and by knowing and loving him, may communicate this knowledge and delight in it, then gird yourself for the study of letters.'[102]

Consequently, all good literature must be measured by God's revealed word in Christ because human words can claim a measure of truth for themselves only insofar as they are commensurate, even if only in a preliminary way, with the measure of God's word, Christ.[103] Their portion of truth is not evident until one discovers how closely they approximate to the truth. So good letters receive their relative value from their approximation to Christ, the *scopus* of all reality: *Scopus autem unicus est, videlicet Christus et huius doctrina purissima.*[104] And that means in general that Christ, the word-medium who has become the mediator between God and the world, stands in the middle between the origin and goal of all language, as the Alpha restoring its goodness in the beginning and as the Omega anticipating its perfection in the end.

Inasmuch as Christ is really present in Scripture, the sacred text constitutes the highest and most perfect source of truth. It teaches true wisdom; it contains the teaching of heaven in contrast to all earthly knowledge. This is so because God, instead of human beings, is the author of Scripture: 'But now that Jesus was at the point of starting on the heavenly task of the gospel, for which he meant only his Father to be his authority, he did not allow any human authority to be superimposed.'[105] In Scripture, the author of all speech, God, has so become flesh in the incarnate word, Christ, that the *philosophia Christi* bears the sign of divine authority. As a result, the word of Christ possesses also the supreme drawing power to persuade its readers and to transform them into itself, much more so than any human speech in good literature can achieve.[106] And the rapport between the content of the word and the readers is of such a kind that, transformed into what they hear, their heart becomes a library of Christ as they devote themselves to imitating and realizing the message.

Since Scripture occupies such a dominant place in the hierarchy of literature, restoring this source to its pure origin is the primary task of the humanist theologian. For as things are, the Bible has been swept downstream from its spring. It has been diverted into artificial channels and polluted by foul tributaries.[107] Just as language and literature in general are caught up in a historical process of deterioration, the Bible, too, has been contaminated over time by mistakes and errors, that is, by *lapsus linguae* as regards its form and content, causing misinformation as well as misinterpretations and, at worst, heresies that rend the seamless coat of Christ asunder.[108] Also, human accretions, not the least the presumptuous interpretations of the scholastic dialecticians, have burdened the sacred text so grievously as to sap its power to edify the church, confront the heretic, and convert the heathen. The simplicity of the biblical message has been distorted by the proliferation of complex readings.

For this reason the Scripture must regain the freedom to speak for itself. The divine word must be liberated from centuries of accretions, distortions, copying mistakes, and downright errors. The biblical source must be purified so that its truth is restored from dilution and superficiality to its pristine consistency and integrity. Only then will it be able again to exert its full power of persuasion. Nothing short of text-critical restoration of Scripture to its original form will return the truth of Scripture to its original unity.[109] Therefore, it is the duty of the theologian to cleanse the text – an ancillary occupation, to be sure, but one not to be disdained for its servant role. In fact, this philological function is of the utmost theological importance because it enhances the freedom of the word. For whoever refines the divine word by lifting its burden serves the Holy Spirit, whereas those who knowingly corrupt the text commit a sin against the Holy Spirit.[110]

The restoration of the original text of Scripture is in a way the philological equivalent of Erasmus' overall reform principle: *instauratio bene conditae naturae*.[111] Restoring things to the natural goodness of their beginning was for him a desideratum. He was concerned with returning the divergent interpretations of the epigones of intellectual traditions to the founders of the respective schools and the authors of the original thoughts – a task which he accomplished with his numerous editions of ancient writers and church Fathers. But the biblical humanist saw his foremost duty to be the purifying of the sacred text so as to draw the philosophy of Christ from its very own source: 'Our chiefest hope for the restoration and rebuilding of the Christian religion ... is that all those who profess the Christian philosophy the whole world over should above all absorb the principles laid down by their Founder from the writings of the evangelists and apostles, in which that heavenly Word which once came down to us from the heart of the Father still lives and breathes for us and speaks with more immediate efficacy ... than in any other way. Besides which I perceived that that teaching which is our salvation was to be had in a much purer and more lively form if sought at the fountain-head and drawn from the actual sources than from pools and runnels. And so I have revised the whole New Testament ...'[112] His text-critical efforts certainly answered humanist concerns, but in the end they served the theological purpose of understanding God's revelation.

However corrupt the present biblical text may be, the authenticity of Scripture itself, its majesty in its source, remains unimpeachable. To be sure, after the time of the prophets and apostles, history had a detrimental effect on the sacred text. For all the different text traditions, copying mistakes, inadvertent changes, scholastic misinterpretations, and heretical falsifications, however, scriptural authority itself has remained inviolate.[113] Textual criticism by means of the oldest available manuscripts did not mean for Erasmus that the textual critic has the right to judge the text by extraneous authority. Rather, as the text is restored to its original form, it is returned to its author and thereby is given its due, namely, respect (*pietas*) for its inherent authority. For Erasmus, author, authority, and authenticity belong together and demand reverence.[114] Therefore, the humanist textual critic did not intend to criticize the truth of the divine revelation by human standards, but aimed at liberating it from any alien ballast, that is, from human impositions, in order to reach an understanding that accorded with its self-authenticating authority.

While the freedom of God's word is vulnerable to human incursions, its authority is beyond human reach. This is so because *auctoritas* signified the power of an original act – a privilege due first of all to God, the creator. According to the classical tradition, author and authority are virtually synonymous with source, beginning, and origin. Authority denotes the property of the author's identity which in the act of creation is bestowed on what is initiated and set in motion. The originator also confers such an effective power on the creation that the follower is persuaded to imitation by the truth inherent in the creation, rather than by external coercion.[115] The divine authority of Scripture as an expression of God's identity and power in the word, then, could not be diminished by human usurpation. Instead, it was enhanced by text-critical work.

So Erasmus himself set about to restore the freedom of the

New Testament, and exactly thereby he sought to honour its authority. The result of his spadework was a purged Greek text and a new Latin translation, the *Novum Instrumentum* of 1516 (plus the more radical second edition *Novum Testamentum*, 1519). He added copious annotations to justify the numerous deviations of his translation from the time-honored Vulgate.[116] While his edition of the New Testament represents, at least for our modern historical methods, less than an exact textual criticism on the basis of the first Greek manuscripts (he did not bother to track down the oldest codices but used three minuscules from the twelfth century), it did correct the Vulgate so thoroughly that he produced in fact a novel Latin translation – a translation that could not sit well with church authorities for whom the Vulgate was sacrosanct.

As was to be expected, Erasmus' edition of the New Testament caused among staunch Catholics severe criticism ranging from philological cavils to attacks for doctrinal reasons.[117] On the other hand, it was welcomed by humanists and reformers alike, even by Luther, who readily used it for his translation into German, the *September Testament* of 1522. Also Tyndale's 1525 translation into English and the King James version of 1611 were based on Erasmus' groundbreaking work. It is thus one of those ironies of history that the humanist who had such a low opinion of the vernacular, laid not only the foundation for the recovery of the New Testament by the reformers but also enabled its rendition into the language of the people. The holy book became available and accessible for everyone who could read – and, in turn, everybody was to be trained to read in order to read, first of all, the Bible.

For all its impact, however, Erasmus' philological work on the New Testament was not intended to be an end in itself. Since philology serves theology, he was not content with editing and translating the sacred text. He went on to interpret it in his New Testament *Paraphrases* and *Commentaries* on the Psalms. Moreover, in his introductory writings to the New Testament he laid down his principles of interpretation, an outline of the philosophy of Christ, and his ideals for the spiritual rebirth of Christianity.[118] Although he had prepared himself for this task by studying Greek since 1500, editing Valla's *Adnotationes in Novum Testamentum* in 1505, and occupying himself with preliminary studies for a commentary on Romans, it is the edition of the 1516

Novum Instrumentum that marks the real beginning of his theological work. What importance he himself attributed to this enterprise of interpreting Scripture is, for instance, clear from the fact that he dedicated his *Paraphrases* on the gospels to no one less than the four leading rulers of his time, Charles, Francis, Henry, and Ferdinand.[119]

Erasmus' hermeneutical principles as spelled out in both his *Ratio verae theologiae* and his *Ecclesiastes* (and as applied in his exegesis of New and Old Testament passages) certainly controvert any contention that his philology had to do only with establishing the accuracy of the biblical text in historical, literal terms. Moreover, his hermeneutical practice belies the inveterate cliché that his exegesis was motivated by practical, moralistic purposes alone. Of course, the humanist did engage in textual criticism following especially Valla. But his aim was to return the text to its original purity exactly in order to reform theology, the church, and society rather than to ascertain its factuality by means of criteria similar to those of modern historical criticism.[120] To restore the original nature of the text was for him a labour of piety. He meant to recover the authenticity of the word by serving its divine authority in such a way that the transcendent truth of the author would again be free to shine forth in a true theology which would restore Christianity to its original integrity.

Since God, the ultimate source of all that is, cannot be known except through God's revelations, the truth arises for human beings from the divine speech that ordered nature and salvation, that is, God's creation and restoration of the world by the word, Christ.[121] Accordingly, even the text-critical work of Erasmus served a given ontological and theological order elicited by means of the rhetorical structure of divine speech.[122] For the letter can reflect the truth only if it is again translucent to the reality for which it stands. And for that to happen the text must be original and pure. Moreover, we shall see that both the exegetical method and the hermeneutical principles of Erasmus rely in the final analysis on a systematic framework that is ordered by what he takes to be the objective order of divine truth. The criteria by which he understands reality are not derived from the contingencies of subjective, human experiences and so do not constitute a historical consciousness akin to that of modern historicism.

Already his move from history to tropology demonstrates

this.¹²³ But what is more, he was not content with staying on the tropological level of nature and culture. To be sure, he refused to diminish the relative importance of both the literal, historical and the practical, moral interpretation. But he was convinced that to get the full picture one had to move on to the highest level of a religious interpretation where one perceives the text within the context of the divine revelation in Christ. Only then is it possible to apply the word, in turn, to the personal and social conditions of particular times and circumstances.

On the whole, then, it seems that Erasmus concerned himself with freeing the text from its constricted literal sense by interpreting it in the context of the universal orders of nature, culture, and salvation. In doing so, he ultimately brought the words within the unique *scopus*, Christ, the focus of all reality. Therefore, the liberation of the text leads to a specific concentration in Christ, not to the multiple choices of an arbitrary libertinism. That is to say, the deliverance of words from their historical contingency moves them finally to an order around a fixed point, the Christological centre, rather than to the open field of unbounded anthropological notions. The fact that the word is for all seasons does not mean that there is an open season on the word. For it is precisely the concentration in God's *verbum*, Christ, that endows the letter with the freedom of the spirit to convey its true meaning.

With their approximate reference to this ultimate goal, words acquire a new meaning as their place within the divine arrangement of things becomes clear. More precisely, the measure of meaning that words attain is proportionate to the extent to which they agree with Christian teaching and life, and are in accord with the equity of nature.¹²⁴ So, as far as the dynamic of freedom and authority is concerned, the expansion of interpretation carries the text from its detention over into a freedom that is qualified by the authority of the divine revelation in Christ.

6 THE APPROACH TO SCRIPTURE

To gain access to the sacred word, one must approach it in a way appropriate to its nature. Just as the text is genuine only if it corresponds with its original, so interpreters fail to reach a germane understanding unless they conform to the character of the word. Inasmuch as Scripture is pure in its source, persons approaching it must be clean.[125] The interpreters' moral innocence and simplicity of faith are collateral to the *puritas* of the text. If they enter the divine word with unwashed hands (or dirty feet),[126] i.e., without a single heart and pure affections, they not only defile the sanctum but also deprive themselves of its revelation. Besides the *illotis manibus* (*pedibus*) image, Erasmus uses the metaphor of the low door (*humile ostium*), meaning that Scripture admits only those who bow their head in humility and faith: 'But be careful that you do not rashly break into the secret room. The doorway is low; make sure that you do not strike your head and be thrown backwards.'[127]

Innocence, simplicity, and humility, then, are the preconditions for entering the sacred precinct of the text. Only the believer who is properly prepared is attuned to the nature of the word. This is so because the essence of Christ's word is, after all, innocence, simplicity, and humility.[128] Not until readers have been conformed to the word, will it release its meaning and transform them into what it says. The moral and spiritual preparation of the reader is the foremost prerequisite for the biblical text to speak and also to work.

Erasmus applies here, as he does throughout his work, the principle *similia similibus* ('like attracts like').[129] Just as in the beginning the creation symbolizes the author, and the text corresponds to its original, so reader and text must be similar if there is to be an interaction between author and reader by way of the text. Only by adjusting to the text can the reader be transported into it and consequently be transformed into the author's image in it. The principle *similia similibus* governs all correlations between author, text, and reader, that is, between the beginning, middle, and end of the hermeneutical process. Only like can attract like. In fact, Erasmus' understanding of reality as a whole is predicated on the notion that similarity, sympathy, and likeness attract each other to effect unity and harmony, whereas dissimilarity, antipathy, and divergence repel each other to cause dissension and chaos.[130]

Already the task of purifying the text, preliminary and ancillary as it is, demands the moral preparation of the philologist in addition to respect for the authority of the text. While textual criticism does concern itself with the external side of the word, the textual critic is nevertheless not exempt from the requirement of purity. For cleansing the text already calls for decisions as to its content and therefore requires some preliminary interpretation, much as *paraphrasis*, one level higher, has already to do with commentary, even though it basically intends to say the same thing in other words.[131] Interpretation and commentary, however, deal with the content of the word, with reality in its authoritative form. And that reality is pure, simple, and true in its origin.

Because of the symbolic relation between word and reality, neither refining nor reading the text is simply a mechanical undertaking but rather requires, beyond a thorough knowledge of the languages, expertise in grammar, rhetoric, and poetry. Of course, one must not dally in these preliminary disciplines, for if one drinks too much absinthe everything one consumes afterwards tastes like absinthe, and if one stays too long in the sun, one is blinded and sees everything in its light.[132] What is of propaedeutic value in the exposure to good literature, however, is that it gives training in allegory and begins to shape the moral character of the student.[133] Even the formal means of dealing with the text, linguistic and rhetorical proficiency, encourage the moral formation of the humanist, the *vir bonus apte dicendi peritus*. Being learned and knowing how to express oneself appropriately depend on the moral life: 'Good learning makes men, philosophy makes superior men, theology makes holy men.'[134]

For the theologian the demand for purity is heightened. Over and above morality in general terms, those dealing with sacred literature must conform with the spiritual nature of the sacred text: 'Orators agree on the definition of one of their number as "a good man, skilled in speaking." So why should we be dissatisfied with "A theologian is a pious man, skilled in speaking of the divine mysteries," or "Theology is piety linked to skill in speaking of the divine"?'[135] The broader prerequisite of moral innocence is now specified by the need for a simple heart and humble faith.[136] Leading a life of moral integrity must issue in a spiritual movement toward holiness. Only the spiritual can come to the spiritual, the holy to the holy. For Holy Scripture is not a matter of philosophy but of prophecy.[137] Unless theologians are attuned to its sanctity, they cannot be transformed into the sacred word. It seems that the relation between rhetoric and theology is, at this juncture, one of the general to the specific, of the lower to the higher. As we shall see, this distinction between morality in general and Christian spirituality, specifically, prevails also in

Erasmus' differentiation between tropology and allegory, piety and faith, and the classical and Christian virtues.[138]

Erasmus considered the formation of the theologian's moral and spiritual character of extreme importance. This is especially evident in his advice to students preparing for the clerical office. To be sure, he insists on the formal instruction in the three languages fundamental to the interpretation of Scripture. Greek, Hebrew, and Latin supply the grammar and syntax for a direct access to the fountain of theological knowledge. Exercises in the *bonae litterae* and readings in various church Fathers provide supplementary studies to develop that sound judgment and shrewd prudence which distinguishes a sincere and strong mind. Studies in the precepts of rhetoric (that is, the comprehension of the rules of speaking and exercises in the *copia* of language) must accompany and supersede the training in grammar. Beyond intellectual education, however, the meditation upon the Bible day and night is the indispensable prerequisite.[139]

Rhetoric, the human art of speech, serves theology, the understanding of divine speech. Spiritual wisdom is superior to the natural knowledge. Despite this subordination, Erasmus never drew an absolute line of demarcation between the natural and the spiritual. This comes out prominently in his discussion of the young scholar's preparation. The spirit does not render unnecessary but rather perfects the natural gifts a student brings to the study of theology. Prudence, for instance, is often a natural rather than acquired disposition, which the Spirit takes up and surpasses. Similarly, natural diligence is not eliminated, but the Spirit's energy latches onto it. In short, the love of God perfects the moral endowments of nature, and the evangelical doctrine both restores and brings to completion a person's natural sincerity. Therefore, natural gifts like sincerity, prudence, and industry, brought out in rhetorical training and heightened in theological formation, render a person suitable for the office of the church.[140]

Finally, the study of rhetoric and theology together with the development of spiritual and ethical behaviour pass over into the student's nature in such a way that they form a habit. They turn into a second nature[141] on the basis of which the humanist theologian reacts spontaneously, almost instinctively. Rhetorical art, moral character, and theological knowledge have become truly natural. Art is no longer artificial. It loses even its appearance of art as it is reunited with the original goodness of nature.[142] The habits acquired by rhetorical, ethical, and theological training have again become an ontological habit, an essential quality of life and characteristic trait of nature's primordial integrity. In the unity of person and study, the wholeness of original nature is restored.

We took a general look in this chapter at Erasmus' concept of language, literature, literacy, and Scripture, and saw first of all that language not only enables communication between human beings but also makes them understand their place in the world and their role in culture. Language is either constructive or destructive according to its use. By situating humanity between God and the devil, Erasmus built a theological framework that derives its structure from the beneficial and destructive origin of language. Since language has degenerated in the course of history, humanists must restore it to its original integrity – a project that distinguished Erasmus' reform program from the Ciceronians and the scholastics alike. The following brief analysis of how Erasmus saw the relation between *verba* and *res* helps to clarify the ontological, basically Platonic, background that supports his rhetorical theology. It is especially metaphorical language that provides a bridge between opposites and therefore serves a mediatorial function. This role of metaphorical language is central to his concept of literature and literacy in general, but in particular to his appreciation of the linguistic nature of Scripture.

The examination of the symbolic function of language in good literature led us to the task of understanding Erasmus' concept of the incarnational nature and allegorical function of sacred literature. His reform plan to return language to its original integrity focused on both restoring Scripture to its pure sources and bringing theology and Christianity back to their true origin. He acquitted himself of this task by his text-critical work on the New Testament and his interpretation of Old and New Testament texts. Essential to his biblical exegesis is the unravelling of allegory, the middle between the external side of the word and its real meaning, and that so much the more since Christ, the divine word in human form, is the mediator between humanity and God. Now we have to take a closer look at the *Ratio* and *Ecclesiastes* in order to give specific attention to his allegorical interpretation of the divine revelation as it arises from the Christological mediation in the biblical word.

THREE

The Allegorical Nature of Scripture

1 LETTER AND SPIRIT

We have seen that for Erasmus language in general possesses a mediating quality, enabling it to perform both a symbolic and a transforming function, provided that it is restored to its origin and kept from falling into the service of evil. More importantly, where the divine revelation is concerned, God's word has progressed in history and finally become incarnate in Christ, the *scopus* of all reality. When God's word took on human speech in a final form, the mediating quality of language was brought to the height of perfection. The medium became the mediator: 'He (Christ) interposed himself between God and men in such a way that he included in himself the nature of both, for he intended to reconcile the one to the other. But a conciliator who intercedes has to intercede among several parties. For no one disagrees with himself. However, God is one, and there was discord between him and the human race. Consequently, a third party was necessary who would share both natures and reconcile them to each other. He would placate God by his death and lure men by his teaching to the true worship of God.'[1]

Christ, the incarnate word of God, represents that final mediation between God and the world which restores nature, renews human beings, and reconciles humanity with God and among itself. Yet, because beginning and end coincide in Christ,[2] he is also the original word-mediator between God and the world in the creation of the world. Precisely as the original word of the divine author, Christ is also its restoration after the fall.[3] Therefore, he is the criterion of all language, specifically of biblical language. Moreover, since he possesses the supreme power of persuasion he is the ultimate source of all transformation, specifically of Christian regeneration.

In both these modes of expression, symbolic and incarnational, language serves as a bridge between two mutually exclusive regions, the letter and the spirit, the flesh and the spirit, the visible and the invisible:

> All of this simply means that we should become numb to material things and render ourselves insensitive to them so that we may have more taste for things that pertain to the spirit as we have less taste for material things. Let us begin to live the interior life all the more sincerely as we live less exteriorly. To sum it all up in simple language, we should be less influenced by transitory things as we come to know more fully the things that are eternal, and we should have less esteem for insubstantial things as we begin to raise our thoughts to those that are real.
>
> Therefore let this rule be ever in readiness, that we do not linger over temporal matters at any time, but move on, rising up to the love of spiritual things, which are incomparably better, despising visible things in comparison to those that are invisible ... This is how we should act in the face of all those things that daily present themselves to our senses and variously influence them according to the diversity of their appearance ... The same rule applies for all literary works, which are made up of a literal sense and a mysterious sense, body and soul, as it were, in which you are to ignore the letter and look rather to the mystery. The writings of all the poets and the Platonist philosophers belong to this category, but especially the sacred Scriptures, which like those images of Silenus ... enclose unadulterated divinity under a lowly and almost ludicrous external appearance ... Therefore you must reject the carnal aspect of the Scriptures ... and ferret out the spiritual sense.[4]

Whether used by human beings to communicate or chosen by God to speak the first and last word, language provides a metaphorical transition between opposites in that it not only enables human agreement but, what is more, effects divine reconciliation. It is this way of thinking, we maintain, that characterizes Erasmus' theology and reform program as a whole. While acknowledging a basic dualism in the world, he inserted a mediating link between the opposites by bringing a trichotomous structure (in which the middle serves as a transition from the higher to the lower by accommodation and from the lower to the higher through transformation) to bear on the dualistic state of affairs. 'Just as in the natural transformation of things the change is facilitated by an intermediate stage that has an affinity with both sides, so John stood between the carnal law of Moses and the spiritual law of the gospel to facilitate the transformation of men from creatures of the flesh into creatures of the spirit. Earth does not suddenly become air; water forms the intermediate stage – it is gradually thinned out into the lighter element ... Christ became his (John's) successor, so to speak. For it is fitting that carnal things form the earlier stage and spiritual things the later; that imperfect things precede and perfect things follow. Grace imitates nature: grain grows first a stalk, then an ear, and infancy is followed by a more robust age.'[5]

Erasmus no doubt believed that a pervasive dualism is determining the present state of things. At worst, this split is liable to harden completely. Words become divisive and language disruptive through violent speech. If language separates rather than unites, opposition polarizes. Speech turns antagonistic as soon as it finds its orientation in the author of discord, the devil, who incites confusion and chaos. Becoming addicted to the gravitational pull of destruction, language not only loses its mediating quality but confuses the opposites, calling the bad good and the true false. But although perverted language bespeaks the *perturbatio ordinis*, it does not lose its power of persuasion and transformation. For whoever uses diabolical language is drawn into it so as to imitate its author and turn into what it says. As a result, the existing dualism turns into an irreconcilable opposition as the good order is disastrously turned upside down.[6]

Despite the conflicting, potentially diabolical state of things, however, dualism does not have the last word (since it did not have the word in the first place). It is characteristic of Erasmus' theology and reform program that he attempted to reorient language in God, the author of concord and harmony. His confidence in the divine order prevailed on the whole, whether in the broader order of symbolic language encompassing God's general omnipotence and governance in nature and culture, or in the proper order of God's special word of revelation in Christ for the salvation of humankind. In either case, the present dichotomy can be overcome by a process of assimilation through accommodating and transforming language.

As to universal discourse, then, language stands either between God and the world, calling forth order and salvation through God's law and gospel, or it stands between the devil and the world, giving rise to disorder and condemnation through Satan's law. Human beings find themselves by their speech either raised into the context of divine jurisdiction, answering God's speaking of the law, or they fall for the diabolical diction of Satan's jurisdiction, complying with Satan's speaking of the law.[7] Accordingly, the good word evokes balance, order, and unity in the world, whereas evil language engenders division, violence, and destruction. Erasmus derived his ontology and ethics from the human faculty of speech and the use of language according to either God's or Satan's speech.

Inasmuch as everything is essentially informed by the word, all reality is originally and finally oriented in God's word. But because human beings use language in such a way as to cause a deep gap to open up between God's original and final word, language appears actually distorted. Regardless of the present aberration, however, Erasmus sees the whole world, nature, human beings, society, and history, through the filter of a pervasive word-realism and word-finalism: Language reveals in its original and ultimate form that God, by virtue of the *logos* creating and fulfilling everything, is the beginning and end of all being. For this reason, all speaking beings find happiness in affirming both God's intention in creation and goal in perfection as they use good language to realize the harmonious order of the world. If oriented in this original and final purpose of God, human language is the means to restore the divine order.

By virtue of its mediatorial capacity, language is the medium to build consensus and to reconcile opposites. If not, it causes dissension and renders dissimilarities absolute. When it restores the original harmony of order, language recovers a balanced world by way of accommodation and transformation. Otherwise, it perverts the natural order of things by destroying the equilibrium of the world. In other words, the mediatorial power of language can have a holistic effect, or else the dualistic state of things is aggravated so grievously that the original unity is irretrievably lost. This is why the reconciling power of Christ is of such paramount significance. For in Christ, the divine word is overcoming the dichotomy of the world and thereby restoring wholeness. Bringing salvation to human beings and rendering whole all the world, Christ both restores the integrity of the universe's original relation to God and anticipates its perfection in the end. In Christ the mediatorial power of the word has become central, unique, universal, and final.

It is our task now to see how the mediating and reconciling function of language expresses itself in Erasmus' exegesis of Scripture. It is plausible to assume that there is a certain analogy between his understanding of the general function of language and the specific method of interpreting the sacred text. But it is important to make out the extent of this analogy, for the quality of the sacred word requires a qualified exegetical method.

Scripture is for Erasmus a text superior to all others: 'God has willed that the happy state of freedom from error be reserved for the sacred books alone.'[8] This is no doubt so because they contain the philosophy of Christ, revealing salvation above human integrity, teaching a truly Christian life beyond human morality, and leading to everlasting bliss in excess of human happiness: 'In order to achieve eternal salvation it is enough for now to believe about God those things that he himself has openly made known about himself in Holy Scripture ... To hold fast to these things in simple faith is the philosophy of Christ; to revere them in purity of heart is true religion; to strive through them towards preparation for the heavenly life is godliness; to be steadfast in them is victory; to be victorious by means of them is the height of bliss.'[9]

Nevertheless, even *sacrae litterae* are not immune to the present dualism of things. Word and meaning have fallen apart: 'The gospel has its flesh and its spirit. Although the veil was lifted from Moses' face, Paul still "sees in a mirror obscurely," and Christ said in John's Gospel: "The flesh is of no profit, it is the spirit that gives life."' But Erasmus is ill at ease with this dichotomy. While submitting to the authority of Christ's word, he chafes under it and tries to talk himself out of a fundamental dualism by attributing to the flesh some usefulness: 'I would have had scruples to say: "It is of no profit"; it would have been sufficient to say: "It is of some profit, but the spirit is much more profitable." But Truth itself said: "It is of no profit." Indeed it is of so little profit that according to Paul it is fatal unless it is referred to the spirit. In another respect the flesh is useful in this sense, that it leads our weakness to the spirit by degrees. The body cannot subsist without the spirit, but the spirit has no need of the body. But if on the authority of Christ the spirit is so great that it alone gives life, then we must strive that in every written word and in all actions we regard the spirit, not the flesh.'[10] So Erasmus must agree that the spirit and the letter in fact diverge because the original unity between language and God has been lost, inasmuch as the perfect unity between history and mystery has not yet come about. Even so, he leaves the door open for a gradual movement from letter to spirit. The dualism is not absolute; it is moderated by a development between the extremes.

As far as its historical condition is concerned, sacred literature is a text like any other good literature and requires the same literary methods of interpretation.[11] In spite of the fact that Scripture contains the sublime truth of the philosophy of Christ, as a text is it not accorded special privileges. As we have seen, however, the philological approach to Scripture must not touch its authoritative truth. And since this truth is of a religious kind, thus superior to the knowledge of nature and culture, the rhetorical means of interpretation must be specified so as to fit a theological understanding.

What seems to be an apparent ambiguity, namely, that Scripture is essentially distinct from all other good literature but as a text is actually similar to other texts, points again to Erasmus' characteristic way of thinking. As the incarnate word of God, sacred literature is different from other literature. But as literature, Scripture shares in the symbolic function of all good language. Regarding the relation of Scripture to profane literature, then, we can observe again Erasmus' attempt at recognizing distinction and similarity at the same time. He acknowledges a fundamental dichotomy, expressed by distinction, while yet working with a trichotomous structure, expressed by the mediating concept of similarity.

This way of thinking seems to derive in part from the Platonic principle of *chorismos* and *methexis*, of separation and participation, and it pervades, we maintain, Erasmus' entire thought.[12] Scripture as the word of God in Christ is unique, universal, and final. Even so, it shares in both the dualistic predicament and the symbolic function of human language as well. It is precisely the mediating quality of the symbolic function of language that provides a bridge across sacred and profane literature. Therefore, rhetoric and theology can be coordinated in such a way that the superiority of divine speech is preserved while its connection to human speaking at its best is yet not severed.

Once again, since even sacred literature remains subject to a dualistic split, it is by way of the symbolic, mediating quality of language in general that the biblical letter and spirit are connected. The Scripture is characterized by symbolic, mediating language like other good literature. What makes the Bible unique, universal, and final, however, is that Christ, the ultimate word of God, is incarnate in it as by a real presence.[13] This means that human mediation has been raised into the power of divine reconciliation. Therefore, Christ is at once symbolically and really present in the sacred word, symbolically as to the human nature of the word and really in terms of the divine nature of the word. The apparent ambiguity underlying Erasmus' view of the relation between *sacrae litterae* and *bonae litterae* reflects his Christology. He must insist on Christ's real, divine presence in the word while also conceding Christ's symbolical, human representation by the word.[14]

2 THE FOURFOLD SENSE OF SCRIPTURE

When he treated exegetical method, Erasmus mentioned several times the fourfold sense of traditional Scriptural interpretation (*littera, allegoria, tropologia, anagogia*).[15] But unlike 'meretricious interpreters'[16] or those ecclesiastical dialecticians who used the *quadriga* to deduce established doctrine from the biblical text, he revised this method according to the rules of humanist rhetoric: 'It is not enough to consider how the eternal truth reflects itself variously in diverse things according to the simple and historical sense, according to the tropological sense that refers to morals and common life, according to the allegorical sense that deals with the mysteries of the head and of the whole mystical body, and according to the anagogical sense that touches on the heavenly hierarchy. One also will have to consider which degrees there are in each of these, which differences, and which method of treatment ... The type receives as it were another form in proportion to the variety of things to which it is accommodated, and according to the diversity of times.'[17]

It is not too much to say, then, that Erasmus tried to liberate the biblical word from what he considered to be the burden of spurious interpretations and from captivity by scholastic theology. He modified the traditional method in order to free the living biblical word from what he saw as the monstrosity of scholastic rubbish and from the constraints of a deadening dogmatism, by eliciting from Scripture the harmony of Christ's teaching as it is accommodated to a variety of things, persons, times, and places.

For Erasmus the theologian, the biblical text bears a self-authenticating authority and therefore must not be violated by heterogeneous canons of interpretation. The sacred word neither releases its genuine meaning nor exerts its transforming power unless it speaks for itself. In this way, the sacred text manifests its fundamental freedom. But Erasmus as humanist maintains also that any text in *bonae litterae* can claim the same right. His attempt to let any good text speak for itself implied that Scripture, as literature, had no prerogative over profane writings. *Bonae litterae* and *sacrae litterae* are to be interpreted by means of the same philological method, regardless of the fact that there is indeed a qualitative difference between them. So since sacred literature is a human text, it must be approached by means of a grammatical-rhetorical analysis. Even so, since sacred literature contains the divine word as well, human means of interpretation must be adjusted to fit theological discourse. And it is, as we shall see, a Christologically based allegorical interpretation that properly responds to the divine authority of the sacred text: 'For that spring (divine Scripture) represented Christ himself, who even now in his might lying hidden in the mysteries of Scripture opens the eyes of the blind, if only they acknowledge their darkness.'[18]

Even in the Bible, the spirit remains bound by the letter. Erasmus believed that Scripture is not exempt from the qualitative distinction between the inner content and the external appearance of the word: 'The divine Spirit has his own peculiar language and modes of speech ... Break through the husk and extract the kernel.'[19] Like Origen, he followed the exegetical rule based on the philosophical axiom of the split between the visible and invisible world in both ontological and anthropological terms: *Littera occidens, spiritus vivificans* and *Caro non prodest quicquam, spiritus est, qui vivificat.*[20] This dichotomy impels the exegete to move from the surface toward a recondite meaning, which is not possible unless one recognizes that sense which mediates between the outer and the inner sides of the word by reconciling them. To discern the spirit in the letter, then, Erasmus used the two middle links of the fourfold method of interpretation, tropology and allegory, as a bridge between the literal and the spiritual sense, between history and mystery: 'Of the interpreters of divine Scripture choose those especially who depart as much as possible from the literal sense.'[21]

Certainly, Erasmus' biblical interpretation aimed above all at the spiritual meaning of the word: 'Ignore the letter and look rather to the mystery.'[22] Nevertheless, he refused to abandon its literal, historical sense. For the letter constitutes the irremovable fundament and substratum of the hidden content.[23] Therefore, just as one must not look down on philology and rhetoric for their service to theology, so also the literal and historical form of the text must not be disdained when compared with its spiritual content. Even as tropology and allegory lie concealed in history, their interpretation yet builds on the historical sense rather than removing it. History, after all, is a form of narrative literature to be read for moral and spiritual truth. When disclosing the truth, tropology liberates the confined word into its own broader, moral import and allegory frees the text by revealing its deeper, spiritual meaning.[24] Thus there is more to the word than its first impression, namely, its hidden content,[25] to be uncovered by the tropology and allegory. The movement from the visible to the invisible, so fundamental to Erasmus' thought as a whole,[26] governs also his understanding of the exegetical process.

Adopting the *Rule of Tychonius*, Erasmus took the allegorical meaning to point not only to Christ, but also to the church, the body of Christ, and to the Christians, the members of this body. Allegory, when applicable, performs an essentially Christological and ecclesiological function.[27] Tropology, on the other hand, uncovers the moral instruction of the word aiming at ethical utility for individuals, society, and church alike. In fact, there is no biblical text that does not imply a moral significance.[28] The final, anagogical sense, however, adumbrates the last things of God's mystery.[29] Since anagogy touches on an eschatological reality of the triune divinity itself, it remains by and large beyond the exegetical reach. This is so because the essence of divinity, God *in se*, lies beyond human comprehension, renders us speechless, and therefore must be worshipped in silence: *Quae supra nos, nihil ad nos.*[30]

To uncover the cache of truth in the divine words, Erasmus preferred the allegorical and tropological sense of Scripture to its anagogical meaning. While leaving the literal sense intact as the inevitable starting point of the exegetical process and keeping its end point (the anagogical consummation and perfection) veiled in the mystery of God's spirit, he concentrated on the middle and mediating part of interpretation, where allegory and tropology function in the intermediary region between the outer and inner side of the word and thus facilitate the *transitus* from the visible to the invisible.

Both allegory (the specifically Christological, ecclesiological, and Christian understanding) and tropology (the general moral instruction in terms of utility, civility, and humanity) proceed from the immediate, literal sense of the text. While continuing to adhere to history as their *declaratio*, they yet open new perspectives by casting light on the letter, in such a way that they at once render it a shadow and reveal its true meaning. Therefore, even otherwise orthodox church Fathers are wrong when they reject the obvious literal sense.[31] Nevertheless, should a literal interpretation lead to nonsense, run counter to Christ's teachings, or undermine morality, an allegorical and tropological interpretation must prevail. Then the spirit must do without the letter.[32] It is true that not all scriptural passages, especially certain Old Testament ones, are conducive to Christian allegory. Some are so frigid that they fail to kindle the fire of Christ's love. But to draw a moral lesson from any good source, and most of all from biblical history, is always possible: *Tropologice nusquam non est locus*.[33]

The allegorical, Christological interpretation fathoms the proper meaning of the word, whereas the tropological, moral interpretation grasps its broader import. Tropology, we can say, has more to do with symbolic language in the general order of God's governance of the world. Allegory, on the other hand, concerns itself primarily with the incarnational language in the specific order of God's revelation in Christ for the salvation of the world. Tropology is common to both *bonae litterae* and *sacrae litterae*. But allegory, in terms of a Christological and ecclesiological interpretation, applies properly to Scripture.[34] It would be misleading, though, to assume that allegory belongs to theology alone or, for that matter, tropology only to rhetoric. Both, tropology and allegory are legitimate means of interpreting the sacred text, except that the tropological method (which in good literature is virtually the same as allegory) is raised in biblical interpretation to the level of theological discourse since it serves Christ and the church as either forerunner or attendant.

The historical sense establishes the only basis from which the exegete can move to any higher meaning.[35] Even so, it is allegory and tropology that perform a metaphorical function since they provide a medium between the letter and the spirit. The Christological interpretation, properly speaking, and the moral interpretation, broadly speaking, carry the meaning of the text over from the confinement of the letter to the freedom of the spirit, and from there onward to the final mystery. History denotes the beginning of the text; mystery bespeaks its consummation. Yet Erasmus concentrates on the exegetical middle region, the transition between beginning and end, the progress from origin to fulfillment.[36] Without eliminating the historical meaning of the text as the point of departure, Erasmus placed tropology and allegory in the centre of the exegetical process, considered them as metaphorical means for the transition from the letter to the spirit, interpreted them in terms of Christology, ecclesiology, and ethics, and left the endpoint of insight, the divine mystery, in the darkness of the future.

Applying this insight to the larger framework of Erasmus' thought, we can conclude that just as language itself functions within the world order as the medium for knowledge and action, so the Christological-ethical exposition of biblical texts marks the mediatorial area between letter and spirit. Allegory and tropology represent a metaphorical passage from history to mystery, a mediating *transitus* between the visible and the invisible, by pointing to similarities.[37] This concentration on the middle process between source and goal, origin and fulfillment, is in my opinion the most important element of Erasmus' hermeneutic. The overcoming of a basic dualism by a trichotomous structure that reconciles opposites characterizes the thinking of the biblical humanist.

This concentration on the middle is also the salient point in Erasmus' theology, cosmology, and anthropology. Christ, the word, stands as the incarnate mediator between God and humanity.[38] Human response to Christ is the means by which human beings, placed as they are in the middle between God and animals, can move upward toward divinity, provided they yield to the drawing power of divine love (*eros*).[39] The same can be seen in Erasmus' cosmology, where water and air are located between earth and fire. The middle region can either be reduced to earthly matter in a downward move or liquefied and rarified when yielding to fire, the all-consuming supreme power of attraction.[40] Similarly, failure to respond to the divine love, symbolized by fire, makes human beings fall easy prey to the gravitational pull of brutish passions. Like the soul, psychologically speaking, between spirit and body, and the *affectus*, ethically, between virtue and vice,[41] human beings themselves are placed in a position where by word and deed they can either strive heavenward or go downhill, become increasingly spiritual or mundane. And their movement, whether toward improvement or degeneration, expresses itself in speech as it affects others, uplifting them or degrading, enhancing or diminishing, enlivening or destroying.[42]

3 ALLEGORY AND ACCOMMODATION

If we take a closer look at the function of allegory both as the way in which Scripture reveals the truth and as the method of an interpretation that suits this form of the biblical message, it becomes apparent that allegory is akin to the single most important concept in Erasmus' hermeneutic, accommodation. For the transition from the literal to the spiritual is made possible by accommodation of the divine Spirit to the letter, which in turn also effects by virtue of its power of persuasion the human transformation from the flesh to the spirit: 'He (Christ) accommodated himself to those whom he strove to draw to himself. To serve men, he was made man; to heal sinners, he intimately associated with sinners.'[43]

The pivotal role which allegory plays in Erasmus' exegesis is analogous to the crucial place which accommodation obtains in his theology.[44] But along with theology comes ontology and ethics. We can conclude that allegory is to language, what accommodation is to reality. Since reality precedes language, accommodation comes before allegory as its necessary ontological condition. Moreover, since ethics expresses language in action, ethical accommodation realizes allegorical language in practice. Erasmus' exegetical method did not function as a mere mechanistic device, but was in line with his overall view of reality. We cannot understand the specific function of allegory without exploring the nature of accommodation in general.

As for revelation in Scripture, allegory serves a double purpose. For one thing, the divine wisdom employs allegory to accommodate itself to the level of human comprehension. It lowers itself to the human condition. But then the Spirit also uses allegory to persuade human beings to rise to the truth: 'Divine wisdom speaks to us in baby-talk and like a loving mother accommodates its words to our state of infancy. It offers milk to tiny infants in Christ, and herbs to the sick. But you must hasten to grow so that you may receive solid food. It lowers itself to your lowliness, but you on your part must rise to its sublimity.'[45] Since the author and the recipients of the revelation are essentially dissimilar, a process of accommodation is required to bridge the gap between them. This is so because, generally speaking, only like can join like, according to the principle of similarity (*similia similibus*).[46] Given the separation between the visible and the invisible, between the sensible and intelligible, an adjustment is necessary to reduce the distance in order to make assimilation possible and similarity viable.

Inasmuch as the lower is at first incapable of rising to the higher by its own power, the higher must be pleased to lower itself. Accommodation thus reduces a dualistic opposition in that the higher condescends to the lower without losing its virtue of being superior. That is to say, the higher is free to relate to the lower while yet maintaining its authority. As a result of accommodation, however, the lower is enabled to become similar with the higher, even though this assimilation will fall short of an absolute identity. This is why the lower needs to improve by imitating the higher until a final perfection consummates the process of approximation. Accordingly, Erasmus' concept of similarity must not be understood in terms of identity but as qualified by the dialectic of separation and participation (*chorismos, methexis*). Being capable of participation, the higher possesses the power of accommodation. Being subject to separation, the lower is enabled by the accommodation of the higher to become similar with the higher through imitation.[47]

These are obviously ontological grounds for accommodation. But the philosophical principle *similia similibus* ('like to like') in the area of nature and culture is raised to the biblical maxim *omnia omnibus* ('all to all'), which similarly expresses the motif of adaptation, but now in the specific area of salvation: 'He (Christ) was made all things to all men in such a way that in nothing was he dissimilar to himself.'[48] And imitating Christ, his disciples must accommodate themselves to others in Christian love: 'You, too, must be all things to all men, so that you may win everyone to the side of Christ, as far as it is possible, without giving offence to piety.'[49] It seems that for Erasmus the general principle *similia similibus* is to the specifically biblical maxim *omnia omnibus* as genus is to species.[50] Either signifies accommodation, whether in the general region of human insight and behaviour, or in the specific area of God's revelation in Christ and in Christian life. In Scripture, general reasons for accommodation are perfected by the power of theological discourse as God accommodates the divine word to human understanding.

The highest expression of accommodation is Christ's incarnation in the biblical word. Moreover, his attitude on earth in his teaching and life is also characterized by accommodation. Accommodation thus distinguishes his being, teaching, and doing. Not only in his nature did Christ adjust himself to human nature, but in his word he also adapted his doctrine to the various levels of human comprehension. And he acted toward others in such a way as to observe *decorum*, that is, he adjusted to the variety of persons, times, circumstances, and things in particular situations.[51] In all of this, however, neither his divine nature, nor his being the centre of Christian doctrine, nor his representing the prototype of moral behaviour were compromised at all. Christ is the incarnate model of the divine participation in, and separation from, human nature, thought, and action. Likewise, the disciples, especially Paul, imitated Christ in that they adjusted to the level of others, even though as Christians they were different from the world by virtue of their spiritual regeneration, heavenly teaching, and Christian living.[52]

Accommodation and its linguistic correlative, allegory, are instrumental for the restoration of nature and the promotion of culture. Just as the harmony of nature is owing to the power of sympathy by which the cosmos, threatened as it is by antipathies, maintains its balance, so kinship, friendship, familiarity, political alliances, and intellectual consensus engender concord in a precarious human world: 'It is easy for friendship to be made and kept between those who are linked by a common language, by the proximity of their lands, and by the similarities of temperament and character.'[53] 'Eternal concord should unite those whom nature has made one in many things and whom Christ has unified in more, and all should join in a united effort to bring about what concerns the happiness of one and all. Everything points the way, first natural instinct and what we might call the human principle itself (*humanitas*), then the Prince and Author of all human happiness, Christ.'[54] Harmony in nature, happiness in the body politic, and health in the human body belong together: 'A balanced state of things preserves good health. But when the parts are at war with each other and the body is buffeted, it is an indication of the imminent ruin of the whole.'[55]

Accommodation is required to bring about at first similarity and eventually unity in the present dichotomy of the invisible and the visible, the intelligible and the sensible, spirit and matter. This is why nature already abounds with similes, images, symbols, signs, and allusions offering insights into its balance and harmony. What is more, on the higher level of literature, human language, particularly poetry, resounds with allegories, metaphors, similitudes, proverbs, and parables, inviting the readers to understand their human nature more deeply and inspiring them to realize their humanity in a peaceful and happy community. Last but not least, God chose in Scripture, specifically, to accommodate in Christ the divine wisdom to human diction so as to be understood in human terms and to transform human beings into a life of godliness.

Conversely, this divine accommodation to human speech by way of allegory calls for a reciprocal adjustment on the part of those who read and interpret the Bible. The spiritual nature of the revelation requires first of all that the person approaching it be spiritually suitable. Whoever advances to the inner sanctum must have a pure heart, clean feet, and the humble faith without which one cannot enter the narrow gate of Scripture.[56] These spiritual, ethical, and theological qualifications are a *conditio sine qua non*.

But these higher prerequisites, indispensable as they are to understand the spiritual meaning of the sacred text, do not exclude those grammatical and rhetorical skills which are necessary to grasp the literal sense and moral import of the text. In the first place, proficiency in the biblical languages, including Latin, is mandatory so that the student is able to accommodate to the diction of the text. Nothing substitutes for the immediate contact with the sources. Next, since allegorical interpretation already can be practised in good literature, learning how to read the symbolical language of the ancients constitutes a training preliminary to biblical exposition. This elementary education is significant not simply because it instructs in the necessary philological skills, but because it begins to form the individual's moral character in preparation for the transformation by the sacred word: 'For my part, I should certainly not disapprove a kind of preliminary training in the writings of the pagan poets and philosophers ... provided that one engages in these studies with moderation ... and only in passing ... You will find many things there which are conducive to a holy life, and the good precepts of a pagan author should not be rejected ... These writings shape and invigorate the child's mind and provide an admirable preparation for the understanding of the divine Scriptures, for it is almost an act of sacrilege to rush into these studies without due preparation.'[57]

It is not surprising by now to find that Erasmus does not bother much about protecting from a certain ambiguity the relation between the reader's subjective preparation for understanding the word and the objective transformation of the reader by the word itself. It is probably less theological inconsistency that makes him leave this problem unresolved than his prudent conviction that to draw a firm conclusion in favor of either side would lead to irreconcilable differences. So, on the one hand, students must adapt themselves to sacred wisdom by a process of formal education, moral development, and spiritual adjustment. On the other hand, the transformation into what the divine word says is supposed to be entirely an effect of the word itself, which, in turn, is nevertheless persuasive in such a way that the volition of the person is not altogether ruled out.[58]

Also unclear is the relation between this human preparation and that 'admirable metamorphosis' or 'restitution to original innocence' which happens in baptismal regeneration.[59] The ambiguity we found in Erasmus' attitude toward rhetoric and theology in general, specifically toward Scripture as a sacred and human text, and to Christ's presence in Scripture as a real and symbolic presence at the same time, surfaces here again, now regarding the salvific effect of human effort, word, and baptism. Rather than insisting on an absolute 'either-or,' as Luther certainly did, Erasmus, the man of the middle, opted for the 'not only-but also' approach which applies the principle of separation and participation in such a way as neither to compromise the superiority of the higher nor to absolutize the inferiority of the lower. Erasmus, the judicious humanist, left open those questions, on which ecclesiastical authority had not yet decided, to avoid forcing a logically consistent conclusion that would harden an issue into categorical polarities.

Accommodation in Scripture, both as the accommodation of the word to the reader and of the reader to the word, is for Erasmus analogous to accommodation in education as such, both as the accommodation of the teacher to the student and of the student to the subject matter. Erasmus believed that it is incumbent on the pedagogue to adjust to the student's natural disposition, mental capacity, and level of learning: 'The teacher must, of course, be careful in his choice of subject matter and put before his students only what he finds to be especially agreeable, relevant, and attractive material, which flowers, so to speak, with promise.'[60] In this way the teacher imitates the allegory of good literature, which in the first place adapted itself to the receptivity of the reader. In fact, from interpreting allegorical texts, the teacher learns the pedagogy for a useful and effective instruction of students. Evil in children, on the other hand, is not so much due to nature as to bad schooling.[61] While original sin is 'a disposition to evil that has been deeply ingrained in us ... we cannot deny that the greater portion of this evil stems from corrupting relationships and a misguided education.'[62]

Similar to the drawing power in good literature (*eros*) and God's Spirit in Scripture, the tutor's love (*caritas*) attracts impressionable students with parental affection: 'It is also beneficial if the prospective teacher deliberately adopts a fatherly attitude towards his pupils; in this way his students will undertake their studies with great enthusiasm, while he himself finds less tedium in his work. Love will overcome almost any difficult challenge. The old saying is that like rejoices in like; so the teacher must, as it were, become a child again and thus win the affection of his students.'[63] Teachers are to be so devoted to their subject matter that by example they draw the student to it, with the pupil in turn learning to love letters for their own sake, and to love the teachers for their love of letters.

Such humanist charity naturally excludes all mechanistic

instruction, whether by enforced conformity with a formalist set of abstract laws or by psychological repression through punishment, humiliation, coercion, and intimidation – in short, by violence of any kind. Violence disrupts, oppresses, and destroys, whereas love brings to bear the supreme power of attraction that enables accommodation and eventually brings about reconciliation. In fact, the persuasive power of the word ultimately springs from the love of its author, whether it is God's in revelation or the teacher's in instruction.

Therefore, education in humane studies should be pleasant and playful (*per lusum discere*),[64] but also suited to the students' natural tendencies and individual disposition (*ingenium*).[65] Respect for each person's individuality and natural gifts marks an education that is liberal because it enables formation by evocation instead of enforced conformity, by emulation rather than by competition. It is the teachers' accommodating attitude of love, balanced by their authority, that keeps the freedom-authority dialectic of education in proportion.[66] The teachers' love and respect for the student derives, we conclude, from the dynamic of participation and separation, that is, from their freedom to accommodate themselves while at the same time keeping distance on account of their authority. In this way, they imitate God's relation to humanity.

4 ALLEGORY, SIMILITUDE, AND PERSUASION

A closer look at allegory in sacred letters helps us to understand how its symbolism is related to its power of persuasion and transformation. As we have seen, Erasmus claimed that the purpose of allegorical language is to persuade readers to let themselves be drawn into the truth so as to be transformed. Language is allegorical insofar as it possesses the mediating quality of transcending the letter toward the spirit, in the process carrying the reader with itself. Allegory provides language with the medium to bridge the gap between contrary sides by showing up similarities and effecting attraction. It is not only transitional in that it moves the reader from the letter to the spirit, but it is persuasive since it opens the person to the drawing power of the Spirit. The persuasive and transforming power of allegorical language rests on its quality of mediation.

Allegorical language in good literature already possesses a

certain power of conviction, even if its reach is limited. But it is biblical allegory, the Christological sense of Scripture, that is eminently capable of carrying common language over into a higher meaning. Symbolic language at its best, biblical allegory possesses the supreme power of persuasion that draws the reader into its content. What is more, by virtue of its being incarnational language, it renders its import really present as a power of transformation that carries the reader over into itself. What unites good literature and sacred literature is, besides the letter, allegory. What makes Scripture pre-eminent, however, is that Christ, the ultimate reference point of all reality, is incarnate in scriptural allegory.

The unexcelled power of persuasion and transformation in biblical allegory arises from Christ's being not only symbolically but also really present in Scripture. In other words, the superior metaphorical power of biblical allegory springs from Christ's symbolic and incarnate presence in the word. It is the divine accommodation to language, the adaptation of Christ's meaning and presence to human speech, that creates biblical allegory, which for its part then enables the translation of human speech into a divine meaning. The allegorical nature of Scripture originated when the higher condescended to the lower. This inverbation of Christ in Scripture in turn makes an allegorical exegesis, the hermeneutical progress from the lower to the higher, possible.

By elevating allegory to such a prominent position, namely, as an expression of the presence of the divine mediator in incarnational language, Erasmus raised it far above its place of a figure of speech in traditional rhetoric.[67] Along with allegory, metaphor received a similar theological significance; indeed, it could even serve as a sign for the Christians' translation from old to new beings, their rebirth or *metamorphosis*.[68] Biblical allegory, then, was for Erasmus more than a rhetorical figure, even though it was that, too. It represented the very nature of God's revelation and thus characterized the foremost method of understanding Scripture – a view that Erasmus shared with the Platonizing Fathers of the church. Certainly, he could use allegory and metaphor as part of the general inventory of elocution.[69] But the special function he saw allegory perform in sacred literature was that it referred to the Christological, ecclesiological, and Christian meaning of the text.[70]

Rhetoricians in the classical tradition had assigned allegory and metaphor to the sub-category of similitude (*similitudo, parabole*). The rubric *similitudo* in turn was defined as a rhetorical figure of the semantic amplification of sentences that points, like its companion *simile*, to a common attribute (*tertium comparationis*) underlying two seemingly opposite things. Showing that they are in fact comparable, similitude discloses their essential similarity and thereby encourages the comparison with other things of a similar kind so as to see them fall into an overall order (*collatio*).[71] As Erasmus said for instance: 'John has a style of his own; he strings his words together as though they were links in a chain, held together sometimes by a balance of contraries, sometimes linking like with like, sometimes by repeating the same thing several times.'[72] However, should it be impossible to compare these opposites, then they are obviously dissimilar (*contraria*),[73] which means in the case of utter incompatibility that they lead, in the final analysis, to the perversion of order. 'Old suits old and new suits new. If you mingle them, you not only labour in vain but also make worse men out of those whom you are trying to improve ... A mixture of incongruous things is useless.'[74]

When he wished to indicate the basic dualism of things, Erasmus used the scheme of *contraria* (*pugnantia, dissimilia*).[75] He especially reverted to it when he tried to show the fundamental opposition between God and the devil, their kingdoms and laws, virtues and vices, and the end of good and evil persons – as he did in the *Elenchus* of the fourth book of his *Ecclesiastes*, his systematic overview of theology.[76] On the other hand, he took great pains to compare things, persons, times, and circumstances in order to draw forth similarities, and this was possible only by introducing a trichotomous view in which the middle link functioned as a *tertium comparationis*. So he used not only antithesis to express a duality but also analogy to express a duality that was to be moderated by a mediating similarity. A symbol for this is, for instance, John the Baptist: 'John, on the borderline between law and grace, like a mixture of both, had some of the old law in him ... he also had in himself something of the new law.'[77]

This Erasmian method of employing the rhetorical devices of both contrast and similarity provides a clue for the way we must understand his work as a whole. *Contraria* obviously express a dualist perspective, whereas *similitudo* is predicated on a basic,

The Allegorical Nature of Scripture 115

if often hidden compatibility. Accordingly, our interpretation of Erasmus' thought should be sensitive to the way he used a dualistic or trichotomous view, or a combination of both, whatever the case may be in particular instances.[78] It is necessary to establish in each case whether he tried to indicate a basic duality by using the language of contrariety, or wished to express, from a trichotomous perspective, a possible assimilation on account of similarity. Similarity, however, is impossible without introducing a middle link between opposites, the *tertium comparationis*. While the language of contrariety (and, accordingly, an exclusively literal interpretation) divorces the letter from the spirit, the external from the internal, to the point of absolutely hardening their distinction,[79] allegory (both as the nature of scriptural revelation and as the method of interpreting it) points out similarities by showing transitions between opposites.

Erasmus adhered to the normal definition of metaphor and allegory. Both perform the same rhetorical function except that metaphor is a single word, whereas allegory is a continuous narrative, for instance, a parable.[80] Allegory thus represents an extended metaphor embracing larger contexts of meaning. Metaphor, we can say, is to word what allegory is to continuous text. Where Scripture is concerned, however, allegory has assumed an incarnational quality, so that the Christian exegete must utilize a Christological interpretation to understand the real meaning of the sacred text, because 'Christ clothed nearly everything in parables, something which is peculiar also to the poets.'[81] Allegory therefore marks an overall Christological understanding while similitude characterizes the literary form of Christ's own parables. Allegory is the word about Christ; parable is the word of Christ. Allegory is to incarnational language (Christ present in human terms) what similitude is to symbolic language (Christ using parables to teach the divine truth in human terms).

Tropes and allegories, similes and parables carry the word from an ordinary, well known context to a higher level of meaning. 'No other kind of teaching is more familiar or more effective than comparison through similarity, for Christ, who wished for his doctrine to be most popular, takes the parables from the most common things ... And he wonderfully renews these commonly known things in that he accommodates them to his philosophy.'[82] 'This kind of speech pleased Christ above all, because it is especially effective for persuasion, accessible and familiar to learned men and unschooled folk alike, and most of all according to nature, particularly if similitudes are drawn from those things which are well known to the common people ... In fact, the parable is not only effective for teaching and persuading but also for moving the affections, for delighting, for clarity, and for impressing the same meaning so deeply into the mind that it cannot slip away.'[83]

Whether it is metaphor or allegory, the similarity between figure and content is possible only in the presence of at least a minimal compatibility. But this affinity cannot be established except in that the higher accommodates itself to the lower, meaning to letters, things to words, the philosophy of Christ to nature and history. The resulting similarity then enables the interpreter to compare corresponding passages and associated ideas (*collatio*). 'How much more worthy of Christian equity it is that, as with the Holy Scripture, if we come across anything ambiguously or obscurely phrased, we explain it by comparing other passages, so with books dealing with sacred Scripture, if we meet anything ambiguous in meaning, we should either interpret it in the more favourable sense, or else elicit the meaning of what is written from other passages.'[84] This condition (that two levels of discourse must not only be potentially compatible or sympathetic for similarity to be effective, but also potentially comparable for collation to work) demonstrates again why the similarity principle (*similia similibus*) plays such a decisive role in Erasmus' hermeneutic. Rhetorical collation is analogous to metaphorical translation: 'As metaphor is a brief similitude, so similitude or comparison (*collatio*) is a metaphor unfolded and accommodated to the thing it implies.'[85] But neither can operate in the absence of compatibility, affinity, or similarity.

Since it is the higher that has assumed similarity with the lower, its accommodating word possesses the metaphorical quality of allegory and parable, enabling the interpreter to translate biblical language from common speech into the higher arena of discourse: 'Jesus therefore once again lowered himself to the humble state of his people and, leaving the mountain top, descended to the rest of the disciples and to the multitude. Remember, then, teachers of the gospel, how much more it becomes you to lower yourself to the level of the weak.'[86] Divine translation into human speech is the necessary condition for the translation of human language into theological meaning. Just as God became similar to humanity through accommodation in Christ, so the divine wisdom uses the rhetorical device of similitude to speak human language: 'And these are the mysteries of God the Father, these the secret purposes of the divine mind, whereby it seemed good to him to make God into man, and to make mankind in a fashion into gods, to mix the highest with the lowest and raise the lowest to the heights.'[87] The presence of similitude in the Bible is indicative of the divine having become similar to the human through accommodation: 'At first doctrine must be adapted to their uneducated minds, until they have made progress ... [Jesus] offered them parables, that is, similies drawn from things that are very familiar to everyone, for this is the simplest and most suitable way of teaching uneducated men ... [Evangelical parables] are subtle in their simplicity, wise in their foolishness, lucid in their obscurity. For under this lowly and laughable garb they conceal heavenly wisdom.'[88]

Similarity is for Erasmus more than a potential state of likeness. It is also the motive power for assimilation, a movement to realize similarity. What characterizes Erasmus' thinking as a whole comes here to light, namely, that a state is never divorced from an overall movement. The gospel spreads and the kingdom grows: 'Under the cover of this allegory the Lord covertly taught his disciples the beginning, progress, and perfection of the gospel, the beginning and end of which he himself would act out publicly in his visible body; the intermediate stage, that is progress, is supplied by the invisible grace of the Holy Spirit. Being the beginning himself, Christ spread the seed of the gospel ... And to this day the evangelical seed is sprouting forth ... and grows in secret increments day and night alike ... through the invisible power of his Spirit. And he will not return to be seen by the world until the business of the gospel has progressed to the point that he himself has predetermined and alone knows – then he will come a second time, visible to all ... Although this parable pertains specifically to Jesus, who leads, advances, and perfects the evangelical kingdom, it nevertheless also touches on the apostles and the successors of the apostles, whom God wishes to have but one concern: that the word of the gospel be disseminated as widely as possible. For the time of sowing lasts until the end of the world.'[89]

It is this thought pattern that prompted him to lay out his world view not only in terms of a framework of thought but also of an organic development within it.[90] Accordingly, likeness carries with itself both the possibility of liking (that is, a measure of attraction[91]) and the actualization of it in a movement from a beginning toward an eventual union. Likeness, liking, and oneness; similarity, assimilation, and union; affect, affection, and consummation; accommodation, persuasion, and transformation go hand in hand. Just as there can be no metaphor without potential similarity, there can be no similarity without virtual attraction, that is, the drawing power of the divine *eros* and the response of human affection in general piety and specifically in Christian *caritas*.[92] So, since the persuasive power of language arises from the mediating property of the word, persuasion too depends on both the potential similarity and virtual attraction between two otherwise incompatible levels of discourse.

5 OPENNESS AND HIDDENNESS

Erasmus holds that the split between letter and spirit causes the hiddenness of Scripture, whereas the openness of Scripture results from the mediating, revelatory power of allegory. The sacred word conceals its treasure from the carnal view of the senses while rendering it accessible to a spiritual understanding. God's word never reveals itself to anyone beholden to the letter alone. Without humility and faith in Christ, the reader is possessed by the flesh, recognizes only the outer shell of the word, and consequently lacks a sense for the essentially spiritual nature of the sacred text: 'Since the historical sense is like the body of Scripture, and the concealed sense like the soul, it is certain that those who reject what is the best of Scripture draw back from Scripture itself.'[93]

Erasmus linked the hermeneutical statement: 'the letter kills,' with the anthropological and ontological statement: 'the flesh profits nothing.'[94] This is especially evident in his *Paraphrase on John*: 'What is the bulk of a human body if spirit is not there? So my words, understood according to the flesh, will not bestow life unless you understand them spiritually as coming from heaven.'[95] 'What is born from the flesh is only flesh, but what is born from the spirit is spirit ... Those who are born according to the flesh know nothing other than the flesh; they think there is nothing except what they perceive in their senses. But things that are not seen are the most important and have the greatest power, while the flesh is weak and helpless. But if in your heart you still do not follow, take an example from things that have some similarity to the spiritual, and yet are perceived by the physical senses.'[96]

But things are a bit more complicated than this straightforward dualism. For allegory remains at first hidden even to those to whom it will reveal itself. The power of allegory therefore takes effect in two ways: Allegory is hidden in order to reveal itself; allegory is hidden to remain hidden. While it encourages pious and teachable folk to seek its meaning, it does not release its meaning at all to the impious interpreter. Christ used tropes and allegories, similies or parables to hide the truth up to the point of enigmatic obscurity 'to vex our sluggishness, so that the fruit of our labor would be the more pleasing ... and to conceal and cover his mysteries from profane and godless people, but in such a way that pious searchers would not be shut off from the hope of understanding.'[97]

So even someone who piously searches Scripture in tune with the spiritual nature of the word will find its truth at once closed and open. A full understanding of the truth comes only at the endpoint of the spiritual development, perfection or consummation, when the dualism between letter and spirit, flesh and spirit, is finally overcome and there is need for allegory no more. For the time being, however, allegory itself is both covert and overt. It is a paradigm for the hiddenness and openness of Scripture itself.

This becomes clearer when we compare allegory with Christ's incarnation, which is fitting since Christ, after all, is the prototype of allegory. Although the two natures of Christ, divine and human, are altogether distinct, they did become similar by virtue of the incarnation, without the divine, however, losing its superiority. Divinity certainly reveals itself, yet it maintains at the same time the secrecy of its mystery.[98] And what is true of incarnation holds good also for the divine accommodation in allegory, Christ's inverbation in Scripture. Allegory joins letter and spirit, yet it preserves at the same time the integrity of the spirit. Erasmus' rhetorical understanding of allegory is obviously modelled on his theology of incarnation.

But similitude, allegory, and parable connect biblical interpretation also with nature. The allegory of Scripture opens a view to reality through discourse that conforms with nature: *Facile* *descendit in animos omnium, quod maxime secundum naturam est.*⁹⁹ Since Christ's allegories and parables are 'in closest accordance with nature,' they are most suited 'not only for teaching and persuading but also for moving the affections, for delight, for clarity, and for impressing the same meaning deeply into the mind.'¹⁰⁰ Allegorical language in Scripture, like in any good literature, is naturally pleasant, agreeable, and attractive, insinuating its truth into the reader. After all, similitude and *suavitas*, the mode of suasory speech, belong together: 'As for style, insofar as it depends on the employment of rhetorical tropes and figures, we are there on a level with Cicero ... If you do away with allusions ... speech loses much of its attractiveness.'¹⁰¹ Yet in contrast to good literature, the compatibility of divine Scripture with nature is so unexcelled that 'no other doctrine is more consonant with nature'; 'in faith and grandeur of subject-matter we are his (Cicero's) superiors by far.'¹⁰²

This consonance with nature characterizes the harmony of Christ's teaching: 'Just as the whole circle of doctrine is in harmony with itself, so it is in agreement with his life, even with the discernment of nature itself.'¹⁰³ Therefore, *aequitas naturalis* becomes a criterion for the true interpretation of Scripture: 'The meaning which we draw forth from the obscure words must respond to that circle of Christian doctrine, to its life, and finally to natural equity.'¹⁰⁴ Natural equity in turn has to do with *consensus naturalis*, with the harmony and balance of nature: 'The conflicting forces of the elements are evenly balanced so as to preserve unbroken peace, and despite their fundamental opposition they maintain concord by mutual consent and communication.'¹⁰⁵ Besides signifying, then, that biblical language is in accord with nature, that interpretation must be in harmony not only with Christ's doctrine and life but also with nature, *aequitas naturae* also means the equity of nature itself as it shows its cosmic equilibrium by consensus and communication.

What is more, the truth revealed by the equilibrium of nature has ethical implications: 'Virtue is in accordance with nature, vice is against nature.'¹⁰⁶ Because the harmony of God's creation is attractive on account of its beautiful balance, it serves as a paradigm for moral behaviour, advising moderation in the exercise of justice by balancing justice with love: 'Prudence corresponds with faith, justice with love, fortitude with hope. Temperance is a species of justice, teaching how much is to be conceded to the affections, how much to the body, how much to the mind, and how much is to be denied.'[107]

Small wonder that the humanist is quite in line with the rhetorical tradition in combining the pedagogical rule which relates language allegorically to nature with the rhetorical principle of *delectare* which aims to convey the moral import of allegory (tropology) by appealing to the milder *ethos* of human beings. And even though this ethical appeal is still preliminary (because not yet having the full impact of *movere*, that is, the appeal to the sharper human *ethos*), allegory is connected with tropology. *Aequitas naturae*, then, is a concept that brings together allegory and nature, expresses the harmony in the balance of nature itself, and points to an ethical attitude of virtue in general and to temperance specifically, which makes justice equitable by love. It is in this way that Erasmus coordinates word, nature, and virtue, or hermeneutic, ontology, and ethics.

However, beyond this aesthetic and ethical appeal of, and to, nature, the truth of the divine wisdom captivates the heart by its own supernatural attraction: 'Nothing is more splendid than the heavenly philosophy, nothing sweeter than the name of Jesus Christ.'[108] That is to say, the aesthetic and ethical appeal of allegory is perfected by its theological significance. Accordingly, over and above its mirroring of the splendour of the natural order, biblical allegory reflects the light of the divine revelation itself. It refracts God's glory as if through a prism, revealing the heavenly doctrine and inspiring a Christian life. Just as the beauty and goodness of the word are functions of its truth, so aesthetics and general moral principles are subservient to theology and Christian ethics.

Regardless of its openness, though, the truth in allegory remains hidden. While inviting human beings to approach it in humble faith, it retains its sublimity. This is so because things 'are more pleasing if they are shining through a crystal or a piece of amber than if seen with the naked eye ... Sacred things display more majesty if they are brought to view under a veil than if they are laid bare just like that. We discover the truth more agreeably if it first has baffled us by the cover of an enigma.'[109] Besides this aesthetic aspect, Erasmus can see the hiddenness of the truth from an eschatological perspective. So, for instance, Jesus did not wish to have his words understood until his prophecy was made clear by their fulfillment in subsequent events:

'Almost all the language which the evangelist put into the mouth of the Lord Jesus is highly figurative and obscure ... The way in which the Lord says many things shows that he knew they could not be understood, and did not wish them to be understood, until the course of events should make his meaning plain.'[110]

Scriptural truth also protects itself against any improper access, particularly the impudent incursions, the irreverent prying of *impia curiositas*: 'What is open to view, lean forward to kiss! What is not given to see but rather covered to whatever extent, worship in simple faith and honor from afar: Absent be godless curiosity!'[111] Erasmus had in mind here those modern theologians who 'reduce theology to dialectical subtleties and Aristotelian philosophy,' when 'it is enough for us to believe, hold on to, and worship what is written.'[112] If philosophy is used to 'examine everything inquisitively rather than piously, certain reasons suggest themselves that destroy and corrupt the strength of faith.'[113] 'Such a dangerous inquisitiveness,' says Erasmus in another context, 'has generally arisen in us from the study of philosophy, a fact which the illustrious Tertullian, the most learned by far of the Latin theologians, has asserted in several places, although he himself was a philosopher of the first rank.'[114] We see that the mystery of Scripture remains covert in order both to attract the pious and to maintain its authority and integrity over against the impious. Attraction and repulsion, then, are the effects of the participation-separation tension as expressed in the openness and hiddenness of Scripture.

We have already come across another reason why the truth remains hidden. It is for the most part pedagogical, namely, to arouse human beings from their sluggishness or sleep and prompt them to make an effort to learn.[115] Certainly, starting the process of knowing is generally hard, as is the beginning on the way of virtue, exactly because 'what is excellent is also difficult.'[116] But continuing the effort becomes increasingly easier: 'What seems at first to be unattainable becomes more accessible as one progresses, easier with practice, and in the end even pleasant through custom.'[117] And as far as rhetorical training is concerned, repetition and memorizing give way to a habit that eventually turns into a natural disposition, a second nature of the student. When it comes to the study of Scripture, however, the beginner must have from the start a singular aim in view: 'Let this be your first and only goal, this your commitment, strive for this only, that you let yourself be changed, drawn, inspired, and transformed into what you learn. The food for the spirit is useful only when it does not remain in the memory as if in the stomach but spreads into the very affections and the inmost parts of the mind. Do not believe that you are making progress if you dispute more acutely, but only when you realize that you are gradually becoming another person.'[118]

This pedagogical motive can be intensified to include a eudemonic element. So, for instance, it pleased Christ to imitate the language of the Old Testament prophets to work on our dullness, in order that we afterwards find the fruit of strenuous effort the more enjoyable.[119] But for the most part, the motive of accommodation prevails. Always the perfect educator who monitors the students' progress, Christ adjusted his teaching to the level of his disciples' comprehension. That meant that several times he 'deceived them for the time being by riddles of allegories so that what he wished them to understand would later stick the deeper in their minds.'[120]

In his understanding of accommodation, Erasmus could even go so far as to see Christ use the rhetorical strategy of *dissimulatio*,[121] at times to the point of 'dissembling his divine nature – yet without obscuring the truth.'[122] Dissimulation, the hiding of one's true intentions for pedagogical purposes, is for Erasmus neither reprehensible nor unethical, if only it leads the student toward being drawn into the truth. 'Your rhetorical theorists allow the orator on occasion to misrepresent the truth, to magnify the unimportant and to make the splendid look small, which is a kind of conjuror's trick, to infiltrate the hearer's mind by deception, and finally to carry his intelligence by storm through rousing his emotions, which is putting a kind of spell on him.'[123] As long as the instructor's intentions are pure, deception can be pedagogically justified in certain circumstances and for certain time periods. 'Plato, in imagining this ideal republic, realized that people could not be governed without lies. Far be it from a Christian to tell a lie, and yet it is not expedient to tell the whole truth to ordinary people no matter how it is done.'[124]

It is all right to conceal what one really intends, or to act on a hidden agenda: 'We need a sort of holy cunning; we must be time-servers, but without betraying the treasure of the gospel truth from which our lost standards of public morality can be restored.'[125] Concealment of truth is, after all, the way Scripture accommodates itself to its readers. It is therefore appropriate for the teacher to imitate the manner of baby-talk (*balbutire*) by which the divine parent communicates with children of underdeveloped, limited insight.[126] Dissimulation is justified not only on pedagogical and rhetorical grounds but also for theological reasons. Accordingly, the pedagogical adjustment to the student's progress in the development of insight, the art of ordering speech (composing discourse so that it is fitting, convenient, and accommodating to particular circumstances), and last but not least the nature of the biblical revelation call for indirect language up to the point of dissemblance.

All the same, the truth is hidden, in the last resort, because reality is basically split into a duality. Therefore, the pedagogical, rhetorical, and theological reasons for indirect language imply an ontological perspective. Sacred Scripture resembles the *Sileni Alcibiadis* (those statues concealing beautiful images of gods beneath panels decorated with ugly flute players), because it 'encloses unadulterated divinity under a lowly and almost ludicrous external appearance.'[127] And Christ appears as a Proteus: 'Although there is indeed nothing more simple than our Christ, yet by a certain secret plan he acts the role of a kind of Proteus in the variety of his life and doctrine.'[128] To be sure, the truth is kept hidden from the surface of the word because of the corruption of, and the human accretions to, the sacred text. But more fundamentally, word and true meaning fall apart because of the dualistic state of things in general. This is why the truth of sacred letters 'is usually covered and skewed by tropes and allegories, by similes and parables, sometimes to the point of having the obscurity of an enigma.'[129]

So the hidden and open nature of Scripture is analogous to the ambiguous and mediating function of allegory. Allegory in Scripture remains ambiguous regardless of its metaphoric capacity. And yet, its ambiguity notwithstanding, the language of the divine revelation as expressed in allegory is indeed metaphoric, mediatory, and persuasive. Thus Erasmus viewed allegory from both a dichotomous and trichotomous perspective. Expressing the wisdom of God, allegory is fundamentally distinct from human speech. Even so, it also accommodates itself to human perception by expressing itself in human terms. Situated as it is at the intersection of divine and human language, as it were at the linguistic line of demarcation between the holy and profane, allegory must function as indirect speech, for it is able to represent the real presence of the divine only in symbolic terms.

Christ spoke in human terms as he used parables foremost drawn from nature and human life. But because human language is inadequate to pronounce the things which are of God, the divine mediator transferred human language to a heavenly level of meaning. This translation is at once mediatorial and ambiguous, drawing near in participation with human diction and remaining distant in separation from it. Maintaining his divine authority and exercising at the same time his freedom to lower himself to human language, Christ is present in his word as the prototype of allegory and divine persuasion. The ambiguity of symbolic language and the mediation of incarnational language are therefore corollaries of God's accommodation to the human condition.

The ambiguity and mediation of the sacred text together signal the dialectic of distinction and participation. And it is Christ, the supreme allegory, in whom this dialectic became incarnate: 'Fullness of grace and truth was received by his only-begotten Son alone, who was made man and has come down to us in such a way that through his divine nature he is forever in the bosom of God the Father.'[130] Christ is the focus in which both dimensions of reality, human and divine, converge and intersect. As the *scopus* of everything, Christ constitutes not only the hermeneutical principle of Scripture, but also, in a preliminary way, the criterion of good literature. Moreover, Christ is the paragon of the metaphorical property, of the persuasive power, and of the transforming effect of language. Precisely as the center of everything, he enables the transition from the lower to the higher. In him the middle is the medium, the medium is the mediator, and the mediator is the reconciler.[131]

This is why the only key to Scripture is Christ 'who so closes it that no one can open it, and so opens it that no one can close it.'[132] For human comprehension, in turn, the divine revelation is both difficult to grasp and attractive to seek; it is at once beautiful and homely. The biblical word is appealing and hard to crack. God's wisdom draws human beings unto itself precisely in that it encourages them to strive for it.

Erasmus' understanding of the allegorical nature of Scripture and of the allegorical presence of Christ in Scripture informed his own Protean way of thinking and writing. It is the hidden nature of Scripture and the ambiguous function of allegory that determined the ambiguity of his language. It is, on the other hand, the revelatory nature of Scripture and the mediating function of allegory that encouraged him to seek consensus through his own writings, trusting as he did the reconciling power of language to bring about harmony and balance. He practiced what he believed, namely, that Christians ought to imitate not only the spirituality and ethics of their prototype, Christ, but also his manner of speaking.

A rhetoricial theologian imitating the divine speaker and his manner of speaking, Erasmus expressed himself in both ambiguous and mediating terms, whereby he always aimed at the transformation of individuals and society into the ideals of the philosophy of Christ. In his personal lifestyle and attitude, too, hiding and publicizing, seeking friends and being a *homo pro se*, association and solitude, reaching out and pulling back became his second nature. Regardless of whether he did so consciously or by the influence of dealing with allegorical texts, Erasmus was accustomed to thinking, writing, and behaving in terms of accommodation, revealing and concealing himself at the same time but with the intention at heart that his readers be drawn into, and transformed by the truth.

It would be erroneous, then, to assume that ambiguity was for Erasmus a matter of doubt calling for a sceptical stance. He was far from being nothing but a fellow of the Academy.[133] Instead, he followed Ciceronian scepticism in that he suspended judgment and pursued probability when a question defied the judgment of logical conclusions.[134] What is more, ambiguity reflected for him the essential character of the sacred word, which he saw as being equivocal by its very nature, since it offers a double meaning, human and divine. However, exactly by showing up the distinction between the two sides, Erasmus pursued, in imitation of Scripture and Christ, the ultimate goal of mediation. The biblical humanist was in the final analysis not a dualist. He saw his vocation in building bridges.

6 THE ALLEGORICAL METHOD

After having reflected on how Erasmus viewed allegory as the way in which Scripture expresses the divine truth, we turn now to his understanding of allegorical exegesis as the method that corresponds with the allegorical nature of biblical language. We shall find, to no great surprise, that the middle is again of central significance, this time in terms of the golden mean between too much and too little allegorizing.[135]

In line with Augustine, Erasmus insists: 'There is nothing false in sacred Scripture, nor trifling or written in a human vein, but everything is full of heavenly philosophy and worthy of the Holy Spirit, in whatever form it offers itself, if it is properly understood.'[136] But since Scripture is covered with types, schemata, tropes, similes, parables, and allegories,[137] the reader must be attuned to this mode of expression to arrive at the genuine meaning of the text. Of course, one must not 'strain for tropes if the plain word has a pious and sound meaning that squares with other scriptural passages.'[138] Nevertheless, necessity compels us to draw away from the letter 'as often as the words of Scripture ... are clearly false or absurd, or otherwise run counter to Christ's doctrine and pious morals.' Similarly, utility persuades us to forgo the grammatical sense 'as often as the words of Scripture ... indicate no usefulness or little in comparison with the far richer moral import in the mystical sense.'[139] It is therefore no sin to deviate from the obvious sense of a passage if one adds a pious meaning that is also contained in other scriptural passages, even though the writer perhaps had not had this in mind.'[140]

Beyond good common sense (*sanus sensus*), then, it is the consensus of Scripture as a whole (*collatio*) and the moral usefulness of piety (*utilitas*, *pietas*) that are the basic criteria for both plain reading and allegorical reading. In addition, there is also the criterion of the doctrine of faith: 'Any interpretation at odds with the inviolable doctrines of faith must be rejected.'[141] Obviously, good common sense has to do with insight into nature, utility with the conduct of life, and doctrine with the teachings of Christ. So the passages from the *Ecclesiastes* we have just analysed confirm what Erasmus had put in his *Ratio* in both a succinct way and in the reverse order of significance: 'The meaning which we draw forth from the obscure words must respond to that circle of Christian doctrine, to its life, and finally to natural equity.'[142]

Let us now amplify this basic rule of allegorical interpretation. 'Several times,' says Erasmus, 'the meaning of the words is openly false, even ridiculous and absurd, if taken at face value.' This is, he goes on saying (and we paraphrase), why the divine wisdom interspersed the course of reading with bogs, pits, and similar obstacles (throwing in certain things that could not have happened or, if they happened, surely were absurd) in order that our mind, closed by such stumbling blocks from a vulgar understanding, wanders on more remote paths and finally arrives at the point where the treasures of deeper insight open up. But the fact that there are some places where the divine providence forces, as it were, our minds to search for the spiritual understanding does not permit us to remove all historical meaning. 'For the most part it happens that both senses [the historical and the spiritual] are present.'[143]

In normal cases, then, the meaning of a biblical text rests on a mixture of the immediate, literal sense and mediated, allegorical meanings. The exegete must therefore make every effort to discover whether any, and if so which, of the meanings beyond the historical are present. Only after the various levels of the text have been explored, can exegesis be true to the text. The integrity of the word requires that its exposition be commensurate with the extent of its signification. In other words, exegetes must accommodate their interpretation to the possible depth dimension of the word. Similarity and accommodation characterize not only the relation between the expression and content of the word (*verbum-res*), but also between the text and its interpretation. It is not surprising to find that the axiom *similia similibus* surfaces here again.

In interpreting allegories in sacred Scripture, theologians should above all follow the example of Christ, the apostles, especially Paul, and the orthodox Fathers (in that order). 'It was the purpose of the Holy Spirit ... to wrap up the mysteries of heavenly wisdom under these layers of metaphor. The way to unwrap the mystery has been marked out for us by Christ himself in the gospel and by the writings of the apostles. Following in their footsteps orthodox Fathers have shown us the rest.'[144] Taking their clue from these, the greatest interpreters, theologians will be able to walk the fine line between overallegorizing and underallegorizing. The rule guiding them along their way cautions them to stay in the middle by avoiding excess and observing moderation, that is, to keep the delicate measure of proportion (*mediocritas*) between exegetical amplitude and concision, *hyperbole* and *ellipsis*.[145] For to read too much into an allegorical text is as inept as to read too little out to it. A frigid interpretation ensues if one observes all external details of a story so scrupulously (*superstitiose*) as to turn every triviality into a spiritual meaning. On the other hand, Old Testament regulations concerning sacrifice and food do not literally apply to the present situation but must be interpreted spiritually. In fact, to reject the spirit of Scripture in favour of its body is to reject Scripture as such.[146] Nonetheless, allegory must not be left to the whims of the reader's fancy, either: 'It is enough to accommodate what we find in sacred letters to allegory, without inventing anything in addition to it.'[147]

The literal meaning of a biblical text may be absurd and insipid, even futile and pernicious, unless one fathoms its allegorical import. But this does not give the interpreter the licence to use the allegorical method in such a way as to twist the divine oracles into an alien, even contrary sense: 'No one is a more deadly enemy of the gospel teaching than one who skews sacred Scripture to his own base passions.'[148] For example, there are those who misuse biblical authority to condone public mores. While it is quite legitimate to draw inferences from the sacred text for the teaching of true morality, one must not use God's word to authorize crude customs. To draw ethical implications for ideal conditions is one thing, but to sanction the vulgar status quo by biblical authority is quite another.[149]

A true understanding of Scripture, then, arises from faithfully deriving its meaning from what it says instead of reading one's own arbitrary notions into it.[150] The interpreter must render the genuine sense of the text rather than impose a heterogeneous meaning on it. This is why *paraphrasis*, that is, the interpretation of a text (as more than translation and less than commentary) was for Erasmus such an important rhetorical exercise.[151] In fact, burdening the text with a sense other than its own amounts to doing violence to it. The words become distorted and lose their integrity, though not their authority.

Consequently, one must not force the text to say what one (before reading it) presumes to know. Just as force and violence are in general the reversal of accommodation and persuasion, causing as they do division and hardening opposition, so also specifically in the interpretation of sacred literature they impede rather than open the access to the truth.[152] These hermeneutical admonitions make it quite clear that Erasmus was aware of the perennial objection raised against allegorical interpretation, namely, that it amounts to *eisegesis* rather than *exegesis*.[153]

On the whole, then, allegorical exegesis must first of all rely on the historical sense of the word. Should the literal meaning yield absurdities and lead to superstition, then interpretation can do without its foundation in history, as long as it elicits a meaning that conforms to piety and agrees with other biblical passages. As for allegory, specifically, the following rule obtains: 'The meaning which we draw forth from the obscure words must correspond to that circle of Christian doctrine, to its life, and finally to natural equity.'[154] That is to say, allegorical exegesis must read the text analogous to the equity of nature – a step in the hermeneutical process, as we have seen, that already introduces moral perspectives. Most importantly, however, allegorical interpretation must be centrally oriented in the harmony of Christ's teachings. But because the doctrine of Christ is inseparable from the way of life he taught, allegorical exegesis always includes a definitely Christian ethic. Inasmuch as this ethic perfects rather than eliminates natural morality, the allegorical (Christological) method links up with the tropological method that looks for clues to moral implications in general (nature) and to Christian behaviour in particular (the life within the circle of Christ's doctrine).

While Erasmus did not bother to delineate clearly between his allegorical and tropological interpretation, there is yet a pattern to be found in his own exegesis. On the one hand, he can go so far as to identify the allegorical method with the tropological method. It is this circumstance that gave rise to the contention that he was nothing more than a moralist. At times, the tropological interpretation can stand alone, which happens when a text does not admit of a specifically Christological understanding. Since there is always a moral import to any symbolic text, the tropological interpretation is always applicable to determine *utilitas* in general, and that is true even of a biblical text when it is barren of a specifically Christological meaning.[155] Consequently, allegory as tropology is common to good and sacred literature. Following the rhetorical tradition, Erasmus can thus combine tropology and allegory.[156] As is the case with *bonae litterae*, tropology possesses an accommodating, transitional, mediatorial, and persuasive power similar to allegory, except that it aims at the good life (*bene vivere*) issuing in natural happiness, the goal of all human beings (*finis*). 'It is natural for all mortals to seek happiness.'[157] Just the same, while in good literature there is more of an identity between the moral and the allegorical meaning, in *sacrae litterae* the two methods of interpretation are more distinct.

On the other hand, if a text indeed yields the specifically Christological sense, tropology plays a servant role by preceding allegory as its harbinger and/or following it as its retinue. Preceding allegory, the ethical meaning of the text serves for the preparation of the Christian life. Following allegory, tropology applies Christ's doctrine to the life of the Christian. By itself, tropology in Scripture uncovers the general moral meaning of the text, as in good literature. In either case, it is the higher order of Christian life that qualifies common morality as propaedeutic and/or attendant. In other words, tropology is ancillary to allegory, whether preparing the way for it (even if standing alone) or following after it. It is therefore plausible to conclude that for Erasmus tropology is to Christological allegory what rhetoric is to theology, what good literature is to sacred literature, what antiquity is to Christianity, and what *genus* is to *species*.[158]

Although the allegorical interpretation of the Bible subsumes the literal and tropological interpretation under its Christological purview, it does not rule them out. Just as the divine revelation does not destroy history, nature, and culture but rather perfects them, so also the translation of the text into its higher significance does not abandon its historical and moral sense. The literal, we can say, constitutes the particular meaning of the text. The tropological represents the general, extended meaning of the text. The allegorical presents the specific meaning of the text, that is, the extended meaning focused on the unique *scopus*, Christ. But it is precisely the specific meaning that illuminates the text in its particular and general meaning. While literal particularity can be dispensed with if absurd, the ethical import is always present. The allegorical meaning, however, exactly because it is Christological, gives literary form to the specific, hidden centre of the text, essential even if not readily at hand.

Looking at the function of tropology and allegory from the perspective of transformation helps to spell out their relation more clearly. The biblical word aims at the reader's transformation. Now the ethical instruction of tropology can come either after transformation as instruction in the Christian life, or before transformation as a moral preparation for the proper approach to Scripture. In the first case, tropology functions subsequent to allegory by showing the moral import for Christian life: faith active in love.[159] The resulting Christian piety is then following from the cardinal virtues. In the second case, tropology serves a preparatory, pedagogical function. But since tropology can occur also in the absence of allegory, the general ethics of the Bible confirms the moral philosophy of the ancients, as it appeals to that natural piety which is based on the classical virtues.[160]

To illustrate, the relation between allegory and tropology (that is, between the proper, specific, Christological meaning and the broader, general, moral meaning) is analogous to that of faith and piety.[161] Faith has to do with the allegorical interpretation, and piety with the tropological interpretation of Scripture. Faith expresses a person's specific relation to Christ, whereas piety concerns the general scope of moral behaviour. Faith reveals the absolute priority of grace over nature. But piety relates the natural virtues to both the preparation for, and the advancement on, the way of salvation. Erasmus insisted on the exclusiveness of grace and faith. But under the rubric *pietas* he reserved for natural morality a function not only preliminary but also ancillary to faith, and as Christian charity a function concomitant with faith.

With the addition of the tropological interpretation, all three components of rhetoric (*docere, delectare, movere*), now raised to the higher level of theological discourse, have finally come together: The sacred text teaches and attracts readers by persuading and transforming them; it moves them to the good life of Christian virtues, with the classical virtues playing a necessary supporting role. As Erasmus said it, biblical allegory 'is not only effective for teaching and persuading, but also for moving the affections, for delight, for transparency, and to impress the mind deeply with the same teaching so that it cannot be lost.'[162]

In all of this there is obviously a snag as far as the Scripture's capacity to delight is concerned. For, try though he may, it is difficult for Erasmus to find in the Bible the same stylistic elegance and rhetorical eloquence that distinguishes the polished writings of classical literature. Biblical language is simply not up to par with the exquisite style of Ciceronian Latin. Although Scripture excels in terms of teaching and moving, its literary attractiveness leaves something to be desired. Its power of persuasion is therefore due to its superior substance, less to its eloquence. To solve this problem, Erasmus reverts to a *topos* of the early Christian apologists. He attributes the rustic language of the New Testament to the fact that the divine wisdom accommodates itself to the *rusticitas* of the unschooled folk.[163] The Scripture talks to beginners in faith as if to children, reserving the solid food of doctrine for those who have grown up in the faith.

We have concentrated in this chapter on Erasmus' understanding of the allegorical nature of Scripture within his overall world view. The common thread running through all sections is the concept of the mediatorial power of allegorical language, its capacity to throw a bridge over the chasm between letter/flesh and spirit, the visible/material and the invisible/spiritual world. Erasmus modified the fourfold method of scriptural exegesis to accommodate a humanist-rhetorical interpretation. Without sacrificing the initial historical sense of the text, he highlighted the middle of the exegetical process, the allegorical (Christological/ecclesiological) and the tropological (moral) meaning of Scripture as the medium and means for passing from history to mystery.

Taking a closer look at the relation between allegory, accommodation, similarity, persuasion, and transformation, we found the focus on mediation helpful for clarifying some of the Christological implications of Erasmus' theology. The supreme mediation, Christ's presence in the word, is characterized by the principle of separation and participation at the same time. Just as he mediated between God and humanity in his person and work, so he mediates between the letter and the spirit by accommodating himself to the human condition while remaining at the same time fully divine. The expositor of God's mind, Christ persuades the reader to consensus, love, and concord. Moreover, the Christological principle of closeness and remoteness is also key to Erasmus' understanding of the spiritual, mysterious hiddenness and the natural, historical openness of Scripture.

Finally, the medium as *mediocritas* is central to Erasmus' allegorical method of interpreting Scripture. Just as allegory is the way in which Scripture expresses the divine truth, so the allegorical method of interpretation must conform to the specific nature of biblical language. It is not surprising, therefore, to find that the middle is again of central significance, this time in terms of the golden mean between too much and too little allegorizing.

FOUR

Speech and Interpretation

1 INVENTION

From all that has been said so far it is clear that for Erasmus the source of theology is Scripture (and also good literature), and the subject matter of theology is the commonplaces (*loci*) drawn from the divine wisdom in Scripture (and also from nature). What is more, Christ is the centre of Scripture and therefore the central hermeneutical principle of interpretation (even of good literature). But the way Erasmus interpreted Scripture and arranged theology was informed by rhetoric. The present task is, therefore, to explore in detail how interpretation, theology, and rhetoric are intertwined. To begin, it might perhaps help to suggest that Erasmus' formal principle of interpretation was theological (or better, Christological), while his material principle was rhetorical.

In applying the rules of grammar and rhetoric to the interpretation of Scripture, Erasmus gave grammar the first place: 'Grammar claims primacy of place.'[1] But this discipline ranges beyond establishing the lexical connotation of single words, their grammatical connections, and their location within the syntax of clauses and sentences. Determining in a passage the meaning of words and phrases as well as seeing the text within its context is propaedeutic to grammar, for 'grammar is the art of speaking correctly (*emendate*).'[2] As such it is the foundation of all other disciplines: 'The first task of education should be to teach children to speak clearly and accurately.'[3] Grammar includes training in the classical languages and reading the best authors, that is, those whose good literature is especially conducive to moral utility.[4] Speaking correctly already involves discovering the broader and deeper dimensions of a text. So the line separating grammar and rhetoric is blurred; grammar serves rhetoric and interpretation in a preliminary way.

Even so, to make out the significance of a text as part of a larger linguistic context, the interpreter must apply, over and above the rules of grammar, the norms of rhetoric.[5] Only then is it possible to integrate the text into the order of nature and culture as reflected by language itself. Still, a theological understanding is not reached until the text is viewed as an integral part of the whole, namely, within the sweep of God's progressive revelation culminating in Christ's presence in Scripture. Scriptural interpretation provides the *topoi* which allow theologians to see God's speech in an order, a divine disposition reflecting the economy or dispensation of salvation.

Rules of grammar, principles of rhetoric, and theological *topoi* drawn from the story of Christ are instrumental for understanding Scripture on three increasingly significant levels.[6] These incremental stages of interpretation correspond to the historical, tropological, and allegorical methods of exegesis. In the same way that tropology and allegory make the transition from the letter to the spirit possible,[7] rhetoric and theology enable the move from the particulars of grammatical knowledge to an understanding of an ordered whole that includes, respectively, the perspectives of nature and culture, and of salvation. Rhetorical theology thus helps not only to convey knowledge, morality, and a sense of the overall end in the process of human development in general but, what is much more, to inspire faith, love, and hope as the fundamentals of Christian existence.[8] Where theology is concerned, interpretation receives its hermeneutical principles from the teachings and life of Christ. Where rhetoric is concerned, the interpreter selects those of its norms that are useful to theology and accommodates them to sacred literature.[9] They are drawn particularly from the five functions of oratory: *inventio, dispositio, elocutio, memoria,* and *pronuntiatio* (finding, arranging, and expressing subject matter for discourse, plus memorizing and delivering speech).[10]

When Erasmus mentions these five offices in his *Ecclesiastes*, he at once allegorizes them in reference to a living body. Since invention supplies the subject matter of speech, it compares with the bones of the body, which must be firm or else everything collapses. Next, disposition joins the parts of discourse fitly together and therefore is similar to the nerves. Because disposition orders speech to render it harmonious, it also makes the hearers teachable and facilitates the memory of the speaker. For one learns more easily and remembers better if what is said is properly ordered rather than scattered and confused. Elocution supplies the appropriate words and figures of speech. It thus resembles the flesh and skin of the living body, the comely clothing for bones and nerves. Memory is like the spirit, the life of the body, without which everything falls apart. Pronunciation is similar to the act and motion of the mind whereby the animal nature of the body is transformed into the spirit. This movement is as it were the life of life.[11]

This view suggests that oratory proceeds by means of a process with a beginning, middle, and end. Invention and disposition make up the beginning, elocution the middle, memory and pronunciation the end. This is the way authors compose speech. Interpreters, however, approaching a finished text, start in the middle, with identifying the signs of words and understanding the figures of speech. Then they move backward, through analysing the disposition of the text, to the beginning, to the invention of subject matter. Last but not least, they advance toward the end, where they internalize the subject matter of the text by committing it to memory in order finally to deliver it, as expository discourse, into life. This delivery is reciprocal, both active and passive. Precisely as readers appropriate the subject matter for delivery, so the subject matter by virtue of its authority transforms them into what it says. In other words, by acquiring the text for delivery readers are being delivered by it; delivery and deliverance belong together.

We turn now to the question of how rhetorical invention functions in Erasmus' biblical exegesis and theology. We shall take first a look at the link between interpretation and invention in Erasmus' hermeneutic. In the next section we shall try to find out what interpretation and disposition have to do with one another. The relation of interpretation to elocution will be discussed in the final chapter.[12]

What interpreting a text has in common with both inventing and arranging it is that it is nothing less than the inversion of the process whereby the author conceives of, and orders, the subject matter under discussion. Author and interpreter are involved in the same hermeneutical process but they move in reverse directions.

The author begins by gathering thought (*res*) pertaining to the subject in question and suited to argumentation (*inventio*).¹³ After that the author marshals these ideas by dividing and amplifying them, arranging them in such a way that the parts conveniently fit the order of the whole (*dispositio, ordo*).¹⁴ That is to say, invention is to disposition what thought is to structure. The interpreter, on the other hand, traces the text in a secondary move from its ideas and structure to its origin in the author's mind. Therefore, the author's original move is more authoritative, whereas the interpreter's secondary move is more imitative. The interpreter is not at liberty to understand the text other than originally intended by the author. It is in this way that the dynamic of freedom and authority expresses itself regarding thought and structure: The freedom of interpretation is limited by the principle of imitation in terms of the interpreter's relation to the authority of the text.

Just as the author conceives of the subject matter, recognizes its internal structure, and arranges it coherently, so the interpreter analyses the end product, discovers its structure, and follows it back to its beginning in thought. By analysing the original disposition of the text, the interpreter becomes increasingly aware of the author's invention of thought so as eventually to participate in the original conceptualization of reality. More importantly, arriving at the origin of thought, the interpreter is so drawn into the author's world of ideas as to share in the same view of reality. Accordingly, while the author originally moves from the invention to the disposition of thought, the interpreter subsequently understands the particular text by moving toward, and finally becoming one with, the view of the whole. This movement of the mind toward the whole takes place by virtue of both memory, the internalization of the text, and delivery, the transformation of the body into spirit.

What the rhetoricians in the classical tradition meant by invention differs from our understanding of the term, namely, thinking out and producing something new. The modern mind is not at all squeamish about claiming originality for itself.¹⁵ In the rhetorical tradition, however, invention seems to have been more a matter of imitating the best examples than of producing something novel. Even though some room was left for human individuality, particularly in the enthusiasm of poetic inspiration,[16] imitation of authority had not yet given way to the modern celebration of human autonomy and creativity. Rather, human individuality was understood more in terms of a commonly shared human nature.[17]

Erasmus insisted that imitation conform with one's own nature rather than being 'enslaved to one set of rules, from the guidelines of which it dare not depart.' 'I welcome imitation ... but imitation which assists nature and does not violate it, which turns its gifts in the right direction and does not destroy them. I approve imitation – but imitation of a model that is in accord with, or at least not contrary to, your own native genius.'[18] Just as in general one should imitate models that reflect one's own nature, the biblical interpreter is not free to invent but must imitate Christ in order to have a nature that can really interpret the biblical text. This was a given which called for the reader's imitation of the divine word, Christ, not only by words but also by deeds. Erasmus raised the rhetorical concept of natural imitation to the higher power of the spiritual *imitatio Christi*.[19]

The importance of imitation is clear also from the part it plays as one of the four faculties that enable human beings to speak: *natura, ars, imitatio sive exemplum*, and *usus sive exercitatio*.[20] In fact, Erasmus deals with how these four capacities enable speech even before he turns to the rhetorical offices. But the four faculties are not all equally significant. The ability to speak derives above all from a natural tendency to imitate. 'Already infants show a natural disposition for a certain teachableness by being able to imitate.' Study and practice are only ancillary to nature, for 'the usual obstacles of nature can be overcome by study and practice,' inasmuch as they lend strength to the body and render both the mind keen and the memory reliable.[21]

There is for Erasmus an order of precedence governing the relation between nature, art, and use – and that precedence is indicated by the function of imitation. Nature and art belong together in such a way that, according to Quintilian, nature constitutes the origin of art, i.e., the beginning of the knowledge and skills of speaking. Art thus arises from the observation of nature. 'Nature provides the material for knowledge. Nature forms, knowledge is formed. Art is nothing without material; material without art possesses value; but the highest art is better than the best material.'[22] Art must not be 'art for art's sake.' For artful speech makes the hearer wary of artificial traps and therefore reluctant to agree with sound insight: 'Indeed, a speech that gives the impression of artifice is received coldly, viewed with suspicion, and feared as deceptive. For who would not be on his guard against someone setting out by the use of false glitter to get a hold over our minds?'[23] Rather, 'it is the highest art to conceal art.'[24]

Therefore, imitation must assist nature rather than violating it, improving its gifts rather than destroying them, being in accord with, rather than opposed to, one's own natural disposition.[25] And what is true of the imitation of nature by art in general, applies also to memory and delivery. Knowledge, care, practice, and order must be added to a felicitous nature so as to prevent an artificial memory. Further, as for delivery, nature forms, and knowledge and use perfect, the human being: 'it is best to follow nature' by imitating what is decent and avoiding what is indecent.[26]

In that sense, then, art imitates nature. This primary function of imitation governs its secondary function of acquiring and using the skills of art through study and practice. The use of art by imitating the best models serves, after all, nature in the first place and then art. Imitation links not only nature with art but also art with its use. In like manner, interpretation imitates the invention and disposition of the author's art, whereas the invention and disposition of the author's art imitates nature, its origin and goal.

While some people are endowed with such a happy natural disposition, says Erasmus, that they can clearly judge without the knowledge of dialectic and eloquently speak without the rules of rhetoric, our feeble nature is aided by rules and practice. Using art in imitation of nature thus makes the natural ability more certain and mature. Art by its use becomes a second nature. 'The precepts of art do not help much unless through frequent use they go over into the habit as if into nature. Just as the experienced musician plays properly without thinking of measures and harmonies, so the preacher spontaneously knows what the present argument requires, even though he does not think of rhetorical precepts at all. In order to speak well it is expedient to take art lightly, even though from its use comes the ability of speaking.'[27] Since this is so, it is the highest art to conceal art, to speak and write naturally, which is impossible unless art has been translated into nature, has become a second nature through imitation and use.

The rhetorical tradition taught that invention is imitative because it is predicated on *lectio, repetitio,* and *memoria* – a process that establishes images in certain places of the mind. 'We must not neglect memory, the storehouse of our reading. Although I do not deny that memory is aided by "places" and "images," nevertheless the best memory is based on three things above all: understanding, system, and care. For memory largely consists in having thoroughly understood something. Then system (*ordo*) sees to it that we can recall by an act of recovery even what we have once forgotten.'[28] To aid memory and to organize what has been read, the student 'should have at the ready some commonplace book of systems and topics, so that wherever something noteworthy occurs he may write it down in the appropriate column.'[29]

In the process of invention, the rhetorician first draws out from memory those ideas (*res*) that are suitable for the subject in question. Then words (*verba*) are chosen in such a way that they not only conform with these ideas and appropriately express the subject matter at hand, but also carry an intellectual, aesthetic, and affective appeal through *docere, delectare,* and *movere*. Therefore, reading and memorizing good authors (memorizing and repetition impress the ideas more firmly upon the mind) are the necessary prerequisites for invention, disposition, and elocution. There is no question that also for Erasmus this whole process of the mental formation of the orator (and conversely also the process of interpretation) was marked more by the ethos of imitation than by that of creative originality.

Once fixed upon the mind, ideas and their verbal images are available in the *copia verborum ac rerum*, the abundant storehouse of memorized knowledge.[30] But the mind does not stock this information at random. Inasmuch as the abundance of ideas and words already is shaped by an overall perspective of reality, that is, the system (*ordo*), the choice of ideas for a question to be considered and the selection of proper stylistic means to express it are largely dependent on a given, fairly solid but not rigid, linguistic structure. Accordingly, the rhetorical theorists understood memory to be a region with different places (*topoi, loci*) for different concepts. These proper places in which ideas and their corresponding words are embedded point to the significance of words and ideas within the overall order and consequently to their relevance for speech. The topography of words and ideas in the mind provides a system of coordinates expressing a world view.[31]

2 DISPOSITION

In the process of disposition (arranging, ordering),[32] the *loci* or *topoi* that were invented are arranged so as to function as constituent parts of speech. Ideas must be so aligned that they are integral to the order of the whole.[33] In this way, a natural order of discourse emerges that reflects as nearly as possible the order of nature. Now it was a generally held notion that nature manifests itself in two ways, namely, in the form of rest and motion, being and becoming.[34] The rhetoricians accordingly organized discourse as either reflecting a natural state or a movement, or as a combination of both. Further, the *ordo naturalis* could be changed into an *ordo artificialis* by means of *figurae* (*schemata*). Along with the *copia rerum ac verborum* for natural speech, then, the orator had to collect the *copia figurarum* to be able to render natural discourse artificial.[35]

While the principle of rest implied circularity, the principle of motion gave speech a linear direction. Without extension in time and space, the circle served as a symbol for the truth in a permanent, ontological system consistent in itself. The linearity of motion, on the other hand, expressed a process in time and space with a beginning, middle, and end (*initium, medium, finis*).[36] There is no doubt that these two principles decisively informed Erasmus' thinking as a whole. Both *ordo* and *gradatio* characterized his thought.[37] As we shall see, his understanding of Christ's teaching as *orbis* and of his life as *fabula* is the most important case in point.[38] Moreover, while he could simply place the literary form of rest side by side with that of motion, he preferred to combine natural circularity with historical movement in terms of an organic progress toward perfection (or, negatively, in terms of degeneration).

For instance, his view of the three cycles of the history of salvation (preceding Christ, concentrated in Christ, and following Christ) presents the gospel as both the fixed norm of Christ's teaching and the dynamic cause for a progressive development in the mission, tradition, and life of the church. However, this organic development turns out to be either positive or negative, depending on whether it gradually realizes the ideal norm or constitutes an increasing defection from it. Therefore, upon the period of preparation and revelation of the gospel followed a period of growth and decay.[39] Erasmus thus brought to bear on history two different but complementary perspectives, an optimistic and a pessimistic one (which are based on his dualistic notion of contrast and his trichotomic notion of transition, respectively). His theory of decay criticized historical conditions on the basis of the evangelical norm, while his theory of development respected the historical process as an organic development toward the goal, which is, however, already anticipated in the beginning by the evangelical norm.[40]

Dispositio included ordering the whole discourse by dividing it into its components (*divisio*). Now Aristotle had distinguished in the human constitution three dispositions, one of excess and one of lack, with moderation in the middle keeping the balance between too much and too little. The rhetorical tradition adopted this advice for the disposition of discourse as much as for the disposition of the speaker.[41] Accordingly, the unity of the whole must not be sacrificed to the diversity of its parts, nor must the parts lose their particularity for the sake of the integrity of the whole. The part stands for the whole as much as the whole stands for the part.[42] It was inconceivable to classical thinkers that the order of speech should not follow the order of nature, which maintains its equilibrium by reducing the extremes of excess and want to a measure of proper proportion as far as the whole and its parts is concerned.

Erasmus made this rhetorical principle of *moderatio* a main criterion not only of his hermeneutic but also of his ethics (*temperantia*) and of his own life style. *Ego sum moderatior*: 'My misdeeds amount to this: I am all for moderation, and the reason why I have a bad name with both sides is that I exhort both parties to adopt a more peaceable policy. Freedom I have no objection to, if it is seasoned with charity.'[43] 'My hesitancy and moderation have no other aim than to make myself useful to both parties.'[44]

That Erasmus opted for the middle can be shown, where the *genera causarum* in the area of invention are concerned, by his preference for the *genus suasorium* over against the *genus iudiciale*.[45] Also, with regard to the *genera dicendi* in the area of elocution, he was partial to the *genus moderatum* between the *genus humile* and the *genus sublime*.⁴⁶ Instead of setting one side against the other by either accusing and defending (judicial discourse) or praising and blaming (epideictic discourse), the deliberative discourse prudently weighs arguments on both sides of an issue in order to arrive at a probable solution. Similarly, the middle style serves to reconcile (*conciliare*) and to delight (*delectare*) by appealing to the milder *ethos*, in comparison with the simple style of proving (*probare*), on the one hand, and with the exalted style of moving (*movere*) and changing (*flectere*) by appealing to passion (*pathos*), on the other.⁴⁷ So moderation, deliberation, and reconciliation belonged for Erasmus together.

Moderation is for Erasmus impossible unless one stands in the middle, seeks a balanced view, and lives a modest, temperate life. Only by avoiding too much and too little does the rhetorician acquire that sense of proportion (*modus*) which shows things, persons, and circumstances in their proper, convenient place within an overall order (*commoditas*).⁴⁸ Not until Christians think, speak, and live from the centre, Christ, can they accommodate to others (*similia similibus*), being all things to all people (*omnia omnibus*) by coming to terms and by the meeting of minds. A moderate approach persuades others to balance things out in their own minds so as to come to their senses and become levelheaded in their own behaviour. Beyond the life of the individual, moderation should also govern the life in church and state, with regard to both doctrines and laws. It was this way of thinking that not only shaped Erasmus' method of interpretation (his emphasis on allegory reconciling letter and spirit) but also influenced his theological understanding (his view of Christ as mediator and reconciler).

As to *divisio*, both a dichotomous and a trichotomous pattern was at the rhetorician's disposal. The division into two parts was largely used to express opposition, even as the two opposites were taken as being ultimately held together by a basic unity. Or the whole could be structured in three parts, beginning (*exordium, caput, initium*), middle (*medium, progressus, profectus*), and end (*finis, consummatio, perfectio*).⁴⁹ The tripartite division could be changed into a duality in case the extremes of beginning and end were taken together and contrasted to the middle.⁵⁰ No matter how the whole was divided into its parts, however, the rhetorician was advised to observe moderation in the disposition of thought by avoiding too much or too little of ordering and dividing.

Erasmus' thinking, as we have emphasized repeatedly, was determined by a basic dualistic structure. Even so, he was never content with stark opposition. Irreconcilable differences did not have the last word. Rather, harmony was the goal. However severe the split of reality, he made every effort to find a middle link that would throw a bridge across the gap.[51] The discovery of a connection between opposites established some kind of similarity and made the possibility of rapprochement appear on the horizon. With a third element inserted between two previously exclusive sides, the static structure of opposition yielded to a dynamic pattern of development, whereby the middle now functioned as progress between start and finish.[52] This rhetorical division of thought as a means of ordering discourse in accordance with the order of nature provides a crucial key to understanding Erasmus' way of making sense of reality.

While normal discourse was divided into three parts, drama followed a twofold rhetorical division, the thickening of the plot and the change in fortune as dénouement (*catastrophe*). But the thickening of the plot could be subdivided into a preparation (*protasis*) and an intensification of the dramatic development (*epitasis*), which then rendered drama tripartite (*protasis, epitasis, catastrophe*). Erasmus saw in the tripartite division of drama an important rhetorical device to understand both the development of events in the gospel accounts and the order of the history of salvation in general. In fact, for him the divine economy of salvation as articulated in the Apostles' Creed ran along the lines of a dramatic development from preparation to conflict to solution.[53]

To conclude our analysis of Erasmus' use of rhetorical disposition for his theological purposes, the last item to be dealt with is *amplificatio*. Amplification is that part of the disposition of thought which, in order to effect *utilitas*, enlarges and intensifies by means of art what is naturally given in speech.[54] Whether through *incrementum, comparatio, ratiocinatio*, or *congeries*, amplification was a favored means to extend a limited question concerning individual people and concrete situations (*quaestio finita*) into a general question or universally applicable thesis (*quaestio infinita*). Accordingly, the rhetorician used abstract commonplaces (*loci communes*), drawn from the topography of the mind, to seek probable answers, with the intention of eliciting a common sense, thereby moving the hearer/reader to agreement. However, the freedom of amplification had to be kept from becoming licence by the demands of concision.[55] Therefore, the rule of moderation applied also here in term of a balance between too much and too little expansion. The ideal for Erasmus was 'artful artlessness, and copious brevity.'[56]

The interplay of amplification and concision affected Erasmus' rhetorical style, his way of thinking, and his theology. Amplification became a paradigm for spiritual freedom. Erasmus' concept of expansion in terms of freedom prevailed especially in his understanding of the spirit: 'The flesh makes narrow, the spirit enlarges. Where there is the spirit, there is charity; where there is charity, there fear is cast out; where there is no fear, there is freedom; where there is freedom, there is nothing that constricts.'[57] 'Sparse and confined are the banquets of the Jews who follow the flesh of the law, while the spirit spreads out far and wide and accepts all kinds of men. All love liberty, all need clemency.'[58]

Just as rhetorical amplification raises speech from nature to art, so increasing and heightening occurs, theologically speaking, when one transcends the natural toward the spiritual, when one moves from narrow confines toward the spirit. Allegory widens the horizon from the restriction of the letter to the amplitude of the spirit.[59] The gospel spreads and becomes universal: 'Unlike all else, the truth of the gospel seized, permeated and conquered within a few years every region the whole world over, attracting Greeks and barbarians, learned and unlearned, common folk and kings.'[60] Charity enlarges by giving freely and abundantly (*largiri*); and above all the gifts of largesse of the spirit set the human being free from the anxiety of the mind.[61] And what is true of the individual applies also to the church: 'Thus was the kingdom of the gospel born and thus it grew and thus spread widely and was thus established, though for various reasons we see it now contracted into a narrow space and almost done away with, if you consider how large the whole world is. Fallen, we must rebuild it; contracted, we must spread it wide; unsteady, we must uphold it, using the same resources by which it was first born, increased, and grew strong.'[62]

Again, the movement of spiritual freedom must not lead to libertinist excesses, but is to be balanced by what one can call theological concision; not the narrowness of the letter, the law, and the flesh, where freedom is constrained, but the concentration on Christ, where freedom is qualified by imitation. Rhetorical amplification, then, is checked by the notion of concision. Freedom is limited by authority. Even as art transcends nature through amplification, art nevertheless must imitate nature. Likewise, the freedom of the spirit is kept in balance by the concentration on Christ's teaching and by the requirement of imitating him.

As we return to interpretation in the light of what has been said about rhetorical invention and disposition, it is obvious that the interpreter must learn first to identify the parts in order to integrate them into the whole. However, the whole is more than the sum of its parts. The 'one' excels the 'many' because many parts pull apart while the 'one' binds them together. This is why, on the one hand, rhetorical disposition has to be traced back to invention. But the grammatical, literal exegesis, on the other hand, needs to be enlarged by the tropological and allegorical method. The reduction to invention and the progression toward allegory go hand in hand. Concentrating on what the author said and enlarging the text to its spiritual meaning belong together the same way as concision and amplification, as authority and freedom do. But it is for Erasmus precisely the concentration on Christ as the divine word and on God as the author of divine speech that provides the freedom of spiritual interpretation and life.

The axiom that the whole is larger than the sum total of its parts implies also that the whole must be received as given and therefore as lying ultimately beyond the reach of the interpreter[63] – a fact that Erasmus acknowledges by his open-ended anagogical method and his admission of a sense of mystery. Despite our limited insight into the divine mystery, however, the whole is in fact revealed to the extent that God has spoken in the beginning and the end, by the original word in nature and the final word in Christ. And this whole is more important than the parts because it shows the larger significance of a text within the context of God's order of the world and of salvation.[64] Indeed, what the part is finally all about becomes clear only when it is viewed as a part of the whole rather than apart from the whole.

In other words, details are relevant in proportion to the way they fit in place in the overall picture. Beyond the general setting of nature and culture, it is the specific context of salvation as concentrated in the *scopus* Christ that elucidates the real *locus* each part holds within the whole. The importance of a variety of times, places, things, persons, and circumstances depends on their respective proximity to the centre of reality, Christ. The proximity of a text to Christ qualifies it as having a corresponding measure of spiritual and moral value. The authority of a word rests on the extent to which it reflects Christ's teaching and life. The *topoi* in the mind of the interpreter which reflect the natural order must therefore be amplified by, and at the same time concentrated in, those theological *loci* that spring from the teaching and life of Christ. As the order of reality receives its ultimate focus in the *scopus* Christ, so the general *topoi* in the mind of the interpreter are now freed to be determined by the specific *topoi* of Christ's teaching.

3 THE HARMONY OF CHRIST

The true meaning of the biblical text arises from its reference to Christ, the *scopus* at the centre of the *orbis Christi*, the circle of his teaching and life. In his *Ratio verae theologiae*, Erasmus said: 'The meaning which we draw forth from the obscure words must correspond to the circle of Christian doctrine, to its life, and finally to natural equity.'[65] A more fully developed form of his statement reads: 'As the whole circle of doctrine is in harmony with itself, so it is in agreement with his life, even with the judgment of nature itself ... The books of Plato or Seneca may contain teachings not dissimilar to Christ's. And Socrates' life may show certain similarities with that of Christ. Still, nowhere but in Christ do you find that circle and harmony in which all things are congruent in themselves. However inspired the words and pious the deeds of the prophets, no matter how renowned the holiness of Moses and others, such a circle is found in no human being.'[66]

Accordingly, Christ's teachings are as consistent in themselves as they are consonant with his life. Doctrine and ethics belong together, allegory and tropology. This supreme unity of truth and harmony of life is what makes the *philosophia Christi* unique in comparison with all other philosophical schools. In addition to harmony and consonance with life, the truth of Christ's speech is clear from its simplicity and artlessness.[67] Only Christ's doctrine therefore is worthy of the symbol of the circle, the symbol of perfection.[68] Like the circle, Christ's gospel is congruent with itself from start to finish (because it returns to its origin whence it came), is equidistant from its centre at all times, and numberless, i.e., fundamentally indivisible. As the concept *consensus* seems to express more the harmonious unity and inner consistency of the truth, so the concept *concentus* seems to bespeak more the euphony of the truth and the harmony of the virtuous life.[69] The truth is not only true to itself but also pleasant and therefore evokes both trust in agreement and love in concord. As doctrine and ethics belong together, we can say, so also doctrine, ethics, and aesthetics, that is, *docere, movere,* and *delectare*.[70]

Furthermore, the teachings of Christ are in agreement with the equity of nature,[71] meaning that the consensus of truth in his doctrine and life reflects the equilibrium by which natural equity so balances justice with love that unity and harmony, concord and peace, arise instead of division and discord, violence and war. The symmetry by which nature balances justice and love to achieve harmony is thus a preliminary revelation of the truth in Christ. Likewise, the interpretation of the truth will reach consensus and concord only if it follows the principle of moderation.

Next to the symbol of the circle, Erasmus uses also the term *fabula*.[72] He thus complements the rhetorical notion of rest, namely, of Christ's teaching in terms of fixed, permanent, and standing *topoi*, with that of dramatic development, narrating Christ's life story and beyond that recounting the history of salvation. Rather than signifying a myth or fiction, the *orbis totius Christi fabulae* tells the story of Christ, beginning before his birth and continuing after his death.[73]

Old Testament allegories and prophecies foreshadow him; angels, shepherds, and sages witness to him; and John the Baptist points to the lamb, the symbol of innocence. Then follow the events of Christ's earthly life: He increases in age and makes progress with God and humans; he speaks in the temple, a secluded place, and performs his first miracle in private at the wedding of Cana. This means that he makes his public appearance only after having been properly initiated by his baptism by John, his confirmation by his Father, and his temptation by the devil. Now that he is ready to begin his preaching office in public, he steps out of the arcanum.

After his death, Christ shows himself to his disciples and

teaches them by his ascension to know the place to which they must strive. Finally, the divine Spirit renders them such as the master wished them to be. Begun with the prophets, the circle of Christ's story closes with the apostles. 'But in all of this Christ was as it were his own prophet. Just as he did nothing that was not foreshadowed by the types of the law and announced by the oracles of the prophets, so nothing of note took place which he had not foretold his apostles.'[74]

From this circle of Christ's story, the theologian can extract the main points (*topoi*) of Christian doctrine. 'Examine his birth, education, preaching, or death, you find nothing but the perfect example of poverty, humility, indeed innocence.' Another summation reads: 'Innocence, gentleness, poverty, and aversion to ambition and arrogance.' Boiled down to their shortest form, then, Christ's teaching and life reveal the three characteristic traits of innocence (and purity), simplicity (and gentleness), and humility (or lack of ambition and arrogance).[75]

Even before Erasmus recounted the story of Christ, he anticipated these three cardinal points in his summary of Christian doctrine on the basis of the New Testament sources: 'Christ, the heavenly teacher, has established on earth a new people that totally depends on heaven. Because it distrusts all worldly protection, it is rich, wise, noble, powerful, and happy in quite another way. It strives for happiness by contempt of all earthly things ... It knows neither hate nor envy because its simple eye beholds no violent desires ... It is not titillated by vainglory since it applies everything to the glory of the one Christ. Nor is it ambitious ... but rather of such innocence of character that even the heathens approve of its conduct. It is born again to purity and simplicity ... It considers concord the highest value ... This is the *scopus* put forth by Christ ... This is the new doctrine of our author, which no school of philosophers has ever handed down.'[76]

While Erasmus' account of the *fabula* attributes these modes of conduct to Christ, the description of Christ's people applies them to ecclesiology.[77] Whether in their Christological or Christian significance, however, these qualities have obviously to do with a spiritual attitude issuing in a specific moral behaviour. As the circle of Christ's teaching and life is characterized by consensus and harmony through innocence, simplicity, and humility, so Christian teaching and living imitate Christ and for this reason are conducive to concord and peace in both community and world. Now this orientation of Erasmus' thinking has frequently led to the conclusion that his philosophy of Christ is nothing but spiritual and/or moral. But it is precisely the connection of the *orbis totius Christi fabulae* with the equity of nature that points to an ontological ground for this Christian way of life. What is more, the theological ground for this Christian ethic is indicated by its connection with Christ, the divine mediator and reconciler, indeed the redeemer and author of salvation.[78]

It would be erroneous for us to assume that the essence of Christ's (and Christian) teaching and life consists only in moral instruction. As if to dispel this notion, Erasmus connected, in his further elaborations, these ethical qualities with the theological *topoi* of faith and love: 'Christ impressed especially and continuously two things on his disciples, faith and love. Faith shows that we should place our confidence in God rather than in ourselves. Love urges us to deserve well from all.'[79] Even though hope receives in the *Ratio* short shrift[80] and faith figures in this passage less than love, Erasmus makes it clear in other contexts, that he concentrates the theological significance of Christ's teaching in the virtues of faith, love, and hope.[81] Nevertheless, in the *Ratio*, where he is primarily concerned with enjoining a theology of consensus in contrast to the scholastic dissensions, he emphasizes love as that source which engenders unity, peace, and concord in the face of division, violence, and discord: 'Peace is our religion.'[82]

Christian ethics, then, learns, in a preliminary way, a lesson from nature and therefore rests on an ontological foundation. But it is ultimately informed by a theological identity. While already the knowledge of natural equity gives Christians a general sense of unity, balance, and moderation, it is faith that marks their relation to God, love that characterizes their attitude toward God and their fellow human beings, and hope that orients them to the final goal, the happiness of the eternal communion with God. It is quite in line with Erasmus' thinking to conclude that Christ's harmony signifies a doctrine of faith, love, and hope in conjunction with a life of innocence, simplicity, and humility.

4 THEOLOGICAL LOCI

Identifying in Christ's story both the essentials of his teaching and the characteristics of his attitude does not complete the task of interpretation. It is extraordinarily useful, says Erasmus, to prepare or adopt a list of theological *loci* into which everything one reads should be appropriately placed. Such commonplaces are, among others: faith, fasting, bearing evil, helping the sick, tolerating ungodly magistrates, avoiding offense to the weak, studying Holy Scripture, piety toward parents and children, Christian charity, honouring ancestors, envy, disparagement, and sexual purity. After the topics have been arranged in the order of the affinity or opposition of words and things (as in his *Copia*), whatever is found to be noteworthy in the books of the Bible should be incorporated according to concordance or dissonance. If appropriate, one could also glean from the ancient interpreters of the Bible, and even from the books of the heathens, what might be of future use.[83] Erasmus thus advised the theologian to systematize theological subject matter (drawn above all from Scripture, but also from patristic interpretation, and even from classical authors) according to the principles of rhetorical invention.

This string of *topoi* in the *Ratio* gives at first sight the impression of having been thrown together at random. On closer inspection we do find, among various practical concerns, faith and love mentioned, if only in passing. Even so, this juxtaposition of *topoi* fails to give us a clue as to what Erasmus might conceive of as a systematic order of theological commonplaces. We have to look elsewhere.

Fortunately, some eighteen years later he penned an outline in which faith, love, and hope figure prominently. Our search for an order of theological *loci* arranged by Erasmus himself leads us to the *Elenchus* and *Sylva* of the fourth book of his *Ecclesiastes*.[84] Here, in what comes closest to a systematic blueprint of his thinking, he lays out a dualistic framework, with God, Christ, and the Spirit on one side, and the devil on the other.[85] Then follow God's hierarchies and the kingdom of Satan, God's and Satan's laws, virtues and vices in general and in particular, and finally the extreme boundary line of virtue and vice, and the end of Christian life. In all, then, two dominions are contrasted with each other, each different in origin, association, laws, modes of behaviour, and ends, ranked in the order of rhetorical disposition (*initium, progressus, consummatio*).[86]

The way Erasmus associated the three theological key concepts with this schema indicates that faith has primarily but not exclusively to do with the beginning (the triune God and God's rule, people, and law), that love functions foremost but not alone in the middle (virtues), and that hope orients the Christian especially though not totally to the end (death, and the future glory and happiness). This movement between *exitus* and *reditus* is to be organic, i.e., cumulative, and coalescent, meaning that in each stage, as one of the three theological concepts assumes a major role, the two others are not eliminated. Still, quite in line with his characteristic emphasis on *profectus* as the transition between beginning and perfection, Erasmus greatly expands the middle section on virtues and vices.[87]

Faith, love, and hope indicate three stages in the overall scheme. But they function also in the middle part where they are translated into the category of Christian virtues and correlated, as *species* to *genera*, with the natural virtues. Here the theological virtues of faith, love, and hope are seen as specific expressions of their corresponding counterparts, the philosophical virtues of prudence, justice, and fortitude. The fourth philosophical virtue, temperance, is by no means left out but receives a prominent place in the middle of the middle. Erasmus manages to fit it into his schema by assigning it the function of a subspecies of justice-charity, thereby giving it a place in the centre of the centre.[88] This shows how singularly important the concept of temperance is in Erasmus' system. Balancing justice with love, temperance is the moral equivalent of the rhetorical principle of moderation which itself is predicated on the equity of nature.[89]

This triad in the centre of the macrocosmic schema is again structured along the lines of the order of origin, progress, and end. Accordingly, charity-justice-temperance between faith-prudence and hope-fortitude obtains a middle place, marking it as that region where the progress happens between origin and end, faith and fulfillment, God and eternal bliss. Moreover, it is important to observe that it is temperance (or moderation, for that matter) that functions as the specific balance between justice and charity, insuring that there is neither too much nor too little of either one or the other. This is why, in comparison with the other *loci*, the *chorus temperentiae et intemperentiae* commands much more space in the systematic outline of Erasmus' theology.[90]

From what has been shown so far, this much is clear: The

circle of Christ's story (as ascertained by the historical method) offers insights into his way of life from which the interpreter abstracts (by means of tropology) the modes of his, and Christian, behaviour (innocence, simplicity, and humility). But what is more, Christ's teachings are identified (by way of allegory) and concentrated in the theological concepts of faith, love, and hope. These are then interpreted as theological virtues and aligned with the philosophical virtues. Last but not least, the theologian is instructed to arrange these and other *loci* in a theological system of coordinates, into which all pertinent *topoi* are to be incorporated according to their concordance or dissonance, their similarity or dissimilarity.

This sequence of steps indicates that ethics precedes and succeeds theology. Nonetheless, Erasmus seems to insist that ethics does not give its quality to theology but rather receives its quality from theology. Just as allegory is the ultimate criterion of tropology,[91] so theology governs ethics. Faith, love, and hope are first theological *topoi* before they become theological virtues, revealing then their affinity with the philosophical virtues. While servants proceed before the queen as harbingers and follow her as her train, they do not have priority and authority. Therefore, appearance notwithstanding, where the relation of teaching and life is concerned, it is on the whole clear that Erasmus intended for doctrine to come before life, for teaching to be prior to acting, for thought to go before deed. Just as epistemology constitutes the basis of morality, so theology is the foundation of ethics. Although Christian ethics is generally foreshadowed by the *aequitas naturae*, the natural virtues are to the theological virtues as *genera* to *species*, meaning that it is the special revelation in Christ that discloses what natural reality is all about. Specificity is more valuable than generality.[92]

Another point about the relation between teaching and life needs to be made. In the *Ratio* and in his *Paraphrases*, Erasmus narrates Christ's story in terms of growth toward maturity, with the pivotal point coming at the opportune moment when after a preparatory period Christ is ready to step out of the arcanum to preach his gospel in the open.[93] Two important motifs govern Erasmus' telling the story of Christ's circle: the gradualism of an organic development and the dualism of hiddenness and openness. We shall take a look at the privacy-publicity issue in connection with Erasmus' concept of *prudentia* and *opportunitas*, where it belongs.⁹⁴ What concerns us at this point is the relation of the dynamic of Christ's life to the stability of his teaching.

Just as the first period of salvation history, Old Testament prophecy, is the time of preparation for Christ's coming, so in the beginning of his life, Christ is made ready for his preaching office. Then comes the central period of his public work up to his death. With his resurrection begins the third and final period that ends with the apostles' teaching and the outpouring of the Spirit. The first period is linked with the middle one, like the middle period to the last one, by prophetic prediction and fulfillment.⁹⁵ It is prophecy that provides the mediation between the three periods. In the middle period, however, Christ's life is marked by the stages of a beginning, progress, and an end, the same tripartite development as the larger framework of the three periods of salvation history, with a preparation leading up to the middle part and its after-effects concluding it.

It is interesting to compare this arrangement in the *Ratio* of the three periods of beginning, middle, and end, including a tripartite middle part, with Erasmus' systematic layout of theological *topoi* in his *Ecclesiastes*. While the *Ratio* concerns more the dynamic of salvation history and Christ's life, the *Ecclesiastes* has to do more with the firm doctrines and the perennial teachings of Christ. Nevertheless, in the *Ratio* Christ's teaching is concentrated in permanent, indivisible *topoi*, symbolized by the circle, whereas in the *Ecclesiastes* the systematic layout of theological *topoi* is couched in the tripartite arragement of beginning, progress, and end.

Two patterns emerge that appear to characterize Erasmus' thinking as a whole: the *via* motive with a tripartite movement of beginning, middle, and end, and the *topoi* motif indicating the stability and coherence of the truth in a dualistic context. While the first pattern reflects the development of Christ's life, of salvation history, and of the Christian's improvement, the second pertains to both the perennial teachings of Christ and the firm doctrines of the church. The first seems to be oriented in the rhetorical notion of development in the *ordo artificialis*, the second seems to rest on the rhetorical notion of the *ordo naturalis*. In the disposition of speech, however, the rhetorician makes sure that there is an effective distribution of both.⁹⁶

This double perspective has much to say about the permanence of Christ's teachings over against the development and reformability of ecclesiastical practices that are to apply Christ's teachings to the various conditions in the history of his people.[97] While there are definite elements of doctrine that remain unchangeable (*akineta*),[98] others can become irrelevant, though not superfluous, as history progresses towards its consummation. And the same is true for the individual Christian's spiritual progress on the way of salvation. In other words, the teachings of Christ represent fixed points of Christian existence and the institution of the church. And yet they become the markers of the way in the development of Christian life and in the progress of the church toward perfection.[99]

This relation of the *via* motive and *loci* motif gives us clues to the peculiarity of Erasmus' own theology. He uses, on the one hand, a system of *loci* within which topics are arranged according to similarity and dissimilarity, with Christ representing the universal fixed point, the head and goal (*scopus*). This systematic layout of topics around a Christocentric focus is, on the other hand, animated by the notion of progress between beginning and end, whether in dramatic development in the telling of a story, the development of an argument in rhetorical discourse, the movement toward an allegorical understanding of a text, or moral improvement in life. In general, then, it is the coordination of form and dynamic, doctrine and narration, circle and progression, of the firm and movable, of motif and motive, of *topos* and *gradatio*, principles and application, teaching and life, that brings the characteristic manner of Erasmus' thinking to light.[100] This double perspective of his rhetorical theology (the cause, obviously, for his having been so often charged with ambivalence and ambiguity) can be ultimately traced to the relation between the freedom of organic growth and the authority of constant truth.

5 LAW AND GOSPEL

Examining the function of law and gospel in Erasmus' thought helps better to understand the relation between his hermeneutic and theology. Since his understanding of Scripture cannot be separated from his theology, the theological content Erasmus draws from the concepts of law and gospel must have something to do with the role law and gospel play in his interpretation of Scripture, particularly where the connection of the Old and New

Testament is concerned.[101] The theology of law and gospel is thus critical for his biblical exegesis. As the humanist theologian traced the rhetorical disposition of the sacred text back to its divine invention, the *topoi* of law and gospel, expressing the way in which God acts in human history, served as hermeneutical criteria to understand the divine truth in Scripture.

A survey of Erasmus' most representative references to law and gospel produces at first an ambiguous picture. True to the rules of rhetorical disposition, he viewed these two concepts from both a dichotomous and a trichotomous perspective. Take for example the statement: 'Those who had been true worshippers of the law of Moses, by the evidence of that very law had advanced to the perfection of the gospel, that is from faith to faith, while the Pharisees in their perverted zeal for the law persecuted him whom the law had commended to them.'[102] We see that Erasmus, on the one hand, distinguishes sharply between law and gospel, particularly with regard to the dualism of letter and spirit, or flesh and spirit, slavery and freedom.[103] On the other hand, this mutual exclusiveness again and again gives way to a mediating structure that opens up a transition between the two to enable an organic process. This explains why Erasmus can make, on the literal level of his interpretation, negative comments about the law, the Old Testament, the Jews, and ceremonies, etc., all the while maintaining that they do represent, if interpreted tropologically and allegorically, a propaedeutic stage in a progression toward the gospel. As far as the letter is concerned, the law cannot lead to the gospel. However, when understood spiritually, the law is a harbinger of the gospel.

Taken allegorically or typologically, the spiritual side of the Old Testament exemplifies the pre-Christian time of promise that foreshadowed the brightness of the New Testament fulfillment. 'For we owe our faith in the gospel in large part to the Old Testament, which outlined Jesus Christ to us so many centuries ago in shadows and figures, and promised and depicted him in the oracles of the prophets.'[104] The correspondence between the Old and the New Testament is so strong indeed that nearly nothing happened in New Testament times that had not been prophesied in the Old Testament.[105] Yet in its literal meaning, the Old Testament law stands for the sub-Christian darkness in opposition to the gospel light. 'The darkness of prison corresponds to the shadows and figures of the law; they had to yield to the dawning light of the gospel.'[106] Similarly, while the synagogue symbolizes in its mystical sense the birthplace of Christ and thus represents in reality the prototype of the church, as an external realm of servitude it also signifies exactly the opposite of the spiritual community of God's free children.[107] The same double perspective obtains regarding flesh and spirit, external ceremonies and spiritual worship, coercion and free response, works and grace, misery and joy, limitation and universality, multiplicity and unity, strict justice and forgiving love.[108]

We will now consider some of the detail of the *topoi* of law and gospel. Erasmus can contrast the light of the gospel truth to the darkness of the Mosaic law, the devotion to true piety to superstition and arrogance.[109] Besides light-darkness imagery, he uses the opposites of frigidity and fire, shell and heart, contraction and dilation, external and internal when pointing to the distinction between the old and the new.[110] Moreover, the Jewish religion is to the Christian faith as restriction is to universality, for the law has been given to one people, whereas the grace of Christ pertains to all nations.[111] The theme of geographic and racial bounds in contrast to universal expansion occurs frequently and serves to indicate the opposition between confinement and release in general and between religious servanthood (yoke, burden) and freedom (grace, spirit) in particular, especially in terms of spiritual enlargement (*amplitudo, largitas*) versus carnal confinement (*contractio, angustia, anxietas*). So for instance: 'The severity of the law inflicts punishment as a deterrent; the grace of the gospel does not seek the death of the sinner but rather that he repent and live.'[112] This perspective is clearly due to a dualistic split of reality into the two mutually exclusive regions of flesh and spirit. In this sense, the law has been annulled by Christ.'[113] But the dualism is not confined to the Old Testament texts. Rather, even the gospel has its letter and spirit. Consequently, there is in both biblical books first the letter as flesh, then the mystical sense as spirit.'[114]

In order to avoid literal, carnal misinterpretations, the exegete must see the law in the light of the gospel, the Old Testament from the Christocentric focus of the New Testament. This is necessary because the Old Testament in and by itself is covered with a blanket of figures and enigmas, whereas the New Testament discloses the mysteries. To be sure, the Jews lack the spirit of the new prophecy and thus fail to unlock the mystical sense of their holy book: 'This is the perverted religion of the Jews, who embrace the appearance of religion and thus subvert the source of true religion, clinging tenaciously to the shadows of the law and stubbornly persecuting him for whose sake the law was written.'[115] But with the New Testament now clearly revealing the truth, the Old Testament is found to adumbrate it, as the gospel sheds light on the enigmas of the law and therefore leads it to perfection. 'Yet this present (Jewish) form of religion, though not perfect, is a step on the way to perfect religion. That is why the beginning of salvation has come from the Jews, who through the prophets have the promise of the Messiah to come and through the law have the shadowy outlines of the gospel religion.'[116] The law of Moses lost its splendour no sooner than the glory of the gospel began to shine forth.[117]

What is true of the Mosaic law applies also to the Old Testament prophecies. They were at best enigmas, at worst imagined nonsense (*somnia*), before the heavenly Spirit infused itself more liberally into the minds of the new prophets, the evangelists, who by afflatus were so led into all truth that they were able to unravel the enigmas of the law and remove the covers from the prophecies. Now they could see that the law functioned in fact as a pedagogue toward Christ, restraining as it did the carnal desires of the people until they were ready for spiritual freedom. Now it becomes clear that the ceremonies stipulated by the law were God's concession for the time being to a people as yet caught up in external things. Now it is revealed that the messianic prophecies in reality predicted Christ.[118]

When Erasmus absolutized the contrast between the old and new in terms of flesh and spirit, he spoke of a double law (*gemina lex*), carnal and spiritual.[119] It is in this absolute dualistic context that he made his harshest statements about the Jews. The strict observance of the letter of the law means nothing less than superficality. Superficiality is, literally, hanging on to the surface and taking the outward appearance of things for true reality, in short, being confined within externals. 'Nothing is more irreligious than the Jewish religion, which consists in things visible.'[120] Such superficiality engenders religious illusion (*superstitio*), meaning that one confuses body and spirit, letter and spirit, the temporal and eternal, the visible and invisible by perverting the order of things: 'Think how rightly the Jews are criticized for empty superstition which does not put first things first.'[121] It is the nature of hypocrisy that it deceptively imitates true piety through the devotion to external things. 'Indeed such are the judgments of the Pharisees: for ever wrong. They value a beast more than a man, a garment more than the body, food more than life, body more than soul, human things more than divine, flesh more than spirit, man more than God. Thus nothing is more noxious than perverse religiosity.'[122] No wonder that 'superstition is contentious, whereas true piety is quiet and tranquil.'[123]

Moreover, the superstitious belief that one has fulfilled God's expectations by obeying the letter of the law and engaging in formal ritual finally amounts to religious arrogance (*supercilium*), the claim to works-righteousness before God and to superiority over the heathens.[124] And in his worst moments Erasmus accused the Jews of that extreme pharisaic *hubris* which arises from the claim of religious exclusiveness and leads to contempt of Christ and, in the end, to deicide: 'So great was their lust for vengeance that they voluntarily committed themselves to everlasting slavery in order to execute Jesus the author of liberty.'[125]

While this superficial, superstitious, and supercilious attitude applies foremost to the Jews, Christians too are liable to fall for the illusion that the heart of religion lies in the outside of things, that religious ceremony equals spiritual worship, and that external practices, such as monastic observances or pilgrimages, amount to true piety. Similarly, as far as hermeneutics is concerned, *judaizare* means for Erasmus to remove the tropes and allegories from Scripture so as to render the spiritual carnal, and to take the shadow tenaciously for the real thing, even though the scriptural tropes signify a spiritual amplitude over against literal narrowness. In a word, 'the superstition of the letter contracts the mind, whereas spirit and charity enlarge it.'[126]

A superstitious practice of religion, or interpretation of Scripture for that matter, stems from that perverse judgment (*praeposterum iudicium*) which takes the last for the first and 'attributes more to that which is of lighter moment and less to what properly pertains to the subject matter.' Reversing the appropriate order of speech, rhetorically, the superstitious interpreter perverts also the order of all things, ontologically. This is due to the fact that one is oblivious of the middle (*mediocritas*), particularly as it marks the transition between extremes.[127] And the absence of a sense for the middle engenders a lack of moderation. The true disciples of Christ, however, 'are not led by perverse judgments since they recognize what lies between the beginnings of piety and the heavenly philosophy, between beginning and end, between foundation and summit, without despising these (initial things) for the time being as they hasten with all their heart to the more excellent path that the Lord himself has paved.'[128]

So Erasmus himself moved in his theological hermeneutic from a dualistic distinction to a trichotomous view that sees Christ mediating between the Mosaic law and the grace of the gospel. As Christ embraces the divine and human nature in such a way as to reconcile them, he is also the mediation between the law and the gospel. The middle as a transition between beginning and end signifies both the end of the beginning and the beginning of the end. Therefore, Christ is the end of the law and the beginning of the gospel. Yet the end of the law is in this case not its termination. On the contrary, it is its fulfillment, for Christ did not come to abrogate the law but to free and complete it. 'The Lord Jesus who restored nature ... did not abolish the law but perfected it.'[129] Precisely as the end of the law, then, Christ is the perfection of the law for all believers.'[130] In a similar way, John the Baptist stood in the middle between the old and new prophecy. While the old was waning, certain of its vestiges remained until they were gradually darkened as the evangelical sun began to radiate throughout the whole world.[131]

While John the Baptist represented the transition between the old and the new, Christ excelled him in that he fulfilled the old by bringing in the new. That is to say, in him the law was taken up into the gospel, with the result that the gospel represents the law in its perfect form. So the gospel is at the same time a law which fulfils the old law: The law of Moses is now transformed into the law of Christ, the evangelical law, the law of love, and of the spirit, given for the perfection of the Christian.'[132] Moreover, the spiritual law brings forth works of charity. Christ's law of love always shines before the believers, who advance in the narrow path of piety, with grace incessantly helping them to make progress toward perfection, the fullness of Christ.'[133] There is also true concord in the church only when the law and the prophets are in consensus with Christ, when preaching is oriented in the spirit rather than the letter, in contrast to the synagogues of the Jews and the assemblies of the heretics, where Scripture is not accommodated to Christ but twisted to fit a human sense.[134]

Christ is the medium not only between the Old Testament and New Testament law but also between the natural and spiritual law. This is so because the redeemer did not extinguish the natural good but restored and perfected it; he did not destroy nature but completed it.[135] Within this context of an organic development from the *lex naturae* (written in the hearts of all human beings)[136] to the law of Christ, Erasmus could maintain that there remains in humanity, despite original sin, the natural light of reason, and consequently also natural piety, the seed of virtues and of religion, and a sense of natural freedom, glory, and judgment.[137] After all, grace perfects the natural good, and what is imperfect is not necessarily impious. So the progress from imperfect to perfect moderates the contrast between evil and good. Also, the motif of partial-universal can now be used to show a growth from few to many: 'Under the law of nature some served God, under the law of Moses many, under the evangelical law most, even though salvation is properly owing to no law but rather to God's mercy through Christ.'[138]

When Erasmus applied this trichotomous perspective to the entire history of salvation, he correlated the law of nature, of Moses, and of Christ in various ways.[139] The law of Moses can stand in the middle between the law of nature and the grace of the gospel. Or the law of Christ can mark the transition between the natural law and the law of Moses, on the one side, and the perfection of the world to come, on the other. Even more, just as the middle signifies the *incrementum* between *exordium* and *summa*, so the growth of the human race, which had its origin in the paradise and will have its completion at the end of the world, stands under the authority of a threefold law, the law of nature, the law of Moses, and the law of the gospel. Finally, when Erasmus considered universal history from a dualistic perspective, he introduced the law of God as manifesting a progressive revelation in the law of nature, of Moses, and of Christ, in diametrical opposition to the law of Satan.[140]

6 THE VARIETY OF PERSONS, TIMES, AND THINGS

In addition to identifying ideas and analysing their arrangement, the interpreter must clarify from the text the setting of the story. What the rhetoricians meant by *circumstantia* was not so much a set of independent facts as a state of affairs informed by the question to be argued, whether in juridical, deliberative, or laudatory discourse.[141] Circumstance belonged to, and therefore was dependent on, the *status* of the question. This primary connection between a 'position' or 'essential point' (*status*) and 'that which stands around it' (*circumstantia*) is, of course, largely inconsistent with our modern understanding of historical circumstances as 'concrete situations.' Except in juridical discourse, the circumstances were more like the scenery in a literary context (that is, they had to do with the assemblage of persons, times, and things) than they were like what we call factuality. In other words, rhetorical circumstance was a matter of the place persons, times, and things obtain in rhetorical presentation.

Accordingly, in his *Ecclesiastes*, Erasmus placed *circumstantia* under the heading of the invention of arguments, used to prove or confirm a proposition determined by the status of the question.[142] Yet the rhetorical concept of *argumenta* was so broad that for Quintilian it had included, besides the detail which served as proof in juridical discourse, all sorts of subject matter for narrative, fable, or drama. He organized these arguments into those from persons and those from things.[143] Moreover, the variety of circumstances was also part of the *loci argumentorum*, the places in the overall order of argument where the circumstantial material can be found.[144]

Consistent with the rhetorical concept of *circumstantia*, although not expressed in the same terminology, was Erasmus' use of the term *varietas* in his *Ratio*.[145] Here variety denoted the particular setting of times, persons, and things in the biblical narrative, whereas the rhetorical textbooks had for the most part taken *varietas* to mean alternating the style of speech to prevent tedium or modulating the voice to prevent monotony.[146] At this point they admonished the orator to observe moderation to insure the proper balance between the continuity or uniformity of speech and the diversity or variation of speech, with regard to both its arrangement and delivery. While Erasmus was aware of the aesthetic need for discourse to be varied so as to hold the attention of the readers and preclude their boredom, he nevertheless took *varietas* as being coterminous with what the rhetorician normally called *circumstantia*.

Thus he advised: 'To use Scriptures correctly, it is not enough to cull here and there four or five little words without considering from where the statement arose. For the meaning of this or that passage frequently depends on earlier ones. One should examine by whom it was said, to whom, at which time, on what occasion, in what words, in what spirit, what preceded, what follows. For from the consideration and collection of these matters one discovers what the statement intends.'[147] In other words, the text remains obscure as long as one fails to recognize the *varietas personarum, temporum,* and *rerum.* And in persons themselves there is a *varietas animorum, affectuum,* and *ingeniorum* as well.[148]

Yet it is not sufficient to have identified the various factors coinciding in particular situations. Literary criticism is for Erasmus not an end in itself, nor does it supply anything but preliminary criteria for interpretation. The interpreter must move on to integrating all historical details into the coherence of a larger context of meaning (*collatio*).[149] The various settings remain incoherent unless they are brought into an order that is governed by a fundamental unity. While a set of peculiar circumstances represents a variety of conditions, the overall order is in reality oriented in both the *scopus,* Christ, and the *harmonia* of his teaching and life. Constituting as they do the centre and the concentric circle surrounding it, Christ and his harmony represent the essential *consensus* that reveals the coherence and consistency of the ultimate truth.[150]

Erasmus is therefore not content with listing examples for the variety of situations in New Testament passages but goes on to suggest that the interpreter should have an order at hand so as to understand times, persons, and things as integral parts of a larger whole. To this end he outlines the history of salvation (*varietas temporum*) in five periods, two preceding and two following the central time of Christ.[151] Besides, he divides the universal people of God (*varietas personarum*) into three circles around the unique centre, Christ Jesus, with the clergy occupying the circle nearest to the centre, the princes situated in the next, and the common folk relegated to the third circle.[152] This sociological schema is then correlated with the order of things in nature (*varietas rerum*), where fire takes the highest place, air and water constitute the middle region, and earth makes up the lowest element. Yet the borders between the circles serve for the transformation to the higher and better rather than to the lower and worse. It is for this reason that the higher accommodates to the lower.[153]

With this historical, sociological, and natural framework Erasmus intended to offer a hermeneutical system to assist the interpreter in identifying particular constellations of times, persons, and things. Any concrete situation receives its actual meaning from its location in the general order of the world. But what is more, the real import of a text derives from its proximity to the centre, Christ. Since the order is centred in Christ, the allegorical interpretation can disclose the authentic significance of the particular situation. Because the order encompasses people in history, society, and nature as well, the tropological interpretation is able to show the moral import of the particular situation.

So at the centre of history, society, and nature stand Christ's teachings and life, characterized as they are by the harmony of truth. But even the *harmonia Christi* is subject to the conditions of variety because Christ adjusted to particular circumstances (*varietas Christi*). Consequently, it is the principle of accommodation that explains why Christ spoke and acted diversely in various situations. At times he acted according to his divine nature, at other times he disguised his divinity and behaved like a human being. He performed a variety of miracles, gave various answers, and conducted himself differently toward different persons, so much so in fact that on occasion his words appear at first sight to be contradictory.'[154] Christ himself adapted his word and deed to the conditions of a variety of persons, times, and things, even to the point of dissimulation.[155]

'But the variety of Christ does not at all confuse that harmony. On the contrary, just as a fitting arrangement of different voices makes for the sweetest symphony, so the variety of Christ renders a fuller harmony. He indeed became all to all, but in such a way that in nothing he was dissimilar to himself.'[156] This is why the interpreter must not take offense at the variety in a biblical text, even the puzzling variety of Christ, but rather strive to explain all ambiguity by referring it to Christ's harmony. For the text gathers meaning in proportion as it resembles the harmony of Christ, as the particulars fall into the picture of the whole. 'It is therefore an error to gather from the sacred books, which relate different things according to the variety of times, things, and persons, only those details which appeal to one's liking. After all, even a human law cannot be understood unless one considers the single parts in the light of its heading. Hear the divine word, but hear all of it.'[157]

The harmony of Christ's teaching and life makes any variety the more agreeable. It brings forth in a particularly excellent way consensus and concord among the disciples. This is so because the apostles' faith directly corresponded to Christ's words and their love immediately emulated his conduct.[158] As a result, believing and doing in the imitation of Christ go hand in hand, for the harmony of Christ's teaching and life is of such a kind that it unites the apostles' faith and love, even as they are accommodated in various ways to various circumstances. The apostolic consensus in doctrine and apostolic concord in practice are a corollary of the harmony of Christ's teaching and life. This is why the *orbis totius Christi fabulae* closes, as it returns to its origin, with the apostles.

The relation between Christ and the apostles is decisive for the authority of the apostles in the church. Just as the harmony of Christ's teaching and life engenders the authority of the apostles, so the harmony of the apostles' imitative faith and love becomes the unifying principle for ecclesiastical doctrine and practice in the various circumstances of the history of salvation. To be sure, the harmony of Christ, the author, is the origin of apostolic authority. But apostolic authority in turn becomes, next to the original, the criterion for the tradition of the church. Since the patristic interpreters faithfully persevered in the spirit of the apostles, the *consensus patrum* serves as a supplementary hermeneutical guide for both the interpretation of Scripture and, together with Scripture, for the discernment of church doctrine and practice.[159] For Erasmus, the line of Christ's harmony leads thus from Christ and the apostles to the Fathers and the early church.

This chapter focused on the question of how invention and dispostion operate in Erasmus' theology. Rules of grammar and rhetoric facilitate not only the interpretation of Scripture on its historical, tropological, and allegorical level but also the arrangement of theological *topoi* into a dualistic system which becomes tripartite by the insertion of a middle link. How the dynamics of a trichotomous sequence overcome a static dualism was demonstrated specifically by an analysis of Erasmus' treatment of the law-gospel issue. The interpreter derives the true meaning of Scripture from its reference to the harmony of Christ, the unifying focus for his accommodation to a variety of persons, things, times, and places. In addition, the interpreter can also extract the main *topoi* of Christian doctrine from the story of Christ. For these theological commonplaces Erasmus suggests in his *Ecclesiastes* a systematic matrix. Two dominions, their origin in God or Satan, their respective communities, laws, modes of behaviour, and consequences, are arranged in the order of rhetorical disposition from start to finish in which the middle, the progress between origin and outcome, is central, whether in positive or negative terms.

FIVE

The Virtues of Speech

1 ELOCUTIO; PURITAS, PERSPICUITAS

Rhetoricians generally defined elocution as the formulation of thought in words (diction) and discourse (style).[1] Elocution was likened to the becoming garment of speech (Cicero), or the sword unsheathed (Quintilian), or 'the flesh and skin of the living body; the decent clothing for bones and nerves' (Erasmus).[2] In other words, elocution served to express mental images in linguistic terms. Elocution expresses thought in words.

Because of this crucial function, elocution occupied in rhetorical theory the middle place between conceiving and delivering speech, that is, between invention and disposition on the one side, and memory and pronunciation on the other.[3] While we are nowadays inclined to link elocution primarily with oratorical performance, classical rhetoricians saw it more akin to the conceptualization and arrangement of thought.[4] Certainly, when delivering an oration, speakers had to adjust their tone of voice, gestures, and facial expression to the particular wording of the topic.[5] But elocution was first of all concerned with the content of discourse. It translates ideas into words, even though as the third part of rhetoric, it has also to do with memory and delivery. Just as invention supplies the mental *topoi* and disposition organizes them in proper order, so elocution finds suitable figures of speech and helps to arrange them in a fitting literary composition.

Strictly speaking, invention and disposition are to *res* what elocution is to *verba*. Rhetorical theory, however, did not absolutize this distinction. Elocution tended to overlap with the invention of things, if only because mind and language are intimately related in the first place.⁶ For instance, metaphor and allegory are already instrumental in accommodating ideas to words, regardless of the fact that they are, strictly speaking, figures of speech. In addition to articulating words for speech, elocution also played a role in the disposition of speech. For instance, *aptum*, the process of matching the parts of speech to form a harmonious whole, is at once a *virtus dispositionis* and a *virtus elocutionis*.⁷ So elocutionary devices and figures of speech already perform a significant function in the area of invention and disposition, even though they actually belong to *ornatus*, a branch of *elocutio*. Inventing and ordering a topic were considered to be impossible without choosing words in proper form and giving the text an appropriate texture.

The way Erasmus treated elocution reflects this ambiguity. As the third of the five offices (*inventio, dispositio, elocutio, memoria, pronuntiatio*), elocution is an integral part of the overall rhetorical scheme. Even so, it functions at the same time as a component part of the first two offices, invention and disposition.

Now, on the face of it, Erasmus does not absolutely adhere to the sequence of the five offices of rhetoric. In the *Ratio*, he fails to mention them in so many words.⁸ They do not occur *expressis verbis* in *Ecclesiastes* I. *Ecclesiastes* II refers once (and in passing) to what he calls the five 'singular offices,' with elocution placed between disposition and memory. But the first three (invention, disposition, and – as we learn later – elocution) are at once integrated into the framework of the *partes operis* (*exordium, narratio, divisio, confirmatio, confutatio*, and *conclusio*). The 'parts of the work' in turn are correlated with the *officia oratoris* (*docere, delectare* and *flectere*) which are conditioned, in the first place, by the *genera orationis* (especially the *genus suasorium*).⁹ So, instead of giving his *Ecclesiastes* an external structure along the lines of the five offices of rhetoric, Erasmus follows the outline: *The speaker* (book I); *the duties of speaking* (based on the kinds of speech) and *the parts of speech* including invention, disposition, and elocution (book II).

Nevertheless, the beginning of *Ecclesiastes* III reveals that the five offices of rhetoric do provide an internal structure for the entire work after all.¹⁰ Erasmus gives us to understand that in the previous volume he had covered the offices of speech only insofar as *inventio* is concerned, even as he had begun to deal there also with *dispositio* under the heading of *divisio*. To finish this segment, he now continues to treat *dispositio sive ordo*, but in a summary fashion, and adds a brief passage on *memoria* plus a lengthier section on *pronuntiatio*.[11] After that, he attends for the most part of book III to what obviously has to do with *elocutio*, even though he fails to call it that by name.[12]

Characteristically, however, while elocution is indeed the main subject for the remainder of the volume, it is associated from the outset (just like invention and disposition before) with the *officia oratoris* and the *genera orationis*. Since the preacher's duties arise primarily from the *genus suasorium*, Erasmus lifts up *delectare* and *flectere* (while not dismissing *docere*) as the two foremost offices and connects the former with *jucunditas*, the latter with *vehementia*, as the two most important *virtutes elocutionis*. These two qualities, together with *amplificatio*, were already announced at the end of book II as the subject of book III.[13] Therefore, book III in fact deals with *elocutio* (i.e., *loci communes, amplificatio, adfectus, schemata, sententia, metaphora*, and *allegoria*), albeit in terms of the two most significant virtues of speech, *jucunditas* and *vehementia*.

In order to assess Erasmus' use of elocutionary devices, we must briefly look at the system of elocution in general. The doctrine of *elocutio* (*lexis, phrasis*) contained the principles of eloquent literary expression drawn primarily from the style of those classical authors who were regarded as normative authorities to be imitated. While imitation limited the freedom of the disciple's individual expression, outfitting thought with suitable words still left some room for personal ingenuity.[14] However, both excessive imitation and inflated originality were rejected as violating language inasmuch as they cause mannerism and affectation. It is moderation, therefore, that guards against either too much reliance on models or too much trust in one's own natural faculty of speech.

Traditionally, elocution covered the areas of grammar, rhetoric, and poetry. In grammar, elocution was defined as the art of correct language (*ars recte* [*emendate*] *loquendi*), in rhetoric as the art of good speech (*ars bene dicendi*).[15] Moreover, elocution was subdivided into the four qualities of style (*virtutes elocutionis: puritas, perspicuitas, aptum, ornatus*)[16] and the three kinds of style (*genera elocutionis*: the *genus subtile* [*humile, summissum, gracile*], the *genus medium* [*modicum, mediocre, moderatum*], and the *genus grande* [*sublime, vehemens, amplum*]).[17]

As we shall see, Erasmus did not scrupulously follow these classifications. In the *Ecclesiastes*, he simply lumps selected qualities of style (*probabilitas, perspicuitas, evidentia*) and kinds of style (*jucunditas, vehementia, splendor sive sublimitas*) together, calls them *virtutes orationis*, and mentions them in passing under the heading of *schemata* (*figurae*).[18] Then he divides the figures of speech according to whether they are conducive to either *acrimonia, vehementia,* and *gravitas* or to *jucunditas, perspicuitas, splendor, festivitas,* and *venustas*.[19] Further on, still within the section on figures of speech but now under the rubric of *similitudo*, he lists the three traditional *genera elocutionis*, calls them *characteres orationis*, and distinguishes further divisions among them.[20]

It is clear that Erasmus freed himself from the rigid structure and strict terminology of rhetorical theory to pursue his theological intention. He subordinates the qualities of style to the kinds of style (for instance *perspicuitas* to *jucunditas*). The kinds of style in turn, reduced to *vehementia* and *jucunditas*, are used as criteria to show how the figures of speech can both move the hearers ethically through sharp, powerful, and serious speech and attract them through delightful, clear, brilliant, pleasant, and enticing speech. In the end, though, everything in Erasmus' sacred rhetoric comes down to the moral import of speech that effects change. *Movere* (*flectere*) by way of *delectare* is the single most important motive power of speech in Scripture and in the sermon. It is, after all, the rhetorical equivalent of a spiritual conversion and its moral correlative, progress in the way of salvation.

As for the qualities of elocution in general, the advice cautioning rhetoricians to avoid the extremes of either stylistic excess or dearth[21] became an essential point for Erasmus both in his exegesis of biblical tropes and in his homiletical use of figures of speech. For the supreme virtue of the virtues of elocution consisted in keeping the mean between too much and too little. The sharp, challenging high style of *vehementia* and the low style of *humilitas* were kept in balance by the moderating, accommodating style of *jucunditas*. The virtue of moderation held the rhetoricians back from deviating from the norm as it prevented either the elocutionary vice of excess (*hyperbole*) or of omission (*ellipsis*) except in the case of poetic licence.[22] Consequently, they were cautioned to exercise prudent judgment in adjusting their individual faculty of speech to the virtues of elocution.

Quintilian had listed four qualities essential for speech to conform to established standards.²³ The first quality of style, *latinitas* or *puritas*, falls into the grammarian's province as it concerns the correct, idiomatic use of language (*emendate*). Pure phraseology rests on *ratio* (the rational argument that relies, in case of doubt, on similarity); on *vetustas* (the ancient forms lending majesty to language and upholding the continuity of the literary tradition yet without perpetuating archaisms); on *auctoritas* (the use of classical models as the linguistic norms approved by the *consensus eruditorum*); and, most importantly, on *consuetudo* or *usus* (the language spoken in the present, but as authorized by the *consensus eruditorum* to avoid neologisms). Grammatical excess or lack, though, offend against the nature of correct language because they amount to either artificial purism or vulgar barbarism and solecism. Rhetorical art had to comport with nature in its linguistic expression. Only the inspired flights allowed by poetic licence enjoyed, for artistic reasons, a certain freedom from the rules guarding the integrity of natural language.²⁴

For Erasmus, rational arguments did not play a critical role in theological speech since this particular use of *ratio* belongs primarily to the province of *probatio* in judicial discourse, which in and by itself is less important to the ecclesiastic, except in the convicting of heretics. Certainly, the *genus suasorium* relies in part on evidence too, but it does so by virtue of a *ratiocinatio* that evinces probable truth through comparison of similarities. This kind of reasoning, however, leads to verisimilitude which appeals to the truth in itself, rather than to that rationally arrived at certainty of truth which leaves no margin for mystery or, for that matter, error. Erasmus thus connected reasoning with *probabilitas* for the sake of *perspicuitas* and submitted them to the ultimate purpose of *jucunditas*.²⁵ Just as Scripture convinces by attracting and transforming the hearers rather than catching them in the net of dialectic conclusions, sacred oratory persuades by clear evidence, but in a way that delights the listeners and moves them toward the truth. Instead of arguing and proving a legal case to win a conviction in court, theological language evokes spiritual change and moral progress in persons.

However, the other grammatical qualities receive Erasmus' full attention. We have already seen how he applied the grammatical virtue of purity in his text-critical work on the Scripture, aimed as it was at restoring the text to its correct original, i.e., to the originally good nature of its language. It was this humanist concern for purity (not a modern attempt to establish the historical factuality of the events such as they were reported in the text) that informed his textual criticism. 'I have always been attracted, I confess, by purity of style, even in sacred authors.'[26] His return to the sources was due to his reverence for the authority of the sacred text – a kind of literary *pietas* that motivated the restoration of biblical language to its original authority.[27] Moreover, he accepted the early tradition of scriptural interpretation as authoritative because of both its *antiquitas* (that is, its proximity to the origin) and its unity as expressed in the *consensus patrum*.[28] Further, the problems he had with the contemporary usage of customary language also shows a committed grammarian who followed the first rule of elocution, *latinitas* or *puritas*, even though he was willing to make concessions as to vernacular translations of the Bible as well as to the rusticity of biblical language itself.[29]

The second quality of style, clarity (*perspicuitas*), functioned normally as a transition from grammar to rhetoric. First of all, language must be lucid to be understood on the face of it. This requires words with unambiguous meanings, a simple word order, short phrases and sentences. But more importantly, if speech is to be persuasive, it must be transparent to thought in order to be intellectually plausible and morally credible.[30] Perspicuity thus straddled as it were the grammatical nature of the text and the rhetorical art of discourse. As to its rhetorical function, perspicuity shared the device of amplification with *dispositio* in that it enlarges and intensifies by means of art what is naturally given.[31] Although perspicuity presents facts (*evidentia*) objectively and visually, it possesses the metaphorical power to make the density of concreteness translucent to a higher reality by raising evidence to the level of ideas, that is, by enabling a movement from the perception of the sensible world to the intuitive level of the intelligible world.[32]

The principle of moderation determined naturally also the perspicuity of speech. Too much perspicuity renders language so superficial that it loses its depth and therefore turns into platitudes. Too little perspicuity, on the other hand, results in obscurity. *Obscuritas* becomes a rhetorical vice as soon as hearers are unable to make out any meaning at all.[33] This happens particularly when *dissimilia*, *contraria*, or *pugnantia* seem to vitiate understanding by obstructing analogy and comparison, the necessary means for making sense.³⁴

Obscurities in Scripture arise, according to Erasmus, not only from the nature of its tropes but also from technical problems like incorrect translations; incorrect ideas about antiquity; mistaking the meanings of words with similar sounds; confusing the things expressed by the same noun; incorrect punctuation; incorrect pronunciations; contradictions, untruths, absurdities; and difficulties of telling in whose name a discourse proceeds.³⁵ There are scriptural passages that seem to be at variance or even at odds with themselves. Still, instead of doubting the truthfulness of Scripture we must take particular circumstances into account and look for ways to explain each crux.³⁶ Unless we recognize the idiomatic use of words or phrases, certain biblical passages appear ambiguous if not absurd. Even plain language often vexes the reader with contrariety. Preachers must therefore elicit the germane sense of Scripture. This is made easier when they find out the patristic interpretation, collate places (*loci*), consider the variety of persons and times, hear the tenor of what precedes and follows, compare various commentaries, meditate at length, and pray faithfully.³⁷ To remove ambiguity (by interpreting it in a positive light rather than a negative one) and to elucidate metaphors – that is the task of the professional theologian.³⁸

Nevertheless, there is a positive side to obscurity. Authors were at liberty to use dissimulating language by literary licence for reasons of persuasion: *Verum ubi nulla est ambiguitas, ibi nulla est deliberatio.*³⁹ Leaving more than one interpretation open (*ambiguitas, amphibolia*⁴⁰) was a legitimate rhetorical scheme intended to invite readers to participate in making meaning by being drawn into the text so as to reach their own judgment on the matter. Similarly, the artist left a work of art unfinished to encourage the public to complete it by their imagination. The resulting clarity of vision was then a fruit of the beholder's effort as well as the artist's, and for that reason it was the more enjoyable.⁴¹ In literature, tropes, figures, metaphors, and allegories were deliberately chosen both to conceal the true meaning and to attract the reader. Even though the process of understanding (or progress in piety, for that matter) was thereby made more arduous in the beginning, the insight reached was expected to be the more pleasurable in the end.⁴² This is why metaphors and allegories were so essential to the delightful speech of persuasive rhetoric.

Erasmus was, of course, expert in obliqueness. The interplay of direct and indirect speech had become his second nature as he composed and interpreted texts, not to speak of his polemics. But he was no obscurantist, no cynical elitist who deliberately kept others in the dark. Rather, oblique language reflected his effort to acknowledge and overcome the dualism between the visible and intelligible world. When he discussed a question in deliberative discourse, for instance, ambiguity served as a foil for comparing different interpretations in order to arrive at the most probable solution.[43] Interpreting Scripture, he concentrated on the ambiguity of allegory between the literal and the spiritual meaning as the linguistic means capable of reconciling opposites. No matter how devious he appeared to his opponents, he could justify ambiguity as a pedagogical accommodation to both subject matter and readers. What is more, he could warrant his protean attitude as an imitation of scriptural revelation itself, namely, the divine accommodation to human comprehension. The truth draws and moves the human affections all the more effectively if it is concealed. For that reason, the biblical text looks at first like a *humile sermo* – no platitude, to be sure, but the ground level for advancing to a spiritual meaning. In the same way, Christ appears at first sight in the lowly attitudes of humility, simplicity, and innocence, only to be revealed as divinity in the word.

2 APTUM; COLLATIO, COMMODITAS

Aptum had first of all to do with fitting the parts of speech into a harmonious whole. Due to its connection with *decorum* and *expedientia*, however, it also served to link rhetoric with ethics, to connect speech with *vita* and *mores*.[44] Just as *perspicuitas* throws a bridge from the grammatical nature of language to the rhetorical art of speech, so *aptum* orients rhetorical art toward the final purpose of oratory, moral change. Rhetorical virtue (that is, correct and good speech according to the rules of grammar and rhetoric) becomes a paradigm for moral virtue, for living in tune with the harmony of nature. Conversely, rhetorical vice is recognized for what it really is, a linguistic aberration expressing perverse if not evil conduct which itself is symptomatic of the disturbance of order. So the *ars bene dicendi* resonates with moral overtones as the quality of speech reflects the character of the orator. With good speech revealing the life of the good orator, language, based as it is on nature and cultivated by rhetorical art, reaches for perfection. This is why for Erasmus the *vir apte dicendi* is the ideal orator: 'According to the rhetoricians, no one speaks well, unless speaking aptly, even if otherwise using ornate, copious, and splendid language.'[45]

It goes without saying that Erasmus was vitally concerned with the moral character of the speaker, so much in fact that he devoted the whole first book of his *Ecclesiastes* to describing the integrity of the preacher. Erasmus' preacher must not only surpass the orator's ordinary moral qualities but also receive the gifts of the Spirit and acquire skills in understanding the gospel. He must be taught by God and learn from the gospel the art of accommodating the sermon to the circumstances of the congregation. In an obvious parallel to the classical definition of the orator as *bonus vir*, Erasmus calls the Christian orator 'a man not only extraordinarily good but also instructed by God and endowed with evangelical prudence.'[46]

That Erasmus raised the preacher's moral standards beyond the already high expectations of the classical orator is also apparent from a passage where he enumerates, following Aristotle, three things that engender the hearer's confidence: *prudentia*, *virtus*, and *benevolentia*. Lacking prudence, the speaker may persuade to perverse rather than right things. Next, it is not enough to intend what is right, unless the speaker is a virtuous person who knowingly will not deceive the hearer. Yet without benevolence both right judgment and virtue may yet have harmful effects. When speaking to an enemy or a tyrant, for instance, a virtuous man knowingly may persuade to what is harmful to the hearer. Preachers, however, should be benevolent to friend and foe alike. Preachers should be instructed by the wisdom that makes for right judgment, virtuous enough to never deceive anyone knowingly, and charitable enough to desire to do good even to their enemies.[47] Obviously, the rule for orators: 'No right judgment without prudence; no prudence without virtue; no virtue without benevolence' applies to preachers in a more excellent way. Christian wisdom so qualifies prudence that it is unfailing in judgment; Christian virtue absolutizes and radicalizes classical virtue; Christian love perfects ordinary benevolence.

Aptum and its cognates (*decorum, decens, conveniens, accommodatum*) run a full gamut of meanings covering a variety of operations: to fit together, adapt, adjust, make appropriate, and make suitable; to embellish, beautify, adorn, make graceful, comely, becoming, and handsome; to meet, come together, assemble, fit to agree, make congenial, concordant, unanimous; to make suitable and agreeable by taking the measure, to make commensurate and proportionate.[48] *Aptum* seems to be a term connoting the fitting together of elements in appropriate form. *Decorum* and *decens* appear to be more a matter of aesthetics and ethics, therefore akin to *ornatus* and aiming at pleasurable and moving speech (*jucunditas* and *vehementia*). *Accommodatum*, given its relation to *commodum* and *modus*, seems to have more to do with the measure that makes oratory rhythmic and harmonious. Nevertheless, Erasmus used all these terms more or less interchangeably. *Commodum*, for instance, appeals also to moral utility inasmuch as it synchronizes virtue with the harmony of nature. In fact, the moral goal of speech ultimately qualifies all uses of *aptum* and its cognates. Moral change, however, is for Erasmus, as we have seen, not an end in itself but subsidiary to spiritual transformation.

Speech is rendered apt in a number of ways. First of all, thought must be fitted to words, and language must be accommodated to the subject matter, to the audience, and to the circumstances. Moreover, the parts of speech must be matched one with another to form a proportionate whole. Last but not least, speech must be adapted to a moral goal. In other words, *aptum* includes: the linguistic adaptation of *res* to *verba*; the pedagogical adjustment of the speaker to the hearers and their circumstances; the rhetorical fitting of discourse into its proper order, relating harmoniously the parts to the whole and the whole to the parts, embellishing oratory so as to make it attractive and persuasive, and synchronizing it with the moral goal so that it brings about transformation, which happens most conveniently when the propriety of speech fits the probity of the speaker, when the speaker's life agrees with the content and style of speech.

We can discern here in general two seemingly opposite directions for making oratory appropriate: The orator must adapt speech to concrete situations and at the same time must refer it to a transcendent norm. But these two sides, actual variety and real harmony, are for Erasmus not as far apart as they first appear. Since *convenire*, the coming together of particular circumstances under natural conditions, already implies some kind of agreement, it enables to a certain degree *conferre*, the rhetorical comparison of similarities. It is true that the ideal harmony accommodates itself differently to various times, places, and persons. But doing so it does not surrender its essential unity to the accidents of contingent conditions. So we conclude that Erasmus used *convenire* as practically synonymous with *conferre*.

Indeed, *collatio* turns out to be a predominent concept in Erasmus' rhetorical theology, more prominent than the rhetorical tradition had it, where it functioned for the most part as a synonym for parable or similitude.[49] Not just in *De libero arbitrio*, where it is used as the literary genre, but in the *Ratio*, in the *Ecclesiastes*, and in many other works as well, collation is the single most important method for finding analogies that issue in consensus and harmony. *Collatio* is for the rhetorical theologian the most suitable way of interpreting Scripture. This is so because it imitates the allegorical nature of Scripture itself. 'No other kind of teaching is more familiar and more effective than comparison through simile.'[50]

A hermeneutical equivalent of similitude and therefore related to metaphor and allegory,[51] *collatio* performs the same mediating function of accommodation. It compares the various components of a text to discern similarity and thereby to identify their integral place within a larger order. Overall, Erasmus used *collatio* in three ways, all intended to establish unity and harmony among diverse expressions. On a grammatical level, *collatio* establishes the original by comparing a text with its source.[52] When it comes to interpretation, *collatio* serves to compare similar meanings so as to uncover the *consensus* underlying the various expressions of truth in particular circumstances. In deliberative rhetoric, finally, the rhetorician employs *collatio* to compare both sides of an open question with an eye to that eventual agreement which is suggested by the most probable solution, by the 'equilibrium of truth' at the end of the persuasive process.[53]

Accordingly, *collatio* functions either as a literary method to ascertain an original text, or as an exegetical method to understand the divine word in Scripture, or as a heuristic method to arrive at the truth through discussion. The difference between biblical interpretation and theological discussion, though, is whether the truth at stake is definitively revealed in Christ and the essential articles of faith, or remains an open question on which ecclesiastical authority has not yet decided. In either case, accommodation, the motive power of collation, aims at bringing about agreement. For comparison moves toward concord rather than collision: 'In disputation, soberness and the highest moderation of mind must be observed so that collation, not conflict might occur.'[54]

However, beyond its exegetical function of comparing similarities in a text and its heuristic function of arriving at the equilibrium of truth through discussion, *collatio* serves also a systematic purpose. So Erasmus advised the exegete to employ the rhetorical method of comparison to arrange theological *topoi* into a system: 'to place everything you read as if in little nests. What you wish to reveal or conceal is thereby readier at hand ... Having arranged these topics in the order of affinity or opposition of words and things ... everything notable in the Bible should be incorporated in proportion as it is concordant or dissonant. One could also register in this list anything of future use from the ancient interpreters of the Bible, at last even from the books of the heathens.'[55] This systematic collation of theological commonplaces, however, depends on the exegetical *collatio locorum* within Scripture. The best method of interpreting the divine letters is to clarify an obscure place by comparison with other places. If several agree, they are conducive to belief. If they are at odds or even contrary, they inspire us to a more determined examination. The collation of places is also of advantage for recognizing more certainly the idioms and tropes of the secret word.[56]

A text-critical, exegetical, heuristic, and systematic procedure alike, collation is instrumental in collecting, selecting, and organizing subject matter according to similarity. Yet for collation to work, the interpreter must first identify the literary circumstances in the text, that is, the coincidence of a variety of persons, things, times, and places.[57] 'To use Scripture correctly, it is not enough to cull here and there four or five little words without considering from where the statement arose. Rather, one should examine ... by whom it was said, to whom, at which time, on what occasion, in what words, in what spirit, what precedes, what follows. From considering and collecting these matters one discovers what the statement intends.'[58] A genuine reading of the text arises from the sequence of the discourse itself: what precedes a locus, what follows, where does it start, how far does it go, where does it end? The comparison of other places is also of great value. 'Often the same meaning is expressed in one place by ambiguous words, in another by clear language.'[59]

These references to speaker, hearer, time, occasion, words, things, intention, context, and stages are so important for Erasmus that they qualify the fourfold method of interpretation. 'One will also have to consider which degrees (*gradus*) there are in each of these [sc the four senses], which differences, and which method of treatment (*ratio tractandi*) ... The type (*typus*) receives as it were another form (*figura*) in proportion to the variety of things, to which it is accommodated, and according to the diversity of times.'[60] No doubt, Erasmus' concern for the literary circumstances in the text and for the actual conditions at a given time modifies the traditional method of interpreting Scripture to such an extent that dogmatics can no longer impose its abstract assertions on the word of God. It is the other way around. The *loci* must first be drawn from the text in its historical, literary setting before they can be organized so as to reflect unity and harmony – or their opposite, as the case may be.

The interpreter accommodates the interpretation to the particular set of literary and historical circumstances. The bringing together of elements from the text (*collatio*) must correspond to the coming together of items and details in the text (*conventio*). We can conclude from this that just as history is prior to allegory, so the coming together of items in the text precedes the comparison of similarities from the text. But this priority is one of time, not of significance, temporal, not essential because the harmony of Christ precedes the variety of Christ, and comparison (like allegory) may proceed without its historical foundation in case the conventional (historical) setting is absurd, in conflict with Christ's teaching and life, naturally inequitable, and morally counterproductive.[61] Should the literal sense run afoul of natural equity, the *scopus* Christ, and ethical utility, it lacks harmony, and its obscurity and ambiguity signals disorder. It then figures more likely in the sweep of the devil's reign and promotes the perversion of order.[62]

Accommodating their interpretation to the particular setting of the text, interpreters certainly must not impose a heterogeneous canon on the text but rather must adapt themselves to the circumstances in the same way in which God in Christ has accommodated divinity to human language. Therefore, the rhetorical method of bringing together the variety in different texts imitates the process of divine accommodation in Christ's incarnation. Yet just as God in Christ did not surrender divinity[63] but rather aimed at drawing humanity into the Spirit, so the interpreter must not give up the whole for the part but rather draw the part into the whole. The identification of the particularity in the text, important as it is, serves finally the purpose of seeing to it that it becomes an integral part of the divine order. Therefore, the variety of contingent settings, like the letter, must be translated into the consensus of a spiritual harmony that is oriented in the fundamental unity centred in the ultimate *scopus*, Christ.

As to its goal, comparison is to arrive at consensus. Accommodation, the motive power of collation, serves in the final analysis to bring about agreement. But the move toward agreement is certainly also a progress toward the whole, which is possible because the particular meeting of conditions so brings similarities and dissimilarities to light that the interpreter is able to translate the text into the larger context. Prudently the interpreter integrates a particular set of circumstances into their proper place in the overall picture. The more the text fits into the larger context and eventually into the whole, the more the interpretation acquires the quality of agreement, of the meeting of minds in consensus. What is more, consensus, the intellectual expression of unity in truth, most certainly goes hand in hand with concord, the ethical expression of truth in love.[64]

The means providing the measure and manner (*modus*) for collation to work its way toward integration is *commoditas*.[65] Erasmus adopted the full range of meanings of this concept, all the way from proportion and symmetry to accommodation and adjustment. We find *commoditas* functioning in his hermeneutic as a rhetorical criterion, especially in aesthetic and moral terms. Like a tuning fork, so it seems, it measures whether or not a text or speech appropriately resonates the larger order by being commensurate with harmony, in tune with the true, conducive to the good, and attractive to the beautiful. The rhythm of *commoditas* must be consonant above all with the metre of the harmony of Christ. But it must also resound with the equilibrium of natural equity and echo the moderation of ethical utility. Like a metronome, it beats time, revealing what is 'in sync' with the ideal, and precisely as the rhythm of harmony *commoditas* is the measure of reality.

When it comes to arranging speech through invention and disposition, *commodum* renders the order of words appropriate by making it not only perspicuous and giving it rhythmic measure (*modulatio*) but also by putting a moral edge on it (*acrimonia*). An inept composition, on the contrary, confuses the order of words and thus obscures the meaning of the text. Further, as far as the division of speech is concerned, *commodum* orders the principal propositions in such a way that there is a proper gradation (*gradus*) between the first proposition and the ones which follow. A reversal of that order gives rise to spurious persuasion because things fail to come together and will not fall into their proper place.[66] Moreover, just as the amplification of thought appeals to the affections, so rhythm (*modus*) results from the amplification of words.[67] In addition, it is the aim of speech (*finis*) to persuade the hearer to acquire, increase, and strengthen useful things (*commoda*) and to avoid, lessens, and remove disadvantageous things (*incommoda*).[68] In terms of time, finally, *commoditas* helps to determine whether or not an occasion is appropriate and a moment suitable (*kairos*) for persuasion to succeed.[69]

The moral import of *commoditas* governs the tropological interpretation of Scripture. For *commoditas* is, in the first place, the reason on account of which a metaphor moves from one meaning to another: 'Metaphor transfers by means of similitude a word from its particular significance to another for the sake of any benefit.' The purpose for this translation is to accommodate speech to the hearers in such a way that they understand what is in their best interest, what is useful and advantageous for them in their particular circumstances. Accordingly, the intent and goal of persuasive rhetoric, *utilitas*, is based on providing advantageous things and removing disadvantageous things. In sacred rhetoric, moreover, the intended benefit for the hearers acquires a more excellent quality as *commodum* encourages them to move from the flesh to the spirit and to advance in piety.[70]

Because the *modus* of *commoditas* is like the measure of reality, it motivates appropriate behaviour. Setting proper limits, it generates the impulse for decent conduct in that it inspires the hearers to be moderate and stimulates their ethical accommodation to the conditions of others. *Moderatio* (*mediocritas*) is no doubt one of the cardinal concepts in Erasmus' rhetorical theology. Scholastic disputations, for instance, call for a balanced attitude based on measure and discretion: 'Moderation will prevent us from questioning everything, discretion from questioning anything at will.' And regarding his own attitude in general: 'I have always exhorted to moderation,' says Erasmus in the *Sponge*. In the same way, sober moderation must be observed in interpreting allegories by neither removing them from Scripture nor rejecting the underlying historical sense. Also regarding *actio* or *pronuntiatio*, the voice, facial expression, and mien in general of the speaker must be tempered so as to fit the subject matter of speech.[71] Last but not least, the relation between *commoditas* and *aequitas* in terms of just proportion is the reason why equity moderates the law and temperance balances justice with love.[72]

As interpreters take the measure of the text, they are by the same token called upon to take the measure of themselves and to keep measure for themselves by submitting themselves to the measure of language in harmony with nature. Rhetoricians should exercise self-control by being moderate and temperate both toward the text and other human beings. They must not arrogate to themselves the measure of all things, nor consider themselves superior to other human beings. This is why moderation looks to expedience,[73] meaning that one must resist the temptation of ambition and arrogance to make oneself the purpose of one's action. Instead, one must always have the benefit of others in mind, being useful, kind, pleasing, obliging, serving, and giving, not to confront, reject, and hurt them, but to heal, accept, and encourage them to make progress in the way of salvation. This behaviour pattern takes its cue from Christ's innocence, simplicity, and humility. The more the moderation of the imitators conforms with that perfect modesty which has become incarnate in Christ's mildness and humility, the more they are rendered capable of the divine Spirit.[74]

3 ORNATUS; JUCUNDITAS, VEHEMENTIA

While some rhetoricians subsumed *aptum* under the heading of *ornatus*,[75] Erasmus apparently considered rendering speech appropriate as more important than decorating it with ornaments. When it comes to the question of whether *aptum* or *ornatus* has priority, he sided with those rhetoricians who maintained that: 'no one speaks well, unless speaking aptly, even if otherwise using ornate, copious, and splendid language.'[76] The virtues of appropriate speech were so paramount for him that he mentioned them prominently at strategic points in his *Ratio* and especially his *Ecclesiastes*. Nonetheless, he set a high value on those figures of speech that embellish for reasons of amplification, that adorn in order to convey a metaphorical meaning. He listed these tropes and figures in separate sections, reduced their vast number to those that are relevant to biblical interpretation and preaching, concentrated on those that adorn for the sake of accommodation, and gave in the end his full attention to allegory, the foremost figure of speech in Scripture.[77]

Contrary to the impression one gets from Erasmus' treatment of embellishing techniques in *De copia*,[78] his theological writings at least, if not also other pieces, make it quite clear that decoration is not an end in itself. Unlike a literary garnish serving its own purpose, *ornatus* equips oratory with the means to carry out its proper business and achieve its appropriate goal. Literary art for art's sake distorts the nature of language by making speech artifical instead of affective. Therefore, ornamental devices, just as the means of *aptum*, are subservient to both the duties of speaking and the virtues of speech within a specific genus of speech. Regarding persuasive discourse, then, the figures of speech are significant to the extent to which they attract and transform the hearer by their amplifying and metaphorical power.[79] This is why Erasmus used the devices of *ornatus* selectively, adjusted them to the duties of the *genus suasorium*, and focused them on the task of interpreting Scripture and composing sermons.[80]

Erasmus mentioned certain figures more often and treated them more extensively than others because of their singular capacity to transfer meaning from one level to another, especially from the visible world to the intelligible world. For instance, *hyperbole* says more than the facts indicate.[81] *Synecdoche* expresses one thing by another (like the whole by the part, the genus by the species, and vice versa).[82] The *emphasis* of words lends a statement such depth that we are prompted to draw inferences that go without saying.[83] *Ironia*, sparked as it is by an intense moral sensitivity, depicts exactly the opposite of what we expect in order to shock us out of our complacency and make us alert to what really ought to be.[84] *Metaphor* transfers a word from its particular signification to a similar meaning for the benefit of the reader.[85] Using external, corporeal things to express an inner, spiritual truth, *allegoria* says in one way what is to be understood in another.[86]

Direct speech, particularly when restrained by the force of dialectic syllogisms, tends to press language into the Procrustean bed of once and for all, cut and dried, foregone conclusions, admitting no amplification of meaning. Yet the naked truth is better served when it is not only decently covered by, but is also attractively dressed up in, the clothing of an indirect speech that suggests more than the obvious, that invites the readers to read between the lines, to pass through the text to a larger context, to stretch themselves toward a wider horizon, and to lift up their hearts to the spiritual world. Such a veiled way of speaking renders language ambiguous, to be sure, but not dubious or deceptive. Therefore, the fact that Scripture gives rise to a variety of meanings is for Erasmus a sign of its fecundity rather than uncertainty.[87] Suggestive language, then, becomes a medium for disclosing unknown dimensions of insight as soon as decorative allusions point away from themselves to values that enlarge the nature of language into a second nature – a culture of spirit and truth, and ultimately a religion of faith and love.

Erasmus did not strictly adhere to the traditional division of *ornatus* into single words (*tropi*) and words joined together (*figurae, schemata*).[88] He used the terms 'tropes' and 'figures' indiscriminately. In the *Ratio*, he shows under the heading of tropes how *heterosis, synecdoche, hyperbaton, hyperbole*, and *ironia* function in biblical passages. The figures of speech are subsequently not spelled out but introduced summarily: 'There are several other figures of words and thought that add to composition the weight or pleasantness of speech. While the meaning of mystical Scripture indeed would be certain without them, they do flow the more delightfully and effectively into our minds and are the more fruitfully treated and communicated.'[89] Erasmus saves himself the trouble of going through an extensive list of these figures by simply refering the reader to Augustine's *De doctrina Christiana*, to Donatus and Diomedes, and to the nineth book of Quintilian's *Institutio*. After an excursus dealing with the vice of *amphibologia* and *abusus vocis*, he devotes a section to *emphasis* and then swiftly moves on to a lengthy discussion of allegory.[90]

In the *Ecclesiastes*, tropes and figures are part and parcel of 'those things that make oratory powerful, delightful, and abundant.' The list begins with (1) the *loci communes* (which already had been treated under the heading of disposition),[91] followed by (2) *amplificatio*,[92] especially the amplification of thought directed toward (3) *adfectus*.[93] Metaphor, *schemata, parabola, allegoria, abusus* and *imago* are already mentioned in connection with *emphasis* under the heading of *amplificatio*,[94] *imago* and *evidentia* under the heading of *adfectus*.[95] At length, (4) the *figurae* or *schemata* are treated in their own place and divided according as they are conducive to sharp, powerful and serious speech (*vehementia*)[96] or suitable to delightful, clear, brilliant, pleasant, and charming speech (*jucunditas*).[97] The next section (5) deals with *sententiae*.[98]

(6) *Metaphora*, however, holds the first place among all the virtues of speech: 'None persuades more effectively, presents the matter to the eyes more evidently, moves the affections more powerfully, or adds more dignity, charm or delight, or even abundance to speech.' Although *exempla* in general are very powerful both to persuade and to inflame the minds by the emulation of virtue, the foremost power is exerted by those examples that belong to the irrefutable authority which in Christ is so supreme that there is hardly any other to compare with it. What we find in the history of the Old Testament patriarchs and prophets and of the New Testament saints is suitable for the rule of living only if it is in accord with the indubitable truth or else is confirmed by Scripture itself. But images of virtue can also be drawn from nature, from animals, plants, and the elements.[99] Figures derived from metaphor are: *abusio*, *allegoria*, *similitudo* or *collatio* (which is an explained metaphor), *imago* (a species of similitude), and *effictio* (a species of *hypotyposis*).[100]

(7) The quality of similitude changes the *character orationis*. A section follows to exemplify how the use of *schemata* in a biblical text (Matt 9; Luke 5) effects *jucunditas*, *splendor*, *vehementia*, and *adfectus*.[101] (8) The grammarians list also tropes other than those mentioned, and then there are those which have not yet been named by the rhetoricians or grammarians.[102]

(9) Finally, Erasmus has worked his way up to discussing allegory at length. 'No other trope nor any schema causes more trouble for the ecclesiastic than *allegoria*.' After proposing (a) general hermeneutical rules for how to elicit the genuine sense of Scripture,[103] he devotes (b) a section on *De ratione allegoriarum*. Here he connects allegory again with metaphor. Metaphor is the fountain of several related tropes: *collatio*, *imago*, and *abusio*, *aenigma*, *allegoria*, *proverbium*, and *apologus*. Metaphor is a brief similitude; similitude or *collatio* is a metaphor unfolded and accommodated to the subject matter. The rhetoricians defined allegory simply as a continuous metaphor, whereas in sacred

literature and with the doctors of the church the term has received a wider meaning, sometimes standing for *tropus*, sometimes for *typus*. Modern theologians teach a fourfold sense of Scripture: *historicum sive grammaticum, tropologicum, allegoricum* and *anagogicum*. But the ancient doctors knew only two senses: grammatical (or literal, or historical) and spiritual (which they variously called tropological, allegorical, or anagogical).[104] A long section (c) on allegorical interpretation[105] precedes the conclusion of *Ecclesiastes* III where Erasmus returns to *judicium* and *consilium*, the two sides of prudence.[106]

Seen altogether, it is clear that the figures of speech play a key role in the theologian's exegetical and homiletical work. The knowledge of the various tropes and schemata is essential for understanding first of all Scripture, but also patristic interpretation, and then classical literature. In addition to quoting frequently from these literary sources to provide illustrations, Erasmus does not grow weary of pointing to the way in which the figures of speech are useful for composing effective sermons.[107] The fundamental reason why figurative language is so important lies in its aim and purpose, that is, in its effect on the reader or hearer. For this reason Erasmus assessed the value of the figures of speech according to their capacity to accommodate those virtues of speech which have the best effect on the reader or hearer. The figures of speech are significant insofar as they are conducive to the *virtutes orationis (dictionis, artis)*.[108]

While Erasmus used on occasion the various terms for the virtues of speech indiscriminately by mingling, for instance, grammatical virtues (probability, perspicuity, and evidence) with elocutionary virtues (delight, vehemence, splendor, and sublimity)[109] he did suggest an order by singling out *vehementia*, *jucunditas*, and *amplificatio* (*copia*).[110] So commonplaces make for vehement and copious speech. And metaphor, allegory, and their kin accommodate the full range of virtues, for they are conducive to copiousness, perspicuity, evidence, probability, vehemence, splendor, amplitude, charm, delight, and grace.[111] Vehemence and delight are no doubt highlighted because of their moral appeal. And since metaphor and allegory are the best conduits for these two supreme virtues of speech, they hold the first place among the figures of speech. Amplification seems at first to function as a general device for enlarging meaning. But its ethical orientation appears as soon as Erasmus concentrates on the amplification of thought which appeals specifically to the human affections.[112]

Vehementia clearly produces an ethical effect. But does *jucunditas* make speech nothing but pleasant? No, delightful speech is not an end in itself; it serves in the end an ethical purpose as well. For what is truly delightful is healthful, and what is healthful is useful. An orator, says Erasmus, who employs histrionics to entertain by facetiousness, levity, trivia, and immodest jokes, will leave the audience with nothing useful. Real delight, instead, springs from that wholesome grace which runs through the entire speech just as blood flows through the whole body and thereby makes it sound. Therefore, 'it is the most healthful things that delight the hearers the most.' Eloquence is most powerful when it changes (*flectere*) the person, when it seizes (*rapere*) the affections.[113]

Like its kin, vehemence, the elocutionary virtue of delight appeals to the virtues of the moral life, only more indirectly than incisively, alluring more than challenging, healing rather than cutting. *Delectare* (the function of *jucunditas*) eventually joins the transforming purpose of *movere* or *flectere* (the function of *vehementia*). Both virtues serve the same moral end of speech, even as vehemence addresses the intense passions, whereas delight appeals to the milder emotions.[114] Erasmus generally mentioned vehemence and delight together. But when it came to the question of which of the two is to be preferred he seemed to opt for mediating delight because he associated it with both the harmony of nature and the healing function of medicine, an important image of Erasmus' reforming program. Uncontrolled, confrontational vehemence of speech, on the other hand, can turn into linguistic coercion. Therefore, if probability, evidence, and perspicuity constitute the lower virtues of speech (even though they are also part of delight), and vehemence, gravity, dignity, and keeness represent the higher virtues of speech, Erasmus settled on the middle virtues of attraction and delight which in the long run effect the same transformation as vehemence. It is thus the middle that keeps the extremes on both sides in balance.

The same can be observed with regard to the three kinds of style. Erasmus coordinated the figures of speech not only with the virtues of speech and the functions of speaking but also with what Quintilian called *genera dicendi* and what he himself termed *character orationis*.[115] Accordingly, 'the quality of similitude changes the character of speech' into *jucundus, grandis, acris, mediocris,* and *humilis,* respectively. But beyond the three traditional kinds of elocution (*humile, mediocre* [*jucundum*], *grande* [*acre*]), Erasmus mentioned several others. It is important to note, though, that the characters of speech, just like the virtues of speech, are concentrated on similitude (or *collatio,* or allegory, for that matter), for 'divine Scripture everywhere abounds with this schema, especially the evangelical manner of speaking.'[116]

The three kinds of style traditionally had been associated with the functions of speaking: teaching and proving with the low style; delighting and conciliating with the middle style; moving and changing with the sublime style.[117] While Erasmus could join *docere* with *probatio, delectare* (*conciliare*) with *jucunditas,* and *movere* with *vehementia,*[118] he obviously was loath to follow strict classifications. Style is not an end in itself. It is rather determined by the figures of speech (especially metaphor, similitude, and allegory) which in turn depend on the virtues of speech (copiousness, delight, and vehemence), on the functions of speaking (teaching, delighting, and moving) and ultimately on the kinds of speech (judicial, persuasive, and laudatory rhetoric). Since Erasmus fixed his attention on persuasive rhetoric and on the function of delighting as the most suitable means to interpret and use the figurative language of Scripture, he preferred also the middle style of conciliation – a literary expression readily applicable as a theological symbol for the reconciliation in Christ.

It is the *genus suasorium* (and secondarily the *genus encomiasticum*) that is decisive for speaking in the ecclesiastical office.[119] Teaching by the method of proving does not play a significant role in the preacher's work – except in case of convicting heretics. Far from being a *patronus forensis,* the preacher has little in common with the *genus judiciale.*[120] For sacred oratory appeals to the consciences of all human beings, not just the judge's; it does not treat of human laws, but divine oracles; it does not expose the causes of human errors, but accuses the consciences of all who are bad, and defends all who make simple mistakes. The preacher does not attempt to win over a judge in favor of the accused but attempts to reconcile all equally to God.[121] On the whole, then, Erasmus assigned teaching by proving to the judicial kind of speaking, delighting and moving to the persuasive kind of speaking, and praising to the epideictic kind of speaking.

Nevertheless, even if teaching as proving is remote from the ministerial office, instruction as such is certainly not dispensable, provided that it serves the purpose of persuasion. Like delighting and moving, teaching is part and parcel of persuasive speech.[122] Indeed, among the special duties of a bishop/priest (administering the sacraments, praying for the people, judging, and ordaining) the highest is teaching. 'Teaching includes sound doctrine, admonition, reprove, consolation, and bearing down on those who rail against the evangelical truth.' The usefulness of teaching surpasses even the celebration of the Eucharist, the central function of traditional priesthood.[123]

The preacher's duties, says Erasmus in another place, consist of teaching, persuading, exhorting, consoling, counselling, and admonishing. 'We teach so that the hearer understands ... We persuade the hearer to willingly embrace what is honest and useful.'[124] While persuasion concerns primarily the ethical aspect of speech, teaching is persuasive as well if it brings the hearer not only to understand but also to believe what is being said. In a passage where Erasmus joins teaching, delighting, and changing, he maintains that 'by teaching we bring it about that the subject is understood and believed (*persuadeatur*) ... For people are not delighted or moved by what they neither understand nor believe.'[125]

Teaching, then, is a necessary part of theological persuasion, except that it is preparatory because it concerns knowledge (that is, understanding and believing) more than enjoyment and emotion. Presenting the subject clearly and evidently, it makes the subject matter insightful. Showing verisimilitude by means of probability, it renders the subject matter convincing so that it becomes plausible. In other words, teaching is the epistemological side of persuasion, whereas delighting and moving are the ethical side of persuasion. In theological terms, teaching appeals to the hearers' faith, delighting and moving to their love.

4 PRUDENTIA; JUDICIUM, CONSILIUM

Although Erasmus appealed to the rhetoricians for his notion of prudence, he expanded this concept beyond its traditional scope. In fact, the idea of prudence informed his thinking so pervasively that it must be regarded as a one of his leading hermeneutical principles. With the rhetoricians he affirmed: 'No one speaks well unless speaking aptly, even if otherwise using ornate, copious, and splendid language ... The precepts of art must yield to prudence.' This means that the bond between *prudentia*, *aptum*, and *bene dicere* is so strong that the precepts of art are useless unless guided by prudence. In fact, rhetoric and prudence are at bottom one and the same: 'Rhetoric is nothing else than prudence of speaking (*dicendi prudentia*).'[126] Mentioned in the *Ratio* and elaborated in *Ecclesiastes* I, the notion of prudence is fully developed in *Ecclesiastes* II and III. No wonder that it makes up the subject of the conclusion of book III, the culmination of the whole work (if one takes book IV to be a sort of appendix). The virtue of prudence provides no doubt a fundamental rhetorical and theological principle for both biblical interpretation and sacred oratory.

From the beginning, Erasmus linked the rhetorical virtue of prudence with the Christian virtue of faith. The *Ratio* speaks of 'simple prudence and prudent simplicity' along with the Christian's innocence, charity, mildness, and most certain faith.[127] 'Evangelical discourse,' explains *Ecclesiastes* I, 'requires not only the preacher's faith, but also prudence. Faith pertains to the simplicity of the dove, prudence to the caution of the serpent.' It goes on to say that faithful preachers teach nothing but the divine commandments and in all things look to both God's glory and the advantage of the sacred flock. It is, on the other hand, the purpose of prudence 'to discern from the circumstances of time, places, and persons, what is to be applied to whom, when, and by what moderation.'[128] The preachers thereby imitate Jesus who showed 'the shape and model of a teacher of the gospel, who is wise (prudent) enough not to entrust the mysteries of an elevated doctrine to the hearts of the ignorant all at once, and who is gentle enough to bear with those who are still weak and imperfect until they advance to higher things.'[129]

Therefore, whoever prepares for ministry must not only know the mysteries of sacred Scripture but also develop sound judgment and uncommon prudence.[130] 'A prudent steward will husband the truth – bring it out, I mean, when the business requires it and bring it out so much as is requisite and bring out for every man what is appropriate for him.'[131] 'It is this gentleness in teaching, this prudence in husbanding the word of God that conquered the world and made it pass under the yoke of Christ as no military force, no subtle philosophy, no eloquent rhetoric, no human violence or cunning could ever have done.'[132] In a word, the preacher must be a *vir prudens et pius* who knows how to select from the mysteries of Scripture that which is appropriate and beneficial for the Christian congregation.¹³³

Erasmus divided prudence into *judicium* and *consilium*. Judgment and counsel are human faculties that arise from the speaker's natural disposition rather than from the precepts of art. Notwithstanding that, judgment and counsel become subsequently also human abilities acquired along with the speaker's skill in examining the circumstances of the subject matter under discussion.¹³⁴ Consequently, prudence is first of all a gift of nature; but then it is confirmed by education and practice. With natural prudence present, students acknowledge the precepts of art as something familiar instead of learning them as something new.¹³⁵ Without natural prudence, art can produce but poor and affected speech. This is why 'no one reasons more ineptly than those who are naturally stupid and have learned [the rules of] dialectic too scrupulously (*superstitiose*).' Rather than letting art stifle nature, 'it is often the highest art to conceal art,' but only after one has appropriated the skills of speaking by using the precepts of art.¹³⁶

Just as natural prudence is first an innate endowment, so is spiritual prudence above all a gift of the Holy Spirit. Moreover, just as natural prudence profits also from those dialectical and rhetorical skills that are acquired by putting the precepts of art to use, so the Holy Spirit does not destroy the individual's inborn talents but uses and completes them.¹³⁷ With the Holy Spirit enhancing their natural ability, sacred orators should therefore practice, for a time and moderately, the art of dialectic to develop the skills to judge prudently the circumstances of a subject matter under consideration. Yet these skills must become habitual. They must turn into a second nature and exactly thereby conceal the artist's art. In other words, the functional habit of art cultivates the ontological habit of nature in such a way that art returns to nature. Language is regenerated to its true nature. Similarly, the gift of the Holy Spirit perfects both nature and art in such a way that they are again capable of reflecting the invisible world.

It seems therefore that for Erasmus prudence itself is objectively given, on the one hand, by nature, and on the other hand by the Spirit who perfects it. But then it is also subjectively acquired by the use of the precepts of art. This being so, does the same go for its offspring, judgment and counsel? As we might expect, Erasmus does not always make clear distinctions. Nevertheless, on closer examination it appears that for him judgments derive for the most part from the use of the precepts of art,[138] whereas counsel seems to come predominantly from prudence proper. For judgment concerns the speaker's discernment of certain and manifest things. Counsel has more to do with the speaker's intuitive perception of doubtful and obscure things that are not close at hand. 'We apply judgment to what is obvious and accessible; we use counsel for the more remote and uncertain things that are sometimes derived from a distance beyond a cause.'[139] Since hardly anyone possesses such a felicitous natural *habitus* as to be able to arrive at a clear and correct judgment of what is obvious and accessible, the rules of dialectic must be known. But these precepts of art are of little help unless they pass through frequent use over into one's dispositon as if into nature.[140]

Judgment, we venture to say, relates indirectly to prudence; counsel relates directly to prudence. A judgment is prudent when it arises from the orator's intuition which is first instinctive[141] but then also cultivated by a limited and reasonable use of the precepts of art. To be sure, prudence itself originates in the natural *habitus* of the speaker. But the capability of judging, although it relies on the art of dialectic, eventually becomes an acquired, cultivated habit that turns into a second nature. To develop this habit, temporary and moderate studies in the precepts of dialectic are necessary. They facilitate more certain and prompt judgments in the same way as learning the rules of rhetoric enable a more eloquent speech. Yet the goal of both the art of dialectic and the art of rhetoric is to conceal art.

Certainly, Erasmus never failed to reject any claim of dialectic to hegemony. If dialectic sets itself up as an independent discipline by attempting to lord it over grammar and rhetoric instead of submitting to their authority, whatever persuasive power it possesses turns into a coercive force: *Dialectica cogit*.[142] Nevertheless, Erasmus considered the knowledge of judging to be so elementary that it precedes, temporally though not essentially, the act of speaking: 'It is necessary that judgment comes before eloquence, judicious discernment before speaking, just as in nature the spring comes before the river, and in art, the outline before the picture.'[143] This judgment is a matter of 'reason or intellect by which we know and judge ... Related are conjecture (*opinio*) and knowledge (*scientia*). Conjecture has to do with probable things, knowledge with evident things.'[144]

That is to say, judgment operates in a double way. For one thing, it produces knowledge by using dialectical syllogisms to ascertain direct evidence from the causal connection of actual facts. But more importantly, it also infers verisimilitude of probable things indirectly by conjecture, that is, by using rhetorical syllogisms (*enthymema*).[145] In the first case, cogent reasons bring about conclusive judgments. In the second case, deliberation arrives at verisimilitude. As the first use of reason produces *scientia*, so the second produces *opinio*. It is not clear, though, what *opinio* has to do with prudence or even with *sapientia*, especially if wisdom is enobled by virtue and raised to the level of divine wisdom, or the wisdom of Christ, which is in stark contrast to the wisdom of this world, or preposterous wisdom.[146] Regarding both dialectical and rhetorical reasoning, however, Erasmus was not loath to recommend the study of Aristotle, as long as the preacher conceals the art of dialectic and 'clarifies the subtleties of reason in such a way that the people find him speaking truly rather than cleverly, making obscure things clear, the hidden obvious, the troublesome easy.'[147]

It would be erroneous, though, to conclude that Erasmus assigned judgment to grammar alone, whereas counsel belongs exclusively to rhetoric. The competence of judgment reaches farther than the external side of language. The rational capacity of judging not only determines facts and draws logical conclusions but also orders material for speech and makes comparisons (*collatio*). Certainly, correct, clear, and evident judgments serve the grammatical virtue of purity and perspicuity. This is why expertise in the original languages is necessary, for 'dialectic is blind without grammar,' depending as it does on words by means of which it enunciates, defines, divides, and collects.[148] However, also for rhetorical invention and disposition, judgments are indispensable in that they collate material in an intelligent order. The art of dialectic is particularly useful for argumentation in *probatio* as long as one keeps in mind that the faculty of reasoning is an intellectual power of nature that precedes dialectical art.[149] On the other hand, proof by arguments rests no less on prudence as leading to right judgment.[150]

The role that dialectic plays in rhetoric is especially clear from

Erasmus' understanding of *ratiocinatio* or reasoning[151] within the area of disposition and proof where reasoning serves the purpose of comparison. So for instance, reasoning determines the circumstances of persons and things. Or, in a case where no certain law applies, reasoning summons proof from other laws.[152] Moreover, it may come as a surprise but reasoning renders a service in elocution too (even though in this area prudence as counsel is primary as far as figurative language is concerned). Reasoning in terms of comparison (*collatio*) is definitely part of elocution. So *ratiocinatio* is not only instrumental for determining the proper place of *loci* within the order of speech but is also conducive to amplifying speech.[153] As a figure of speech, *ratiocinatio* as *dialogismon* is 'most appropriate for the preacher to accommodate to the crowd ignorant as it is of eloquence, for it arouses their attention and is suited to make them teachable; it renders speech lucid, lively, and pleasant.' Indeed, similitude or comparison (*collatio*) involves a strong component of reasoning.[154] Last but not least, comparative reasoning applies even to scriptural interpretation: 'Since there is no Scripture that clearly defines what we inquire about, the divine will is gathered by reasoning from various places in Scripture compared among themselves.'[155]

All the same, Erasmus spared no pains to point out the dangers of a scrupulous, superstitious, anxious use of dialectic reasoning, devoid of natural intuition and spiritual discernment. At the worst, dialectic arrives at *praeposterum judicium*, meaning that the orator puts last things first, makes the most of the least, and thus reverses the order. This inversion can amount to the perversion of the order, a situation worse than a mere disturbance of the order (*perturbatio ordinis*). Together with *oblivio mediocritatis*, Erasmus thus put preposterous judgment in line with *superstitio* and *supercilium*.[156] Preposterous judgment 'attributes more to those things that are of lesser moment, less to those things that properly pertain to the matter.' It also does not recognize what lies between beginning and end, between foundation and top, lacking discretion about those things which need to be observed for the time being, even as the Christian hastens to the more excellent way that Christ has paved.[157]

As examples of the effects of preposterous judgment, we see that the right to ordain is relegated to factious and mercenary bishops; the power to baptize and absolve sins is committed to unexamined priests; the faculty of consecrating the Lord's body and blood is permitted to those who sometimes are unworthy of feast and consolation. What is the most excellent of all, the office of teaching, is thrown to the most common priests and monks.[158] As a rule, topsy-turvy judgment is common among the vulgar crowd who choose the worst for the best, embrace the least good for the greatest, the belly for the brain, the temporal for the eternal.[159] Such is the preposterous judgment of mortals that they admit to the angelic office men neither of tamed affections, nor pure from vices, nor instructed in letters, nor inspired by the Spirit, or firm in faith, or fervent in charity, not to speak of moderation or sound understanding.[160]

Preposterous judgments make for perverted speech. Incorrect judgments produce inept speech. But correct judgments perform a positive rhetorical function in that they rightly ascertain a particular setting of persons, things, times, and places. It takes *consilium*, however, to provide the power of discernment to accommodate to a variety of persons, things, times, and places so as to select what is of advantage to the hearer. In terms of rhetorical theology, therefore, counsel is a function of *aptum* or *decorum*. It not only accommodates itself to Scripture to recognize the divine harmony in a variety of circumstances but also adjusts to the audience to apply the divine truth in proportion to the specific conditions of a variety of human situations. 'With a clear eye we determine more certainly the differences of external things; with a clean heart we more rightly see God concealed under the covers of Scriptures.'[161] Since the 'eternal truth reflects itself variously in diverse things,' it is also not enough to interpret Scripture according to the fourfold sense but also to 'consider which degrees (*gradus*) there are in each of these, which differences, and which method of treatment (*ratio tractandi*).'[162] Rhetorical counsel determines for Erasmus even the traditional, fourfold interpretation of Scripture.

Counsel is in this connection synonymous with prudence. It is characteristic of prudence in general 'to discern from the circumstances of time, places, and persons, what is to be applied to whom, when, and by what moderation.'[163] As to sacred oratory, specifically, it must be the preacher's goal to cultivate a prudent and single-eyed heart so as to discern easily 'what is to be left unsaid, what to be said, before whom, at which time, in what way speech should be moderated, knowing with Paul to change one's voice and to become all things to all men, whenever it seems expedient for the salvation of the hearers.' After an overall theme for a sermon has been made clear, for instance, prudence serves as a criterion for teaching, moving, and delighting since it chooses 'what seems to be more useful for teaching, more effective for moving the souls of the hearers, and more appropriate to hold the minds of people by some kind of pleasure.'[164] In short, the purpose of prudence is accommodation; the motive power is Christian love; the goal is to lead to Christ.[165]

Accommodation and moderation go hand in hand. Given the significance of moderation in Erasmus' thinking as a whole, it is not surprising to find him stressing repeatedly the moderating effect of prudence. So with reference to human licence, prudence not only tempers the excessive freedom of the people but also qualifies what is permitted to preachers. Their freedom from the outdated rules in the old law of external observations is limited by the standard of expediency contained in the new law of love. For instance Paul, possessed as he was with singular prudence, 'did not always consider what is allowed but what is expedient ... He so accommodated himself to all that he sometimes seemed to be at odds with himself and make contradictory statements, although he was in every respect utterly at one with himself.'[166] As Horace had already said, 'Strength wanting in counsel collapses under its own weight; strength moderated, even the gods raise in higher degree.'[167]

In the same way, the preacher's speech to the people must be moderated by prudence so as to take 'a variety of gender, age, conditions, natural dispositions, opinions, stations in life, and customs' into account lest 'while healing the errors of some he gives to others an occasion to err, and while hunting out vices he teaches vices, or while exposing evil deeds he inadvertently incites to sedition.'[168] Two things, says Erasmus at the end of *Ecclesiastes* I, help teachers to render hearers teachable: the teacher's love and authority. But both must be tempered by prudence which so accommodates to the hearers' circumstances as to insure their advantage, their advancement toward piety. While preachers should strive in love to please all, they must nonetheless have Paul's word in mind: 'All is allowed, but not all is expedient.' Likewise, the preachers' authority must offend neither the people's backwardness nor their customs.[169]

Moreover, prudence has not only to do with expediency but also with opportunity. While prudence enables the Christian orator to find the proper means and suitable ways to accommodate to a variety of conditions, what is decisive for a successful accommodation is the choice of the opportune moment. This does certainly not mean that Erasmus was an opportunist in our modern, derogatory sense of lacking principle and character. Rather, the humanist understood *opportunitas* in the classical sense of a fit time, an appropriate coming together of persons, things, and circumstances for speech to be useful.[170]

Erasmus took opportunity to be something like a temporal correlative of prudence. For one thing, simple time (*tempus*) falls under three heads: past, present, and future. However, there is also a quality time which the Greeks call *kairos* and the Latins *opportunitas*.[171] 'To every thing there is a season' (*omnia suum habent tempus*,) says the Ecclesiastes of the Old Testament, showing 'what is fitting for each time so that the pious person adjusts to every time.'[172] And 'consider the due time' (*nosce tempus*) says the adage.[173] As far as pedagogy is concerned, Erasmus advises: 'When something is done at the right time progress will be smooth,' and 'We learn best when the time is right.'[174] It is therefore of extreme importance for the theologian to know how to discriminate between the times (*ratio temporum*) as much as it is for the Christian to adapt all deliberation of time to an occasion for good deeds, even if that means on occasion to wait for a better, more suitable moment.[175]

As for biblical interpretation, that means that 'the truth is to be opened to different people in different ways according to the deliberation of times and persons, yet without suppressing it when circumstances require.' *Opportunitas* and *dissimulatio* come together. For it is allowable to conceal the truth at a time when the hearer is either unworthy or not yet submissive to the mystery. Speaking with prudence, therefore, the preacher neither diminishes the truth when holding something back for the moment nor adds anything when accommodating the naturally fecund Scripture to various meanings, provided that they are pious and useful.[176] 'We must not disclose everything to everyone, ... but the gospel doctrine must be dispensed only at the appropriate time and according to the understanding of the listeners.'[177] 'Indeed, while it can never be lawful to go against the truth, it may sometimes be expedient to conceal it in the circumstances. And it is always of the first importance how timely, how opportune, and how well judged your production of it is.'[178] 'I know that sometimes it is a good man's duty to conceal the truth, and not to publish it regardless of times and places, before every audience and by every method, and everywhere complete.'[179]

This discrimination of times applies particularly to the time difference between the Old and New Testament, which often clarifies a question concerning law. Many things that were allowed to the Jews before the law was proclaimed are not allowed to them under the law. But what was allowed to the Jews under the old law is not allowed to us under the new law. Conversely, much is required of us that was not required of the Jews.[180] Also, while the gift of the Spirit is the same, it is given differently according to the provision of time.[181]

Altogether, then, prudence is a rhetorical virtue akin to the Christian virtue of faith and covering judgment and counsel. Prudence is governed by *aptum* (or *decorum*) and *moderatio* (or *temperantia*). Caution, discretion, and forebearance serve the purpose of accommodation, whether it is adapting the interpretation to the nature of the text; adjusting the literary genre and style to the nature of the subject matter to be treated; fitting the instruction, according to Socratic maieutic and irony, to the natural disposition of the student; or adjusting the divine truth in Scripture to the the times and conditions of the hearers. Accommodation and moderation call for a discriminating decision as to whether or not an intended word will turn out useful for others. As a result, Erasmus in his own attempt at reformation chose suitable moments for reasons of expediency, after having thought things over prudently and anticipated consequences carefully. Rather than preaching the gospel in and out of season, the man for all seasons observed the motto 'all in due course' in order to hurt nobody and to enable everybody to make progress in piety, faith, and love.

5 ADFECTUS; ETHOS, PATHOS

Speech of the suasory kind aims at drawing the audience toward the advantage of moral virtue (*honestum, utilitas*). According to Erasmus, this goal is best achieved by means of *amplificatio rerum*, an elocutionary device that enables the orator at least to influence if not to inflame the hearers' affections. While the amplification of words modulates speech so as to please the hearers, the amplification of things appeals more or less intensely to their disposition of mind (*adfectus*).¹⁸² Beyond teaching and delighting, therefore, the speaker is charged with moving the audience by 'the foremost power of eloquence ... that changes the direction (*flectere*) of, i.e., that seizes (*rapere*) the affections of the hearers.' Especially the conclusion of a speech calls for an appeal to the affections, since they 'are more readily excited in a hearer already persuaded and willingly inclined ... to a vehement movement of the mind.'¹⁸³

For moving speech to be appropriate and therefore effective, prudence must guide the orator in determining the particular circumstances of persons, things, and times. Judicial discourse, for instance, is most persuasive when it impels the judges to reveal by their tears and total bearing even before they pronounce a verdict that they have changed their mind. However, the preacher would be amiss to stir the intense passions of a rude and unschooled crowd whose sins are for the most part due to corrupt affections instead of ignorance of the truth. It is one thing to move the affections of a civil, teachable congregation. It is quite another thing to stir up the violent passions of a crass and listless mob by forcing rather than teaching them, by dragging instead of leading them. Nevertheless, no crowd is so dull that persistent teaching would not yield some moral advantage.¹⁸⁴

Erasmus rejected 'the dogma of the Stoics according to which none of the affections are worthy of approval.'¹⁸⁵ He accepted the psychological and moral importance of the human affections which he saw, true to the structure of his overall thought, from both a dualistic and a trichotomous perspective. He not only divided them into two distinct groups but also interposed a middle region of moderate affections between the base and the pure ones. So the affections come first in two forms, 'the one milder and as it were comic, the other more vehement or tragic.' The first kind is called by the Greeks *ethos*, *mores* in Latin. The Greeks call the other kind *pathos*, whereas the Latins have no proper word for it, even though some take the genus for the species and call them *adfectus*, others call them confusions (*perturbationes*), intense motions of the mind (*motus animorum*), passionate desires (*cupiditates*), or mental diseases (*morbi*).¹⁸⁶

Yet nothing, Erasmus goes on to say, speaks against arranging a third group in the middle between them, as Quintilian had done. For neither *ethos* nor *mores* express properly 'the common or more moderate affections which everyone experiences, which are in accordance with nature and are recognized by all, which delight more than upset, even if they sometimes move to tears.' Such natural dispositions are parental love and other affections of person, family, nation, or gender. These affections move the heart more mildly or more strongly according as they border on the higher or lower affections. So Quintilian distinguished between love that belongs to *ethos* and love that is akin to *pathos*. *Caritas* signifies the natural affection between parents and children, or between friends or relations, whereas *amor* denotes 'a vehement affection that torments us by pulling us into two directions and snatches away judgment and peace of mind.' Foremost among the passionate affections are compassion, indignation, love (*amor*) and hate.[187]

In another passage, Erasmus distinguished between the dense (*crassi*) affections of the heart (like rage, ire, hate, love [*amor*], shame, fear, hope, and joy) and the more concealed (*retrusiores*) affections of the heart (like modesty or arrogance, fear or contempt of God, disregard or love of riches, firmness or levity, chastity or lewdness, knowledge or ignorance, and last but not least the most spiritual affections, namely, sincerity of faith, hope, and love [*caritas*]).[188]

From the circumstances of persons and things the orator will draw both kinds of affections, ethos and pathos, in order to show what is to be sought and what is to be avoided. But the middle affection, charity, serving as it does as the way to unite human beings with God, is of paramount importance. Always charity is to be inflamed, especially 'Christian charity which above all loves God as the highest good, and for this reason so loves whatever it loves at all in the created world that it loves God himself and glorifies him in all things. For what excites love in us, is found in God in the highest and ineffable form ... Like is favourably inclined toward like ... Love begets love ... Charity unites family and friendship ... Whoever loves God, has God.' Affinity and affection go hand in hand. *Simile similis amicum est* and *amor gignit amorem* – these are for Erasmus proverbial expressions of the link between natural human love and love of God. However, he goes out of his way to say that God's love in Christ for us, even as enemies, always precedes our love to God.[189] Our love of God is a response to God's love for us.

Regarding sacred rhetoric, nothing stirs the hearers' pious

affections more effectively than if a preacher is filled with pious affections. Conversely, no one calms bad affections better than a preacher who is free from bad affections.[190] But since the pious affections in the preacher's heart are sometimes seemingly asleep (for even those who are inspired by the gift of the Spirit have this precious treasure but in earthen vessels), there are three ways to arouse them: first through *imaginatio* or *phantasia* by which one represents to oneself through concentrated thinking the images of the things to be articulated ('for we are more vehemently moved by what we see with our eyes than by what we only hear'); then by *evidentia* which presents the whole form of the subject matter so to the hearer's mind that it appears to be displayed to the eyes rather than spoken; and finally by reading passages of Scripture fit for inflaming the affections, plus fervent prayer.[191]

Thus we see that for Erasmus the affections are not only dispositions of the mind but also movements of the heart (emotions) as they are directed by the mind's orientation either toward moral character or toward turpitude. Suasory speech confirms and intensifies the positive inclinations of the mind as much as it negates and changes the negative proclivities of the mind. The positive affections in both speaker and hearer are a matter of natural and pious disposition, aimed as they are at the good and eventually perfected by the most spiritual affections of faith, love, and hope. The negative affections in turn so deviate from nature and spirit as to lead at least to confusion, if not to perversion and destruction.

It would be erroneous, though, to assume that the affections constitute nothing but internal dispositions and emotions. On the contrary, 'the internal form of the mind migrates into the external human being and transforms him altogether into its image ... It happens more often than not that the affections of the heart shine forth in the outer appearance of the human being.'[192] Moreover, the mind not only produces the images of things to be articulated in speech but also forms ethical opinions that issue in moral conduct. And it is in this way that the affections link up, and become virtually synonymous, with their corresponding virtues (or vices). Pious affections arise from natural affection. But then they surpass their origin in nature, become capable of the spirit, and are conducive to the Christian virtues. Erasmus chose in this connection the metaphor 'feet' to symbolize the ethical disposition of the mind. 'Reason is in the head; the affections are in the feet.' The feet, the lowest part of the body and closest to the dirty ground, must be continually cleansed from all worldy filth for the preacher to climb up the mountain toward the lofty Christian virtues.'[193] For this reason, 'the theological profession rests more on affections than on clever arguments.'[194]

Erasmus apparently found the traditional division of the affections into milder and harsher ones, or into more concealed (rarefied) and more obvious (dense) ones, insufficient on two counts. For one thing, it did not adequately account for the moderate affections, particularly love, straddling as it does both sides and therefore making possible transition. For another thing, he apparently thought it was not as such suitable for a theological perspective. It neither provided for an extension into a trichotomous structure nor was it based on the sharp contrast of an absolute dualism necessary to accommodate a Platonizing theology. Therefore, he adopted a more polarized view of the affections by aligning them with the dualism he received from the patristic interpretation of Scripture, all the while emphasizing the moderating effect of the natural affections in the middle as transitions between vices and virtues.

Because it is God who is in the last analysis the author of love, concord, order, and unity, and the devil who is the source of hate, discord, perversion, and ruin, the natural affections can turn toward God as much as they can fall prey to the flesh, the world, and the devil, the parent of vice.[195] The human affections, neutral as they originally are, exhibit therefore a double tendency. On the one hand, they can become flesh in contrast to the spirit; they can corrupt even the mass of common Christians; they can distort scriptural interpretation; they can so cloud the judgment of the mind that there is no judgment at all or preposterous judgment; they often draw the clergy away from sincerity of office. They must be uprooted if they are unwholesome.[196] On the other hand, if the human affections are neither unbridled nor attached to vice, they are to be used for progress in piety. For even the passionate movements of the mind are never so violent that they cannot be restrained by reason and redirected toward virtue. So after the affections nearest to the senses have enabled us to judge what to seek and to avoid, they should be abandoned altogether, while the affections similar to virtues, even if they appear at first sight ambiguous, can be corrected and appropriately deflected towards their adjacent virtue.[197]

6 VIRTUS; HONESTUM, UTILITAS

Within the triad of virtue, honesty, and utility, the most significant concept for Erasmus was that of virtue – a concept he used in the first place to align *honestum* with the philosophical virtues and then to relate these to the theological virtues, their Christian perfection. The civic quality of honesty (the 'honourable' in the classical meaning) was, of course, the main goal of traditional suasory speech, even though it had as *rectum* and *legitimum* also to do with the aim of judicial discourse, justice, and as *decorum* and *laudabile* was part of the objective of epideictic oratory, praise.[198] Free human beings derive the rules of conduct from their sense of honesty. But it was only when Erasmus transferred the idea of honesty into the larger context of virtue that he was able to connect rhetoric with moral philosophy and finally with theology. Virtue combines honesty with faith, love, and hope by way of prudence, justice, fortitude, and temperance.

The concept of utility was for Erasmus closely associated, though not identical, with that of honesty as it provides the motive and means to achieve the goal of suasory speech or, for that matter, to prevent the opposite, i.e., the dishonourable. 'Utility depends on putting forth advantageous things (*commoda*) and driving out disadvantageous things (*incommoda*).' But since in human affairs both kinds are mixed together, the orator must choose and emphasize the advantageous things, while speaking against the disadvantageous things, or at least belittle them in case they cannot be denied or readily concealed. By negating what is disadvantageous, we teach what is advantageous, and vice versa.[199]

The orator persuades to a virtuous life by showing not only what is beneficial (or harmful) to the hearers but also what is, through their good words (*benedictio*), their good will (*benevolentia*), and their good office (*beneficentia*), of service to others.[200] Consequently, the speaker must be aware of the hearers' situation in order to discern what kind of profit it is expedient to speak of in the circumstances. 'Although the preacher persuades to nothing but honesty, we nevertheless speak of virtue in one way to the pious, in another way to the wicked and seditious, in one way to those corrupted with depraved opinions, in another to the doubtful.'[201] Utility is thus akin to prudence as it determines expediency within a particular situation. Yet it comes also close to the meaning of virtue inasmuch as it intends the same effect. In a word, utility connects prudence with virtue by way of expedience.[202] Beyond encouraging the audience to make progress in the way of the general virtues for reasons of personal and civic advantage ('We persuade the hearer to be willing to embrace what is honest and useful'[203]), the preacher instills the Christian virtues of faith, love, and hope as singularly useful for salvation. The classical virtues are therefore propaedeutic, ancillary to the Christian life, just as rhetoric is to theology.

Utility looks to what is expedient not only in terms of the variety of persons but also in view of the variety of times. Erasmus reminded the preacher that although it is the same Spirit who imparts salvation to the human race, there is nevertheless more utility to evangelical preaching than to Old Testament prophecy, since the spiritual gifts are distributed in proportion to the conditions at the time.[204] Indeed, even in the church there is an increasing usefulness for the believers as the dispensation of the gospel advances from external matters toward the perfect doctrine of Christ.[205] Therefore, to have the benefit of the Lord's flock at heart is a fundamental prerequisite for election to church office, for no one deserves the title of pastor who does not benefit the congregation.[206]

In the section of the *Ecclesiastes* where Erasmus deals with the parts of the suasory genre, he mentions the Stoics as those who admit only one proposition, honesty, since 'nothing is useful unless it is honest, and whatever is honest is useful exactly because it is honest.' On the other side, those who distinguish between utility and honesty believe that *utilitas* can be subdivided into other parts. The concept *honestum* is not simple, either, for it can be understood as that which is right by itself (*rectum*) and as that which is beautiful (*pulcrum*) and proper (*decorum*). What is right according to nature includes: the divine law (*fas*), piety, justice, equity, magnanimity, and mildness, in short, all species of virtues. One can add to this what is lawful (*legitimum*), that is, what is prescribed by the laws and the legacy of divine writings, commended by the examples of celebrated humans, and received by long custom.[207]

Returning to the same point, as if dissatisfied with the rather sweeping statement he just made, Erasmus is more specific: 'Therefore, to the genus of *honestum* belong divine law (*fas*) and its violation (*nefas*), whether according to nature or contrary to nature: piety and impiety toward God and gods, toward the fatherland, toward parents and children, toward teachers and those whose kindness protects us, and all the countless virtues and vices. Add to these what is lawful (*legitimum*, with its companion, equity, which is the moderation of laws), what is customary (*consuetum*), and what is approved (*probatum*) by the authority and examples of dignified men – or the contrary.'[208] That is to say, honesty corresponds (1) to the divine law as revealed in nature, thus coinciding with natural piety and natural virtues. Next, honesty arises also from a positive attitude toward (2) human laws and (3) received custom. Besides these major qualities of moral excellence (*pium*, *justum* and *aequum*, *decorum* and *laudabile*), Erasmus lists further parts of suasory speech (*utile*, *tutum*, *jucundum*, *necessarium*, *possibile*, and *facile*).[209]

It is important to note that Erasmus defined honesty first of all as that which is right by itself (*rectum*) because it corresponds to the divine law (*fas*) and is in accordance with nature (*secundum naturam*). The relation of honesty with both the divine law and with nature has priority. While honesty is also concerned with human law and equity and with established custom and mores, the divine law as reflected in the harmony of nature constitutes the foremost authority to which honesty must submit itself. And what is true of honesty holds also good for piety and virtue: *Virtus secundum naturam est, vitium contra naturam.*[210] Therefore, what is pious 'sinks easily into the minds of all because it is greatly in accordance with nature,' especially the philosophy of Christ which, after all, represents the restoration of nature.[211] Just as Christ and virtue are nearly synonymous, so the devil and vice clearly belong together: 'Whoever moves toward virtue alone, strives after Christ. Whoever is a servant of vices, gives himself up to the devil.'[212] 'The love of Christ, the love of heavenly and honorable things, will naturally bring with it a repugnance for passing things and a hatred of dishonourable things.'[213]

Virtue, according to Socrates, concerns the knowledge of what to seek and what to flee,[214] that is, *honestum* on the one side, and *turpia* on the other, with *necessaria* in the middle.[215] So, as Christians hasten toward the goal of the highest good, whatever they happen to encounter in the way should be rejected or accepted according as it eases or hinders their progress. These things fall generally into three classes: Some are so dishonourable that they never can be honourable, such as avenging injury or bearing ill will toward others. These are always to be shunned. Some things are in themselves so honourable that they cannot be dishonourable, like good will toward all, aiding friends with honest means, hating vice, and enjoying pious talk. Some are in between, such as health, beauty, strength, eloquence, learning, and the like. Of these none should be sought for their own sake or indeed used except as they are conducive to the supreme goal.[216] The natural dispositions of human beings, says Erasmus in another context, are no doubt greatly varied. If something deeply implanted in our nature is connected with vice, we must strive to conform it with virtue. If our natural constitution is not complicated, we must beware that it does not fall into a related vice, like gravity turning into fierceness, harshness, and wildness, or gentleness into carelessness and disdain, or charm into seeking flattery.[217]

The genus of virtue includes the species of justice, liberality, prudence, fortitude, and temperance.[218] In a later passage, Erasmus reduced the the 'origins of all rightful actions' to the four philosophical virtues (prudence, justice, fortitude, and temperance) and correlated them as genera to the theological species: prudence to faith, justice to charity, fortitude to hope. 'Temperance is a species of justice teaching how much is to be assigned to the affections, how much to the body, how much to the mind, and how much is to be negated. To this extent it coincides equally with faith and hope inasmuch as it puts reins on the passionate desires, which by their commotions often both disturb the judgments of faith and obstruct the impulse of charity.'[219] Temperance moderates justice[220] (and charity) in that it looks for expedience and moral advantage in particular circumstances. It therefore functions in a similar way as utility and, further down the line, prudence.

At the end of the *Ecclesiastes*, where Erasmus brought his theology into a final synopsis, he drew a parallel between faith and reason (mind), knowledge, judgment, and prudence. Likewise, he related love with heart (soul), natural affections, will, and justice.[221] At first sight, then, faith is a matter of intellectual insight and love has to do with intention and moral action. Applying this to rhetoric, especially the duties of the speaker, it is safe to conclude that for Erasmus the teaching part of speech concerns knowledge in faith, while the moving part of speech aims at action in love. Faith and knowledge keep *flectere* from becoming too vehement by holding speech to its object; love and action prevent *docere* from turning static by moving speech to its objective. Keeping each other in balance, both make for the third duty of the speaker, mediating speech and mediatory action (*conciliare*).

But we have come to know Erasmus better than to assume that this is all. *Fides perficit intellectum; caritas perficit voluntatem* – that is the end of it all. It is faith that brings understanding to completion, just as it is charity that 'perfects the natural power of the will by which we strive after the wholesome and flee from the contrary.'[222] As to the definition of faith, it 'is a certain persuasion of all that is necessary for salvation,' or more specifically, 'a certain persuasion about the stories and teachings of sacred Scriptures, a certain trust in God's promises, and a full obedience by which the human being submits completely to the divine will.'[223] Faith perfects our natural, albeit obscured, power to know and judge. It holds the first place because it is the door to salvation.[224] For through faith God bestows on us the other gifts, and without faith we are unable to please God. Moreover, hope is more a part of faith than a different species. So the Bible sometimes speaks of faith in terms of trust and certain hope. To be sure, no one hopes who does not believe. But faith is not at once hope. For 'that part of a living faith is called hope by which we expect the promises of God.'[225]

To be sure, faith holds the first place among the theological virtues in terms of sequence. But the pre-eminent rank undoubtedly goes to Christian love. 'By charity we love God above all as the highest good, desire to enjoy him (*frui*), and for the sake of God are well disposed toward the neighbour.' Natural affections do not qualify as a theological virtue unless we love parents, spouses, and children for the sake of God and help them to walk in the way of salvation. So, love of God and love of neighbour belong together. For no one really loves God who does not love the neighbour, and vice versa. 'These two [sc faith and love] are the gist of human happiness: Through the eye and light of faith the human being may see without error what to seek and what to flee, and through charity carry out the dictates of faith. Faith begets charity; charity in turn nourishes faith by good works ... And increased faith again renders charity more lively. These two are the fountains of all virtues and good works – the fruit by which a good or bad tree is discerned. Faith is the root, charity the branches.'[226]

Erasmus sums up 'the whole gospel teaching, the whole life of Christ,' in his address *To the Pious Reader* of his *Paraphrase on John*: '[It] breathes a new and marvelous love ... This is of course the Christian love which teaches in brief whatever is taught in all the volumes of the Old Testament, all the books of the philosophers, all human laws; this is the love that of its own accord brings with it every virtue there is, and once and for all shuts out every vice. For since our highest happiness lies in knowledge, trust, and purity of life, we learn nothing more quickly or willingly than what we love passionately. Faith is as it were our eye, with which we see and know God, and that is enough for our eternal salvation and in accord with Holy Scripture. Love, which views nothing falsely, all things clearly, makes this eye pure, simple and dove-like ... True love urges upon us most convincingly this too, that we cast ourselves wholeheartedly upon him whom we wholeheartedly love.'[227]

Elocution, the art of expressing thought with appropriate words and in proper order, was the subject of this chapter. The elocutionary virtues most suitable for the task of biblical interpretation and preaching are for Erasmus those that organize speech in accordance with the equity of nature and the harmony of Christ. He therefore concentrated specifically on the clarity (and obscurity) of speech; on the comparison of similarities as the most appropriate way of communicating truth; on the appealing power of the figures of speech (*jucunditas*) that moves an audience toward moral transformation more gently than *vehementia*; on the central role allegory and metaphor play in theological discourse; on prudence which allows the speaker to accommodate to a variety of situations; on moderation as the balance between too much and too little; on *affectus*, a rhetorical and human quality that draws the hearers to the final goal of suasory speech, the moral life. The philosophical virtues are stepping stones to the theological virtues of faith, love, and hope, whereby faith perfects the natural intellect and charity perfects natural piety.

Conclusion

Instead of concluding with a number of propositions which define in concise form the findings of our research, we prefer to present, as Erasmus probably would have done, a synopsis of the highlights of our study.

Searching for Erasmus' biblical hermeneutic has led us to a distinct block of material from the mature period of his theological work: the *Ratio verae theologiae* at the beginning and the *Ecclesiastes* at the end, with the *Paraphrases* on the New Testament, the *Commentaries* on the Psalms, and other pertinent writings in between.

Our examination of his exegetical and homiletical method showed that Erasmus interpreted Scripture by means of a rhetorical theology that focused on the metaphorical quality of language. He believed that allegory, above all, mediates between similar things, while yet keeping opposite things apart. This double function of figurative language, separation and similarity, explains the apparent ambiguity in Erasmus' thought as well as his constant effort at conciliation. Equivocalness and balance characterize Erasmus' rhetorical stance, a stance that prefers consensus by persuasive dialogue to indoctrination by syllogistic dialectic.

But persuasive speech was by no means unsystematic. Rhetoric required that the *topoi* of discourse be arranged in an organic plan. Good speech must reflect the order of nature, which happens only when the art of rhetoric imitates nature. More importantly, since God accommodated the divine word to human speech, the Bible reveals an order higher than nature, that is, the arrangement of theological *loci* around the *scopus* Christ. Therefore, theologians are to imitate the invention, disposition, inverbation, and delivery of divine speech by recognizing the composition of its human expression, ordering its subject matter, internalizing its content, and communicating its power. Rhetoric provided Erasmus with the implements for finding theological commonplaces in Scripture, drawing from it a repertoire for knowing and living, and translating it into sacred oratory. But even as rhetoric served as a method of interpretation and communication, a Christocentric theology determined the substance of teaching and life.

Erasmus' appreciation for rhetoric placed him at the culmination of a tradition that can be called *theologia rhetorica*. Ciceronian rhetoric with its philological realism, philosophical probabilism, and civic moralism provided the means for concentrating on the theological substance of language. On the other hand, the Platonic assumption of a split between *res* and *verba* caused distrust in the external word, urging a *collatio visibilium ad invisibilia*. Like his beloved church Fathers, Origen, Jerome, and Augustine, Erasmus took rhetoric to be the handmaiden of theology. He saw a basic dualism bridged by an analogy between words and reality. Words have not completely lost their natural capacity of mirroring transcendent meanings. Language reveals and conceals the truth at the same time. The spirit enlivens the letter, even though the letter as such kills. Therefore, the dynamic of separation and participation in a language at once dualistic and symbolic is essential for understanding Erasmus' hermeneutic. He tried to overcome a basic dichotomy by assuming a metaphorical transition between word and truth.

Erasmus' comments on the usage of language in his own time reveal perspectives of historical deterioration and linguistic restoration. Words had gone flat and dry, detached from their true meaning and discrepant from reality. Only the ancient *bonae litterae* embody that truth which is useful for the moral life, for they address reality close to the origin and thus possess the power to persuade and transform. As soon as good language generates a second nature in the reader, it brings about a habit of right action: The literate person becomes the true representative of humanity. Speech humanizes in that it informs, forms, and transforms the human being. Therefore, good literature must be restored (*ad fontes*). The resulting literacy renders the reader humane and thus warrants cultural stability in correspondence with the harmony of nature. But what is more, *sacrae litterae* restore true religion through the spiritual renewal of the individual in the community of faith and love.

Language, literature, and literacy are central to Erasmus' world view. Metaphorical speech displays at first sight the natural order of things. But for spiritual insight it reveals the divine economy of the world, its disposition according to the dispensation of God's counsel of salvation. Moreover, metaphorical speech is the medium for this reality of nature and God to become actual in culture and religion. Language therefore communicates by mediating and uniting, creating community through consensus and concord. Or it may disrupt by separating and dividing, causing disagreement and destruction. Orderly speech corresponds to the order of the universe. Vicious speech creates disorder. Good language is a medium for both forming concepts that conform with reality and for framing opinions that inform responsible action. Evil, violent language, on the other hand, perverts the order of things and eventually issues in chaos. Ultimately, language places human beings in the company of God or the devil.

Beyond good literature, however, language has been raised to its highest power by the final and unique inverbation of Christ as God's word in Scripture. Although the Old Testament foreshadowed him, it is in the New Testament that the verbal incarnation of divinity has definitively taken place. Here the medium has become the mediator. Indeed, God's final revelation as contained in the story of Christ's person, teaching, and life supersedes even Jesus' earthly presence. While this divine epilogue perfects rather than destroys all good literature, Scripture possesses the highest authority and therefore also the supreme power of persuasion and transformation. This is so because its author is God and its *scopus* is Christ.

Biblical allegory serves to mediate between the letter and the spirit in the text and to transform the reader from the flesh into the spirit. Overcoming a basic dualism, this mediation (in Erasmus' hermeneutic) restores nature, regenerates human beings, and reconciles the world with God. Opposites are reconciled first in that the higher accommodates itself to the lower through assumed similarity and then when the lower is made similar with the higher through assimilation and imitation. Language restores the divine order of harmony and concord through the reconciling word of Christ. Bringing salvation to humanity and rendering whole all the world, Christ restores the initial goodness of the created world as much as he anticipates its perfection in the end.

However excellent as the mediating word of God, Scripture is still subject to the present dualism of all things. Consequently, it is a text to be treated with the same literary methods as other literature. Rhetorical means of interpretation, however, must be specified so as to suit a theological understanding. This happens when rhetoric and theology come together in such a way that the superiority of divine speech prevails even as its connection to human speaking at its best continues. For Erasmus, rhetoric, the art of human speech, is ancillary to theology, the understanding of the divine word. To be sure, God's revelation does not destroy but rather perfects history, nature, and culture. But since spiritual wisdom transcends natural knowledge, rhetoric functions as a method in the service of the philosophy of Christ. Specifically, the rhetorical device of allegory enables the translation from human to divine speech because it calls for a Christological and ecclesiological interpretation of the biblical message.

Erasmus revised the traditional *quadriga* of scriptural interpretation (history, tropology, allegory, anagogy) according to his humanist sense of rhetoric. Instead of using the fourfold meaning to deduce and solidify abstract dogmas, he brought to bear on it a rhetorical prudence that carefully ascertains the variety of persons, things, times, and circumstances in each instance. Here he took a giant step beyond medieval doctrinalism. Nevertheless, he believed that while keeping the historical, literal sense intact, the interpreter must move from the surface of the word to its spiritual, recondite meaning. This passage is made possible by the two middle links between letter and spirit: Tropology elicits the broader moral import; allegory evokes the proper Christological and ecclesiological meaning. As the anagogical sense foreshadows God's final mystery, it passes human understanding and calls for reverent silence.

Accordingly, history marks the beginning of the word. Mystery denotes its consummation. Yet the middle region is so important because it is where the transition from origin to fulfillment takes place, with allegory and tropology enabling a mediating *transitus*. The tropological method plays in this process a servant role to allegory by preceding it as its harbinger and/or following it as its retinue. Preceding allegory, the moral import of the text serves to prepare for the Christian life. Following allegory, tropology carries Christ's doctrine into Christian practice.

The transition from the literal to the spiritual is made possible by Christ's accommodation (*omnia omnibus*) according to the principle of *similia similibus*. Similarity, rhetorically, depends on whether a *tertium comparationis* can be found underlying two apparent opposites. If so, common denominators emerge that allow comparison between two things, and also between things of a similar kind in other contexts (*collatio*). Even so, what is similar cannot become identical. That means, for Erasmus' theology, God in Christ adapts to humanity – without diminishing divinity. Conversely, human beings are changed to be able to imitate Christ – without achieving full identity. Capable of participation, God possesses the power of accommodation. Subject to separation, humanity can yet become god-like, first by the gift of regeneration and then by the effort of imitation. This is why Christ accommodated himself to human nature. In word and life he suited his philosophy to various human beings in a variety of situations, though he never compromised his divine nature nor impaired the heavenly truth. He is the incarnate model of the divine participation in, and separation from, human nature.

Similarity carries with itself the power of attraction (*affectus*). Accommodation and assimilation, likeness and liking belong together. And the supreme power of attraction is for Erasmus, naturally, love. So allegory receives its power of similarity and attraction ultimately from love. Just as allegory fails without potential similarity, so nothing can become similar unless there is virtual attraction, that is, first of all the drawing power of divine love and subsequently the response of human affection in piety generally and in Christian charity specifically. As love makes all things common, it renders the estranged akin by overcoming confines and thereby creating affinity. Love is the power of life that lends allegory its linguistic power of attraction.

Scriptural allegory is attractive because it is extremely consonant with nature. Erasmus considered equity with nature to be an initial criterion for interpretating Scripture. But in addition to this hermeneutical function, *aequitas naturae* also has ontological and ethical dimensions. It expresses the equilibrium of nature itself as much as it points to a moral judgment that tempers justice with love. Even so, the natural appeal of allegory is perfected by its theological power of attraction, meaning that biblical interpretation must, beyond natural equity, square above all with Christ's doctrine and life. While biblical allegory attracts the reader because it reflects the balance of the natural order, it draws even more to the harmony of Christ as it inspires a Christian life. Just as the beauty and goodness of the word are functions of its truth, so aesthetics and general morals are subservient to theology and Christian ethics.

Erasmus' rules for biblical interpretation warn against over-allegorizing as much as they caution against under-allegorizing. He advised the interpreter to avoid excess by observing moderation, keeping a balance between too much and too little. Of course, reading the meaning from what Scripture actually says rather than imposing one's own notions on it already means to rely on the literal sense. Should the external word turn out absurd and superstitious, though, then it is allowable to allegorize even without a historical basis, provided that the criteria of natural equity and of Christ's doctrine and life prevail. In other words, interpretation must make good common sense, yield moral usefulness, be consonant with Scripture as a whole, and comport with the doctrine of faith. Good common sense comes from insight into nature, utility has to do with right behaviour, and the doctrine of faith concerns the teachings and life of Christ.

A biblical text receives its real meaning from its reference to Christ, the *scopus* at the centre of the *orbis Christi*, the circle of his teaching and life. This circle is harmonious in itself as much as it is congruous with his life and in agreement with the judgment of nature itself. Consensus and concord distinguish Christ's philosophy as the perfect truth which as such far excels all other philosophies. Besides the symbol of the circle, Erasmus used also the rhetorical concept of *fabula*. He identified it with the narrative device in the gospels used to relate Christ's life story as a dramatic development between birth and resurrection. But he also used it as a fitting structure to identify the major stages of the history of salvation from creation to consummation.

The circle of Christ's story intimates the main characteristics of his life: innocence, simplicity, and humility. Though these traits appear to be natural modes of behaviour, the philosophy of Christ represents more than an ethical ideal. The Christian way of life is built on the bedrock of Christ's teaching. Christ is not simply an ethical example. He is first of all the mediator and reconciler between humanity and God, indeed, the author of salvation. Erasmus did not divorce Christology from soteriology. Christ taught his disciples the theological virtues of faith, love, and hope. So, while Christian practice does draw moral lessons from nature, it is ultimately predicated on the Christians' salvation. Faith identifies the Christians' relation to God; love characterizes their attitude toward God and their fellow human beings; and hope orients them to their final goal, the happiness in the eternal communion with God.

The harmony of Christ's teaching and life (*harmonia*) addresses human beings in a variety of circumstances, for Christ accommodated himself to particular conditions (*varietas Christi*), even sometimes up to the point of dissimulation. All the same, the variety of Christ does not confound his harmony. Erasmus used here the image of a symphony which if composed of various voices sounds the more harmonious and agreeable. So the interpreter must clarify in the biblical text the literary scenery with its assemblage of persons, times, and things (*varietas*) in order to discover the specific situation to which Christ adapted his teaching. Moreover, since the teaching of Christ determines how the truth relates to any concrete situation, it becomes the norm for ecclesiastical doctrine and practice to be suited to the various circumstances within the history of salvation. Historical details receive their significance according to their proper place within the divine order of salvation centred in Christ's harmony.

But that is not yet the end. Erasmus advised the theologians to compile a stock of theological *topoi* by arranging their subject matter into a system based on similarity and dissimilarity. To assist them he suggests in his 'Elenchus' and 'Sylva' of the fourth book of the *Ecclesiastes* such a framework. His outline is, unsurprisingly, dualistic in nature: God, Christ, and the Spirit, on the one side, and the devil, on the other, followed by their respective kingdoms, laws, virtues and vices, and outcomes. These two opposite dominions are ordered according to beginning, progress, and outcome. While faith concerns primarily the beginning, love is foremost in the middle, and hope orients the Christian especially to the end. But it is the middle part concerning virtues and vices that receives most of Erasmus' attention because here the transition takes place between beginning and end. Here the theological virtues of faith, love, and hope are correlated with their respective philosophical virtues: faith with prudence, love with justice, hope with fortitude.

As a result, two patterns characterize Erasmus' way of thinking: the *loci* motif and the *via* motive. He developed, on the one hand, a system of *loci*, with Christ representing the universal fixed point, the head and goal (*scopus*). This systematic layout of topics around a Christocentric focus is, on the other hand, animated by the notion of progress between beginning and end, whether in dramatic development, rhetorical discourse, allegorical exegesis, or moral development. In general, then, it is the coordination of form and dynamic, circle and story, teaching and life, that brings the characteristic manner of Erasmus' rhetorical theology to light.

A closer examination of the *Ecclesiastes* shows in detail how and why Erasmus employed rhetoric in the service of theology.

In the first place there is grammar, the foundation of all other disciplines. It encompasses learning the three classical languages, reading the best authors, and practicing correct speech. After that, rhetoric proper teaches students to speak well by becoming skilled in the five functions of speech (*inventio, dispositio, elocutio, memoria, pronuntiatio*), the three offices of the speaker (*docere, delectare, flectere*), and the three kinds of speech (*genus judiciale, genus suasorium, genus laudativum*). Theology, finally, interprets and communicates biblical texts as part of God's dispensation of salvation as it is centred in Christ. Altogether, then, rules of grammar, principles of rhetoric, and theological *loci* drawn from Christ's teaching and life help to understand and preach the Bible on three increasingly significant levels.

Before gathering material for the invention of speech, however, it is important to raise the question: How do *natura, ars, imitatio,* and *usus* prepare for the rhetorical task? Erasmus' answer is clear: Imitation takes the first place. Rhetoric is for him more a matter of imitating established authors than of innovating speech by means of one's own ingenuity. This is especially true as far as Scripture is concerned, where imitation comes to mean, exegetically, paraphrasing God's word and, spiritually, following Christ in a life of discipleship (*imitatio Christi*). But nature is intimately linked with imitation, too, as is art by way of nature. Already children are naturally disposed to imitate. And the art of rhetoric arises from observing and imitating nature. As art seeks to follow nature's example, it produces rhetorical rules and skills that are impressed on the mind by practice. In this way, then, art turns into a second nature. It should eventually come so naturally to the orator that it becomes the highest art to conceal art.

Inventio draws on ideas and their verbal images such as they are located at certain places in the mind (*topoi*, *loci*), as if in a storehouse of memorized knowledge. But this mental reservoir is certainly more than a jumble of words and things. Rather, the topography of the mind must reflect the overall order of things in nature. As a result, each proper place in the mind determines the appropriate meaning of words within a system of coordinates that expresses a comprehensive world view. Moreover, what is true of invention applies also to *dispositio*. For the disposition of discourse is nothing less than arranging the invented commonplaces in such a way that they not only become constituent parts of ordered speech but also stand for the overall order of things. If words and ideas in their arrangement and meaning correspond to the order of the universe, they are appropriate and adroit, capable of presenting a likeness of reality.

Disposition must reproduce as nearly as possible the order of nature. Now, according to the rhetorical tradition, nature manifests itself in two ways, namely, by rest or motion. While the principle of rest implied for Erasmus circularity, the principle of motion gave speech a linear direction. Without extension in time because equidistant from its centre and always returning to itself, the circle symbolizes the truth in a consistent system. Motion, on the other hand, expresses a process in time with beginning, middle, and end. Once this is seen, it is not surprising to find Erasmus apply, as the occasion required, the concept of a perennial *ordo* and a temporal *gradatio*. In other words, both the *loci* motif and the *via* motive, sameness and development, characterize his thought, as for instance in his conception of Christ's teaching as *orbis* and of his life as *fabula*. Similarly, he describes the circle of Christ's teaching and life in terms of *harmonia* and *varietas* at the same time. The gospel thus represents not only a fixed norm but also the dynamic cause for a progressive development as it adjusts to a variety of circumstances.

Moderation plays a decisive role, now where the disposition of discourse is concerned. To keep the whole and its parts (the one and the many) in balance, orators must neither lose sight of the unifying whole in the face of its diversifying parts, nor must they forget the particularity of the parts as they try to maintain the integrity of the whole. All the same, the whole is larger than the sum of its parts in that it enlarges a text to become meaningful within the context of God's order of nature and salvation. In fact, what the part is finally all about does not appear until it falls into its place as a part of the whole. Details are relevant in proportion to their convenient place in the overall structure. As for Scripture, then, various times, places, things, persons, and circumstances become significant according to their respective proximity to Christ. The more closely a text represents Christ, the greater its moral and spiritual value.

When it comes to *divisio*, rhetoricians had both a dichotomous and a trichotomous pattern at their disposal. The one expresses a duality between opposites. The other introduces a third element to suggest an underlying unity. The tripartite division provides speech also with a dramatic pattern of development, whereby the middle enables a progress from start to finish. These rhetorical devices were, of course, conducive to a theology such as Erasmus espoused. While he used the dualistic pattern to show for instance the opposition between God and the devil, or virtue and vice, the tripartite pattern was amenable to the movement of his allegorical interpretation between history and mystery. It also helped him to understand the interplay of persons and events in the gospel story (*fabula*) as a dramatic development between *protasis, epitasis,* and *catastrophe.* Even more, the tripartite division of drama explained the entire history of salvation in terms of creation, restoration, and perfection. Therefore, the division of speech in two and three parts gives a crucial clue to Erasmus' account of reality. Dichotomy served to accommodate his bent for a Platonic dualism. Trichotomy supplied the rhetorical basis for his attempt at achieving harmony by a metaphorical, reconciling transition between opposites.

The delicate balance between *amplificatio* and *concisio*, that is, between enlarging words and things (by developing them more fully) and coming to the point (by cutting them down to size), calls for moderation between too much or too little (*hyperbole* or *ellipsis*). But beyond that, Erasmus used these rhetorical devices as theological paradigms for spiritual freedom and concentration on the *scopus* Christ. Accordingly, allegory widens the horizon from the restriction of the letter, or the confining law, to the amplitude of the spirit, or the inclusive gospel. Charity enlarges

Christians through the largess of the Spirit, freeing them from anxiety. Also, the catholic church expands, as it spreads from small beginnings throughout the world, from anxious and superstitious ceremonies to the freedom of the children of God. Even so, libertinist excesses are checked by the imitation of Christ. Still, while Christians are bound by divine authority, they do receive the spiritual liberty for a liberal interpretation of Scripture and for a life of liberality.

Elocutio, the third function of speech, serves to express mental images in proper, eloquent terms. It translates ideas into words, finding suitable figures of speech and arranging them in fitting literary composition. In this area, too, Erasmus selected, without violating the ground rules of rhetoric, those devices that satisfied his theological purpose. Some he highlighted, others he set aside, but always in an effort to accommodate rhetoric to both the exposition of Scripture and the composition of the sermon. He obviously was loath to produce a formal textbook of rhetoric for theologians. He freed himself from the rigid structure and strict terminology of rhetorical theory to pursue his theological intention. As a result, his treatment of elocution focused on the middle office of the speaker (attracting and conciliating – the medium between teaching and moving), on the middle kind of speech (persuasive discourse – the medium between judicial and laudatory discourse), and on the moderate style (between the plain and sublime modes of expression).

This selective principle can also be seen in Erasmus' stress on certain virtues of speech. He emphasized grammatical *puritas* for the correct, idiomatic use of language (but also *antiquitas, auctoritas, consensus patrum*, and to a lesser degree *ratio* and *consuetudo*, as additional criteria, particularly where interpretation is concerned). Purity, of course, motivated him to restore the original text of Scripture. But the necessity of philological restoration is only the external equivalent for the inner need of cleansing, namely, the person's return to a simple heart and honest intentions. The closer the text, the speaker, and the hearer to the purity of Christ, the purer they are rendered themselves. Consequently, the grammarian's restoring the nature of the text to its original state, Christ's restoring nature to its original integrity, and the Christian's regeneration into a Christ-like life of innocence and sincerity belong together. This is how philology, theology, and ethics are correlated at this point.

Perspicuitas, a virtue that straddles the grammatical and rhetorical side of speech, calls for unambiguous word meanings, simple word order, and short sentences. Its purpose is to make the dense concreteness of the visible world transparent to the clarity of mental images used by the writer. Obscurity, on the contrary, is a rhetorical vice whenever it vitiates analogy and comparison. Ambiguity seems to be of middle quality, in danger of falling into vicious obscurity unless raised to clarity. Removing ambiguity from a text by interpreting contrary statements so as to reconcile them is a therefore a primary task of the theologian. Nonetheless, there is considerable value to a certain kind of obscurity. Writers may employ covert language for reasons of persuasion. After all, deliberative discourse rests on ambiguity, and persuasion requires that readers be drawn into the text so as to reach their own judgment. The truth moves human affections more effectively if it is concealed at first sight. This pedagogical motive makes the use of tropes, figures, metaphors, and allegories all the more appropriate. Even though the process of understanding is thereby made more difficult in the beginning, the insight reached in the end is the more pleasant and lasts longer.

The rhetorical virtue of *aptum* (*decorum, conveniens, accommodatum*) serves to adapt words to things, to adjust speech to the hearers, to fit discourse into its proper order, to embellish oratory to make it attractive and persuasive, and to orient the message toward a moral and spiritual goal. The latter is the most important part for Erasmus since rhetoric connects here with ethics. When the parts of speech form a harmonious whole and thus reflect consensus and concord in *vita et mores*, the rhetorical virtue becomes a paradigm for moral virtue, for living in tune with the harmony of nature. Good speech images the virtuous life of the speaker. This moral origin and goal of speech ultimately qualifies all uses of *aptum* and its cognates. Accommodation to a moral purpose, however, is not an end in itself but subsidiary to spiritual transformation.

The single most important method for discovering analogies is *collatio*. Comparison enabled Erasmus to examine the similarities and differences between words and passages in text and context, but also between words signifying and things signified in figures of speech, and last but not least between the visible and the invisible world. Moreover, the measure (*modus*) for collation to achieve integration is *commoditas*, the rhythm of harmony. It determines whether a text or speech appropriately resonates the larger order, that is, the harmony of Christ, the equilibrium of natural equity, and the moderation of ethical utility. *Commodum* not only lends rhythmic measure to speech but also puts a moral edge on it (*commoda*). So it eventually links up with *utilitas*, the moral goal of persuasive speech, which looks to providing advantageous things and removing disadvantageous things. In sacred rhetoric, however, the intended benefit for the hearers acquires a more excellent quality in that it inspires them to move from the flesh to the spirit by advancing in piety.

The moral quality of *commoditas* applies to writers as much as to writing, to speakers as to speaking, to interpreters as to interpretation. When interpreters take the measure of the text, they are by the same token enjoined to maintain measure for themselves, that is, to imitate the measure of language with their measured conduct, to echo its moral overtones in a tactful life. Commodity implies personal moderation – a temper that carries with it a sense of proportion as it looks to achieve balance. Interpreters must exercise self-control by being temperate toward text and hearers alike, not making themselves the measure of their words and actions but having the benefit of the other in mind, whether it is the benefit of the doubt regarding the text or decency toward other human beings as that has been supremely prefigured by the modesty of Christ.

Appropriate speech (*aptum*) had for Erasmus a higher value than literary ornamentation (*ornatus*), particularly if decoration serves its own end as art for art's sake. Nevertheless, those embellishments that amplify thought, convey metaphorical meanings, and add both an attractive feature and a moral edge received in fact more than a normal share of attention. Figures of speech are significant to the extent to which they serve *aptum* by pleasing and moving the hearer. So Erasmus selected those figures that are relevant to the Bible, appeal through delightful, clear, brilliant, and enticing speech (*jucunditas*), and move to moral action through intense, powerful, and grave speech (*vehementia*).

Among the figures of speech (like *hyperbole, synecdoche, emphasis,* and *ironia*), Erasmus singled out *metaphora* and *allegoria* because they excel in effecting attraction and vehemence. They amplify thought by appealing to the human affections with the intention of changing the person. Not only vehemence but also delight attracts to the virtues of the moral life. So *delectare* ultimately serves the same tranforming purpose as *movere*, though vehemence addresses the intense passions whereas delight speaks to the milder emotions. Although Erasmus often mentioned both together, he preferred delight because it eventually brings about the same transformation as vehemence, except in a milder and mediating way. Without giving up *docere* and *movere*, then, he emphasized *delectare* in the middle, and that so much the more since attraction is conducive to conciliation. It serves as a literary expression for the reconciliation in Christ.

While Erasmus could on occasion associate *docere* with judicial discourse, *delectare* (*conciliare*) with suasory discourse, and *movere* with laudatory discourse, he included teaching and moving more often than not within the *genus suasorium*. It is suasory rhetoric, after all, that is decisive for the theologian's reconciling work (also epideictic discourse in liturgy). The preacher has little in common with the *genus judiciale*, except when proof is needed to convict heretics. But teaching as instruction is indispensable. Indeed, if used to persuade, exhort, console, counsel, and admonish, teaching constitutes an ecclesiastical office higher than the administration of the sacraments, prayer, adjudication, and ordination. As functions of suasory discourse, then, *docere*, *delectare*, and *movere* are essential to Erasmus' rhetorical theology.

Erasmus widened the concept of *prudentia* beyond its traditional scope in the rhetorical textbooks. Indeed, he elevated it to the place of one of the leading hermeneutical principles. Since the precepts of art fail unless guided by prudence, rhetoric is virtually at one with prudence. Furthermore, from the beginning he associated the rhetorical virtue of prudence with the Christian virtue of faith. As faith signifies the pure simplicity of the dove, so prudence is the cunning art of the serpent. It takes simple prudence and prudent simplicity alike to discern the circumstances of time, place, and persons in order to speak aptly and with the benefit of the audience in mind.

Prudence falls under two heads, *judicium* and *consilium*. While both constitute faculties innate in the natural disposition of human beings, they are also nurtured by the art of dialectic and rhetoric – just as spiritual prudence, on a higher level, is first a gift of the Holy Spirit but then also the perfection of natural prudence. Judgment ascertains the causal connections of obvious, accessible, and visible things. Counsel discerns verisimilitude in remote, uncertain, and invisible things.

Judgment applies the rules of dialectic in an exercise of reason (*ratio*), producing both knowledge (*scientia*, the determination of evidence by syllogistic conclusions) and conjecture (*opinio*, the inference of probability by means of rhetorical *enthymema*). Where rhetoric is concerned, reasoning (*ratiocinatio*) operates properly when it helps to determine the appropriate place of *loci* as well as to amplify and compare thought. But it can easily get lost in narrow details. As a result, it is liable to come up with *praeposterum iudicium* that puts last things first, makes the most of the least, and fails to see what lies between beginning and end. Together with *oblivio mediocritatis*, Erasmus put preposterous judgment on a level with superstition and superciliousness.

It takes *consilium* to discriminate between a variety of persons, things, times, and places so as to select what is of advantage. Regarding theology this means that rhetorical counsel must be enhanced by spiritual prudence. For Christian orators cannot administer the divine truth unless they take its measure in proportion to particular situations. Only if they are aware of what to say and what to leave unsaid are they able to moderate speech and thus become all to all. Consequently, prudence calls for accommodation and moderation as it looks to what is expedient. To that end, the choice of an opportune moment (*opportunitas*) is decisive as well. Theologians must reckon with the dispensation of times (*ratio temporum*) in order to apply the truth to different people in different proportions. In doing this they imitate the divine revelation that dispenses the gifts of the very same Spirit in appropriate portions according to the provision of time.

It is the end of suasory speech to draw individuals toward the advantage of moral virtue (*honestum, utilitas*) by appealing to their affections (*affectus*). Erasmus saw the human affections, true to the structure of his overall thought, from both a dualistic and a trichotomous perspective, with moderate affections situated between the base passions (*pathos*) and the milder emotions (*ethos*). The moderate affections inhere in the human being as natural dispositions such as parental love and other affections of person, familiy, nation, and gender (*pietas, caritas*). Love engenders love: This motto expresses the link between natural human love and the love of God. Accordingly, suasory speech confirms and intensifies the positive dispositions of the heart as much as it negates and changes its negative inclinations. But the natural affections are eventually perfected by the most spiritual affections of faith, love, and hope.

Erasmus considered the classical teaching on the highest good as propaedeutic, ancillary to the Christian life. The civil quality of *honestum* concerns that which is right by itself (*rectum*), but also that which is beautiful (*pulcrum*) and proper (*decorum*). More specifically, honesty has to do with the divine law (*fas*) and its violation (*nefas*), depending on whether it is according to nature or contrary to nature. The honest person responds to the divine law as revealed in nature and thus leads a life of natural piety and natural virtues. For what is true of honesty holds also good for piety and virtue: Virtue is according to nature, vice is against nature. Small wonder, then, that Christ's philosophy restores nature, for the love of Christ is the love of both heavenly and honorable things.

Erasmus applied a trichotomous scheme in this connection as well. Just as the moderate human affections are situated between the base passions and the milder emotions, so *honestum* is opposed by *turpia*, with *necessaria* standing in the middle. Necessary things (such as health, beauty, strength, eloquence, learning, and the like) are not to be sought for their own good, like *honestum* itself, nor should they be allowed to fall into vile passions, but they are to be used in proportion as they are conducive to the supreme goal, the love of Christ.

Erasmus coordinated in a final rhetorical move the genera of *virtus* (prudence, justice, fortitude, and temperance) with their corresponding theological species: Prudence is akin to faith, justice to charity, fortitude to hope. Temperance, or moderation, comes significantly into play as a species of justice, holding like charity the middle position between faith and hope. It tempers above all justice with love. But it also moderates prudence with faith and qualifies fortitude by hope. Temperance is the moral equivalent of the rhetorical principle of moderation which itself is predicated on the equity of nature.

In his final synopsis of the theological virtues, Erasmus drew a connection between faith and reason (mind), knowledge, judgment, and prudence. Likewise he related love with heart (soul), natural affections, will, and justice. Faith determines the Christian's insight as it perfects human understanding. Love motivates the Christian's intention and action by perfecting the will. Faith is the door to salvation. But the pre-eminent rank goes to Christian love, the way from beginning to end. Faith and love are the gist of human happiness.

All in all, then, our study of Erasmus' biblical hermeneutics has shown how he put rhetoric in the service of theology. He utilized the allegorical and tropological method so as to coordinate Christology, ecclesiology, and ethics in a unique, humanist way. His exegetical method not only revealed his hermeneutical principles but also the structure of his rhetorical theology. However, this theology did not serve its own end. It was to communicate the word of God through preaching with the intent of drawing people into the power of the divine love that transforms them and enables them to moral action. In that sense, Erasmus' theology was eminently practical. Conceived as it was in the ivory tower of the pious intellectual, it was passionately aimed at the *restitutio Christianismi* by way of both Christ's restoration of nature and the Christian's regeneration into a life of faith and love that creates public peace, harmony, and concord.

There is no better way to conclude our conclusion than to let Erasmus speak for himself with a statement summing up his life's work: 'Has anyone been a more active opponent in print of putting one's trust in ceremonies; of superstition concerning food and liturgy and prayer; of those who give more weight to human inventions than to Holy Scripture, who value the decrees of man more than the commandments of God, who put more trust in the saints than in Christ himself; of academic theology, corrupted as it is by philosophic and scholastic quibbling; of the rash practice of laying down rules for every mortal thing; of the topsy-turvy judgments of the multitude ... This, and very much else, which I have taught according to the measure of grace accorded to me, I have taught steadfastly, but never standing in the way of any man who has something better to teach. And they say Erasmus has taught nothing but rhetoric!' (*Letters* 1341A / CWE 9 340: 1132–44)

Abbreviations

ARG	*Archiv für Reformationsgeschichte*
Aristot.	Aristoteles
Metaph.	*Metaphysica*
Nic. Eth.	*Ethica Nicomachea*
Phys.	*Physica*
Rhet.	*Rhetorica*
ASD	*Opera omnia Desiderii Erasmi Roterodami* Amsterdam 1969–
Aug.	Aurelius Augustinus
De util. cred.	*De utilitate credendi*
Tract. in Ioh.	*Tractatus in Iohannem*
De doctr.	*De doctrina christiana*
CWE	*Collected Works of Erasmus* Toronto 1974–
Cic.	Cicero
Att.	*Epistulae ad Atticum*
Brut.	*Brutus*
De or.	*De oratore*
Div.	*De diuinatione*
Fin.	*De finibus*
Inv.	*De inuentione*
Off.	*De officiis*
Or.	*Orator*
Tusc.	*Tusculanae disputationes*
CR	*Corpus Reformatorum*
Ep	*Opus epistolarum Des. Erasmi Roterodami* ed P.S. Allen, H.M. Allen, and H.W. Garrod, Oxford 1906–58
ERSY	*Erasmus of Rotterdam Society Yearbook*

H	*Desiderius Erasmus Roterodamus: Ausgewählte Werke* ed Hajo Holborn und Annemarie Holborn, München 1933; repr 1964
Her.	*Rhetorica ad Herennium*
HWP	*Historisches Wörterbuch der Philosophie*
L	*De libero arbitrio; Hyperaspistes, liber primus* ed Winfried Lesowsky, Darmstadt 1969
LB	*Desiderii Erasmi Roterodami opera omnia* ed Jean Leclerc, Leiden 1703–6; repr 1961–2
NAK	*Nederlandsch Archief voor Kerkgeschiedenis*
Ov. Her.	Ovid *Heroides*
Petr. De vita sol.	Petrarch *De vita solita*
PG	*Patrologiae cursus completus, series Graeca*
Plat.	Plato
Tim.	*Timaeus*
Phaedr.	*Phaedrus*
Quint. Inst.	Quintilianus *Institutio oratoria*
Reedijk	*The Poems of Desiderius Erasmus* ed Cornelis Reedijk, Leiden 1956
RAC	*Reallexikon für Antike und Christentum*
RHE	*Revue d'Histoire Ecclésiastique*
SCJ	*The Sixteenth Century Journal*
TRE	*Theologische Realenzyklopädie*
WA	*D. Martin Luthers Werke, Kritische Gesamtausgabe* Weimar 1883–
WABR	*D. Martin Luthers Werke, Kritische Gesamtausgabe: Briefwechsel* Weimar 1930–85
WATR	*D. Martin Luthers Werke, Kritische Gesamtausgabe: Tischreden* Weimar 1912–21

Notes

INTRODUCTION

1 *Erkenntnis und Verwirklichung der wahren Theologie nach Erasmus von Rotterdam* Tübingen 1972. F. Krüger largely corroborated my findings and extended his research to Erasmus' exegesis of the gospels (*Humanistische Evangelienauslegung, Desiderius Erasmus von Rotterdam als Ausleger der Evangelien in seinen Paraphrasen* Tübingen 1986).
2 J.W. Aldridge *The Hermeneutic of Erasmus* Zürich–Richmond 1966, 127–8
3 J.B. Payne 'Toward the Hermeneutics of Erasmus' *Scrinium Erasmianum II* Leiden 1969, 13–49; *Erasmus: His Theology of the Sacraments* Richmond 1970, 44–53
4 T.F. Torrance 'The Hermeneutics of Erasmus' *Probing the Reformed Tradition, Historical Studies in Honor of Edward A. Dowey, Jr* ed E.A. McKee and B.G. Armstrong, Louisville 1989, 48–76
5 As for instance in C. Trinkaus *The Scope of Renaissance Humanism* Ann Arbor 1983, 257
6 M. O'Rourke Boyle *Erasmus on Language and Method in Theology* Toronto/Buffalo/London 1978; *Rhetoric and Reform: Erasmus' Civil Dispute with Luther* Cambridge, Mass/London 1983
7 J. Chomarat *Grammaire et rhétorique chez Erasme* Paris 1981
8 P. Walter *Theologie aus dem Geist der Rhetorik, Zur Schriftauslegung des Erasmus von Rotterdam* Mainz 1991
9 *Letters* 1062 / CWE 7 196:23–197:49. 'I saw the saintly Doctors of the church regarded, some of them, as obsolete and out of date, and all in a corrupt, confused, and filthy state. I saw the teaching of the gospel almost overlaid with the petty comments of men, and the gospel texts buried in mistakes as though in brambles and in tares' (*Letters* 1053 / CWE 7 161:513–17).

10 *Letters* 1007 / CWE 7 57:40–3
11 E. Rummel '*Et cum theologo bella poeta gerit*: The Conflict between Humanists and Scholastics Revisited' *SCJ* 23:4 (Winter 1992) 718
12 *Ecclesiastes* ASD V-4 368:64–370:89
13 *Letters* 1334 / CWE 9 252:226–31
14 *Letters* 1341A / CWE 9 340:1137–38
15 *Letters* 1428 / CWE 10 196:61–197:70
16 *Letters* 1139 / CWE 8 41:76–81
17 *Letters* 1183 / CWE 8 150:38–44
18 *Letters* 1379/ CWE 10 56:2–5
19 See ch 3, notes 107–11.
20 On the formula: 'To understand a writer better than he understood himself' see H.-G. Gadamer *Truth and Method* New York 1975, 169–73.
21 A preliminary report on my findings has been published in 'Erasmus on Language and Interpretation' *Moreana* 28:106–7 (July 1991) 1–20.

CHAPTER ONE

1 See W. Kaegi 'Erasmus im achtzehnten Jahrhundert' in *Historische Meditationen* Zürich 1942, 185–219; A. Flitner *Erasmus im Urteil seiner Nachwelt* Tübingen 1952; G. Ritter *Die geschichtliche Bedeutung des deutschen Humanismus* Darmstadt 1963; L.W. Spitz *The Religious Renaissance of the German Humanists* Cambridge 1963, 234; B.E. Mansfield 'Erasmus in the Nineteenth Century, the Liberal Tradition' *Studies in the Renaissance* 15 (1968) 139 ff; M. Hoffmann *Erkenntnis und Verwirklichung der wahren Theologie nach Erasmus von Rotterdam* Tübingen 1972, 10ff; B. Mansfield *Phoenix of His Age: Interpretations of Erasmus c. 1550–1750* Toronto 1979; C. Reedijk *Tandem bona causa triumphat. Zur Geschichte des Gesamtwerkes des Erasmus von Rotterdam* Basel/Stuttgart 1980; R.L. DeMolen *The Spirituality of Erasmus of Rotterdam* Nieuwkoop 1987, 199–203; J.-C. Margolin 'La Religion d'Erasme et l'Allemagne des Lumières' in ibid *Erasme dans son miroir et dans son sillage* London 1987, 197–230; B. Mansfield 'Erasmus in the Age of Revolution' *Erasmus of Rotterdam: The Man and the Scholar* ed J. Sperna Weiland and W.Th.M. Frijhoff, Leiden 1988, 228–39; C. Augustijn *Erasmus: His Life, Works, and Influence* Toronto/Buffalo/London 1991, 3ff, 185ff.
2 *Adages* I iii 86 / CWE 31 304:1–305:36. This phrase was actually used by Erasmus to portray Thomas More; cf G. Marc'hadour '*Omnium horarum homo*: A Man for All Seasons' *ERSY* 1 (1981) 141–7.
3 See for instance M. Pattison 'Erasmus' *Encyclopedia Britannica* 9, 8,

453ff; R.B. Drummond *Erasmus: His Life and Character* London 1875; J.A. Froude *Life and Letters of Erasmus* London/New York 1894; E. Amiel *Un libre penseur du XVIe siècle: Erasme* Paris 1899. This line of interpretation has been continued in modified form by P. Smith *Erasmus: A Study of His Life, Ideals and Place in History* New York/London 1923; and A. Renaudet *Etudes Erasmiennes* Paris 1939. Even J. Chomarat *Grammaire et rhétorique chez Erasme* Paris 1981, 1162 still agrees with the liberal interpretation of Renaudet. M. Mann Phillips 'Visages d'Erasme' in *Colloque Erasmien de Liège* Liège 1987, 17–29 gives a brief overview of this tradition. The best and most thorough treatment of nineteenth century Erasmus interpretations has been provided by B. Mansfield *Interpretations of Erasmus c 1750–1920: Man on His Own* Toronto/Buffalo/London 1992.

4 W. Dilthey 'Auffassung und Analyse des Menschen im 15. und 16. Jahrhundert' in *Gesammelte Schriften* 2 Berlin 1957; E. Troeltsch 'Protestantisches Christentum und die Kirche in der Neuzeit' in *Die Kultur der Gegenwart* Berlin 1909, I, 4:1; 431ff; 'Wesen der Religion und Religionswissenschaft' in ibid. 4:2, 1ff; P. Wernle *Die Renaissance des Christentums im 16. Jahrhundert* Tübingen/Leipzig 1904; *Renaissance und Reformation* Tübingen 1912, 69.

5 '*Erasmus est anguilla*. Niemand kan yhn ergreiffen denn Christus allein. *Est vir duplex*' (WATR 1 55:32f). According to Luther, Erasmus was like an eel because of his *amphibologia* (WATR 3 260:21ff; 27ff; 4 573:18; WABR 7 2093:305). The image of *homo pro se* was brought into circulation by the *Epistolae obscurorum virorum* (ed A. Bömer, Heidelberg 1924, repr Aalen 1978, 2 187:25; H. Holborn *On the Eve of the Reformation: Letters of Obscure Men* New York/Evanston/London 1964, 224), repeated by Hutten in his *Expostulatio*, and perpetuated by Luther; cf C. Augustijn '*Vir duplex*: German Interpretations of Erasmus' *Erasmus of Rotterdam: The Man and the Scholar* ed J. Sperna Weiland and W.Th.M. Frijhoff, Leiden 1988, 219–27.

A similarly negative image has been drawn by the Catholic J. Lortz, even though from different dogmatic presuppositions (*Die Reformation in Deutschland I* Freiburg 1939, 131f; 'Erasmus kirchengeschichtlich' in *Aus Theologie und Philosophie, Festschrift F. Tillmann* Düsseldorf 1950, 271ff).

6 See W. Behnk *Contra Liberum Arbitrium Pro Gratia Dei: Willenslehre und Christuszeugnis bei Luther und in der Interpretation durch die neuere Lutherforschung* Frankfurt/Bern 1982, 76ff; 115ff.

7 *Opus epistolarum Des. Erasmi Roterodami* ed P.S. Allen, H.M. Allen and H.W. Garrod, Oxford 1906–58; J. Huizinga *Erasmus* Haarlem 1924, New York/London 1924 (cf J.-C. Margolin 'Huizinga et les

recherches erasmiennes' in ibid. *Erasme dans son miroir et dans son sillage* London 1987, 258–74). See also J.v. Walter *Das Wesen der Religion nach Erasmus und Luther* Leipzig 1906; W. Köhler *Erasmus, ein Lebensbild in Auszügen aus seinen Werken* Berlin 1917.

8 M. Cytowska 'Erasme et son petit corps' *Eos* 62 (1974) 129–38

9 M. Mann Phillips pictured Erasmus as a champion of the 'middle way' (*Erasmus and the Northern Renaissance* London 1949), while Roland Bainton saw him as a 'battered liberal' (*Erasmus of Christendom* New York 1969).

10 This line of interpretation leads from M. Bataillon (*Erasme et l'Espagne, Recherches sur l'histoire spirituelle du XVIe siècle* Paris 1937), L. Bouyer (*Autour d'Erasme, Etudes sur le Christianisme des humanistes catholiques* Paris 1955), and J. Etienne (*Spiritualisme érasmien et théologiens louvanistes* Louvain/Gembloux 1956) to C. Béné (*Erasme et saint Augustin* Geneva 1969), L.E. Halkin (*Erasme parmi nous* Paris 1987), R.L. DeMolen (*The Spirituality of Erasmus of Rotterdam* Nieuwkoop 1987), and R.J. Schoeck (*Erasmus Grandescens: The Growth of a Humanist's Mind and Spirituality* Nieuwkoop 1988). G. Chantraine ('*Mystère*' et '*Philosophie du Christ*' *selon Erasme* Namur/Gembloux 1971; *Erasme et Luther, libre et serf arbitre* Paris/Namur 1981) interpreted Erasmus' theology in terms of the French *nouvelle théologie* (see my review in *ERSY* 3 [1983] 156–65).

11 A. Renaudet's views (*Erasme, sa pensée religieuse et son action d'après sa correspondance [1518–1521]* Paris 1926; *Etudes erasmiennes [1521–1529]* Paris 1939) bear a striking resemblance to the ideals of the modernist movement in Roman Catholicism; see also F. Heer *Die dritte Kraft, Der europäische Humanismus in den Fronten des konfessionellen Zeitalters* Frankfurt 1959.

12 *Opera omnia Desiderii Erasmi Roterodami* Amsterdam/Oxford 1969–

13 Detailed historical work, as evidenced for instance in his superb introductions and footnotes of ASD IX-1, distinguishes C. Augustijn's contributions (*Erasmus en de Reformatie: Een onderzoek naar de houding die Erasmus ten opzichte van de Reformatie heeft aangenomen* Amsterdam 1962; *Erasmus: Vernieuwer van kerk en theologie* Baarn 1967; 'Erasmus' in *TRE* 10, 1–18; *Erasmus von Rotterdam: Leben-Werk-Wirkung* München 1986, tr *Erasmus: His Life, Works, and Influence* Toronto/Buffalo/London 1991).

14 A. Auer *Die vollkommene Frömmigkeit des Christen nach dem Enchiridion militis Christiani des Erasmus von Rotterdam* Düsseldorf 1954; R. Padberg *Personaler Humanismus* Paderborn 1964; E.W. Kohls *Die Theologie des Erasmus* Basel 1966; J.B. Payne *Erasmus: His Theology of the Sacraments* Richmond 1970; G. Chantraine '*Mystère*' et '*Philosophie du Christ*' *selon Erasme* Namur/Gembloux 1971; M. Hoffmann *Erkenntnis und Verwirklichung der wahren Theologie nach Eras-*

mus von Rotterdam Tübingen 1972; A. Rabil *Erasmus and the New Testament* San Antonio 1972; G. Winkler *Erasmus von Rotterdam und die Einleitungsschriften zum Neuen Testament* Münster 1974; M. O'Rourke Boyle *Erasmus on Language and Method in Theology* Toronto 1978; F. Krüger *Humanistische Evangelienauslegung, Desiderius Erasmus von Rotterdam als Ausleger der Evangelien in seinen Paraphrasen* Tübingen 1986; P. Walter *Theologie aus dem Geist der Rhetorik, Zur Schriftauslegung des Erasmus von Rotterdam* Mainz 1991

15 G. Kisch *Erasmus und die Jurisprudenz seiner Zeit* Basel 1960; K.H. Oelrich *Der späte Erasmus und die Reformation* Münster 1961; J.K. McConica *English Humanists and Reformation Politics* Oxford 1965; R.R. Post *The Modern Devotion: Confrontation with Reformation and Humanism* Leiden 1968; C. Béné *Erasme et Saint Augustin* Geneva 1969; G. Kisch *Erasmus' Stellung zu den Juden und Judentum* Tübingen 1969; H. Holeczek *Humanistische Bibelphilologie als Reformproblem bei Erasmus von Rotterdam, Thomas More und William Tyndale* Leiden 1975; M. O'Rourke Boyle *Christening Pagan Mysteries: Erasmus in Pursuit of Wisdom* Toronto 1981; A. Godin *Erasme lecteur d'Origèn* Geneva 1982; P.I. Kaufman *Augustinian Piety and Catholic Reform: Augustine, Colet, and Erasmus* Macon 1982; J.H. Bentley *Humanists and Holy Writ: New Testament Scholarship in the Renaissance* Princeton 1983; H. Holeczek *Erasmus Deutsch* Stuttgart-Bad Cannstatt 1983; J.K. Farge *Orthodoxy and Reform in Early Reformation France* Leiden 1985; E. Rummel *Erasmus as a Translator of the Classics* Toronto/Buffalo/London 1985; S. Markish *Erasmus and the Jews* Chicago/London 1986; E. Rummel *Erasmus' 'Annotations' on the New Testament: From Philologist to Theologian* Toronto/Buffalo/London 1986; S. Seidel-Menchi *Erasmo in Italia 1520–1580* Turin 1987; E. Rummel *Erasmus and His Catholic Critics* 2 vols, Nieuwkoop 1989

16 G. Gebhardt *Die Stellung des Erasmus von Rotterdam zur Römischen Kirche* Marburg 1966; J.S. Guarneschelli *Erasmus' Concept of the Church, 1499–1524* diss Yale 1966; C. Augustijn 'The Ecclesiology of Erasmus' in *Scrinium Erasmianum* 2 Leiden 1969, 135–55; W. Hentze *Kirche und kirchliche Einheit bei Desiderius Erasmus von Rotterdam* Paderborn 1974; B. Gogan 'The Ecclesiology of Erasmus of Rotterdam: A Genetic Account' *The Heythrop Journal* 21 (1981) 393–411; M. Hoffmann 'Erasmus on Church and Ministry' *ERSY* 6 (1986) 1–30

17 H. J. McSorley *Luther: Right Or Wrong? An ecumenical-theological Study of Luther's Major Work, The Bondage of the Will* New York 1968; G. Chantraine *Erasme et Luther: Libre et serf arbitre* Paris/Namur 1981; M. O'Rourke Boyle *Rhetoric and Reform: Erasmus' Civil Dispute with Luther* Cambridge, Mass/London 1983 (see my review

in *ERSY* 4 [1984] 154–62); O.H. Pesch ed *Humanismus und Reformation: Martin Luther und Erasmus von Rotterdam in den Konflikten ihrer Zeit* München/Zürich 1985 (my article tr 'Erasmus on Free Will: An Issue Revisited' *ERSY* 10 [1990] 101–21).

18 C.R. Thompson 'Erasmus as Internationalist and Cosmopolitan' *ARG* 46 (1955) 167–95; E. v. Koerber *Die Staatstheorie des Erasmus von Rotterdam* Berlin 1967; S. Wollgast *Zur Friedensidee in der Reformationszeit* Berlin 1968; J.C. Margolin *Guerre et paix dans la pensée d'Erasme* Paris 1973; J.D. Tracy *The Politics of Erasmus: A Pacifist Intellectual and His Political Milieu* Toronto/Buffalo/London 1978

19 J. Chomarat *Grammaire et rhétorique chez Erasme* Paris 1981 (see my review in *ERSY* 5 [1985] 65–83)

20 On the older view cf J.B. Payne *Erasmus: Theology of the Sacraments* 7 n1; on more recent opinions see for instance G. Rupp in *Luther and Erasmus: Free Will and Salvation* Philadelphia 1969, 9; J. Chomarat *Grammaire* 16–24, 1159ff; C. Augustijn 'Erasmus und seine Theologie: Hatte Luther Recht?' in *Colloque érasmien de Liège* 49–68 (see my review in *ERSY* 9 [1989] 129f). But cf my book *Erkenntnis* 32; E. Rummel *Erasmus' 'Annotations'* 3ff, and *Catholic Critics 1* 33; J.W. O'Malley in his 'Introduction' to CWE 66, xiiff; and P. Walter *Theologie* 2–5, 16ff, who says: 'In dieser Frage hat sich in jahrzehntelanger wissenschaftlicher Diskussion ein tragfähiger Konsens herausgebildet' (3).

21 *Letters* 108 / CWE 1 203:24–42. 'Pro theologis fiunt mateologi' (*Ratio* H 301: 6). Cf for instance CWE 3 121:320–125:453; H 7:25, 152:24, 183:13, 296:34–300:29. More references in my book *Erkenntnis* sv and E. Rummel *Erasmus' 'Annotations'* sv. On Cicero's concept of *neoterici* see *Att.* 7,2,1.

22 *Letters* 1309 / CWE 9 170:54–171:68

23 *Capita contra morosos* LB VI ˙˙˙3v–4r, quoted by E. Rummel 'God and Solecism: Erasmus as a Literary Critic of the Bible' *ERSY* 7 (1987) 72. 'Let theology by all means be the queen of sciences: no queen is so effective that she can dispense with the services of her handmaidens. Some she allows to counsel and some to adorn her, and she believes it part of her glory that those who serve her should be honourable women' (*Letters* 1062 / CWE 7 197:68–72). 'These studies [sc the ancient languages and the art of writing] do not obscure the dignity of theology, they set her in a clearer light; they are not her enemies but her servants ... If theology joins in honouring these studies, they in turn will prove a credit to her; but if she meets them with insult and calumny, I fear we shall see, in Paul's words, that while they bite and devour one another, it will end in their mutual destruction' (*Letters* 1006 / CWE 7 54:362–3, 371–4). Cf CWE 2 94:147–52; ASD IV-2 66:144; LB II 1053F–1054A.

24 Ep 139:39-40
25 *Letters* 1352 / CWE 9 435:39-436:42
26 *The Yale Edition of the Works of St. Thomas More* vol 15, tr, D. Kinney 13, 15; cf 21. The title of Erasmus' exposition of Psalm 1 reads: *Enarratio primi psalmi, iuxta tropologiam potissimum, auctore Erasmo Roterodamo, sacrae theologiae professore* (ASD V-2 33).
27 *Letters* 1144 / CWE 8 53:21-3. 'At least I have tried ... to recall men from those lifeless details which could bring no result ... and to fire them with zeal for a theology alike more authentic and with higher standards' (*Letters* 1007 / CWE 7 58:64-5; 68-71). 'I have tried to open the fountain-head of true piety and religion, I have done my best to restore theology, sunk far too deep in wrangling with more sophistry than sense, to its ancestral dignity' (*Letters* 1104 / CWE 7 285:5-6). 'My heart is set on the humanities, it is set on truth as truth is found in the gospel' (*Letters* 1157 / CWE 8 83:13-14).
28 *Ratio* H 193:18-22. 'This is indeed the mark of theological learning: to define nothing beyond what is recorded in Holy Scripture, but to dispense in good faith what is there recorded' (*Letters* 1334 / CWE 9 253:244-6). Cf H 284:28, 294:20, 304:14, 305:14, ASD V-4 470:534, LB IX 918B.
29 See my article 'Erasmus on Church and Ministry' *ERSY* 6 (1986) 1-30.
30 *Letters* 1334 / CWE 9 252:232-253:246.
31 L 6; see also *Hyperaspistes* 1 (L 250, 272). Cf J. Chomarat *Grammaire* 32f; M. O'Rourke Boyle *Rhetoric and Reform* sv; A. Rabil 'Cicero and Erasmus' Moral Philosophy' *ERSY* 8 (1988) 70-90.
32 *Ratio* H 297:22-4. 'I have never made any assertions, I have always shunned the character of one who lays down the law, particularly on topics which are already accepted among the articles of our religion; though I admit that some theologians I could name have handed down decisions on some points which, at least in my opinion, might be left undecided without prejudice to the religion of the Gospel' (*Letters* 1183 / CWE 8 150:44-9). Cf U. Claesges art 'Epoché' in *HWP* 2, 594f.
33 *Letters* 1006 / CWE 7 52:283-5. 'I refrain from laying down the law, for I would rather purvey good advice than dogma' (*Letters* 1225 / CWE 8 277:250-252).
34 *Ratio* H 209:6-7. Cf H 209:3; 210:5; 32; 211:1; 29; 222:36.
35 See J.E. Seigel *Rhetoric and Philosophy in Renaissance Humanism: The Union of Eloquence and Wisdom, Petrarch to Valla* Princeton 1968; C. Trinkaus *In Our Image and Likeness: Humanity and Divinity in Italian Humanist Thought* 2 vols, London 1970, esp. 1, 103ff; *The Scope of Renaissance Humanism* Ann Arbor 1983, esp. 388ff; and A. Rabil ed

Renaissance Humanism: Foundations, Forms, and Legacy 3 vols, Philadelphia 1988, esp. M. Lorch 'Lorenzo Valla' 1, 332–49.
36 See for instance J. Chomarat *Grammaire* 153ff, 183ff; G.A. Kennedy *Classical Rhetoric and its Christian and Secular Tradition from Ancient to Modern Times* Chapel Hill 1980, 173ff, 195ff; W.K. Percival 'Renaissance Grammar' in *Renaissance Humanism* 3, 67ff; J. Monfasani 'Humanism and Rhetoric' in *Renaissance Humanism* 3, 171–235; C. Trinkaus 'Italian Humanism and Scholastic Theology' in ibid 3, 322ff; R. Guerlac *Juan Vives Against the Pseudodialecticians: A Humanist Attack on Medieval Logic* Dort 1979, 2ff; *Juan Luis Vives: In Pseudodialecticos* ed by C. Fantazzi, Leiden 1979, 12ff.
37 For basic information see the entries on Agricola, Vives, Budé, Fichtet, Gaguin, Lefèvre, More, Reuchlin, Celtis, etc., in P.G. Bietenholz and T.B. Deutscher eds *Contemporaries of Erasmus: A Biographical Register of the Renaissance and Reformation* 3 vols, Toronto 1985ff.
38 J. Monfasani 'Humanism and Rhetoric' in *Renaissance Humanism* 3, 195–7
39 It seems that Agricola's most important successors before Ramus were Juan Luis Vives and Philip Melanchthon because they also identified invention with dialectic and defined rhetoric primarily in terms of elocution. Agricola apparently began a movement that culminated in Ramus' criticism of rhetoric as mere style without content.
40 On his understanding of dialectic as *judicium* and *ratiocinatio* within the purview of rhetoric, see ch 5, 4.
41 See *studia humanitatis* sv in *Renaissance Humanism* ed A. Rabil; also C. Trinkaus *Scope* 18ff; and L.W. Spitz 'Humanismus/Humanismusforschung' in *TRE* 15, 639–61.
42 G.A. Kennedy *The Art of Persuasion in Greece* Princeton 1963; J.E. Seigel *Rhetoric and Philosophy in Renaissance Humanism: The Union of Eloquence and Wisdom, Petrarch to Valla* Princeton 1968; G.A. Kennedy *The Art of Rhetoric in the Roman World* Princeton 1972; S. Ijsseling *Rhetoric and Philosophy in Conflict: An Historical Survey* The Hague 1976; G.A. Kennedy *Classical Rhetoric* Chapel Hill 1980; W. Eisenhut *Einführung in die antike Rhetorik und ihre Geschichte* Darmstadt 1982; M. Fuhrmann *Die antike Rhetorik* München/Zürich 1987.
43 However one defines the movement of humanism, it seems that 'the strong interest in rhetoric is its most remarkable common feature' (K. Alfsvag 'Language and reality. Luther's relation to classical rhetoric in *Rationis Latomianae confutatio* (1521)' *Studia Theologica* 41 [1987] 86). Cf C. Trinkaus *Scope* 26ff; J. Monfasani 'Humanism and Rhetoric' in *Renaissance Humanism* 3, 171ff; Q. Breen 'Some Aspects of Humanist Rhetoric and the Reformation'

NAK 43 (1960) 1. On Petrarch see C. Trinkaus *The Poet as Philosopher: Petrarch and the Formation of Renaissance Consciousness* New Haven 1979; M. O'Rourke Boyle *Petrarch's Genius: Pentimento and Prophecy* Berkeley 1991.

44 Cic. De or. 1,3,12; Quint. Inst. 1,4,43; 8,pr 25. For Calvin see W.J. Bouwsma *Calvin: A Sixteenth Century Portrait* New York/Oxford 1988, 115.
45 *De recta pronuntiatione* CWE 26 369.
46 Plat. Phaedr. 272c ff; Aristot. Rhet. 1,2,8ff; 15; 2,24,1; Her. 1,9,16; Cic. Inv. 1,21; 29; Quint. Inst. 5,14,1; L 272. On Erasmus' understanding of dialectical and rhetorical syllogisms (*enthymeme*) see ch 5, 4. Cf G.A. Kennedy *Classical Rhetoric* 20f; M. Fuhrmann *Die antike Rhetorik* 16, 27
47 *De libero arbitrio* I. 195. Cf Cic. Or. 71,237; Quint. Inst. 5,14,29. L 194; 272; cf E. Rummel *Catholic Critics* 1, 22.
48 Cic. Inv. 1,1,1. Cf Cic. Or. 4,14; 33,118; Quint. Inst. 1,pr 13; Aug. De doctr. 4,5,7
49 Cf J.E. Seigel *Rhetoric and Philosophy in Renaissance Humanism* 18–30.
50 Identified in detail but over-systematized by H. Lausberg *Handbuch der literarischen Rhetorik. Eine Grundlegung der Literaturwissenschaft* München 1960; *Elemente der literarischen Rhetorik* München 1963; on Quintilian see the useful index by E. Zundel *Clavis Quintilianea, Quintilians 'Institutio oratoria' aufgeschlüsselt nach rhetorischen Begriffen* Darmstadt 1989.
51 Aristot. Rhet. 3,1,3; Her. 1,2,3; Cic. Inv. 1,7,9; De or. 1,31,142; Quint. Inst. 3,3,1
52 'It seems to me that if the religious works of the Italian humanists may be characterized as efforts to develop a *theologia rhetorica*, even more should this conception apply to Erasmus ... Erasmus most perfectly fulfils the promises and programs of the religious thought and studies of the Italian humanists ... More than anyone he made actual what was their ideal' (C. Trinkaus *Scope* 257).
53 *Scope* 253, 26, 29; *Image* xvii, 563ff, 683ff, 770. Cf for instance Salutati's 'Letter to Peregrino Zambeccari' tr R.G. Witt, in *The Earthly Republic: Italian Humanists on Government and Society* ed B.G. Kohl and R.G. Witt, Pittsburgh 1978, 93–114; see also J. Lindhardt *Rhetor, Poeta, Historicus, Studien über die rhetorische Erkenntnis und Lebensanschauung im italienischen Renaissancehumanismus* Leiden 1976, esp. 129ff.
54 C. Trinkaus *Image* 611.
55 C. Trinkaus *Image* xvii, 689; *Scope* 23
56 'It was possible to treat a pagan literary *topos* or philosophical statement in its own historical perspective and with scholarly

precision and yet see it as part of a movement of the spirit toward the subsequently revealed Christian truth' (C. Trinkaus *Scope* 30).

57 Cf my book *Erkenntnis* 33 n83; J.B. Payne *Sacraments* 7 n2; and above all J.B. Gleason's critique of the notion that it was John Colet's influence that made Erasmus turn to the Bible (*John Colet* Berkeley 1989).

58 *Ecclesiastes* ASD V-4 122:806. 'In any case, no matter where you find truth, attribute it to Christ' (*Enchiridion* CWE 66 36). 'The authority of the philosophers would be of little effect if all those same teachings were not contained in the sacred Scriptures, even if not in the same words' (*Enchiridion* CWE 66 47). *Quamquam nemo tradidit haec absolutius, nemo efficacius quam Christus, tamen permulta reperire licet in ethnicorum libris, quae cum huius doctrina consentiant* (H 145:7). *Sed non credimus Philosophis, nisi cum Scriptura consentiant* (L 450). *Imo vero quisquis bonus verusque christianus est, Domini sui esse intelligat, ubicumque invenerit veritatem* (Aug. De doctr. 2,18,28; cf 2,40, 60–42,63).

59 *Ciceronianus* CWE 28 447. 'None of the liberal disciplines is Christian, because they neither treat of Christ nor were invented by Christians; but they all concern Christ' (*Antibarbari* CWE 23 90:10–12).

60 *Encomium medicinae* CWE 29 45

61 'When you take away gleaming Egyptian vessels, prepare to build a noble shrine to the Lord' (*Poems* Reedijk 15:18–19). 'To take away the wealth of Egypt is to transfer the wealth to the adornment and use of our faith' (*Antibarbari* CWE 23 97:20–1). Cf *Letters* 49 / CWE 1 103:110–11; H 32:7; 64:22–3; Aug. De doctr. 2,28,43; 40,60; 42,63; More's letter to the university of Oxford in *The Yale Edition of the Works of St. Thomas More* 1, 139. A similar *topos* is *mulier barbara*: 'Even an Israelite can love a foreign, barbarian woman, taken by her beauty, but by shaving off her hair and cutting her fingernails he makes an Israelite of a foreign-born woman' (*Enchiridion* CWE 66 34).

62 Cf for instance *Letters* 1115 / CWE 7 316:5–317:26.

63 Cf *De ratione studii* CWE 24 683:16–8; *Antibarbari* CWE 23 90:15–8; H 70:16–7; 71:35ff; 278:15; LB V 853D; 854C-D. Cf Aug. De doctr. 2,40,60. See M.A. Screech *Ecstasy and the Praise of Folly* London 1980.

64 *Enchiridion* CWE 66 68. 'Of the interpreters of divine Scripture choose those especially who depart as much as possible from the literal sense, such as, after Paul, Origen, Ambrose, Jerome, and Augustine' (*Enchiridion* CWE 66 34).

65 *Enchiridion* CWE 66 65. 'Indeed, divine wisdom resembles nature itself, leading us by the hand, as it were, from the knowledge of

visible things to the knowledge of invisible things' (*Paraphrase on Mark* CWE 49 13). Cf H 79:5-6; 283:26-8; ASD V-4 218:605ff; LB VII 250E; 520C-D. Aug. De doctr. 1,4,4; 3,5,9.
66 *Ratio* H 193:18-22. *In fontibus versetur, qui velit esse verus theologus* (*Psalmi* ASD V-2 54:606-7). Cf H 284:28; 305:14; ASD V-4 470:534-7.
67 On pre-Reformation biblical interpretation see for instance G.R. Evans *The Language and Logic of the Bible: The Road to Reformation* Cambridge 1985.
68 H. Bornkamm 'Erasmus und Luther' *Lutherjahrbuch* 25 (1958) 6
69 See my book *Erkenntnis* 33; E. Rummel *Erasmus 'Annotations'* 10-12; C. Augustijn *Erasmus* 33; S. Dresden 'Erasme et les belles-lettres' in *Colloque Erasmien* 9f; F. Krüger *Humanistische Evangelienauslegung* 2, 10ff; P. Walter *Theologie* 23.
70 R.L. DeMolen *Spirituality* xv; 15ff; 35ff
71 Similarly, L.-E. Halkin characterizes the vigorous spirituality of his interior life as one neither exclusively intellectual nor rigidly formalist ('La pieté d'Erasme,' *RHE* 74 (1984) 671-708).
72 'Raise yourself as on the steps of Jacob's ladder from the body to the spirit, from the visible to the invisible, from the letter to the mystery, from sensible things to intelligible things, from composite things to simple things. In this way, the Lord will draw nigh in his turn to the one who draws nigh to him, and if you will attempt to the limit of your powers to rise out of your moral darkness and the tumult of the senses, he will obligingly come forth to meet you from his inaccessible light and that unimaginable silence, in which not only all the tumult of the senses, but also the forms of all intelligible things fall silent' (*Enchiridion* CWE 66 84). Erasmus expressed this double movement by the verbs *(e)niti-rapi (trahi, affici, transformari)*; see for instance H 33:20; 57:18; 69:6; 122:23; 30; 139:22; 151:17; 180:22; 203:2. *Donum est Dei, sed vester est conatus* (*Paraphrasis in Joannem* LB VII 548F).
73 *Paraclesis, Methodus, Apologia,* and *Ratio seu methodus compendio perveniendi ad veram theologiam* ed Holborn, München 1933, repr 1964
74 LB VII; ASD V-2, V-3
75 'My purpose in writing paraphrases is not to strike the gospel out of men's hands, but to make it possible for it to be read more conveniently and with greater profit, just as food is seasoned to make us more willing to eat it and enjoy it' (*Letters* 1381 / CWE 10 74:444-7). The paraphrases interpret the word by an amplified sequence of thought that underlies the grammatical surface of the text, therefore 'paraphrase is a kind of commentary' (*Letters* 1255, 1333, 1342 / CWE 9 9:41-2; 243:422; 398:1026).
76 Cf J.J. Bateman 'From Soul to Soul: Persuasion in Erasmus' Paraphrases on the New Testament' *Erasmus in English* 15 (1987-8) 13.

77 ASD V-4. Literature on the *Ecclesiastes*: R.G. Kleinhans *Erasmus' Doctrine of Preaching: A Study of 'Ecclesiastes sive de ratione concionandi'* diss Princeton 1968; C. Béné *Erasme et saint Augustin* 372–425; M. Grundwald *Der 'Ecclesiastes' des Erasmus von Rotterdam, Reform der Predigt durch Erneuerung des Predigers* diss Innsbruck 1969; J. Weiss 'Ecclesiastes and Erasmus: The Mirror and the Image' *ARG* 65 (1974) 83–108; R.G. Kleinhans '"*Ecclesiastes sive de ratione concionandi*"' in *Essays on the Works of Erasmus* ed R.L. DeMolen, New Haven/London 1978, 253–67; J. Chomarat *Grammaire* 1053–1155; J.W. O'Malley 'Erasmus and the History of Sacred Rhetoric' *ERSY* 5 (1985) 1–29

78 A. Auer *Die vollkommene Frömmigkeit*; O. Schottenloher 'Erasmus, Johann Popenruyter und die Entstehung des *Enchiridion militis Christiani*' *ARG* 45 (1954) 109–16; E.-W. Kohls *Die Theologie des Erasmus*; R. Marcel 'L'*Enchiridion militis Christiani*: Sa genèse et sa doctrine, son succès et ses vicissitudes' in *Colloquia Erasmiana Turonensia* 2, 613–46; R. Stupperich 'Das *Enchiridion militis Christiani* des Erasmus von Rotterdam nach seiner Entstehung, seinem Sinn und Charakter' *ARG* 69 (1978) 5–23; A.M. O'Donnell 'Rhetoric and Style in Erasmus' *Enchiridion militis Christiani*' *Studies in Philology* 77 (1980) 26–49; A. Godin 'The *Enchiridion militis Christiani*: Modes of an Origenian Appropriation' *ERSY* 2 (1982) 47–79; J.W. O'Malley ed CWE 66 (1988).

79 Although J.W. O'Malley ('Introduction' CWE 66 xiiff) connects Erasmus' piety with theology and ministry, he fails to include Erasmus' understanding of natural piety; see my article 'Faith and Piety in Erasmus's Thought' *SCJ* 20:2 (1989) 241–58, and A.M. O'Donnell's review in *ERSY* 11 (1991) 130.

80 Excellently annotated by J. Chomarat in ASD V-4.

81 On the historical background see R. Stupperich 'Zur Entstehungsgeschichte der *Ratio seu methodus compendio perveniendi ad veram Theologiam*' *NAK* 67 (1987) 110–19; E. Rummel *Catholic Critics* 1, 63ff.

82 As in S. Wiedenhofer *Formalstrukturen humanistischer und reformatorischer Theologie bei Philipp Melanchthon* Bern/Frankfurt/München 1976

83 I accept P. Walter's critique (*Theologie* 176 n952) of my earlier analysis of this passage (*Erkenntnis* 46).

84 Our outline somewhat differs from J. Chomarat's (*Grammaire* 1061–71, and 'Introduction' ASD V-4 8ff) because it focuses above all on Erasmus' hermeneutic.

85 Quint. Inst. 2,14,5; 12,10,1

86 *Ecclesiastes* ASD V-4 270:490. *An non hoc ipse docuit Cicero, caput artis esse dissimulare artem?* (*Ciceronianus* ASD I-2 625:28–9)

87 *Ecclesiastes* ASD V-4 30:50
88 *Ratio* H 178:7–14; 283:29–32; *Ecclesiastes* ASD V-4 268:486; et al.
89 To sort it out remains the daunting task for the editors of the critical text (*ASD*) and English translation (*CWE*). In his recent edition of *Ecclesiastes* I–II (ASD V-4), J. Chomarat has done a yeoman's job in identifying Erasmus' rhetorical sources.
90 *Oratio contionale* is the speech in the assembly of the people and thus a kind of deliberative oratory; cf Quint. Inst. 3,4,1; 10; 8,11; 14; 65; 67; 10,1,73; 12,10,70.
91 Memory and delivery receive less space, as with Cicero, Quintilian, and Melanchthon (*Et in tribus partibus fere toto ars consumitur*, CR 13,419; see M.J. La Fontaine *A Critical Translation of Philip Melanchthon's 'Elementorum rhetorices libri duo'* diss Michigan 1968, 58).
92 'The way of persuasion was shown to us by the Lord himself, imitated by the apostles, and praised by the doctors of the church' (*Purgatio* ASD IX-1 458:425-6).
93 *Ecclesiastes* ASD V-4 40:111
94 *Ratio* H 236:29
95 *Ecclesiastes* LB V 781B; 1062D; 1080E. For a full treatment of prudence, see below ch 5, 4.
96 *Ratio* H 291:19
97 J. Chomarat concludes: 'Erasme ne pouvait se dispenser de rappeler les règles dites de Tychonius sur l'exégèse; il le fait, à fin du livre III, comme une sorte d'appendice, sans les utiliser lui-meme' (ASD V-4 17). But alongside Augustinian and Dionysian influences, elements of Tychonius' rules (the God-devil dualism, the two communities, Christ and the mystical body, law and gospel, the variety of times, and recapitulation as restitution) are found in Erasmus' theology as a whole and therefore contribute significantly to determining his hermeneutic.
98 *Ecclesiastes* LB V 1071ff; cf 1058ff
99 Bouwsma *Calvin* 126; in his epistle to the final version for the *Institutes*, Calvin wrote that he intended 'to prepare and instruct candidates in sacred theology to read the divine word so that they may be able both to have easy access to it and to advance in it without stumbling' (Bouwsma 29).

CHAPTER TWO

1 J. Chomarat's study (*Grammaire*, see esp. 31–75) has made this abundantly clear.
2 As far as the *Ecclesiastes* is concerned, see for instance: *Qualis est sermo noster, talis est spiritus noster* (ASD V-4 40:117–42:142). *Qualecunque est cor hominis, talis est oratio* (42:161). Cf 460:271–2; et al.

3 Erasmus espoused the *dictum Socraticum: Quae supra nos, nihil ad nos* (*Adages* CWE 32 48; LB VII **3; *Letters* 1334 / CWE 9 251:189–90; see also *De libero arbitrio* L 10; 14). *Quod si ambiguum est quicquid translatitium est, nulla sunt humana verba quibus proprie loquamur de rebus diuinis* (*Purgatio* ASD IX-1 463:581–3). That Erasmus' understanding of the divine mystery differs from Luther's concept of the hiddennness of God (WA 18 685:3–7) is clear from E. Jüngel's article '*Quae supra nos, nihil ad nos. Eine Kurzformel der Lehre vom verborgenen Gott, im Anschluß an Luthers Lehre interpretiert*' *Evangelische Theologie* 32:3 (1972) 195ff. See also C. Christ-von Wedel *Das Nichtwissen bei Erasmus von Rotterdam: Zum philosophischen und theologischen Erkennen in der geistigen Entwicklung eines christlichen Humanisten* Basel/Frankfurt 1981.
4 Cf *De copia* ASD I-6 30:94–31:102.
5 As for instance the interplay between *ordo naturalis* and *ordo artificialis* in the disposition of oratory; see below ch 4 n35 and H. Lausberg *Elemente* 27f. On the relation of movement and rest in all living things cf Aristot. Phys. 2,1,8ff; 13ff. With Erasmus this relation expresses itself in the interplay between *status* and *varietas* (*Ecclesiastes* LB V 1071F), God as *veritas* and *fons* (1072E), *ordo* and *gradus* (1082F), and *autor-materia-forma-finis* (*Explanatio symboli* ASD V-1 213:220).
6 *De pueris instituendis* CWE 26 298. 'But man certainly is not born, but made man. Primitive man, living a lawless, unschooled, promiscuous life in the woods, was not human, but rather a wild animal. It is reason which defines humanity' (CWE 26 304). Cf W.H. Woodward *Desiderius Erasmus Concerning the Aim and Method of Education* New York 1964.
7 'In the common usage of our language we call our sons *liberi*, realizing that they should have a liberal education, which bears no resemblance to anything servile' (*De pueris instituendis* CWE 26 327). Cf G.A. Kennedy *Classical Rhetoric* sv liberal arts; education; H.M. Klinkenberg art 'Artes liberales' *HWP* 1, 531–5.
8 'Coming to one's senses' is for Erasmus primarily a religious term as an expression for conversion (*resipiscentia*). Cf for instance H 46:23; 56:22; 119:13; 124:3; 133:2; 209:25; 218:33; 253:32; 257:29; 260:13; 284:19; ASD V-2 150:680; 198:141; 209:515.
9 For *auctoritas* in Quint. see Inst. 1,4,4; 6,1–2,11; 42; 3,8,36; 5,11,36–44.
10 H 24:4; 38:13; ASD V-4 42:176; V-1 214:233.
11 Cf the work of Trinkaus, Chomarat, and Boyle.
12 A beginning has been made by my work (*Erkenntnis*), followed by Krüger (*Humanistische Evangelienauslegung*). Walter (*Theologie*), though critical of previous approaches, has moved in a similar

direction but failed to take the ontological structure of Erasmus' thought into account, nor could he fully grasp Erasmus' hermeneutic because he concentrated on his biblical interpretation without including the function of preaching.

13 *De recta pronuntiatione* CWE 26 369. Cf Cic. De or. 1,8,32; Quint. Inst. 2,16,12. On Zeno's notion that it is *logos* that distinguishes human being from animals, see M. Pohlenz *Stoa und die Stoiker* Zürich/Stuttgart 1964, x.

14 'Nor can I regard as an error the assertion that order is essential to the existence of nature itself, for without order everything would go to wrack and ruin. Similarly if oratory lack this virtue, it cannot fail to be confused, but will be like a ship drifting without a helmsman, will lack cohesion ... without fixed purpose or the least idea either of starting-point or goal' (Quint. Inst. 7,pr 3; tr H.E. Butler *Loeb Classical Library* Cambridge/London 1986, 5).

15 *De pueris instituendis* CWE 26 304–5. See for instance ASD I-2 1ff; 79 ff; and above all ASD IV-IA 19ff. Cf M.M. Phillips 'Erasmus on the Tongue' *ERSY* 1 (1981) 113–25; L. Carrington 'Erasmus' *Lingua*: The Double-Edged Tongue' *ERSY* 9 (1989) 106–18; and *CWE* 29 249ff.

16 *Lingua* CWE 29 314–15. 'Speech is the reflection of the mind' (*Lingua* CWE 29 326). 'Speech is truly the mirror of the heart' (*Paraphrase on John* CWE 46 16). 'Speech reveals the features of the mind much as a mirror reflects the face' (*Ciceronianus* CWE 28 441). *Sermo hominis verax imago est mentis, sic oratione quasi speculo reddita ...* (*Ecclesiastes* ASD V-4 38:98). *Nam sermo mentis est signum* (*Ecclesiastes* ASD V-4 460:272). Cf ASD I-2 704:10; IV-1 296:96ff; LB VII 88E; J.J. Bateman 'From Soul to Soul' 7 n6.

17 *Adages* CWE 32 36–7. On Quintilian's insistence that the ideal orator is nothing less than *vir bonus dicendi peritus* (12,pr 1,4; cf 1,pr 9) cf Cic. De or. 2,43,184; ASD V-4 358:805; 464:404. See also M. Winterbottom 'Quintilian and the *Vir bonus*' *Journal of Religion* 54 (1964) 90–7; P.A. Meador 'Quintilian's *Vir bonus*' *Western Speech* 34 (1970) 162–9; A. Brinton 'Quintilian, Plato, and the *Vir bonus*' *Philosophy and Rhetoric* 16 (1983) 167–84; and C. Trinkaus *Scope* 369.

18 *Lingua* CWE 29 326; *Adages* CWE 32 37

19 For instance *De pueris instituendis* CWE 26 304. Cf Cic. Inv. 1,2,2ff; 4,5; De or. 1,8,33.

20 Cic. De or. 3,5,20–6,21 (tr H. Rackham *Loeb Classical Library* Cambridge/London 1982, 17–9).

21 *Querela pacis* CWE 27 294

22 *Antibarbari* CWE 23 59

23 *Lingua* CWE 29 277. Cf ASD I-2 704:8–10; LB VII 254A; J.-C. Margolin 'L'idée de nature dans la pensée d'Erasme' *Recherches érasmiennes* Geneva 1969, 9–44.

24 *Letters* 1137 / CWE 8 36:24–7. 'I always pursue what I have once begun. I promote with all my strength good letters and endeavour to restore a pure and simple theology' (*Spongia* ASD IX-1 170:109–10). 'Theology, frigid and quarrelsome, had sunk to such a pitch of futility that it was essential to recall it to the fountain-head' (*Letters* 1127 / CWE 8 18:16–18). Cf *Letters* 1181 / CWE 8 148:36–40; 1191 / CWE 8 163:51–2.
25 Erasmus connected *vulgus* (cf Petr. De vita sol. 352; Cic. Tusc. 1,16,37f; De or. 3,6,24; 24,92; Aug. Tract in Ioh. 30,2) with tumult (*turba*). The crowd admires new things which upset public tranquility, is moved by external apearances, by earthly and transitory things more than by examples of true piety or sound doctrine, and takes them as an occasion for vice (*Ecclesiastes* LB V 969A; 976F: 986F; 878F; 1070B). On *perturbatio ordinis* see H 42:11; LB V 951E; 1074C.
26 H 142:10ff; ASD V-2 54:616ff; LB VII **2v; **3v; L 386; but see ASD V-4 262:360; 264:402; IX-1 448:151.
27 (*De recta pronuntiatione* CWE 26 389). Cf *De pueris instituendis* CWE 26 320. On 'second level' persuaders see J.J. Bateman 'From Soul to Soul' 10.
28 J. Chomarat, *Grammaire* 115–224; R. Guerlac *Juan Vives* 1–16
29 *Paraphrase on John* CWE 46 13; 15. Cf *Letters* 1225 / CWE 8 277:239–42.
30 See ch 5, 4.
31 *Letters* 1334 / CWE 9 250:173–7
32 *Letters* 1033 / CWE 7 112:143–7. Cf *Letters* 1341A /CWE 9 340:1132–44; 1342 / CWE 9 397:966–9. See my book *Erkenntnis* 110–14.
33 *Ciceronianus* CWE 28 349. Cf ASD I-2 611:26; 626:4ff; 16; 702:36.
34 'Cicero's apes' (ASD I-2 626:27; 630:5; 648:24; 649:10)
35 On *utilitas* see below ch 5, 6.
36 On *mediocritas* or *moderatio* see the index of technical terms.
37 'A noble nature desires to be instructed, and will not endure to be coerced. Merely to use coercion is for tyrants; merely to suffer it, for donkeys' (*Letters* 1153 / CWE 8 72:173–5). 'Noble natures desire to be instructed, and will not endure to be coerced. Instruction is for theologians, merely to use coercion is for tyrants' (*Letters* 1167 / CWE 8 116:287–9).
38 *Paraphrasis in Joannem* LB VII 576A; cf Aug. Tract. in Ioh. 72, 3. 'But to restore great things is sometimes not only a harder but a nobler task than to have introduced them' (*Letters* 384 / CWE 3 221:29–222:30). 'It is a greater achievement to heal disorder than to suppress it' (*Letters* 1414 / CWE 10 164:47–8). 'You should not be so eager to overthrow the existing order that you fail to consider

whether what succeeds it will be better. For change, quite apart from the strife that it usually brings with it, often tends toward the worse. Such is the unfortunate condition of human affairs: remedies are sometimes harsher than the very evils we are eager to cure' (*Detectio* ASD IX-1 260:656–60; cf *Contra pseudevangelicos* ASD IX-1 308:699–700).

39 'Error and ignorance are pardonable' (*Paraphrase on Mark* CWE 49 53). 'An error that has its origin not in wickedness but in simplicity has to be either healed or endured for the time being' (*Paraphrase on Mark* CWE 49 130). Cf ASD IX-1 444:34ff; LB VI 696E; ASD V-2 331:70f; 346:585ff. See my article 'Erasmus and Religious Toleration' *ERSY* 2 (1982) 80–106.

40 *Psalmi* ASD V-3 147:14–148:45. *Per linguam potissimum occiditur Christus, per linguam nascitur ac renascitur in nobis* (*Ecclesiastes* ASD V-4 216:547–8). Cf ASD V-2 62:883ff; 302:495ff; ASD V-3 145:937ff; ASD V-4 38:98ff; 42:175–44:186; 216:575ff; 398:783; LB V 967C; 969F.

41 'Instead of the venom of slander, let our tongue offer brotherly rebuke, instead of insults, consolation, instead of curses, prayers to God, instead of denigration, a mild and honest reproof, instead of a hotbed of conflicts, conciliatory speech, instead of the poison of ulceration, sound doctrine, instead of muttering, psalms and hymns, instead of quarreling, spiritual chants, instead of silly tales, the speech of knowledge, instead of accusation against our neighbour, the confession of our own evils, instead of the most bitter persecution of other mens' failures, the desire to give healing' (*Lingua* CWE 29 410).

42 *De ratione studii* CWE 24 666

43 Cf Her. 3,20,33; Quint. Inst. 3,5,1; Aug. De doctr. 1,2; 2,1–5. For the following see J. Chomarat *Grammaire* 86–90, 718f; T.F. Torrance 'The Hermeneutics of Erasmus' 51, 54–6.

44 *De recta pronuntiatione* CWE 26 455–6. Cf ASD V-4 460:273–4.

45 Cf L. Carrington 'Erasmus on the Use and Abuse of Metaphor' *Acta Conventus Neo-Latini Torontonensis* (1991) 111–20.

46 *Ecclesiastes* ASD V-4 254:174–97

47 *Verum vbi ecclesiastae tractanda erit similitudo aut allegoria, non satis videbitur scire, quod ea vox est nomen arboris aut piscis aut gemmae aut fluminis. Talium enim schematum tractatio non sumitur a simplici nomine, sed a forma, natura, vi et effectu rei, a qua similitudo ducitur* (*Ecclesiastes* ASD V-1 254:198–201).

48 *Humile ostium*; see below n127.

49 Cf R. Waswo *Language & Meaning in the Renaissance* Princeton 1987.

50 See below ch 5, 2.

51 *Ecclesiastes* ASD V-4 310:525ff; LB V 951Eff

52 Invention is not a creative process in the modern sense but the

remembrance of the *copia rerum* in the speaker's mind where, according to the Platonic theory of knowledge, *topoi* are located in certain places. (H. Lausberg *Elemente* 24, 40). On the difference between the classical concept of invention and the modern understanding of creativity see A. Hügli and U. Theissmann, art 'Invention, Erfindung, Entdeckung' *HWP* 4, 544–52.

53 On how Erasmus related *natura, ars, imitatio,* and *usus* see below ch 4, 1.
54 *Ciceronianus* CWE 28 441. On the significance of *imitatio* between theory (*ars*) and practice (*exercitatio*) compare Her. 4,2,2; Cic. De or. 2,22,90; Quint. Inst. 3,5,1; 7,10,9; 10,2,1–27.
55 *probare, conciliare, movere* (Cic. De or. 2,27,115); *probare, delectare, flectere* (Cic. Or. 21,69); Quint. Inst. 3,5,2; 5,pr 1; 8,pr 7; 11,1,6; 12,2,11; 10,59; Aug. De doctr. 4,12,27–8; ASD I-1 626:2; LB V 1062. Cf ASD V-4 274:596; LB VII 77B; ASD IX-1 478:996.
56 Her. 1,1,1; 3,16,28; Cic. De or. 1,15,64; 2,22,90; Quint. Inst. 3,2, 1; 5,1; 7,1,40; 8,pr 16; 28; 12,9,20
57 Cf Cic. De or. 2,27,115; 42,178; 43,182; Quint. Inst. 3,9,7; 4,3,9; 6,1,12; 12,10,59; ASD V-4 235:931–236:948.
58 *Paraphrase on John* CWE 46 11
59 ASD I-6
60 See below ch 3, 5.
61 *De pueris instituendis* CWE 26 336
62 *Ecclesiastes* LB V 1016F
63 *Enchiridion* CWE 66 67, 69. Cf H 191:26–30; 210:33–5.
64 See my book *Erkenntnis* sv.
65 *Apologia de 'In principio erat sermo'* LV IX 117A-C; *Letters* 1061 / CWE 7 170:24–35. 'Just as the mysteries of Scripture call the highest mind, than which nothing greater or better can be conceived, God, likewise they call God's only Son the Word of that mind. For though a son is not the same as his father, yet in his likeness he reflects as it were his father, so that it is possible to see each one in the other, the father in the son and the son in the father ... And there is no other object that more fully and clearly expresses the invisible form of the mind than speech that does not lie. Speech is truly the mirror of the heart' (*Paraphrase on John* CWE 46 15–16). Cf M. O'Rourke Boyle *Erasmus on Language* 3–31; E. Rummel *Catholic Critics* 1, 123ff, 142f.
66 *Ecclesiastes* ASD V-4 466:449–63. Cf LB V 903F; 933B
67 See above n16.
68 *Lingua* CWE 29 326
69 Cf ASD V-2 62:883ff; 302:495ff; ASD V-3 122:20; 145:946; 211:499ff; ASD V-4 40:168ff; 216:567ff; 460:272; LB V 982B.
70 *Psalmi* ASD V-3 147:14–148:45

71 'A complete image of a man's way of life and the whole force of his character is reflected in his speech as in a mirror, and the very secrets of his bosom can be detected from clues, as it were, that lie beneath the surface' (*Adages* CWE 32 37). Cf ASD V-3 158:451; ASD V-2 54:614; ASD V-3 146:960.
72 *Psalmi* ASD V-2 70:144ff; *Ecclesiastes* LB V 1080C
73 *Psalmi* ASD V-2 78:416–18
74 *Primus certe gradus est utcunque cognoscere* (*Paraclesis* H 142:19–20). *Primum autem est scire, quid docuerit, proximum est praestare* (*Paraclesis* 145:33). Cf ASD I-2 640:8–10; 651:32; 704:29; ASD V-4 40:130ff; 100:398ff; 252:131ff. See Aug. De doctr. 4,12,28; Quint. Inst. 9,1,19.
75 See above n55.
76 *Lingua* CWE 29 277
77 See below ch 5, 3.
78 That Erasmus put a premiun on *jucunditas* and *vehementia* will be shown. See below ch 5, 5.
79 *Docendo efficimus vt res intelligatur ac persuadeatur ... Quod nisi fit, caetera sunt superuacua. Nullus enim delectatur aut mouetur iis quae non intelligit aut non credit* (*Ecclesiastes* ASD V-4 274:597-600).
80 Cf for instance ASD I-5 90:28ff; I-6 276:13ff; V-4 274:600; H 139:23; 260:11; 271:34. See Quint. Inst. 4,2,46; 5,14,29; 8,3,5; 12,10,43ff. *Delectatio* (or *conciliatio*) is attached to the *medium genus dicendi* (Quint. Inst. 12,10,58–63), thus receiving a place which is also central in Erasmus' rhetorical theology.
81 *Lingua* CWE 29 277
82 See above n74.
83 C. Trinkaus *Scope* 30. Whether or how far Erasmus shared Valla's Christian-Epicurean view of *voluptas* (C. Trinkaus *Image* 103ff) remains to be seen. But that he associated *delectatio* and *voluptas* with the attraction to harmony and love is beyond any doubt (cf *Lingua* ASD IV-1 253:528). Platonic love (*eros*) is perfected by Christian charity which, like *delectare* between *docere* and *movere* (and like *eros* between God and humanity), stands in the middle between faith and hope (see my book *Erkenntnis* 55 n132, 94 n99).
84 J. Chomarat *Grammaire* 387–93
85 Cic. De or. 1,33,150
86 See my book *Erkenntnis* 121f.
87 Cf H 151:25ff; ASD V-2 54:604; ASD V-4 258:255; 262:341. See J. Chomarat *Grammaire* 301–94. On the trilingual college at Louvain see H. de Vocht *History of the Foundation and the Rise of the 'Collegium Trilingue Lovaniense' 1517–1555* Louvain 1951–5.
88 *Letters* 1334 / CWE 9 274:965–7. Cf E. Rummel 'Erasmus and the Greek Classics' CWE 29 xxi–xxxiii, and E. Fantham 'Erasmus and the Latin Classics' xxxiv–l.

89 For a reading list of pagan authors see for instance *Ecclesiastes* ASD V-4 264:416ff; cf H 35:27. But Erasmus advised the fledgling theologians to immerse themselves above all in those authors who are closest to sacred literature, i.e., Plato and the poets: H 70:16; 72:8; 191:28; 210:33.
90 Ov. Her. 15,83. 'For those silent letters are transformed into conduct and feelings' (*Institutio principis christiani* CWE 27 250). And where the gospel is concerned, Erasmus wrote: '... bite off some of this medicine constantly ... chew it assiduously and pass it down into our spiritual stomachs ... do not cast up again what you have swallowed but keep it in the stomach of the spirit until it develops all its powers and transforms the whole of us into itself' (*Letters* 1381 / CWE 10:424–7). Cf ASD IV-1 179:422; H 148:31; 161:10; 180:24; 293:18; 296:33; ASD IV-1 179:420-2; V-2 64:940; ASD V-4 52:364.
91 On the relation between symbolic and allegorical speech see J. Lindhardt *Rhetor* 142ff. But Erasmus goes one step further and sees Christ incarnate, or if you will 'inverbate,' in Scripture.
92 *Lingua* CWE 29 323. Cf ASD IV-2 294:3ff; V-2 214:683; 288:45; V-3 100:180.
93 *Lingua* CWE 29 323
94 *Quum Vetus Testamentum fuerit vmbra ac veluti progymnasma philosophiae euangelicae quumque euangelica doctrina sit instauratio simul et perfectio naturae, vt erat primum condita sincere, mirum videri non debet, si philosophis quibusdam ethnicis datum est, naturae vi quaedam animaduertere quae cum doctrina Christi consentiant ... et maxime congruebat vt nihil adferret Christus, cuius non aliqua vel vmbra vel scintilla praecessisset in Veteris Testamenti libris ...*' (*Epistola de philosophia euangelica* LB VI ***5r). Cf ASD V-3 99:155ff; IX-1 470:789ff; V-4 100:403; 182:942ff; LB V 1062C.
95 *Verbum Dei nemo dictus est praeter Christum, qui solus natura est Deus, iuxta quam naturam hoc titulo designatur Verbum Dei, cuius praecones sunt ecclesiastae* (*Ecclesiastes* ASD V-4 38:96–8). Cf H 146:6ff; 149:2; ASD V-4 36:55ff; 56:429ff; 83:45; 186:8; 415:182f; LB V 1092D; 1093B; LB VII 498E–499D; 576C; et al.
96 On *fabula* see H 209:1ff; 210:4; 35; LB VII **3v; 27F; 243B; 784A; LB IX 563Dff; 1109C; ASD V-1 218:260; IX-1 450:218; 452:260ff; 459:473; 476:938. *Fabula* is for Erasmus part of poetic literature and therefore allegorical in character but not necessarily fictitious (LB IX 654A), even though it contains an element of the miraculous (cf Aristot. Rhet. 2,20,2f; Her. 1,8,13; Cic. Inv. 1,19,27; Quint. Inst. 2,4,2). It is connected with drama (Her. 4,4,6; Quint. Inst. 5,10,9) which for Erasmus includes a set of actors (*varietas personarum*) and a movement from *protasis* to *epitasis* to *catastrophe*, or from *initium* to *progressus* to *consummatio*, whether in the divine *dispositio*

(*oikonomia*) of the development of the church and of the history of salvation in general or in the gospel story specifically. '*Fabula* (drama) ... means a coherent argument involving various persons, each of whom plays his part, the whole action being arranged in such a way that from a reasonable calm beginning it increases in intensity, but finally reaches a happy ending. The metaphor implicitly compares God the Father to the director, who is the author of the entire dispensation. The Son who has taken on the weakness of the flesh, concealing his divine nature, comes in an assumed character, as it were ... The Holy Spirit moderates the church until, at the resurrection of the just, God wipes away every tear from the eyes of the saints. Man being created good is like the beginning (of the drama), the cross is like the completion, the resurrection is like the dénouement ... The word *fabula* is two-headed indeed; certainly if nothing is added to it. For sometimes it means a fictional narrative, sometimes the recounting of true and familiar things ... and sometimes ... it means a coherent argument acted by different persons. Yet I have taken care so that it cannot be ambiguous to anyone' (*Purgatio* ASD IX-1 452:283–96, tr P. Macardle; see ASD IX-1 477:n938–9). Cf CWE 49 xiii; 6; 8; 15; 38; 55; 61; 88; 134; 145; 146; 156; 170; CWE 29 xli. Unlike E. Rummel (CWE 49 and *Catholic Critics* 2, sv), G. Chantraine (*Erasme* 309–12) does not recognize the rhetorical background of *fabula* and therefore misinterprets it in terms of history and mystery. But even history is for Erasmus not altogether factual (LB V 1061D).

97 *In his litteris praecipue praestat, in quibus nobis etiamnum vivit, spirat, loquitur, paene dixerim efficacius, quam cum inter homines versaretur* (*Paraclesis* H 146:23). Cf H 149:2ff; LB VII 609E; 620B; ASD V-4 414:180ff; LB V 984E.

98 See below ch 3, 1.

99 Cf ASD IV-1 294:19ff; ASD V-3 206:321ff.

100 *Paraphrase on Mark* CWE 49 109. 'For this impenetrable mystery (sc Christ's two natures) had to be urged upon the world at the right time, by miracles, death, resurrection, ascension into heaven, and the inspiration of the Holy Spirit, rather than being baldly stated and imposed before its time on people who would not believe it' (*Paraphrase on John* CWE 46 120).

101 Cf H 209:1ff; 210:4; 211:4; 286:2. The circle is a symbol of perfection both in terms of the consistency of truth and of the eternity of life; see H 44:10; LB II 400C; 401A–B; ASD V-1 216:334; LB V 1072E. Aristot. Rhet. 3,6,1; Cic. De or. 3,14,178f.

102 *Enchiridion* CWE 66 62

103 Cf H 35:33; 47:27; ASD I-2 709:24.

104 *Epistola ad Volzium* (H 12:23–4). Cf H 9:30; 20:5; 32:32; 63:10; 65:18;

180:22; 193:18; 194:24; 202:5; 204:12; ASD I-2 709:27; V-2 52:549ff; CWE 32 247. M. O'Rourke Boyle (*Erasmus on Language* 74–81) makes a farfetched argument to prove that Erasmus understood *scopus* as a navigational star-fix – an interpretation with which P. Walter agrees (*Theologie* 56 n311). But *scopus* is for Erasmus originally a rhetorical term, identical with *caput* (or *status*; cf Quint. Inst. 3,6,2): *Roget aliquis quid haec ad praeconem euangelicum? Primum ad hoc valent vt ... ad caput velut ad scopum omnia conferat* (*Ecclesiastes* ASD V-4 342:394ff). *Status* is the essential point of a case or a question on which the speaker focuses everything (ASD V-4 342:375ff). Moreover, the main point of speech anticipates the aim of speech (*finis*; cf Aristot. Rhet. 1,5,1; 6,1; Her. 3,2,3; Cic. Inv. 2,51,155f). *Finis* as outcome in the end already is present in the beginning as *intentio*: *Quicquid autem conditum est, ad certum finem conditum est ... Finis igitur ... qui in euentu vltimus dicitur, in intentione primus* (*Ecclesiastes* ASD V-4 388:543; 550f). *Materia* provides the material for the development between *scopus* and *finis* (ASD V-4 168:698). Erasmus thus sees *scopus* in the context of the development of speech (*initium, progressus* and *consummatio*). In this sense Christ is at once the *scopus* and *finis*, the Alpha and the Omega, and his philosophy is the subject matter of his speech.

105 *Paraphrase on John* CWE 46 38. On the authority and divine inspiration of Scripture see for instance H 56:33; 168:14; ASD I-3 251:615; V-4 83:46; 470:535; LB V 1008B; 1049E; 1062D; 1078A–E. Cf Aug. De doctr. 1,10,10; 4,6,9; 7,21.

106 *Postremo confirmatur effectu sive energia. Nulla enim humana scriptura sic rapit ac transformat totum hominem, quum simplici sermone sit prodita, nec Philosophiae mundanae subtilitate se venditans, nec Rhetorum lenociniis blandiens auribus hominum* (*Ecclesiastes* LB V 1078D).

107 Cf H 152:7; 158:9; 162:22; 165:8; 168:17; 169:3; 182:24; 284:32; 305:2.

108 Cf H 168:27; 172:26ff; 192:25.

109 H 163ff; cf E. Rummel *Erasmus' 'Annotations'* 89 ff.

110 *Qui praedicant inviolabilem divinarum scripturarum auctoritatem, his utroque favemus pollice. Qui has sciens depravat, contumeliam facit spiritui sancto. Fatemur. Verum haec maiestas in ipsis est fontibus* (*Apologia* H 168:13–17). *Is vero subservit spiritui sancto, qui quod per homines depravatum est, pro viribus pristinae restituit integritati* (*Apologia* H 168:29–31).

111 *Paraclesis* H 145:6; *Epistola de philosophia euangelica* LB VI ***5r. Erasmus links the restoration of nature by Christ not only to Christian regeneration but also, within the overall dispensation

of salvation, to creation in the beginning and to perfection in the end. Cf LB VII 173B; 625F; 816D; 862B,D–E; LB V 1073C; 1078D–E.
112 *Letters* 384 / CWE 3 222:44–55. Cf H 155:16ff; 191:16ff; 194:32ff; 284:28ff
113 *Auctoritas illa inviolabilis intra prophetas et apostolos aut euangelistas stetit. Immo haec est summa scripturarum laus, quot in tot linguas toties transfusae, toties ab haereticis vel mutilatae vel depravatae, tot modis incuria scribarum contaminatae tamen aeternae veritatis vigorem obtinet (Apologia* H 168:24–8).
114 Cf my article 'Faith and Piety' 255.
115 Cf H. Wagenvoort and G. Tellenbach art 'auctoritas' *RAC* 1, 902ff.
116 Facsimile repr Stuttgart 1986, intr by H. Holeczek; a facsimile of the final text of the annotations with all earlier variants has been published by A. Reeve and M.A. Screech in two vols thus far: *Erasmus' Annotations on the Gospels* London 1986; *Erasmus' Annotations on Acts-Romans-I and II Corinthians* Leiden 1990.
117 See E. Rummel *Erasmus and His Catholic Critics* 2 vols (reviewed by N.H. Minnich and myself in *ERSY* 11 (1991) 135–45).
118 *Paraclesis, Methodus, Apologia,* and *Ratio seu methodus compendio perveniendi ad veram theologiam* ed H. Holborn, München 1933, repr 1964
119 *Paraphrasis in Novum Testamentum* LB VII **1v; 150; 271; 489
120 This is the basic error of J.W. Aldridge's *The Hermeneutic of Erasmus*; J.H. Bentley *Humanists and Holy Writ* moves on a similar track (see S.H. Hendrix' review in *ERSY* 5 (1985) 84–91).
121 'You created the world through me (sc your Son) so that there might be those who would learn, marvel at, and love your power, your wisdom, and your goodness. Now it is again time for your goodness to restore creation through me. And it will be restored if the world learns how great your love for the human race is, when for the sake of its salvation you hand your only Son over to death; if it learns how great your power is, when you break the tyranny of the devil; if it learns how great your wisdom is, when by such a marvellous plan you turn to you a world separated from you' (*Paraphrase on John* CWE 46 193).
122 See below ch 4. Cf my book *Erkenntnis* 59–101; Krüger *Humanistische Evangelienauslegung* 29–46.
123 See below ch 3, 2.
124 *In his haec quoque servanda regula, ut sensus, quem ex obscuris verbis elicimus, respondeat ad orbem illum doctrinae Christianae, respondeat ad illius vitam, denique respondeat ad aequitatem naturalem* (*Ratio* H 286:1–4). Cf ASD IX-1 472:814–16.
125 H 150:27–151:13; 178:19–179:2

126 *Adages* CWE 32 211–12. Cf H 32:14; 33:13; ASD V-2 52:563; LB VII 86F; 897D; et al.
127 *Enchiridion* CWE 66 34. Cf H 56:32; 141:30; 179:28; ASD V-3 98:122
128 H 63:12; 75:20; 203:23; 210:6ff; 216:31ff; 220:11ff; 264:21; LB VII 229D; 628A–B
129 'Like is affected by like' (*Enchiridion* CWE 66 81). Cf *Adages* CWE 31 167–8; H 35:1; 42:3–4; 68:36; 117:20; 155:23; 292:4; ASD V-2 40:204; V-4 86:100; 182:950; 260:310f; LB V 981D. Aristot. Metaph. 2,4,5.
130 Cf J.-C. Margolin 'L'idée de nature'.
131 Cf above ch 1 n75.
132 *Ratio* H 192:6–13
133 *Ratio* H 187:1–22; 190:12–27
134 *Querela pacis* CWE 27 297. On *vir bonus* see above n17.
135 *Apologia contra Latomi dialogum* CWE 71 55
136 *Ratio* H 178:19–180:9; *Ecclesiastes* ASD V-4 44:187–76:875
137 *Ecclesiastes* ASD V-4 180:925–190:62
138 See my article 'Faith and Piety in Erasmus's Thought.'
139 *Ratio* H 293:13–18; *Psalmi* ASD V-2 53:597–54:610
140 *Ecclesiastes* ASD V-4 68:670–4; 80:983–4; 110:588–96; 236:950–2; 249:73–250:87; LB V 1080B
141 *In naturam ibit, quod usu perpetuo fuerit infixum* (*Ratio* H 293:18); *Iam facile descendit in animos omnium, quod maxime secundum naturam est* (*Paraclesis* H 145:4). Cf H 272:3–4; 224:21–2; ASD V-4 368:41–2. See F. P. Hager art 'Natur' HWP 6, 421–41, esp. 425ff.
142 *Ecclesiastes* ASD V-4 66:649–53; 250:106–12; 260:311; 368:41–3; LB V 977D; see below ch 4, 1.

CHAPTER THREE

1 *Paraphrase on Galatians* CWE 42 112. *Filii persona tribus constat naturis, Divina quam eamdem habet cum Patre & Spiritu sancto, anima humana & corpore humano: sic enim conveniebat, ut medius esset inter Deum & homines* (*Ecclesiastes* LB V 1073B). Cf H 244:19–23
2 As *scopus* Christ is *caput* and *finis*, cf above ch 2 n104.
3 *Explanatio symboli* ASD IV-1 294:19ff; *Psalmi* V-2 288:44ff; V-3 262:125ff; 263:181ff; 377:13ff; 382:448; *Ecclesiastes* LB V 1092D
4 *Enchiridion* CWE 66 67–9
5 *Paraphrase on Mark* CWE 49 21 (cf Plat. Tim. 49c). As John stood between the law of Moses and the law of the gospel, so Christ stands between God and world; water and air between fire and earth; the soul between spirit and body; the natural affections between virtues and vices; *adiaphora* between *turpia* and *honesta*; allegory and metaphor between letter and spirit; etc. On the dichotomy-trichotomy issue see my book *Erkenntnis* sv 'Anthropologie'; on Erasmus' dualism see J. Chomarat ASD V-4, 20–2.

6 *Ecclesiastes* ASD V-4 330:100; 358:807; LB V 980Bff; 1061C; 1074Aff. On *perturbatio ordinis* see H 42:11; LB V 1047C.
7 See the connection between God (Satan, respectively), their laws, and the diametrically opposed communities and behaviour patterns resulting from either God's or the devil's speech: *Ecclesiastes* LB V 1072Dff; 1083Eff; *Paraphrasis in Matthaeum* LB VII 73C–D.
8 *Letters* 1334 / CWE 9 248:92–3
9 *Paraphrase on John* CWE 46 13–14. 'The whole of the Christian philosophy lies in this, our understanding that all our hope is placed in God, who freely gives us all things through Jesus his son, that we were redeemed by his death and engrafted through baptism with his body, that we might be dead to the desires of this world and live by his teaching and example, not merely harbouring no evil but deserving well of all men; so that, if adversity befall, we may bear it bravely in hope of the future reward which beyond question awaits all good men at Christ's coming, and that we may ever advance from one virtue to another, yet in such a way that we claim nothing for ourselves, but ascribe any good we do to God' (*Letters* 1039 / CWE 7 126:245–127:254). Cf H 5:10; 6:37; 7:7; 9:6; 139:8; 140:12; 141:14; 31; 142:30; 144:11; 32; 146:6; 148:21; 150:27; 156:9; 204:4; 283:9; LB V 1019E; CWE 10 72:365–75; ASD V-1 207:n20–1; et al. See C. Augustijn *Erasmus* 75–88; A. Godin 'La Bible et la "philosophie chrétienne"' in G. Bedouelle and B. Roussel eds *Le temps de réformes et la Bible* Paris 1989, 563–86; P. Walter, art 'Philosophie' *HWP* 7, 662–67, and H.M. Schmidinger art 'Philosophie, christliche' *HWP* 7, 888.
10 *Enchiridion* CWE 66 69–70
11 See J. Chomarat *Grammaire* 579–86.
12 Cf E. Cassirer *Individuum und Kosmos in der Philosophie der Renaissance* Leipzig/Berlin 1927, repr Darmstadt 1963, 91.
13 See above ch 2, 5.
14 Since Christ is human and divine at the same time, Christ, the incarnate word, is also seen from both a holistic and dualistic perspective. One could say that the human nature of Christ allows for both good and sacred literature, while Christ's divine nature calls for the uniqueness and superiority of sacred literature. The symbolic presence of Christ in the word is required for dualistic reasons, because the distinction between God and human beings calls for an accommodation of the divine word to human language. For holistic reasons, however, Christ must be really one with the divine word in human language in order to effect the transformation of human beings through the word and consequently their participation in the divine reality. Similarly, the transformation of human beings into the divine word effects their

becoming really Christ-like, indeed God-like, even though naturally they remain human.

15 *Methodus* H 157:25-28; *Ratio* 283:29-284:10; *Ecclesiastes* LB V 1034C-1035A; *Psalmi* ASD V-2 102:187-91; 330:43-51. In the *Ratio*, Erasmus refers in this connection to Dionysius' *On the Divine Names* (PG 3, 585ff), for the *regulae Ticonii* to Augustine's *De doctrina christiana* (3,30,42-37,56; cf LB V 1058Fff) and for Augustine's own methodology (*historia, aetiologia, analogia*, and *allegoria*) to *De utilitate credendi* 2. On the fourfold interpretation see H. Lausberg *Handbuch* 444-6; H. de Lubac *Exégèse médiéval, Les quatre sens de l'Ecriture* 4, Paris 1959-64, 427ff; L. Bouyer 'Erasmus in Relation to the Medieval Biblical Tradition' in *The Cambridge History of the Bible* 2, Cambridge 1969, 492ff; H. Caplan 'The Four Senses of Scriptural Interpretation and the Mediaeval Theory of Preaching' in ibid. *Of Eloquence, Studies in Ancient and Mediaeval Rhetoric* Ithaca 1970, 93ff; J. Chomarat *Grammaire* 570; H. Meyer art 'Schriftsinn, mehrfacher' *HWP* 8, 1431-9.
16 *Institutio principis christiani* CWE 27 250; *Moria* CWE 27 134; *Adages* III iii 1 (Phillips 275-6)
17 *Ratio* H 284:2-10
18 *Paraphrase on John* CWE 46 123
19 *Enchiridion* CWE 66 35. On the *cortex-medulla* dualism cf H 70:13-16; 71:15; 88:17; *Sileni Alcibiadis*: LB II 770Cff; *Proteus*: H 51:1; 214:31ff; 282:32ff.
20 2 Cor 3:6; John 6:64. Cf *Enchiridion* H 34:35-6; 72:17-18; *Psalmi* ASD V-2 221:919; 346:561; ASD V-3 101:240; 112:648f; *Ecclesiastes* LB V 1045C; et al. Aug. De doctr. 3,5,9. Erasmus' biblical interpretation corresponded, like Origen's, to an ontology and anthropology that extended a basic dualism by a trichotomous framework; see H. Meyer art 'Schriftsinn, mehrfacher' *HWP* 8, 1432.
21 *Enchiridion* CWE 66 34. *Sunt qui novi quoque testamenti historiam ad allegoriam trahunt, quod ego sane vehementer approbo, cum aliquoties sit necessarium, saepissime festivum et elegans, si quis modo scite rem tractet* (*Ratio* H 278:18-21).
22 *Enchiridion* CWE 66 67. *Necessitate igitur depellimur a littera, quoties Scripturae verba, ni tropum adhibeas, manifestam habent falsitatem aut absurditatem, aut alioqui sensum pugnantem cum doctrina Christi, piisque moribus* (*Ecclesiastes* LB V 1044D). Cf LB V 1043D; et al.
23 *Ita Scripturae fundamentum & robur subvertunt, qui sensum infimum rejiciunt, quum nulla cogat necessitas* (*Ecclesiastes* LB V 1038E). Cf H 275:3; ASD V-2 100:121; 102:187-190; V-3 98:133; 101:241; 259:48; 336:177; LB V 1028D; 1029D-F; 1030C; 1036D; 1037D.
24 Cf for instance *Ecclesiastes* LB V 1036D-F; 1043B-D.

25 *In verbis alium subest sensum, quam sermo prima specie prae se ferat* (*Ratio* H 293:10).
26 Cf above ch 1 n65.
27 *Ratio* H 284:5; *Psalmi* ASD V-2 156:892; 194:51ff; 224:995; 290:100ff; 330:45f; V-3 112:647ff; 189:693f; *Ecclesiastes* LB V 1034Ff; 1036F; 1059A-B. Cf ASD V-1 216:294-7.
28 *Ratio* H 278:3-5; 284:4; 17; *Psalmi* ASD V-2 102:190f; V-3 391:701; *Ecclesiastes* LB V 1034F; 1035A-D; 1036D-E; 1037A; 1050A
29 *Methodus* H 151:11ff; *Ratio* 284:6; *De libero arbitrio* L 10; *Ecclesiastes* LB V 1034F-1035A; 1037B-D
30 Cf above ch 2 n3.
31 *Ratio* H 276:21; 278:21; 280:6; 23ff; 287:21; *Ecclesiastes* LB V 1020C-D; 1029D-1033F
32 *Ratio* H 274:24-30; 286:1-4
33 *Psalmi* ASD V-2 156:891-3; 102:190-1; *Ecclesiastes* LB V 1050A
34 As a rhetorical figure, allegory certainly occurs also in profane, especially poetic texts. But there it possesses only a general metaphorical quality (and therefore is virtually identical with tropology), not the specifically Christological-ecclesiological meaning.
35 *Nec oportet historicum sensum reiicere, quo locus fiat allegoriae, quum ille sit huius basis et fundamentum, qui cognitus facit, ut aptius tractetur intelligentia retrusior ac mystica* (*Psalmi* ASD V-3 259:48-50).
36 On *initium-progressus-consummatio* see below n90.
37 *Confinia serviunt transformationi non in deterius, sed in melius* (*Ratio* H 203:5-6). *A finitimis cognatisque proclivior est transitus* (*Ratio* H 191:29-30). *Arripitur enim protinus quicquid cognatum est* (*Ecclesiastes* ASD V-4 260:310f). Cf LB V 969C.
38 See above n1.
39 *Enchiridion* H 41:16ff; 52:24ff; 53:32ff; 54:9-17; 67:28ff; etc.
40 *Epistola ad Volzium* H 12:2ff; *Enchiridion* H 68:7ff; *Ratio* 202:32ff; 203:1ff; *Adages* LB II 773A-B
41 On *adfectus* see below ch 5, 5.
42 See for instance *Psalmi* ASD V-3 147:10-148:48.
43 *Ratio* H 222:7-9. Cf H 34:16f; 203:5ff; LB VII 68A; 518E-F; ASD V-2 124:844f; V-3 103:304; 113:689ff; 338:216ff; 372:193f.
44 See my book *Erkenntnis* 90-3; 191f.
45 *Enchiridion* CWE 66 35
46 See above ch 2 n129.
47 See above n12.
48 *Ratio* H 211:31. Cf ASD V-4 40:111-16. Erasmus expressed the relation between Christ's integrity and accommodation by the word-pair *harmonia Christi* and *varietas Christi* (cf H 211:28ff; 214:31ff; 237:3f). On *harmonia-varietas* see below ch 4, 3.

49 *Enchiridion* CWE 66 104. 'Thus does Paul become all things to all men, that he may gain them all for Christ' (*Letters* 1202 / CWE 8 204:101–2). Cf H 211:31; ASD V-3 116:793; 180:331; LB VII 17C; 825D; 894E; ASD IX-1 480:10–11; V-4 68:693; 124:877; 222:662; 240:21; 332:154. Just as Christ's accommodation required his concealing his divine nature (without becoming dissimilar to himself), so the Christians' accommodation calls for *dissimulatio* (without any loss of piety). On the rhetorical device of *dissimulatio* see below n122.
50 But genus is not necessarily superior to species. Rather, through *hypallela* the species can become superior and the genus inferior: *Nihil autem vetat eamdem vocem ad superiora relatam esse speciem: ad inferiora, genus ... Haec vocantur hypallela, quod aliis subsint, allis praesint* (*Ecclesiastes* ASD V-4 410:68–9; 73).
51 See below ch 4, 6.
52 Cf H 223:33ff; 248:31; 264:30ff; ASD V-4 60:585ff; 612ff; 98:378ff; 174:827ff; 222:659ff; 396:740ff; LB V 1067A.
53 *Institutio principis christiani* CWE 27 276
54 *Querela pacis* CWE 27 321
55 *Paraphrase on Mark* CWE 49 151–152. Cf ASD IV-2 62:37ff; IX-1 262:697–9.
56 See above ch 2, 6.
57 *Enchiridion* CWE 66 33. On the secular disciplines as *progymnasmata* see for instance Ep 182:132ff; LB I 1026f; H 180:9ff; 184:23ff; LB IX 104D; ASD V-4 40:187ff; 248:30ff; 252:138ff; 270:489f; LB IX-1 470:784–471:799 (cf LB VI *4v; *5r).
58 Erasmus expressed this relation with *niti* and *rapi*; see above ch 1 n72.
59 *Psalmi* ASD V-2 174:327; 254:979; 985; 260:160; 349:665f; V-3 234:389; 384:500.
60 *De pueris instituendis* CWE 26 337. On Erasmus' pedagogical principles see J. Chomarat *Grammaire* 158–62, 921, 966.
61 *De pueris instituendis* CWE 26 312
62 *De pueris instituendis* CWE 26 321
63 *De pueris instituendis* CWE 26 334. Cf for instance ASD V-4 470:532ff. The students respond to this love with their natural love of *pietas* as reverence toward the teacher; see below ch 5, 5.
64 *De pueris instituendis* CWE 26 340. See W.H. Woodward *Aim and Method* 91, 99; J. Huizinga *Homo Ludens, Vom Usprung der Kultur im Spiel* Hamburg 1956, 93, 152, 174
65 References in my book *Erkenntnis* 182f
66 'He (Arnobius) does something ... which is a great achievement even when the subject-matter is crystal-clear: he imparts instruction quite openly, while at the same time fully retaining his hold over our feelings. His language suggests more than it expresses,

and as he speeds on his way he leaves in the readers' mind plenty
to think about and plenty to spur it into activity, so that you cannot say which is the first effect he produces in you, understanding
or enthusiasm. This again is the hallmark not merely of a good
scholar but of a teacher who loves his subject' (*Letters* 1304 / CWE
9 153:280–7). On the teacher's love and authority see *Ecclesiastes*
ASD V-4 222:641–240:27.
67 Her. 4,34,46; Cic. Or. 27,94; Quint. Inst. 8,6,14; 44–58; 9,2,46; 92.
68 *Paraphrase on John* CWE 46 46. Cf ASD V-2 254:979; 985; V-4 247:21ff.
69 *De copia* ASD I-6 64:795ff; 66:825ff; *Ratio* H 259:28ff; 266:5ff; 274:24ff;
   Ecclesiastes LB V 1008Bff; 1019Aff; 1033Fff
70 *Ratio* H 284:3f; *Ecclesiastes* LB V 1059A–B; cf Aug. De doctr. 3,32,45.
   But Erasmus cautioned that allegory, just as the other meanings of
   the fourfold sense, must not be applied indiscriminately. Rather,
   the traditional method must be qualified by rhetorical prudence,
   according to which the interpreter carefully ascertains the variety
   of persons, things, times and circumstances in each text.
71 Aristot. Rhet. 3,3,4; 10,3; 11,11; Her. 4,45,59ff; Cic. De or. 3,39,159ff;
   Or. 26,92ff; 34,134; Quint. Inst. 5,11,22; 8,3,72–81; 8,6,8; 49. Cf H.
   Lausberg *Elemente* 132–4.
72 *Paraphrase on John* CWE 46 3
73 Aristot. Rhet. 2,19,1; Her. 4,18,25; 34,46; 45,59; Cic. Top. 11,47;
   Quint. Inst. 9,1,34; 3,90; 5,10,2. Cf H. Lausberg *Elemente* 125–130.
74 *Paraphrase on Mark* CWE 49 42–3
75 *Ecclesiastes* ASD V-4 418:285–422:379; LB V 967D; 972D; 1001D; 1007F
76 *Ecclesiastes* LB V 1083E–1087F
77 *Paraphrase on Mark* CWE 49 15
78 A case in point is Erasmus' attitude toward the Jews. Unless one
   discerns in each instance whether he speaks from a dualistic or
   trichotomous perspective, his views appear skewed as either
   anti-Semitic or tolerant. While his dualistic statements show an
   irreconcilable opposition between Judaism and Christianity, his
   trichotomic statements show a progression, for instance, from the
   law of nature to the law of the gospels by way of the Mosaic law
   (see above pp 157–62). See my review of S. Markish *Erasmus and
   the Jews* Chicago/London 1986, in *ERSY* 7 (1987) 136–139.
79 For the most part Erasmus uses in this connection the terms
   Judaismus or *judaizare*: ... *Igitur ad Judaismum vergunt qui Tropos &
   Allegorias excludunt a Scriptura, ex lege, quae, juxta Paulum, spiritualis
   est, reddentes carnalem* (*Ecclesiastes* LB V 1038E). Cf H 16:21; 17:13;
   75:33; 77:5; 35; 80:3; 134:5; 200:24; 216–20; 245:30; etc. On *superstitio*
   and *supercilium* see below ch 4, 5.
80 *Metaphora ipso nomine declarat quid efficiat. Transfert enim verbum a
   propria significatione per similitudinem ad alienam alicujus commoditatis*

gratia ... Quod si totus sermo constat translatitiis, fit Allegoria, hinc dicta, quod aliud loquatur, aliud intellegi velit (*Ecclesiastes* LB V 1010A–B). Cf LB V 1034C; ASD I-6 66:826.

81 *Methodus* H 155:9–10. *Constat igitur Scripturam Canonicam, typis, schematibus ac tropis opertam esse. Nullus autem tropus, nec ullum schema plus exhibet Ecclesiastis negotii, quam allegoria* (*Ecclesiastes* LB V 1019A). Cf H 190:25–6; 259:33–6; 278:18–21; 283:3–6; LB V 1008B.

82 *Ratio* H 283:3–9

83 *Ratio* H 260:5–13. Cf Aug. De doctr. 2,6,8.

84 *Purgatio* ASD IX-1 469:743–7, tr P. Macardle. Cf H 291:34; LB V 1011A; 1019D; 1034A, C. Erasmus used *collatio* not simply as a literary genre for *De libero arbitrio*. It was for him the fundamental way to interpret Scripture, to develop one's own store of theological *topoi*, and to overcome inconsistencies in the interpretation of others.

85 *Ecclesiastes* LB V 1034C

86 *Paraphrase on Mark* CWE 49 110. 'Teachers in their sublime knowledge must not hesitate to lower themselves to the humble state of feeble men so as to win more men over to their Lord' (*Paraphrase on Mark* CWE 49 51).

87 *Paraphrase on John* CWE 46 25

88 *Paraphrase on Mark* CWE 49 55–6

89 *Paraphrase on Mark* CWE 49 61. 'God will not forsake his chosen people, he loves those who are vigilant and alert, but in such a way that while they do everything that can be done through human endeavour, they pray nevertheless, knowing that the beginning, the progress, and the consummation of eternal bliss is a divine gift' (*Paraphrase on Mark* CWE 49 156).

90 Just as Erasmus arranged *loci*, according to the (Platonic) principle of similarity, in a system that is oriented in the unique *scopus* Christ, so he used the rhetorical device of a movement from *initium* through *progressus* toward *consummatio* to account for the dynamics within it. Cf for instance ASD V-4 388:550; 414:155; 430:575; 448:980; LB V 1032F; 1077A; 1138C; 1140C; 1150B; LB X 1410C.

91 Erasmus used the concept *affectus* in four ways: as the divine (the author's) attraction in the word (*rapere*), as natural human affections in general (*pietas*), and as the moral disposition of human beings within the framework of virtues and vices, and especially in terms of Christian *caritas*. Cf for instance H 33:20ff; 180:22ff; on natural and ethical affections see below ch 5, 5.

92 Cf my article 'Faith and Piety' 253ff. It seems that similarity is to persuasion, what attraction is to transformation.

93 *Ecclesiastes* LB V 1043D. Cf *Enchiridion* H 70:13–19.

Notes to pages 118–20   261

94 John 6:63; 2 Cor 3:6. Cf above n20.
95 *Paraphrase on John* CWE 46 88
96 *Paraphrase on John* CWE 46 46
97 *Ratio* H 259:33–260:5. *Expediebat coelestis Philosophiae mysteria sic velati impiis, porcorum exemplo conculcaturis margaritas, ut tamen piis ac docilibus pateret aditus. Conducebant & humanae mentis somnolentiae excitandae. Quod in promptu est, negligimus, juxta Graecorum proverbium, in foribus hydriam; ad recondita semotaque sumus avidiores, & ut magis illa juvant, quae pluris emuntur: ita cariora nobis sunt, quae cum labore sumus adsecuti, quam quae ultro obtigerunt. Praeterea quemadmodum multa per vitrum aut succina pellucent jucundius, ita magis delectat veritas per Allegoriam relucens. Postremo sicut habet plus caloris radius speculo aut aenea pelvi exceptus, ita vehementius afficiunt animos nostros quae per Allegoriam traduntur, quam quae simpliciter narrantur* (*Ecclesiastes* LB V 1047B). Scripture is *arcana, mystica, obscura, operta, obliqua* etc.: Cf H 35:4; 16ff; 285:6f; 300:33f; 31:4; 36:15; 71:19; 31; 151:15; 159:17; 181:18; 272:1f; 288:5; 179:15; 17; 285:7f; and so on
98 *Ratio* II 211:30–1; 214:31–3; 215:32–216:14
99 *Paraclesis* H 145:4–5. *Facilius discimus ea quae secundum naturam sunt quam quae contra naturam* (*Ecclesiastes* ASD V-4 368:41).
100 *Ratio* H 260:7–8; 10–13. Cf LB VII 581D; 608C–D
101 *Ciceronianus* CWE 28· 395. Cf Cic. De or. 3,39,159; Or. 26,91ff. On *delectatio, jucunditas,* and *venustas* see below ch 5, 3.
102 *Ecclesiastes* LB V 1078D; *Ciceronianus* CWE 28 395
103 *Ratio* II 210:3–6. *E compluribus quidem rebus nascitur haec certitudo (sc omnes illi libri afflatu numinis conscripti), sed ex vna praecipue. Primum e consensu naturali. Nam quae in illis traduntur, magna ex parte consentanea sunt natiuo rationis iudicio, cuius scintilla quaedam residet etiamnum in prolapsis* (*Explanatio symboli* ASD V-1 208:78ff). *Gratia naturam imitatur* (*Paraphrasis in Marcum* LB VII 163B; 157C).
104 *Ratio* H 286:1–4. *Mea sententia vehementer confirmat Christi doctrinam, quod cum prophetis consentiat et a naturae sensu non abhorreat* (*Purgatio* ASD IX-1 472:814–16). Cf my book *Erkenntnis* 120-4. P. Walter made an illuminating study of part of the role of *aequitas naturae* (*Theologie* 72–8), whereas K. Eden ('Rhetoric in the Hermeneutics of Erasmus' Later Works' *ERSY* 11 (1991) 88– 104), by simply identifying *aequitas* with *decorum*, skews the concept of equity to show that Erasmus replaced 'the allegorizing techniques of his recent predecessors ... with the strategies of the classical forensic orator'(89). Our study, however, shows that (a) Erasmus himself cheerfully allegorized by means of a Christological-ecclesiological interpretation in consensus with the patristic tradition; (b) equity had to do with balance in, and consent with,

nature; and (c) the recognition of the variety of persons, things, times, and places was for him a matter of *prudentia*. Finally, Erasmus rejected the forensic genre as inappropriate for theological discourse. On equity cf E.J. Jonkers, art 'aequitas' RAC 1, 141–4; and G. Bien, art 'Billigkeit' HWP 1, 939–40.

105 *Querela pacis* CWE 27 294. Cf Cic. De or. 3,5,20; 6,21.
106 *Ecclesiastes* ASD V-4 368:42–3. *Scriptura variis modis nos instruit ad pietatem, interdum seruat naturae ordinem, primum a viciis reuocans, mox ad virtutes adhortans* (*Psalmi* ASD V-2 293:217–18). Cf Cic. Inv. 2,53,159.
107 *Ecclesiastes* LB V 1080E. Erasmus connected the divine law with nature: *Igitur ad honesti genus pertinebunt fas & nefas, sive secundum naturam aut praeter naturam, pietas & impietas ...* (*Ecclesiastes* ASD V-4 313:617–18). Cf LB V 1074D. On Erasmus' understanding of natural law see P. Walter *Theologie* 77, who calls for further study of *aequitas naturae* in relation to the legal tradition as understood by the rhetoricians, as for instance: Aristot. Rhet. 1,13,12–19; Her. 2,11,16; 13,19–20; 3,2,3; Cic. Inv. 1,11,14f; 2,22,68; Quint. Inst. 3,8,26.
108 *Ciceronianus* ASD I-2 709:15–16
109 *Ratio* H 262:2–6. 'Obscurity of speech arouses diligence in investigation, and the words carry more conviction when the facts become clear' (*Paraphrase on John* CWE 46 100). Cf Aug. De doctr. 2,6,8.
110 *Letters* 1333 / CWE 9 233:40–6. 'Jesus, who knows all thoughts, fitted his answer to these ignorant and sinful mutterings, so that what he said was not understood until his death, resurrection, and ascension into heaven were completed' (*Paraphrase on John* CWE 46 111). 'For the impenetrable mystery had to be urged upon the world at the right time, by miracles, death, resurrection, ascension into heaven, and the inspiration of the Holy Spirit, rather than being baldly stated and imposed before its time on people who would not believe it' (*Paraphrase on John* CWE 46 120).
111 *Ratio* H 180:3–5; *Methodus* H 151:13–15. Cf H 141:20; 213:27; 221:16
112 *Ratio* 297:13–15; 298:25–6
113 *Ratio* 299:12–14
114 *Letters* 1334 / CWE 9 251:184–8
115 *Ratio* H 260:1–2; *Ecclesiastes* LB V 1047B
116 *Institutio principis christiani* CWE 27 238. Cf H 46:26–8; 91:9–10; 261:26–8; LB VII 44C
117 *Enchiridion* CWE 66 46
118 *Ratio* H 180:22–28. On the topic, *Abeunt studia in mores*, see above ch 2 n90. This interesting juxtaposition of the active and passive voice indicates the ambiguity in Erasmus' understanding of the

relation between human striving and divine intervention in the
process of salvation. While human effort, indispensable as it is in
general education, submits completely to the power of divine
inspiration and transformation, it is not eliminated – but perfected by grace. 'Human matters are learned with human zeal;
this heavenly philosophy is not grasped unless the secret inspiration of the Father makes the human heart ready to be taught ...
The gift is God's, but the effort is yours. In vain does anyone
hear my words with his physical ears, unless he first hears the
secret voice of the Father within, the voice that breathes on the
mind the imperceptible grace of faith. Then the Father in this
way draws all those who show themselves fit for this inspiration;
and whoever has been drawn at last comes to me' (*Paraphrasae on
John* CWE 46 85). 'All things will come to you by our kindness,
but it is your task to strive to be fit for our kindness' (*Paraphrase
on John* CWE 46 185). It is clear that for Erasmus human striving
surrenders to the drawing power of the revelation – yet without
being eliminated. Human activity yields to divine transformation
– yet without becoming completely passive.

119 *Ratio* H 259:35–260:2
120 *Ratio* H 263:30–2
121 Her. 1,7,11; Cic. De or. 2,67,269; 3,53,203; Quint. Inst. 2,17,6;
   4,1,60; 2,117; 6,3,85; 8,6,59; 9,1,29; 2,14; 93–5; 12,9,5; Latin for the
   Greek *ironia* (9,2,44).
122 *Ipse Dominus quanquam ad tempus dissimulavit naturam divinam,
   tamen veritatem non abscondit* (*Hyperaspistes* I L 408). Cf H 214:31ff;
   291:18; ASD V-4 120:790–2; LB V 983E; VII 112A; 322B; 826A. Because
   dissimulatio is a means of accommodation and therefore related to
   similitudo, it is not the same as *simulatio*: *Nam vbi simulatio est, ibi
   non est veritas* (*Ecclesiastes* ASD V-4 102:435).
123 *Ciceronianus* CWE 28 382
124 *Letters* 1523 / CWE 10 444:90–3
125 *Letters* 1202 / CWE 8 210:323–6
126 *Balbutit nobis divina sapientia et veluti mater quaepiam officiosa ad
   nostrum infantiam voces accommodat* (*Enchiridion* H 34:16–17). *Sic
   autem visum est Divinae sapientiae nobiscum vulgatissimo more
   quodammodo balbutire* (*Ecclesiastes* LB V 1016F). Cf LB V 1072F.
127 *Enchiridion* CWE 66 67–8. Cf *Adages* ASD II-5:159ff
128 *Ratio* H 214:31–3
129 *Ratio* H 259:33–5
130 *Paraphrase on John* CWE 46 25
131 See above n1.
132 *Psalmi* ASD V-2 346:587–99
133 So Luther WA 18 605:30ff; 603:1ff.

134 Cf A. Rabil 'Cicero and Erasmus' Moral Philosophy' *ERSY* 8 (1988) 70–90. On *judicium* and probability see below ch 5, 4.
135 *Ratio* H 280:23–30. Cf *Adages* CWE 32 63–4 (*Ne quid nimis* 'Nothing to excess'). 'That which is not in excess is good, whereas that which is greater than it shoulds be, is bad' (Aristot. Rhet. 1,6,21). Cf Aug. De doctr. 2,39,58; 3,12,18.
136 *Ecclesiastes* LB V 1062D. Cf LB V 1044E
137 *Ratio* H 259:33–4; *Letters* 1333 / CWE 9 233:40–2; *Purgatio* ASD IX-1 452:270–2; 480:9–10; *Ecclesiastes* LB V 1011A; 1016F; 1019A; 1045E; 1051D; etc.
138 *Ecclesiastes* LB V 1019B. *Nec ideo tamen oportet omnem historicum sensum in divinis libris tollere, quod ... aliqua loca reperiantur, quibus divina providentia voluit ingenia nostra veluti cogere ad rimandum intellectum spiritualem* (*Ratio* H 275:3ff).
139 *Ecclesiastes* LB V 1044A–E
140 *Ecclesiastes* LB V 1028C; 1029C. *Quisquis igitur Scripturas divinas vel quamlibet earum partem intellexisse sibi videtur, ita ut eo intellectu non aedificet istam geminam charitatem Dei et proximi, nondum intellexit. Quisque vero talem inde sententiam duxerit, ut huic aedificandae charitati sit utilis, nec tamen hoc dixerit quod ille quem legit eo loco sensisse probabitur, non pernicose fallitur, nec omnino mentitur ... Sed quisquis in Scripturis aliud sentit quam ille qui scripsit, illis non mentientibus fallitur: sed tamen ... si ea sententia fallitur, qua aedificet charitatem, quae finis praecepti est, ita fallitur, ac si quisquam errore deserens viam, eo tamen per agrum pergat, quo etiam via illa perducit. Corrigendus est tamen, et quam sit utilius viam non deserere demonstrandum est, ne consuetudine deviandi etiam in transversum aut perversum ire cogatur* (Aug. De doctr. 1,36,40-1).
141 *Ecclesiastes* LB V 1054D; cf 1047A
142 *Ratio* H 286:1–4
143 *Ratio* H 274:28–275:7. Cf LB V 1019D; VII 80C
144 *Letters* 1304 / CWE 9 158:489–94. Cf H 280:28–30; 282:6–8
145 *Quare qui volet litteras sacras tractare serio, mediocritatem servabit in huiusmodi* (*Ratio* H 280:27f). *Pariter impii sunt, qui ... Allegorias submovent e Scripturis, & qui sectantes Allegoriam, sensum historicum rejiciunt, ubi nulla cogit necessitas. Sed in his sobria mediocritas est servanda* (*Ecclesiastes* LB V 1043B). More on *mediocritas* as moderation below ch 5, 2. Also the virtue of elocution is characterized by *mesotes* and its violation is a rhetorical vice, either as *ellipsis* (dearth, omission) or as *hyperbole*. Erasmus accused Luther of *hyperbole* and *paradoxa*; Luther charged Erasmus with *amphibologia* (*Purgatio* ASD IX-1 430; 432; 438; 454:314; 470:757; 477:955). On *ellipsis* and *hyperbole* cf Quint. Inst. 8,3,50; 6,67–76; H. Lausberg *Elemente* 42.

146 *Ratio* H 281:35–282:10; *Ecclesiastes* LB V 1043D. Adhering to the outside of the word leads to a shallow and frigid reading. Such a spiritless, literal interpretation of the biblical text is superstitious and results in superstitious practices of religion, particularly the observance of external ceremonies. See below ch 4, 5.
147 *Ratio* H 282:3–16
148 *Paraphrase on John* CWE 46 103. Erasmus likes to use the verb *detorquere* to show how the genuine meaning of a biblical text is twisted into an alien meaning: *Coelestis illa veritas, nullius moribus inquinari. At qui Scripturam ad humanos sensus detorquent, funditus tollunt omnem illius auctoritatem, dum e divina faciunt humanam* (*Ecclesiastes* LB V 1020B). Cf H 284:33; ASD V-4 98:365–6; LB V 1019E; 1023A; 1027B; 1039A; ASD IX-1 482:92.
149 *Ratio* H 285:5–15
150 *Optimus divinorum voluminum lector est, qui dictorum intelligentiam exspectet ex dictis potius quam imponat et rettulerit magis quam attulerit neque cogat id videri dictis contineri, quod ante lectionem praesumpserit intelligendum* (*Ratio* H 285:8ff).
151 Cf F. Krüger *Humanistische Evangelienauslegung* 26.
152 On violence as the opposite of truth cf J. Chomarat *Grammaire* 1118–53.
153 *Ratio* H 285:8–12; *Ecclesiastes* LB V 1019E
154 *Ratio* H 286:1–4
155 See above n33; on *utilitas* see below ch 5, 6.
156 H. Lausberg *Elemente* 137–42
157 *Paraphrase on Mark* CWE 49 13. Cf H 50:3ff; 51:30ff; 117:16ff; LB IX 637B.
158 See above n50.
159 See for instance *Psalmi* ASD V-2 261:215; 302:491ff; 349:678.
160 Cf LB V 1080D–E; on virtue see below ch 5, 6.
161 Piety signifies both the natural affections preceding faith and Christian charity following faith; cf my article 'Faith and Piety' 247–56.
162 *Ratio* H 260:10–13
163 On *rusticitas, rudis,* etc. see for instance *Letters* 1304 / CWE 9 149:158–69; *Ecclesiastes* ASD V-4 76: 892ff; *Paraphrasis in epistolam ad Corinthios priorem* LB VII 866C–D. Cf A. Reeve and M. A. Screech eds *Erasmus Annotations, Acts* 298–300; E. Rummel *Catholic Critics* 1, 24f.

CHAPTER FOUR

1 *De ratione studii* CWE 24 667. *Primum illud constat grammaticen esse disciplinarum omnium fundamentum, ex cuius neglectu quanta bono-*

rum autorum ac disciplinarum vel interitus vel corruptela sit profecta (*Ecclesiastes* ASD V-4 252:138–40).

2 *Ecclesiastes* ASD V-4 252:148. *Grammaticam dico ... rationes emendate proprieque loquendi, quae res non contingit nisi ex multiiuge veterum lectione, qui sermonis elegantia praecelluerunt ... Ad ea requiritur vocabulorum cognitio, quibus singulae res declarantur, tum eorum compositio; quorum vtrunque pendet non ab arbitrio disputantium, sed a consuetudine veterum, qui castigate loquuti sunt* (*Ecclesiastes* ASD V-4 252:141–55). Cf Quint. Inst. 1,2,14; 4,1f; 2–29; 5,1; 2–72; 6,1–45; 2,1,1–6.

3 *De pueris instituendis* CWE 26 319; *De ratione studii* CWE 24 669. Cf ASD I-3 585–90; I-4 25:379; V-4 252:138–40

4 *De ratione studii* CWE 24 667

5 *De conscribendis epistolis* CWE 25 194–5. Cf H 180:20f; 187:1ff; 10ff; 190:15; ASD V-4 268:484ff.

6 See the sequence of grammar, rhetoric, and theological *topoi* in both the *Ratio* (roughly H 178:19ff; 259:28ff; 291:13ff) and the *Ecclesiastes* (ASD V-4 252:138ff; 268:484ff; LB V 1071Cff).

7 See above ch 3, 2.

8 Cf the structure and progression of the *Elenchus* (LB V 1071C–1083E).

9 *Ex rhetorum praeceptis aliqua delibemus, quae videntur ad Ecclesiastae munus accommoda* (*Ecclesiastes* ASD V-4 268:484–5). Cf Aug. De doctr. 4,2,3–3,4.

10 See above ch 1 n51.

11 *Ecclesiastes* ASD V-4 279:705–280:719

12 We follow thereby Erasmus' structure of the *Ecclesiastes* (LB V 951E); cf below ch 5, 1.

13 Cf for instance Plat. Phaedr. 236a; Her. 1,3,4; Cic. Inv. 1,7,9; De or. 1,31,142; Or. 13,44–15,49; Quint. Inst. 3,3,1–15.

14 Aristot. Rhet. 3,1,1; 3,13–19; Her. 3,4,7–5,9; 3,9,16–10,18; Cic. Inv. 1,14,19; De or. 1,31,143; 2,76,307–81,332; Quint. Inst. 7,pr 1–4; 7,1,1–63.

15 On the difference between the rhetorical concept of invention and the modern understanding of discovery and creativity see A. Hügli and U. Theissmann, art 'Invention, Erfindung, Entdeckung' HWP 4, 544–52.

16 *Veteres poesim non arti, sed numinis afflatui tribuerunt* (*Ecclesiastes* ASD V-4 260:308).

17 On imitation cf for instance Aristot. Rhet. 1,11,23; Her. 1,2,3; 4,2,2; Cic. De or. 2,22,90; Quint. Inst. 2,2,8; 5,25–6; 8,pr 16; 10,1,3; 24–131; 2,1; 10,5,19.

18 *Ciceronianus* CWE 28 441. 'The true imitation tries not so much to say identical things as similar things, sometimes not even similar

things but equivalent things' (*Ciceronianus* CWE 28 446). 'Imitation is a matter of effort, likeness the result' (*Letters* 1334 / CWE 9 256:344).

19 For the influence of the *Devotio moderna* see for instance R.L. DeMolen *Spirituality* 35–67; R.J. Schoeck *Erasmus Grandescens* 31–40. The relation between the rhetorical concept of imitation and the theological concept of *imitatio Christi* has not yet been explored.

20 Her. 1,2,3; 3,16,28; Cic. De or. 1,25,113; 32,145; 2,22,90; Quint. Inst. 1,pr 26; 2,17,1–19,3; 3,2,1–4; 5,1; 5,10,121; 6,4,12; 9,4,3–4; 120; 11,2,9. Erasmus defines nature, method, and practice in *De pueris instituendis* CWE 26 311–12: 'By nature I mean man's innate capacity and inclination for the good. By method I understand learning, which consists of advice and instruction. Finally, by practice I mean the exercise of a disposition which has been implanted by nature and moulded by method. Nature is realized only through method, and practice, unless it is guided by the principles of method, is open to numerous errors and pitfalls ... Three strands must be intertwined to make a complete cord: nature must be developed by method and method must find its completion in practice.'

21 *Ecclesiastes* ASD V-4 260:303–39. Cf *De pueris instituendis* CWE 26 319; 320; 336.

22 Quint. Inst. 3,2,3; 2,19,3

23 *Ciceronianus* CWE 28 368. *Ecclesiastes* ASD V-4 248:32–5

24 *Ecclesiastes* ASD V-4 66:656; 248:32; IV-1A 153:210; *Letters* 531 / CWE 4 230:243–4; 1304 / CWE 9 146:46; *Ciceronianus* CWE 28 368. *Oportet igitur Ecclesiasten sibi notum esse, nec artem modo, verum etiam naturam suam in consilium adhibere* (*Ecclesiastes* LB V 967A). Cf Aristot. Rhet. 3,2,4; Cic. De or. 2,41,177; Quint. Inst. 4,1,5–6.

25 *Ciceronianus* ASD I-2 704:16–18; 647:37ff; *Ecclesiastes* V-4 236:950–1.

26 *Ecclesiastes* LB V 955C; 956B–D; 958C; cf Her. 3,16,28f.; 22,35.

27 *Ecclesiastes* ASD V-4 250:80ff; 106ff. Cf Quint. Inst. 1,2,8.

28 *De ratione studii* CWE 24 671:5–10. Cf Her. 3,16,28–24,40; Quint. Inst. 10,1,19.

29 *De ratione studii* CWE 24 672:24–7. *Ratio* H 291:13–35

30 *De copia* ASD I-6. Cf Quint. Inst. 10,1,5.

31 Quint. Inst. 11,2,13; 20; 23; 28; 36–8; 44. Cf H. Lausberg *Elemente* 24.

32 *Ecclesiastes* ASD V-4 280:725; LB V 951E–955E. *Ratio* H 291:25. Cf Aristot. Rhet. 3,13–19; Her. 3,4,7–5,9; 9,16–10,18; Cic. De or. 2,74,307–85,349; Or. 15,50; Quint. Inst. 7,1,1ff.

33 Cicero defines *ordo* as *compositio rerum aptis et accommodatis locis* (Off. 1,40,142); cf Quint. Inst. 7,pr 3.

34 Aristot. Phys. 2,1,13ff. See F. P. Hager, art 'Natur' HWP 6, 421–41.

35 H. Lausberg *Handbuch* 245–7; *Elemente* 27–8
36 Lausberg *Handbuch* 242; *Elemente* 31–2
37 See above ch 3 n90. On *gradatio* cf for instance ASD V-4 414:154–64; 346:486–8; 351:649f; 352:667; LB V 970C; 1001F; 1002F; ASD V-3 289:90–1; LB VII 620B.
38 See below section 3.
39 *Ratio* H 199:13–201:34
40 Cf my book *Erkenntnis* 69–70; 189 n146. See C. Augustijn 'Erasmus und seine Theologie' in *Colloque érasmien* 55–6; 61–5. Erasmus cultivated both a Catholic sense for the traditional development of doctrine and a Protestant critique of tradition on the basis of the once-and-for-all evangelical norm. He would neither support the radical reformers who attempted to restitute the church to its primitive state, nor would he join the Catholic theologians who tended to use the gospel to justify the *status quo* of ecclesiastical tradition and practice. True to his moderate stance, he kept a balance between the theory of development and the theory of decay. His aim was the restoration of original goodness together with a process toward perfection. His advice was to nurture simple, steadfast faith as well as variable, accommodating prudence.
41 Aristot. Eth. Nic. 1108b, 11–13; Aug. De doctr. 3,21,31; 4,18,35; 25,55. Cf above ch 3 n135.
42 *Aristotelicum est primum rei summam et quasi capita proponere, dein per eadem vestigia recurrendo ad singulas partes quae sunt exactioris scientiae adiungere, exemplo artificum, qui prima manu deformant rude statuae simulachrum, mox ad singula membra redeunt iterum atque iterum, donec summam imponant manum* (Ecclesiastes ASD V-4 434:668–435:672). Cf ASD V-4 388:550–3; 401:870–424:433; 448:964–72; LB V 1059F. On *synecdoche* see H. Lausberg *Elemente* 69–71.
43 *Letters* 1341A / CWE 9 340:1148–51. Cf *Ecclesiastes* LB V 1080E.
44 *Letters* 1523 / CWE 10 448:202–449:204
45 *Ecclesiastes* ASD V-4 270:502–10; 272:536–7; 310:562ff; et al.
46 See below ch 5, 3.
47 See below ch 5, 5.
48 See below ch 5, 2.
49 *Ecclesiastes* ASD V-4 412:135–414:164
50 Cf H. Lausberg *Handbuch* 241–2; *Elemente* 29.
51 *Paraphrase on Mark* CWE 49 21
52 References to Erasmus' use of the *initium-progressus-perfectio* division are found above ch 3 n90. In addition see LB VII 190 A–B; 257A; ASD V-1 208:68ff; 214:238; 231:774ff; V-3 212:564f; 236:914; IX-1 446:109f; 452:259; LB V 953B; 1084C; L 324; LB X 1523F.
53 *Habes huius salutiferae fabulae protasim, epitasim et catastrophen, habes actus omnes ac scenas coelestis illius choragi ineffabili dispensatione*

Notes to pages 145-7   269

digestas (*Explanatio symboli* ASD V-1 218:358-60; *Purgatio* IX-1 451:252-452:269). *Homo bene conditus veluti protasis est, crux epitasis, resurrectio catastrophe* (*Purgatio* ASD IX-1 452:290-1). *Adages* CWE 31 177:1-178:21 (*Catastrophe fabulae*). Cf above ch 2 n96.

54 On amplification in general see for instance Aristot. Rhet. 1,9,38; 2,18,4; 19,26; 26,1; Her. 3,3,6; Cic. De or. 3,26,104; Quint. Inst. 2,5,9; 8,3,40; 4,1-19; 9,1,27. Erasmus treated *amplificatio* primarily in the context of elocution, especially in connection with *adfectus* (*Ecclesiastes* LB V 968F-976D): The amplification of words produces *modus*, the amplification of things makes for *adfectus* (cf *De copia* ASD I-6 73:992-1002; 197:1ff).

55 H. Lausberg *Handbuch* 145-6; 220-7; *Elemente* 35-9. *De copia* ASD I-6 30:85-32:112

56 *Letters* 1304 / CWE 9 146:46

57 *Psalmi* ASD V 2 240:512-14. *Amplissima est diuina sapientia, quae non est animalis sed spiritualis, eoque cor requirit amplum et capax* (*Psalmi* ASD V-2 240:539-40).

58 *Paraphrase on Mark* CWE 49 39

59 *Scripturae tropis significari spiritualem amplitudinem, ac damnari angustiam. Illud habent peculiare res spirituales, quod ex contrariis gignantur contraria, quodque eadem res gignat contraria ... Sic Christi Spiritus ac diuina charitas eundem hominem, et laxat et contrahit, mollit ac durat, erigit ac deiicit, laxat ad benefaciendum omnibus, contrahit a cautionem, ne quem offendat, mollit ad vindictam, durat ad patientiam, erigit ad contemptum eorum qui obsistunt euangelio, deiicit a obsequendum omnibus amore Christi* (*Psalmi* ASD V-2 241:557-242:570).

60 *Letters* 1381 / CWE 10 69:283-5. For the expansion of the gospel from Old Testament narrowness to the amplitude of Christian life see below section 5 on law and gospel.

61 Cf for instance *Psalmi* ASD V-2 232:268-237:424; 266:352f; *Ecclesiastes* V-4 448:964-72.

62 *Paraphrase on Mark* CWE 49 12. Cf *Ecclesiastes* ASD V-4 182:961ff; 146:304; LB V 953C.

63 Cf Aug. De doctr.: *Ipsa tamen veritas connexionum non instituta, sed animadversa est ab hominibus et notata, ut eam possint vel discere vel docere: nam est in rerum ratione perpetua et divinitus instituta* (2,32,50); *Item scientia definiendi, dividendi, atque partiendi, quanquam etiam rebus falsis plerumque adhibeatur, ipsa tamen falsa non est, neque ab hominibus instituta, sed in rerum ratione comperta* (2,35,53).

64 *Nullo salutis periculo aberratur a germano sensu scripturae, modo quod accipitur congruat cum pietate et veritate; nec est leuis utilitas studii nostri, si quod interpretamur non faciat ad praesentem locum, modo faciat ad bonam vitam, et cum aliis scripturae locis consentiat* (*Psalmi* ASD V-2 246:724-7); cf above ch 3 n140.

65 *Ratio* H 286:1-4
66 *Ratio* H 210:4-211:4
67 *Simplex est, iuxta tragici sententiam, veritatis oratio; nihil autem Christo neque simplicius neque verius* (*Ratio* 280:4-5). 'The language of the gospel is simple and artless' (*Letters* 1381 / CWE 10 73:389-90). Cf *Adages* CWE 31 308:1-25; *Ratio* H 304:26-7.
68 See above ch 2 n101.
69 *Hanc harmoniam, hunc omnium virtutum concentum in nullo sanctorum reperieris praeter quam in uno Christo Iesu* (LB VI *5r). 'Sweet and tuneful indeed is the concerted sound when love, chastity, sobriety, modesty, and the other virtues sing together in harmonious variety ... And this music will be the more pleasing to God if performed by a numerous choir in harmony of hearts and voices' (*Letters* 1304 / CWE 9 158:462-76).
70 *Ratio* H 209:3; 210:33; 211:28-30; 222:36-223:1. Although *consensus* and *concentus* are used interchangeably (cf Cic. De or. 3,6,21, referring to Plato), for Erasmus *consensus* has perhaps more to do with the convincing *vehementia* of the divine word and *concentus* more with its attractive *suavitas* or *jucunditas*. Cf below ch 5, 3.
71 Cf above ch 3 n103-5
72 See above ch 2 n96.
73 *Ratio* H 209:1-211:10
74 *Ratio* H 210:22-6
75 *Enchiridion* II 59:25-6; 63:11-13; 75:20; 91:8; *Ratio* H 203:23-4; 31-2; 210:2-4; 220:11ff; 264:21-2; 280:5. 'But men who are like this child in humility, simplicity, and innocence are held in the highest regard by me. For it is fair that those should be dearest to me who are most like me' (*Paraphrase on Mark* CWE 49 117). These qualities occur again and again in Erasmus' theological writings as character traits of both Christ and the Christians, especially their leaders. By constrast, the catalogue of vices Erasmus repeatedly draws on seems to be derived from Stoic ethics which singles out as the foremost vices *luxuria, avaritia, ambitio* and *superstitio*. Cf R. Staats, art 'Hauptsünden' *RAC* 13, 738.
76 *Ratio* H 193:24-195:1
77 As we have seen above ch 3, 2, the allegorical interpretation combines Christology and ecclesiology. Cf F. Krüger *Humanistische Evangelienauslegung* 109-17; my article 'Church and Ministry' 15.
78 *Est irrefutabilis auctoritas, quae sic summa est in Christo, ut pene sit sola* (*Ecclesiastes* LB V 1008B; cf *Purgatio* ASD IX-1 472:832-41). Christ is not only the *unicus auctor et recte sentiendi et beate vivendi* (*Enchiridion* H 110:18) but also *unicus humanae salutis auctor* (*Paraclesis* H 141:2). Christ is the redeemer (*Purgatio* ASD IX-1 473:850) and 'No

one can find salvation unless he believes that Jesus is the author of all salvation. For the source of evangelical salvation is a divinely inspired belief in Christ, the Son of God' (*Paraphrase on Mark* CWE 49 105).
79 *Ratio* H 237:17-19. *In his enim duobus sita est summa felicitatis humanae, ut per oculum ac lumen fidei citra errorem videat homo quid sit expetendum, quid fugiendum, per caritatem exsequatur quod dictavit fides. Fides gignit caritatem, caritas vicissim alit fidem bonis operibus* (*Ecclesiastes* LB V 1080B). 'This is the first principle of the evangelical doctrine: to believe what you hear and to have faith in what is promised' (*Paraphrase on Mark* CWE 49 79). Cf LB VII 649-50.
80 Dionysius the Areopagite too considered hope the lowest of the heroic virtues (*Hierarchies* 40).
81 For instance *Ecclesiastes* ASD V-4 84:89-85:92; 247:21; LB V 1078E-1080E; *Paraphrasis in epistolam ad Corinthios priorem* VII 901E-F. Cf Aug. De doctr.: ... *Quidquid in sermone divino neque ad morum honestam, neque ad fidei veritatem proprie referri potest, figuratum esse cognoscas. Morum honestas ad diligendum Deum et proximum, fidei veritas ad cognoscendum Deum et proximum pertinet. Spes autem sua cuique est in conscientia propria, quemadmodum se sentit ad dilectionem Dei et proximi, cognotionemque proficere* (3,10,14; cf 15; 16).
82 *Ratio* II 245:34-5. 'Through my Spirit I shall act in them, as you have asserted your truth in me; hence they too, like the limbs of one body, holding fast to one head and quickened by one Spirit, will cling fast to each other in mutual unanimity ... Conflict of opinion deprives teaching of its trustworthiness' (*Paraphrase on John* CWE 46 197). *Summa nostrae religionis pax est et vnanimitas* (Ep 1334:217). *Mea pax, quam vobis do, vos conciliat Deo ... Pax, quam vobis relinquo, mutua concordia conglutinans vos inter vos, reddet sodalitium vestrum invictum adversus omnia, quae potest mundus, aut Satanas hujus mundi princeps* (*Paraphrasis in Ioannem* LB VII 612E).
83 *Ratio* H 291:13-31. 'But principles of this kind, which like ballast in a ship do not allow the mind to be tossed to and fro by the waves of fortune and events, cannot be drawn from any better or more reliable or more effective source than the study of the gospel' (*Letters* 1333 / CWE 9 237:195-9). Cf *De ratione studii* CWE 24 672:24-6.
84 *Ecclesiastes* LB V 1071C-1087F
85 In a way Erasmus' system resembles that of the rules of Tychonius (*Ecclesiastes* LB V 1059A-1061C), except that Tychonius contrasts Christ and his body, the church, in the beginning (rule 1) to the devil and his body at the end (rule 7), whereas Erasmus con-

traposes God and the devil from the start. At this point as elsewhere, the influence of Dionysius the Areopagite on Erasmus should be examined.

86 The letter 'To the Pious Reader' following Erasmus' *Paraphrase on John* summarizes similarly the gospel both in terms of a center (faith, love, and hope) and of two spheres: heavenly-earthly; spiritual-physical; the triune God-the tyrant Satan; the children of God in heavenly fellowship vs Satan's confederates; resources and consolations on each side; and rewards for each in the afterlife (*Paraphrasis in Ioannem* LB VII 649–50; cf CWE 46 226–7).
87 *Ecclesiastes* LB V 1085D–1087E
88 *Ecclesiastes* LB V 1080D–E
89 *Aequitas ... est legum moderatio* (*Ecclesiastes* ASD V-4 313:621). Cf Cic. De or. 1,56,240.
90 *Ecclesiastes* LB V 1087A–D
91 Cf above ch 3, 6.
92 Cf above ch 3 n50.
93 *Ratio* H 209:32–210:2
94 Cf below ch 5, 4.
95 See above nn73, 74.
96 See above nn34, 35.
97 *At Ecclesiastica Hierarchia, quoniam Divinis regitur legibus, & Christi immutabilibus institutis, semper eodem statu sit oportet, licet in ritibus nonnullis ac caeremoniis sit nonnulla varietas* (*Ecclesiastes* LB V 1071F).
98 *Adages* CWE 32 43–4; *Psalmi* ASD V-3 304:619; *Paraphrasis in Mattheum* LB VII 145B–146E; *Hyperaspistes* L 256; 506. 'Another thing ... which would reconcile many nations to the Roman church ... would be a readiness not to define everything over a wide field ... but only such things as are clearly laid down in Holy Writ or without which the system of our salvation cannot stand. For this a few truths are enough, and the multitude are more easily persuaded of their truth if they are few' (*Letters* 1039 / CWE 7 126:235–41). See my article 'Erasmus and Religious Toleration' 102–3.
99 See above n40.
100 In my book (*Erkenntnis* 52–3), I had interpreted Erasmus' combination of *ratio* and *methodus* from this systematic perspective and identified *ratio* with a deductive method and *methodus* with an inductive method of inquiry (see M. O'Rourke Boyle's critique in *Language* 64–5). But Erasmus simply substituted the Greek word *methodus* for the Latin *via* used by the rhetoricians in the formula *ratio et via* (see for instance Her. 1,2,3; Cic. Inv. 1,4,5; De or. 1,15,113; Quint. Inst. 5,1,3). Martin Bucer annotates: 'Called by the Greeks *methodus*; which word Theodorus translates as *viam rationemque docendi*. Quintilian divides grammar into two parts:

method and history. By method he means what Cicero calls *viam, artem et rationem* ... Again, elsewhere he translates *methodus* as *breve dicendi compendium*, as if there were a short cut by which we could travel to knowledge' (*Martini Buceri Opera omnia* 3,128; quoted in T.H.L. Parker *Calvin's New Testament Commentaries* London 1971, 31).

101 Previous work on the law gospel issue can be found in J.B. Payne *Sacraments* 71–4; and C.D. McCullough 'The Concept of Law in the Thought of Erasmus' *ERSY* 1 (1981) 89–112. In the following we can give only a sample of references.
102 *Paraphrase on John* CWE 46 33. See above ch 3 n78.
103 For instance *Enchiridion* H 81:26–82:20; *Paraphrasis in Ioannem* LB VII 510F; 516E; 615F–616A. Augustine already had interpreted the letter-spirit dualism in terms of servitude and liberty (De doctr. 3,5,9–9,13).
104 *Paraphrase on Mark* CWE 49 83. 'Their conversation (Elijah's and Moses') with Jesus manifestly signifies the consensus between the law and the prophets. For the law had outlined Christ in mystical figures, the prophets had predicted in their prophesies that Christ would come in the form in which he did, yet the Jews refused to believe it' (*Paraphrase on Mark* CWE 49 109).
105 *Ratio* H 209:10–13
106 *Paraphrase on Mark* CWE 49 83. Cf *Paraphrase on John* CWE 46 179; 196.
107 *Explanatio symboli* ASD V-1 272:968–273:20
108 See S. Markish *Erasmus and the Jews* 27–47.
109 For instance *Paraphrasis in Mattheum* LB VII 142D; *Paraphrasis in Marcum* LB VII 163C; *Paraphrasis in Ioannem* LB VII 569C; 628B; *Psalmi* ASD V-2 118:679–82; 150:683–4; 198:137f; 217:783–4; *Letters* 1202 / CWE 8 206:172–4.
110 For instance *Psalmi* ASD V-2 51:525–36; 236:378–237:424.
111 For instance *Ecclesiastes* ASD V-4 210:437–8
112 *Paraphrase on John* CWE 46 107. 'Paul preaches the liberty of the Gospel against baneful slavery of the Law' (*Letters* 1202 / CWE 8 206:172–4). Cf *Paraphrasis in Marcum* LB VII 157D; 158F; 212E; *Psalmi* ASD V-2 349:687–350:705.
113 *Paraphrasis in epistolam ad Romanos* LB VII 798B–C; *Paraphrase on John* CWE 46 40. *Ecclesiastes* LB V 1070C–D; 1074–1078E
114 For instance *Enchiridion* H 72:14–15; *Psalmi* ASD V-2 51:531–8
115 *Paraphrase on John* CWE 46 67
116 *Paraphrase on John* CWE 46 58. 'The ascent to the gospel faith is from the obedience of the Mosaic law' (*Paraphrase on John* CWE 46 35). 'Now the breeding ground of a new people had been gathered together to migrate from the letter of the law to the

117 *Paraclesis* H 147:8–12; *Ecclesiastes* ASD V-4 182:941–184:971
118 *Ecclesiastes* ASD V-4 184:987–999; 192:98–107. Erasmus divided the Old Testament prophecies into inarticulate types and figures (*mutae*), on the one hand, and articulate prophecies about Christ (*vocales*), on the other, whereby Christ himself revealed the mute figures and types, while the evangelists explained the articulate prophecies as foretelling Christ (*Ecclesiastes* ASD V-4 196:170–96). Cf *Ecclesiastes* ASD V-4 180:925–182:961.
119 *Psalmi* ASD V-2 250:831. Cf *Enchiridion* H 77:45; 84:17–19.
120 *Paraphrase on John* CWE 46 148
121 *Paraphrase on John* CWE 46 8
122 *Paraphrase on Mark* CWE 49 47. Cf *Paraphrase on John* CWE 46 128.
123 *Paraphrasis in epistolam ad Romanos* LB VII 801D. Cf *Paraphrasis in Marcum* LB VII 164A.
124 *Adages* CWE 32 151. On *superstitio, supercilium,* and *praepostera religio* see for instance *Paraphrasis in Matthaeum* LB VII 71B; *Paraphrasis in Marcum* LB VII 159B; 180B; 211A; *Paraphrasis in Ioannem* LB VII 528D–E; 536A; 594B–C; 621A–B; 640D–E; *Paraphrasis in epistolam ad Romanos* LB VII 781B; *Psalmi* ASD V-3 400:934–40; *Ecclesiastes* V-4 284:856–285:868; 340:334–5. Cf Aug. *De doctr.* 2,20,30.
125 *Paraphrase on John* CWE 46 211. *Paraphrasis in epistolam ad Romanos* LB VII 801C; *Psalmi* ASD V-3 402:945–73. See S. Markish *Eramus and the Jews* 66ff.
126 *Psalmi* ASD V-2 51:535–6. *Epistola ad Volzium* H 16:21; *Enchiridion* 80:3; *Ecclesiastes* LB V 1038E; *Psalmi* ASD V-2 238:444–54; 241:557–8.
127 *Ecclesiastes* ASD V-4 70:760–1; 71:765–72:779; *Paraphrasis in Marcum* LB VII 1804E; *Paraphrasis in Ioannem* LB VII 579F; more on preposterous judgment below ch 5, 4.
128 *Ecclesiastes* ASD V-4 74:862–76:866
129 *Paraphrase on Mark* CWE 49 36
130 *Psalmi* ASD V-3 258:19–20; *Paraphrasis in Ioannem* LB VII 511A–B; 512C; 563E; 564A; *Ecclesiastes* LB V 1075F
131 *Psalmi* ASD V-4 192:99–107; *Paraphrasis in Marcum* LB VII 158F; 162F–163A; 177E; 205C–D
132 *Ecclesiastes* ASD V-4 192:103–7; *Paraphrasis in Matthaeum* LB VII 29D–E; 30A; 32E; *Paraphrasis in Ioannem* LB VII 564A; *Paraphrasis in epistolam ad Romanos* LB VII 784F; 785C; 787E; 800E–F; 801A–D
133 *Psalmi* ASD V-2 50:520–51:531; 52:544; 240:512–21; 349:681–3; 350:689; V-3 289:90–3; 389:650–1
134 *Psalmi* ASD V-3 270:442–271:451
135 *Paraphrasis in Matthaeum* LB VII 103C; *Paraphrasis in Marcum* LB VII 173B; *Hyperaspistes* LB X 1463B; 1493E

Notes to pages 162–4   275

136 *Enchiridion* H 52:30; *Psalmi* ASD V-2 40:221–2; 214:679-83; 288:45– 6; V-3 345:407–8; 377:313–14; 400:933; *Paraphrasis in Marcum* LB VII 211B; *Paraphrasis in epistolam ad Romanos* LB VII 793C; *Ecclesiastes* ASD V-4 122:809; *Hyperaspistes* LB X 1514E
137 Cf *Hyperaspistes* LB X 1459D; 1513C; 1515B.
138 *Psalmi* ASD V-2 288:45–52. Cf *Psalmi* ASD V-2 214:679–86; 293:217–21; V-3 100:18off.
139 For instance *Paraphrase on Mark* CWE 49 13–14.
140 *Psalmi* ASD V-3 262:125–30; *Ecclesiastes* V-4 448:980–1; LB V 1074D–1078A
141 Her. 1,11,18–17,27; Quint. Inst. 3,6,1–103; 7,28; 8,4f; 7,4,2f; 5,10,103–110. Cf H. Lausberg *Handbuch* 64–138.
142 *Ecclesiastes* ASD V-4 270:510–271:535; 341:372–344:451; 370:107–400:850.
143 Quint. Inst. 5,10,23–31: from persons (*genus & natio, patria, sexus, aetas, educatio & disciplina, habitus corporis, fortuna, condicio, animi natura, victus, studium, commotio, consilia, nomen*); 5,10,32–93: from things (*causa, locus, tempus, casus, facultas, instrumentum, modus, finitio* [*genus, species, differens, proprium*], *divisio, remotio, partitio, similia & dissimilia, contraria, pugnantia, consequentia, comparativa*). Erasmus used this list of categories for his purposes by emphasizing *similitudo* with its subheadings *fictio, analogia, exemplum* and *imago* (*Ecclesiastes* ASD V-4 370:107–424:433).
144 *Ecclesiastes* ASD V-4 402:890–1. Cf H. Lausberg *Handbuch* 201–3.
145 *Ratio* H 195:1–201:33
146 Quint. Inst. 4,2,22; 118; 5,14,32; 6,1,2; 8,6,19; 9,1,11; 21; 2,29; 59; 63; 66; 4,58; 60; 146; 10,2,13; 5,11; 11,3,43–51; 145. But the term *varietas personarum & temporum* also occurs, as for instance in Cic. De or. 2,34,145.
147 *Ratio* H 285:28–35. *Accedet hinc quoque lucis nonnihil ad intelligendum scripturae sensum, si perpendamus non modo quid dicatur, verum etiam a quo dicatur, cui dicatur, quibus verbis dicatur, quo tempore, qua occasione, quid praecedat, quid consequatur* (*Ratio* II 196:29–32). Cf Aug. De doctr. 3,12,19.
148 See for instance *Epistola ad Volzium* H 9:15; 17:17; *Enchiridion* H 44:17ff; *Ratio* H 196:29ff; 198:33; 284:13–14; 20–21; 286:7–8; *Ecclesiastes* ASD V-4 66:625–6; 236:966; LB V 1071F; *Hyperaspistes* LB X 1348E; *Psalmi* ASD V-3 336:170f.
149 *Laudatissimum docendi genus est ex collatione locorum divinae scripturae sensum rimari* (*Purgatio* ASD IX-1 450:229–30). Cf *Hyperaspistes* LB X 1364E. On *collatio* see below ch 5, 2.
150 For instance *Paraphrasis in Matthaeum* LB VII 101A–B. See also above n69.
151 *Ratio* H 198:33–201:33. With regard to the law of God, Erasmus

divided the periods of salvation history into four: creation, fall, restitution, and perfection (*Ecclesiastes* LB V 1075A). Elsewhere, and most often, he followed the trinitarian schema of creation, restoration, and consummation (as for instance in *Psalmi* ASD V-3 262:124–36; 377:313–378:328; 382:448–9; *Purgatio* ASD IX-1 452:260–1), to which correspond Christ's incarnation, crucifixion, and resurrection.

152 *Epistola ad Volzium* H 9:29–12:9; *Ratio* H 202:1–208:37; *Adagia* LB II 404B–C; 773E–777A. On Erasmus' reference to the three hierarchies (celestial, ecclesiastical, and political) of Dionysius (PG 3,4) see *Institutio principis christiani* ASD IV-1 151:470–4; *Ecclesiastes* LB V 1071C–D.

153 *Epistola ad Volzium* H 12:2–5; *Ratio* H 202:32–203:6

154 *Ratio* H 211:28–223:31

155 On *dissimulatio* as a rhetorical device see above ch 3 nn121, 122.

156 *Ratio* H 211:28–31; *Ad harmoniam ac decorum faciat varietas, non ad dissidium* (*Paraphrasis in epistolam ad Corinthios priorem* LB VII 898F).

157 *Ratio* H 286:6–11

158 *Ratio* H 223:32–236:35. As Christ is the apostle of God, so his disciples are the apostles of Christ; cf *Paraphrasis in Ioannem* LB VII 604B; 609F; 628B.

159 *Enchiridion* H 57:13–14; *Ratio* 284:35–6; 295:1ff; *Ciceronianus* ASD I-2 643:25–8; *Ecclesiastes* LB V 1026A–E; 1078A–E. Cf *Explanatio symboli* ASD V-1 208:89–95; 290:484–90.

CHAPTER FIVE

1 Aristot. Rhet. 3,1,1–3; Her. 1,2,3; 4,7,10; Cic. Inv. 1,7,9; Quint. Inst. 8,pr 13; 1,1. Cf H. Lausberg *Handbuch* 248–9; *Elemente* 42–4

2 Cic. De or. 1,31,142; Quint. Inst. 8,pr 15; *Ecclesiastes* ASD V-4 279:713–280:715. Cf *Spongia* ASD IX-1 137:375–6.

3 Her. 1,2,3; Cic. Inv. 1,7,9; De or. 1,31,142; Or. 13,43; Quint. Inst. 1,pr 22; 3,3,1–15; 5,10,54; 6,4,1; 8,pr 6; 10,7,9

4 Cic. De or. 3,6,24

5 Cic. Or. 17,55–6; *Ecclesiastes* LB V 956B

6 *Inter praedicentem et praedictum est relatio. Itidem relatio est inter orationem et animi sensum. Nam sermo mentis est signum, vnde qui ficte loquuntur, non promunt orationem, sed voces tantum. Ita inter vocabula rerum et res ipsas est relatio* (*Ecclesiastes* ASD V-4 460:270–4).

7 H. Lausberg *Elemente* 153

8 Except for a short passage on use and memory: *Ratio* H 293:13–294:35

9 *Ecclesiastes* ASD V-4 279:704; 280:724ff; 274:595ff; 270:500ff. As *inventio partium principalium* (*Ecclesiastes* 310:525) and *inventio pro-*

Notes to pages 170–3   277

positionum (*Ecclesiastes* 344:452ff), invention becomes a part of the *divisio operis* (*Ecclesiastes* 304:365ff) which itself is identified with *dispositio* (*Ecclesiastes* LB V 951E). Erasmus includes elocution in this invention of the parts of the work.

10 *Ecclesiastes* LB V 951E. It seems that Erasmus inherited this problem from the author of *Ad Herennius* who had devoted, after treating invention and disposition, separate books to elocution (Her. 4; cf 3,1,1), creating thereby difficulty in coordinating the 'pre-Aristotelian (scheme), based on the *partes* of the discourse, and the Peripatetic, based on the five *officia* of rhetoric' (H. Caplan 'Introduction' to (*Cicero*) *Ad Herennium* Cambridge/London 1989, xviii). Quintilian faced a similar problem in aligning the *ars-artifex-opus* structure with the scheme of the parts of speech and the five offices of rhetoric (Inst. 8, 9).

11 *Ecclesiastes* LB V 951E–955B; 955C–956B; 956B–967A

12 *Ostendam quibus rationibus fit, ut oratio sit vehemens, jucunda & copiosa* (*Ecclesiastes* LB V 967A); the *virtutes orationis* as such are mentioned only *Ecclesiastes* 987F.

13 *Ecclesiastes* ASD V-4 274:596ff; 470:545f; LB V 967A; 987F

14 Cf M. Fuhrmann *Rhetorik* 114ff.

15 H. Lausberg *Elemente* 42

16 Aristot. Rhet. 3,2,1; Her. 4,12,17; Cic. De or. 1,32,144; 3,10,37–9; 24,91; Or. 23,79; Quint. Inst. 8,1,1; 2–3; 2,1–24; 3,1–90

17 Her. 4,8,11; Cic. De or. 3,52,199; Or. 5,20; 21,69; Quint. Inst. 12,10,58–68

18 *Ecclesiastes* LB V 987F

19 *Ecclesiastes* LB V 999E

20 *Ecclesiastes* LB V 1011D–1012A

21 Aristot. Rhet. 3,2,4; Quint. Inst. 5,14,33–5; Aug. De doctr. 2,34,58; 3,12,18; 4,18,35. *Simplex est, iuxta tragici sententiam, veritas oratio; nihil autem Christo neque simplicius neque verius* (Ratio H 280:4–5).

22 Cf above ch 3 n135. Deviation from the virtue of speech amounted for the rhetorician to linguistic vice (H. Lausberg *Elemente* 42). Erasmus was not only aware of this relation between language and life (*virtus autem secundum naturam est, vitium contra naturam*, *Ecclesiastes* ASD V-4 368:41–2), but also stressed *mediocritas* (*moderatio*) as the central virtue for both speech and conduct. And it is the speaker's virtue of *prudentia* that applies the norm of moderation to particular rhetorical and ethical circumstances. See below section 4.

23 Quint. Inst. 8,1,1

24 Quint. Inst. 1,6,1; cf F. R. Varwig *Der rhetorische Naturbegriff bei Quintilian* Heidelberg 1970.

25 *Ecclesiastes* LB V 987F; 1011A; *Ciceronianus* ASD I-2 651:35–652:1. On *ratiocinatio* see below section 4.

26 *Letters* 1304 / CWE 9 146:50–1
27 *Ecclesiastes* LB V 1026D; 1078A. The textual purity of Scripture, the purity of Christ, and the purity of the Christian belong together. The restoration of the nature of the text, the restoration of nature by Christ, and the regeneration of the Christian are correlated in Erasmus' thought. This is how philology, theology, and ethics hang together.
28 *Ecclesiastes* LB V 1026A–E; 1078BA–C; *Ratio* H 205,11. Cf above ch 4 n159 and my book *Erkenntnis* 82 nn43–6.
29 See above ch 3 n163.
30 Aristot. Rhet. 3,2,1; Her. 4,12,17; Cic. De or. 3,10,37f; Quint. Inst. 8,2,22; ASD V-4 100:410f; Aug. De doctr. 4,8,22–10,24
31 *Est enim commoda verborum dispositio, quae non tantum facit ad perspicuitatem & modulationem orationis, verum etiam ad acrimoniam* (*Ecclesiastes* LB V 951E). Cf H. Lausberg *Handbuch* 145.
32 On *evidentia* (*enargeia*) see Aristot. Rhet. 3,11,2; Her. 4,55,68; Quint. Inst. 4,3,63–5; 6,2,32; 8,3,61–71. It is important to note that Erasmus includes *evidentia* in his treatment of *adfectus*. He is therefore less interested in the accurate description of facts than in the moral effect of the story on the hearer (*[evidentia] quae totam rei speciem ita subjicit auditoris animo, ut geri sub oculis, non narrari videatur ... non est nefas quasdam circumstantias addere, quas verisimile est in negotio gerendo adfuisse* (*Ecclesiastes* LB V 983 D–E)). Cf *Ecclesiastes* LB V 997F–998A; *De copia* ASD I-6 202:160–70.
33 On obscurity see for instance Aristot. Rhet. 3,5,7; Quint. Inst. 8,2,12–21; 3,57; cf H. Lausberg *Handbuch* 513–14.
34 *Ratio* H 215:3–4; *Ecclesiastes* ASD V-4 404:941; 418:285–422:379; LB V 967D; 972D; 1001D
35 *Ecclesiastes* LB V 1051D–1056E. Cf *Ratio* H 272:11–273:22; *Ecclesiastes* LB V 1018E; 1019D; 1026C. Aug. De doctr. 2,6,7; 9,14–12,18; 3,1,1–5,9; 26,37; 38; 4,6,9; 8,22.
36 *Ratio* H 215:27–9. *Primum omnis sententia, quae pugnat cum inviolatis fidei dogmatibus rejicienda est. Quod si in variis sensibus nihil est adversum sanae doctrinae, ex ipsa sermonis serie quaerenda est germana lectio. Observandum quid praecesserit eum locum, quid consequatur, unde coeperit qui loquitur, quo progressus sit, & quo evaserit. Hic nonnihil valebit, & aliorum locorum collatio. Saepe fit ut idem sensus hic verbis ambiguis enunciatus, alibi sermone perspicue efferatur* (*Ecclesiastes* LB V 1054E). Cf *Ecclesiastes* LB V 1045C; Aug. De doctr. 3,26,37–28,39.
37 *Ecclesiastes* ASD V-4 344:428–38; LB V 1018E; 1019D–E
38 *Redigenda in concordiam, quae videntur pugnantia* (*Ecclesiastes* LB V 1055F). *Magnifice profitetur se, si detur locus ambiguis, omnia posse in bonam partem interpretari* (*Purgatio* ASD IX-1 468:712–14). Cf *Purgatio* ASD IX-1 453:305; 469:743–7; 470:756ff.

39 *Ecclesiastes* ASD V-4 312:581-2
40 H. Lausberg *Handbuch* 122-3; 514-19. Cf W.B. Stanford *Ambiguity in Greek Literature* Oxford 1939.
41 *Ut postea gratior esset fructus non sine negotio quaesitus* (*Ratio* H 260:2); *Christus aliquoties fallit suos ad tempus allegoriarum aenigmatibus, quo post altius inhaereat, quod volebat intellegi* (*Ratio* H 263:30-2).
42 *Enchiridion* H 46:26ff; 47:3ff; *Ratio* 261:26ff; *Institutio principis christiani* ASD IV-1 168:51-2; Cf H. Lausberg *Elemente* 51.
43 As in *De libero arbitrio*; cf above ch 1 n17.
44 Cf Cic. De or. 3,10,37; Or. 21,70-4; Quint. Inst. 1,5,1; 8,pr 26; 31; 1,1; 9,4,27; 128; 11,1,1-93; 12,10,60. While *aptum* was often treated under the heading of *ornatus*, we give it a separate place because of the moral significance it had for Erasmus.
45 *Ecclesiastes* ASD V-4 66:629-30
46 *Ecclesiastes* ASD V-4 248:39-40. Cf *Ecclesiastes* ASD V-4 48:256-7; 86:114-18; LB V 985D. On *bonus vir* in Quintilian see Inst. 1,pr 9; 2,3; 2,15,1; 33f; 16,11; 17,31; 43; 21,12; 3,7,25; 11,1,42; 12,1,1-45. See above ch 2 n17.
47 *Ecclesiastes* ASD V-4 356:800-358:816. Cf Aristot. Rhet. 2,1,5.
48 C.T. Lewis and C. Short *A Latin Dictionary* Oxford 1958, 137-8
49 Her. 4,45,59; 47,60; Cic. Inv. 1,30,49; Fin. 2,27,75; Div. 2,17,38; Tusc. 4,38,84; Quint. Inst. 5,11,2; 23; 8,3,77.
50 *Ratio* H 283:3-4. Cf *Ratio* H 291:34-292:11; 293:12; *Ecclesiastes* ASD V-4 271:531-3; LB V 1019D; 1054E; 1061D; *Hyperaspistes* LB X 1364E; 1448F; *Psalmi* ASD V-2 53:599. *Collatio* compares first of all words and passages in a text, but then also the words signifying and the things signified in similes, and last but not least the visible with the invisible world (*Enchiridion* H 67:36).
51 *Ut autem Metaphora brevis est similitudo, ita similitudo sive collatio est explicata & ad rem accommodata Metaphora* (*Ecclesiastes* LB V 1034C). Cf *Ecclesiastes* LB V 1010C; 1011A; 1033F; *De copia* ASD I-6 32:119; 66:855; 240:55; 246:214.
52 As for instance in Valla's *Collatio Novi Testamenti* ed A. Perosa, Florence 1970.
53 *Jam si loca nec plane statuerent liberum arbitrium, nec plane tollerent, tamen in argumentando fueram meo functus officio. Sic in argumentis ante oppositum, ut loquuntur Scholastici, citant & colligunt Theologi, nonnunquam in utramque partem, in fine res componitur ad aequilibrium veritatis* (*Hyperaspistes* LB X 1376C). Cf my article 'Erasmus on Free Will' 115-17.
54 *Ratio* H 180:30-1. On *animi moderatio* cf Her. 1,1,1.
55 *Ratio* H 291:13-31. Cf *De ratione studii* CWE 24 672:24-7
56 *Ratio* H 291:33-293:13
57 Cf above ch 4, 6.

58 *Ratio* H 285:28–35. Cf *Ratio* H 196:29–32; *Ecclesiastes* ASD V-4 311:568–312:570.
59 *Ecclesiastes* LB V 1054D–E. Cf Aug. De doctr. 3,26,37.
60 *Ratio* H 284:9–14
61 *Ecclesiastes* LB V 1044D
62 *Iniqua collatio* (*Enchiridion* H 63:4). Cf *Enchiridion* H 47:18; 50:35; *Ecclesiastes* LB V 1074C–D; 1075A.
63 '(Christ) had been with the Father forever before he was sent, and still then was with the Father according to his divine nature, whereby he is never separated from his Father' (*Paraphrase on John* CWE 46 47).
64 *Ratio* H 245:19ff; 247:26ff; 292:10; *Psalmi* ASD V-2 194:36–9; V-3 106:437; 125:166–8; 184:484–5; 186:584–8; 187:599–600; 224:13–15; 237:508; 270:442–271:444; 288:46; *Querela pacis* ASD IV-2 72:249–52; *Ecclesiastes* LB V 1097E–F; *Paraphrasis in epistolam ad Corinthios priorem* VII 875E–F.
65 *Ratio* H 292:5; 303:28–9; *Ecclesiastes* ASD V-4 222:655–6; 310:558; 346:520–347:545; LB V 951E–953C; 999E; 1067B; *Psalmi* ASD V-2 374:532–3; *Paraphrasis in epistolam ad Corinthios priorem* LB VII 882D; 884A; etc. Cf Her. 1,1,1; Cic. Inv. 1,2,3; Or. 16,51; 17,55; 27,95; Quint. Inst. 1,10,14; 27; 31f; 6,2,19; 9,4,10–13; 10,10,60.
66 *Ecclesiastes* ASD V-4 310:557–8; LB V 951E–953C
67 *Ecclesiastes* LB V 969B
68 *Ecclesiastes* ASD V-4 388:547–53
69 *Ecclesiastes* ASD V-4 392:650–393:665; 396:743–51; LB V 1067A
70 *Ecclesiastes* LB V 1010A; ASD V-4 66:621–9
71 *Ratio* H 303:29; *Spongia* ASD IX-1 138:411; *Ecclesiastes* LB V 1043B; 956B; 959C; 977D. *Mediocritas enim finem habet, curiositas semper incipit* (*Ecclesiastes* ASD V-4 258:270–1).
72 *Ecclesiastes* ASD V-4 313:621; LB V 1080E
73 See for instance *Ecclesiastes* ASD V-4 64:581–8; 358:804–7; *De libero arbitrio* L 20. Cf Quint. Inst. 2,13,5–8; 4,2,83; 7,1,2f; 12; 3,18; 11,1,8–14. For Erasmus expedience is the motive for accommodation (*omnia omnibus*).
74 See above ch 4 n75.
75 Quintilian (Inst. 1,5,1) lists only three virtues of speech (*emendata*, *dilucida*, and *ornata*) but then devotes a whole chapter to *aptum* (11,1), which for Cicero (De. or. 3,10,37; 24,91) is the fourth virtue of style. Cf H. Lausberg *Handbuch* 249.
76 *Ecclesiastes* ASD V-4 66:629–30
77 *Ratio* H 274:24–284:28; *Ecclesiastes* LB V 1008B–1011D; 1019A–1051D.
78 *De copia* ASD I-6 38–196; 197–279
79 *Ecclesiastes* LB V 999E. Cf *Ratio* H 271:34.

80 *Eas dumtaxat Figuras recensuimus, quae visae sunt Conciniatoribus Euangelicis convenire* (*Ecclesiastes* LB V 1005E).
81 *Ratio* H 268:5; 270:8; *Ecclesiastes* LB V 970A; 992E–994F; 1005C; *De copia* ASD I-6 74:4–8
82 *Ratio* H 267:29; *Ecclesiastes* LB V 1017B–1019A; *De copia* ASD I-6 70:929–72:946. Cf Aug. De doctr. 3,35,50.
83 *Ratio* H 273:23; 274:1; *Ecclesiastes* LB V 975C; 1005B–E; *Hyperaspistes* L 606
84 *Ratio* H 271:23; *Ecclesiastes* ASD V-4 276:617; LB V 995A. Cf Aug. De doctr. 3,29,41. According to Quintilian (Inst. 9,2,44) *dissimulatio* is not quite the same as irony.
85 *Ecclesiastes* LB V 999E; 1010A; 1034A; *Paraphrasis in Ioannem* LB VII 520D; *De copia* ASD I-6 62:754–66:824.
86 *Ecclesiastes* LB V 1010B; *De copia* ASD I-6 66:825–40
87 *Ecclesiastes* LB V 1047B. Cf *Ecclesiastes* ASD V-4 120:796–9.
88 H. Lausberg *Handbuch* 279–307; 307–455
89 *Ratio* H 271:33
90 *Ratio* H 266:5–274:23
91 *Ecclesiastes* LB V 967A–968E
92 *Ecclesiastes* LB V 968F–976D
93 *Ecclesiastes* LB V 976D–987E
94 *Ecclesiastes* LB V 975C
95 *Ecclesiastes* LB V 983D–E
96 *Ecclesiastes* LB V 987F–999E
97 *Ecclesiastes* LB V 999E–1005E
98 *Ecclesiastes* LB V 1005E–1008B
99 *Ecclesiastes* LB V 1008B–1010A. Cf *Ecclesiastes* LB V 975E; 1034A.
100 *Ecclesiastes* LB V 1010A–1011D
101 *Ecclesiastes* LB V 1011D–1016F
102 *Ecclesiastes* LB V 1016F–1019A
103 *Ecclesiastes* LB V 1019A–1033F
104 *Ecclesiastes* LB V 1033F–1037D
105 *Ecclesiastes* LB V 1037D–1062D
106 *Ecclesiastes* LB V 1062D–1072A
107 For instance *Ecclesiastes* LB V 1012A; 1046F; 1062E.
108 *Ecclesiastes* LB V 987F. Cf *Ecclesiastes* LB V 856D; 975E; 976D; 999E; 1006B; 1012B; 1016C
109 *Ecclesiastes* LB V 975E. Cf *Ratio* H 193:20 (*gravitas*); 260:11–12 (*delectatio, perspicuitas*); 271:34 (*gravitas, iucunditas*); *Ecclesiastes* LB V 999E (*acrimonia, gravitas, jucunditas, perspicuitas, splendor, festivitas, vehementia*); 1005C (*jucunditas, dignitas, acrimonia*); 1006A (*gravitas*); 1008B (*evidentia, dignitas, venustas, jucunditas*); 1012B (*splendor, vehementia, jucunditas*); 1016C (*jucunditas, vehementia*); 1047C (*jucunditas, vehementia*).
110 *Ecclesiastes* LB V 952C; 967A; 1016C

111 *Ecclesiastes* LB V 967A; 975E; 1008B
112 *Ecclesiastes* LB V 968F–976D; 976D–987E
113 *Ecclesiastes* LB V 859Fff; 861E; 879A; 837C. On histrionics cf *Ecclesiastes* 776E; 846A.
114 *Ecclesiastes* LB V 856E; see below section 5.
115 *Ecclesiastes* LB V 1011D; 1062E. Cf Quint. Inst. 12,10,58; Cic. Or. 29,101; Aug. De doctr. 4,17,34. On the three kinds of of speaking in delivery see *Ecclesiastes* LB V 959D.
116 *Ecclesiastes* LB V 1011D–1016F; 1012A. Cf *Ratio* H 259:33.
117 Cic. Or. 20, 69; De or. 3,52,199.
118 *Ecclesiastes* LB V 932B; 1062E
119 *Ecclesiastes* ASD V-4 310:559–312:591; 272:550–274:594
120 *Ecclesiastes* ASD V-4 279:702–3; 344:458–60; 356:796–8; LB V 955B; 968F–969A; 983A. *Tyrannicida* is 'Erasmus' only foray into the genre of forensic oratory' (CWE 29 xv).
121 *Ecclesiastes* ASD V-4 270:502–8
122 *Ecclesiastes* ASD V-4 272:536–49; 274:595–600; 170:842–52
123 *Ecclesiastes* ASD V-4 198:232–4; 200:270–202:285
124 *Ecclesiastes* ASD V-4 272:536–42. Cf *Ecclesiastes* ASD V-4 311:563–312:574. On the difference between persuasion and exhortation see CWE 61 124.
125 *Ecclesiastes* ASD V-4 274:595–600. Cf *Ratio* H 260:10.
126 *Ecclesiastes* ASD V-4 66:629–31; 647–8; 248:36–7. On prudence in the rhetorical tradition see Aristot. Rhet. 1,9,5; 13; 2,1,6; Her. 3,2,3; 3,4; Cic. Inv. 2,53,160; Brut. 6,23; De or. 3,14,55; Or. 8,24; 49,162; Quint. Inst. 2,20,5. Prudence signifies not only the discretion of what to say and what not to say in particular circumstances but also the discrimination between good and bad.
127 *Ratio* H 236:26–32
128 *Ecclesiastes* ASD V-4 64:579–84; 76:897–8. Cf *Paraphrasis in Matthaeum* LB VII 61A. Aug. De doctr. 1,14,13.
129 *Paraphrase on John* CWE 46 44
130 *Ecclesiastes* ASD V-4 44:189–90
131 *Letters* 1202 / CWE 8 203:63–5
132 *Letters* 1202 / CWE 8 204:124–7
133 *Ecclesiastes* ASD V-4 146:298–9; 188:36–7
134 *Ecclesiastes* ASD V-4 66:631–59; 270:493–6; *Ciceronianus* I-2 651:9–10. Other passages on prudence: *Ecclesiastes* ASD V-4 120:797; 180:903; 188:37; 228:762; 250:117; 358:802; LB V 1067 A–B; 1080E.
135 Cf Aug De doctr. 2,36,54; 4,1,1.
136 *Ecclesiastes* ASD V-4 66:649–56; 248:30–5; 250:111–12; 270:492–6. Cf *Ciceronianus* ASD I-2 653:21–5.
137 *Ecclesiastes* ASD V-4 68:670–84; 249:71–250:89
138 *Nec illud, opinor, inutile fuerit, si theologiae destinatus adulescens*

diligenter exerceatur in schematis ac tropis grammaticorum rhetorumque ... in his praecipue partibus rhetorices, quae tractant de statibus, de propositionibus, de probationibus, de amplificationibus ... deque geminis affectibus ... quod harum rerum peritia maiorem in modum faciat ad iudicium, quae res in omni studiorum genere valet plurimum (Ratio H 187:1–17). In his polemic against the Ciceronians, however, Erasmus speaks of the judgment of nature under which he subsumes prudence and counsel: *Scribendi recte sapere est et principium et fons ... Fons igitur eloquentiae Ciceronianae quis tandem est? Pectus opulenter instructum varia rerum omnium cognitione, praesertim earum, de quibus institueris dicere: pectus artis praeceptionibus, tum multo scribendi dicendique vsu, diutina meditatione praeparatum: et, quod est totius negocii caput, pectus amans ea quae praedicat, odio prosequens ea quae vituperat. His omnibus coniunctum oportet esse naturae iudicium, prudentiam et consilium, quae praeceptis contineri non possunt* (Ciceronianus ASD I-2 651:3–10). Cf *Ciceronianus* ASD I-2 640:8–10; 651:35–8; 653:7–8; 709:28–37.

139 *Ecclesiastes* ASD V-4 66:636–8. Cf *Ecclesiastes* ASD V-4 250:117–252:128; 264:419–20. On the difference between *iudicium* and *consilium* see Quint. 6,5,3–11: *Nec multum a iudicio credo distare consilium, nisi quod illud ostendentibus se rebus adhibetur, hoc latentibus et aut omnino nondum repertis aut dubiis. Et iudicium frequentissime certum est, consilium vero est ratio quaedam alte petita et plerumque plura perpendens et comparans habensque in se et inventionem et iudicationem ... Quid dicendum, quid tacendum, quid differendum sit, exigere consilii est ... Illud dicere satis habeo, nihil esse non modo in orando, sed in omni vita prius consilio, frustraque sine eo tradi ceteras artes, plusque vel sine doctrina prudentiam quam sine prudentia facere doctrinam. Aptare etiam orationem locis, temporibus, personis est eiusdem virtutis.*

140 *Ecclesiastes* ASD V-4 249:70–252:137

141 *Hoc enim agit artificis prudentia vt res exprimat non quales sunt, sed quales apparent intuentibus* (*Ecclesiastes* ASD V-4 250:117–18).

142 *Ecclesiastes* ASD V-4 248:43–7. Cf *Ecclesiastes* ASD V-4 172:776–84; 368:64–370:106. Also the persuasion to faith is not a matter of compulsion: *Nullus ad fidem compellitur* (*Paraphrasis in epistolam ad Corinthios posteriorem* LB VII 921A). 'No one should be forced to the gospel faith' (*Paraphrase on John* CWE 46 89). 'Compulsion is incompatible with sincerity, and nothing is pleasing Christ unless it is voluntary' (*Letters* 1334 / CWE 9 257:386–407).

143 *Ecclesiastes* ASD V-4 252:131–3. 'Now good speaking has two main sources: a thorough understanding of the subject to be treated, and sensitivity and passion to generate words' (*Ciceronianus* CWE 28 387). 'Let us first make sure our minds are thoroughly

equipped with the necessary knowledge; let us first take care of what to say and only then of how to say it, and let us fit words to matter, not the other way around ...' (*Ciceronianus* CWE 28:402). 'Above all, you must make sure you thoroughly understand the matter you undertake to treat' (*Ciceronianus* CWE 28 442).

144 *Ecclesiastes* LB V 1079A–B. Cf *Ecclesiastes* ASD V-4 364:965–366:981.
145 On *enthymema* cf for instance Aristot. Rhet. 1,2,8; 2,22,1–3; Quint. Inst. 5,10,1; 14,1–4; 24–32.
146 *Enchiridion* H 38:4ff; 39:12; 40:7–8; *Ratio* H 193:18–19; etc.
147 *Ecclesiastes* ASD V-4 251:120–252:128; 358:13–14; 368:64–370:106. Cf *Ratio* H 263:14–15; *De ratione studii* CWE 24 670:18–671:2.
148 *Ecclesiastes* ASD V-4 252:138–52; 262:357–8.
149 *Ecclesiastes* ASD V-4 368:48–63. 'The exercise of judgment and the ability to make right decisions ... can be observed but not taught by rules' (*Ciceronianus* CWE 28 403). Cf Aug. De doctr. 2,31,48–9; 4,4,6.
150 *Ecclesiastes* ASD V-4 356:799–358:816
151 Cf Her. 4,16,23–24; Cic. Inv. 1,34,57–41,77; Quint. Inst. 3,6,15; 43; 46; 5,10,6; 11,2; 14,5; 12; 8,4,3; 15–26.
152 *Ecclesiastes* ASD V-4 370:107ff; 424:427–9
153 *Ecclesiastes* LB V 973D; 953A
154 *Ecclesiastes* LB V 1001B; 1011A
155 *Ecclesiastes* ASD V-4 271:531–3
156 *Ecclesiastes* ASD V-4 70:760–72:786. Cf *Paraphrasis in Ioannem* LB VII 579F; *Letters* 1225 / CWE 8 277:242–4; *Letters* 1333 / CWE 9 238:238–40.
157 *Ecclesiastes* ASD V-4 72:778–9; 74:862–76:866
158 *Ecclesiastes* ASD V-4 202:299–304. Cf *Ecclesiastes* ASD V-4 126:916–18
159 *Ecclesiastes* LB V 969A. Cf *Ecclesiastes* ASD V-4 194:131–3; 262:368–70; 366:981–2; LB V 1070B; *Enchiridion* CWE 66 18; *Paraphrase on John* CWE 46 78; *Paraphrase on Mark* CWE 49 86; *Letters* 1341A / CWE 9 340:1139; *Detectio* ASD IX-1 259:632–5
160 *Ecclesiastes* ASD V-4 112:635–9
161 *Ecclesiastes* ASD V-4 46:217–19
162 *Ratio* H 284:7–10. Cf *Ecclesiastes* ASD V-4 120:783–122:802.
163 *Ecclesiastes* ASD V-4 64:583–5. Cf *Ecclesiastes* ASD V-4 76:894–900; LB V 1062D–1070B.
164 *Ecclesiastes* ASD V-4 68:685–94; LB V 1062E
165 *Ecclesiastes* ASD V-4 332:152–9. *Christiana caritas vbique spectat quid cuique expediat* (*Ecclesiastes* ASD V-4 384:444–5).
166 *Ecclesiastes* ASD V-4 228:761–3; 64:585–9; 612–15. Cf *Paraphrasis in epistolam ad Corinthios priorem* LB VII 876E
167 *Spongia* ASD IX-1 189:610–12 (Horace *Carmina* 3,4,65–7)

168 *Ecclesiastes* ASD V-4 66:624-9
169 *Ecclesiastes* ASD V-4 222:641-224:690
170 On *occasio* and *opportunitas* cf Her. 2,4,7; 4,41,53; Cic. Inv. 1,27,40; Quint. Inst. 2,13,2; 3,6,26-8.
171 *Ecclesiastes* ASD V-4 392:650-396:751
172 *Ecclesiastes* ASD V-4 396:743-51
173 *Adages* CWE 32 108-10
174 *De pueris instituendis* CWE 26 341-2
175 *Christianae mentis est omnem temporis rationem ad bene agendi occasionem accommodare* (*Ecclesiastes* ASD V-4 395:719-20). Cf *Ecclesiastes* ASD V-4 106:522-3; 110:583-5; 184:996; 188:37-8; 190:96-192:99; 214:532-9; 318:759-67; LB V 1045C; 1067A; *Hyperaspistes* L 362; *Paraphrasis in Matthaeum* LB VII 5B-C; 12E; *Paraphrasis in Ioannem* LB VII 563F; 574D; 619E; 620B; etc.
176 *Ecclesiastes* ASD V-4 12:786-122:802
177 *Paraphrase on Mark* CWE 49 57
178 *Letters* 1167 / CWE 8 113:182-5. 'But it is possible that the spirit of Christ may not have revealed the whole truth to the church all at once. And while the church cannot make Christ's decrees of no effect, she can none the less interpret them as may best tend to the salvation of men, relaxing here and drawing tighter there, as times and circumstances may require ... The Gospel is not superseded, it is adapted by those to whom its application is entrusted so as to secure the salvation of all men. Nor is a thing superseded when it is better understood' (*Letters* 1006 / CWE 7 50:201-13).
179 *Letters* 1195 / CWE 8 173:121-4. 'Plato does not disapprove of pretence and concealment of the truth in a philosopher who has to govern the commonwealth, provided he uses these tricks for the good of the people. A Christian, I admit, ought to be free from all pretence, but even so an occasion sometimes offers when it is right for the truth to remain unspoken, and everywhere the time, the manner and the recipients of its publication are of great importance ... It is better, as the Greek proverb has it, to let the evil lie that's well disposed, than by unskilful physic to arouse its full force' (*Letters* 1202 / CWE 8 205:142-54; cf *Adages* CWE 31:106-7).
180 *Ecclesiastes* ASD V-4 184:993-186:1; 394:689-94
181 *Ecclesiastes* ASD V-4 192:98f
182 *Ecclesiastes* LB V 969B. Cf Aristot. Rhet. 2,1,8-17,6; Cic. Inv. 2,51,156; De or. 1,31,141; 2,51,206; Or. 37,128; Quint. Inst. 2,5,8; 5,14,29; 6,2,1-36; 8,pr 7; et al. See H. Lausberg *Handbuch* 141-4.
183 *Ecclesiastes* ASD V-4 278:695-700; 468:513-470:516

184 *Ecclesiastes* LB V 976E-F; 987D. Cf *Ecclesiastes* ASD V-4 222:647-63.
185 *Ecclesiastes* LB V 951C. For an analysis of the human affections see my book *Erkenntnis* 196-211.
186 *Ecclesiastes* LB V 977C-D; Cf *Ecclesiastes* ASD V-4 264:417-19; *Enchiridion* H 44:17ff; *Paraclesis* 145:13; *Ratio* H 187:13-15; *De copia* ASD I-6 276:7ff. The disturbance of the affections causes *perturbatio ordinis* (in this connection Erasmus can equate *vulgus* with *turba*). Cf for instance *Ecclesiastes* LB V 976F; 977D; ASD V-4 208:410-13; see above ch 2 n25.
187 *Ecclesiastes* LB V 977D; 978A. Cf *Ecclesiastes* ASD V-4 330:88-105. Other passages on natural affections: Cic. Inv. 2,22,66; *Enchiridion* H 42:31-6; *Ratio* H 228:21-26; *Ecclesiastes* LB V 952A; 976Dff; *Paraphrasis in Mattaeum* LB VII 32B; 87C; *Paraphrasis in epistolam ad Romanos* LB VII 810D; *Hyperaspistes* LB X 1463B-1464F; et al. See my article 'Faith and Piety' 254-6.
188 *Ecclesiastes* ASD V-4 247:14-21
189 *Ecclesiastes* LB V 978B; 981C-E. Cf LB V 1080A-C. 'Like is born from like' (*Paraphrase on John* CWE 46 46). 'Friendship can exist only among similar people, for similarity promotes mutual good will, while dissimilarity on the other hand is the parent of hatred and distrust' (*De ratione studii* CWE 24 683:28-685:2). 'The deepest form of love coincides with the deepest resemblance' (*De ratione studii* CWE 24 686:2-3).
190 *Ecclesiastes* LB V 982A. Cf *Ecclesiastes* ASD V-4 44:202-4.
191 *Ecclesiastes* LB V 983C-985D
192 *Ecclesiastes* ASD V-4 247:8-11. *Qualis cujusque animi adfectus esset, talem esse hominem* (Cic. Tusc. 5,16,47).
193 *Ecclesiastes* ASD V-4 88:150-1; 154:414; 208:421-210:430; *Ratio* H 179:12; *Paraphrasis in Ioannem* LB VII 603C
194 *Ratio* H 187:17-18
195 *Ecclesiastes* LB V 980A-982A
196 *Enchiridion* H 47:30-2; 7:22; *Ecclesiastes* LB V 1020A; ASD V-4 164:617-19; 90:200-2; 244:144-7
197 *Ecclesiastes* ASD V-4 222:648-56; *Enchiridion* H 45:7-9; 46:10-25; 44:25-33; *Ecclesiastes* ASD V-4 320:818-30; 238:976-90
198 *Ecclesiastes* ASD V-4 312:592-314:641. Cf Aristot. Rhet. 1,5,9; 7,30; 11,16; Her. 2,11,16; 3,2,3-5,9; 6,10; Cic. Inv. 2,51,155-55,168; Quint. Inst. 2,4,37f; 3,4,16; 8,1-3; 13; 22-32; 55-7; 6,2,11; 10,1,35; 84; 12,1,28; 2,1; 16.
199 *Ecclesiastes* ASD V-4 314:631-4; 669-315:673. Cf *Paraphrasis in epistolam ad Corinthios priorem* LB VII 882D; 883F-884A.
200 *Ecclesiastes* ASD V-4 235:931-236:948; 358:802-16
201 *Ecclesiastes* ASD V-4 312:570-4

202 For instance *Ecclesiastes* ASD V-4 64:587; 358:805; 384:445
203 *Ecclesiastes* ASD V-4 272:541; 238:986
204 *Ecclesiastes* ASD V-4 188:37–41
205 *Ecclesiastes* ASD V-4 194:145–150; 244:120–4
206 *Ecclesiastes* ASD V-4 166:639–41; 118:748–9
207 *Ecclesiastes* ASD V-4 312:592–314:630. *Viderunt Stoici neminem esse sapientem nisi bonum virum, viderunt nihil esse vere bonum aut honestum praeter virtutem, nihil horrendum aut malum praeter unam turpitudinem* (*Paraclesis* H 145:13–16).
208 *Ecclesiastes* ASD V-4 313:617–22. Cf *Ecclesiastes* LB V 1080E–1082A; 1085F–1086D
209 *Ecclesiastes* ASD V-4 314:631–316:719
210 *Ecclesiastes* ASD V-4 368:41–3. *Nam virtus est animi habitus naturae modo atque rationi consentaneus* (Cic. Inv. 2,53,159). *Addam illud coronidis loco, quod nulla alia doctrina magis consentanea sit naturae quam Scriptura divina. Quid enim magis secundum naturam, quam ut creatura se totam submittat suo Conditori. Natura per se sui conservationem appetit ac perfectionem* (*Ecclesiastes* LB V 1078D). Cf *Ratio* H 260:7–8; *Ecclesiastes* ASD V-4 286:909–10; 313:617–18.
211 *Paraclesis* II 145:3–9. Cf *Ecclesiastes* ASD V-4 316:687.
212 *Enchiridion* H 63:14–16
213 *Enchiridion* H 111:7–8
214 *Enchiridion* H 90:4–5 (cf CWE 66 85 n5). *Summa legum omnium est caritas: per hanc compendio discitur, quid fugiendum, quid sequendum* (*Paraphrasis in epistolam ad Romanos* LB VII 822A).
215 *Necessarium bifariam accipitur, partim pro eo ad quod maioris metu mali adigimur, partim pro eo quod simpliciter vitari non potest ... Nimirum hinc est quod proverbio dicitur, ex necessitate facere virtutem* (*Ecclesiastes* ASD V-4 314:642–53). Cf *Ecclesiastes* ASD V-4 400:865–401:872; 422:380f; LB V 1064F; *Paraphrasis in Matthaeum* LB VII 70B; *Paraphrasis in epistolam ad Romanos* LB VII 820C–822E. Pursuing the concept of *necessarium* would lead us too deeply into Erasmus' ethics (see my critique of R. Padberg in ERSY 9, 122–3).
216 *Enchiridion* H 63:30–64:5 (cf CWE 66 61 n4).
217 *Ecclesiastes* ASD V-4 238:976–90
218 *Ecclesiastes* ASD V-4 410:67–8
219 *Ecclesiastes* LB V 1080E
220 *Summum ius, summa iniuria* (*Adages* CWE 32 244–5).
221 *Ecclesiastes* LB V 1079A–B; 1080A–C
222 *Ecclesiastes* LB V 1079A; 1080B. *Virtutes enim heroicae non reiiciunt obsequia, si quas dotes humanas vel indidit natura, vel addidit institutio atque industria, sed eas comiter amplectuntur, purgant ac perficiunt* (*Ecclesiastes* ASD V-4 236:950–2). Cf *Ecclesiastes* ASD V-4 68:683–4.

Affectum naturae vicit amor religionis (*Psalmi* ASD V-3 264:214). *Euangelica pietas non abroget affectus naturae* (*Explanatio symboli* ASD V-1 312:208–313:213).
223 *Ecclesiastes* LB V 1078F–1079A. For a fuller picture see my article 'Faith and Piety' 247–53.
224 Cf above ch 2 n127.
225 *Ecclesiastes* LB V 1079E–F
226 *Ecclesiastes* LB V 1080B–C; 981C–E
227 *Paraphrase on John* CWE 46 226

Bibliography

Aldridge, J.W. *The Hermeneutic of Erasmus* Zürich–Richmond 1966
Alfsvag, K. 'Language and Reality: Luther's Relation to Classical Rhetoric in *Rationis Latomianae confutatio* (1521)' *Studia Theologica* 41 (1987) 85–126
Amiel, E. *Erasme: Un libre penseur du XVIe siècle* Paris 1889
Auer, A. *Die vollkommene Frömmigkeit des Christen nach dem Enchiridion militis Christiani des Erasmus von Rotterdam* Düsseldorf 1954
Augustijn, C. *Erasmus en de Reformatie: Een onderzoek naar de houding die Erasmus ten opzichte van de Reformatie heeft aangenomen* Amsterdam 1962
– *Erasmus: Vernieuwer van kerk en theologie* Baarn 1967
– 'The Ecclesiology of Erasmus' in *Scrinium Erasmianum* 2 Leiden 1969, 135–55
– 'Erasmus und die Juden' *Nederlands Archief voor Kerkgeschiedenis* 60 (1980) 22–38
– 'Erasmus und seine Theologie: Hatte Luther Recht?' in *Colloque érasmien de Liège* 49–68
– '*Vir duplex*: German Interpretations of Erasmus' in *Erasmus of Rotterdam: The Man and the Scholar* ed J. Sperna Weiland and W.Th.M. Frijhoff, Leiden 1988, 219–27
– *Erasmus von Rotterdam: Leben-Werk-Wirkung* München 1986, tr J.C. Grayson *Erasmus: His Life, Works, and Influence* Toronto 1991
– 'Erasmus' in *Theologische Realenzyklopädie* 10, 1–18
Bainton, R.H. *Erasmus of Christendom* New York 1969
Bataillon, M. *Erasme et l'Espagne, Recherches sur l'histoire spirituelle du XVIe siècle* Paris 1937
Bateman, J.J. 'From Soul to Soul: Persuasion in Erasmus' Paraphrases on the New Testament' *Erasmus in English* 15 (1987–8) 7–16
Behnk, W. *Contra Liberum Arbitrium Pro Gratia Dei: Willenslehre und*

Christuszeugnis bei Luther und in der Interpretation durch die neuere Lutherforschung Frankfurt/Bern 1982

Béné, C. *Erasme et Saint Augustin ou l'influence de Saint Augustin sur l'humanisme d'Erasme* Geneva 1969

- 'L'exégèse des Psaumes chez Erasme' in *Histoire de l'exégèse au XVIe siècle* ed O. Fatio and P. Fraenkel, Geneva 1978, 118-32

Bentley, J.H. *Humanists and Holy Writ: New Testament Scholarship in the Renaissance* Princeton 1983

Bien, G. 'Billigkeit' *Historisches Wörterbuch der Philosophie* 1, 939-40

Bornkamm, H. 'Erasmus und Luther' *Lutherjahrbuch* 25 (1958) 3-22

Bouwsma, W.J. *Calvin: A Sixteenth Century Portrait* New York/Oxford 1988

Bouyer, L. *Autour d'Erasme: Etudes sur le christianisme des humanistes catholiques* Paris 1955

- 'Erasmus in Relation to the Medieval Biblical Tradition' in *The Cambridge History of the Bible* 2, Cambridge 1969, 492-505

Boyle, M.O. *Erasmus on Language and Method in Theology* Toronto 1978

- *Christening Pagan Mysteries: Erasmus in Pursuit of Wisdom* Toronto 1981

- *Rhetoric and Reform: Erasmus' Civil Dispute with Luther* Cambridge Mass/London 1983

- *Petrarch's Genius: Pentimento and Prophecy* Berkeley 1991

Breen, Q. 'Some Aspects of Humanist Rhetoric and the Reformation' *Nederlands Archief voor Kerkgeschiedenis* 43 (1960) 1ff

- 'The Terms 'Loci communes' and 'Loci' in Melanchthon' *Church History* 16 (1947) 197-209

Caplan, H. 'The Four Senses of Scriptural Interpretation and the Mediaeval Theory of Preaching' in ibid *Of Eloquence, Studies in Ancient and Mediaeval Rhetoric* Ithaca 1970, 93-104

Cassirer, E. *Individuum und Kosmos in der Philosophie der Renaissance* Leipzig/Berlin 1927, repr Darmstadt 1963

Carrington, L. 'Erasmus' *Lingua*: The Double-Edged Tongue' *Erasmus of Rotterdam Society Yearbook* 9 (1989) 106-118

- 'Erasmus on the Use and Abuse of Metaphor' *Acta Conventus Neo-Latini Torontonensis* (1991) 111-20

Chantraine, G. *'Mystère' et 'Philosophie du Christ' selon Erasme: Etude de la lettre à P. Volz et de la 'Ratio verae theologiae' (1518)* Namur/Gembloux 1971

- *Erasme et Luther, libre et serf arbitre. Etude historique et théologique* Paris/Namur 1981

Chomarat, J. *Grammaire et rhétorique chez Erasme* 2 vols Paris 1981

Christ-von Wedel, C. *Das Nichtwissen bei Erasmus von Rotterdam: Zum philosophischen und theologischen Erkennen in der geistigen Entwicklung eines christlichen Humanisten* Basel/Frankfurt 1981

Claesges, U. 'Epoché' in *Historisches Wörterbuch der Philosophie* 2, 594–5
Colloques Erasmien de Liège: Commémoration du 450e anniversaire de la mort d'Erasme ed J.-P. Massaut, Paris 1987
Colloquia Erasmiana Turonensia: Douzième stage international d'études humanistes Tours 1969, 2 vols, Paris 1972
Colloquium Erasmianum: Actes du Colloque International réuni à Mons Mons 1968
Contemporaries of Erasmus: A Biographical Register of the Renaissance and Reformation ed P.G. Bietenholz and T.B. Deutscher, 3 vols, Toronto 1985–7
Cytowska, M. 'Erasme et son petit corps' *Eos* 62 (1974) 129–38
DeMolen, R.L. (ed) *Essays on the Works of Erasmus* New Haven 1978
– *The Spirituality of Erasmus of Rotterdam* Nieuwkoop 1987
Dilthey, W. 'Auffassung und Analyse des Menschen im 15. und 16. Jahrhundert' in *Gesammelte Schriften* 2 Leipzig/Berlin 1914
Dresden, S. 'Erasme et les belles-lettres' in *Colloque Erasmien de Liége* 3–16
Drummond, R.B. *Erasmus: His Life and Character* 2 vols, London 1873
Eden, K. 'Rhetoric in the Hermeneutics of Erasmus' Later Works' *Erasmus of Rotterdam Society Yearbook* 11 (1991) 88–104
Eisenhut, W. *Einführung in die antike Rhetorik und ihre Geschichte* Darmstadt 1982
Etienne, J. *Spiritualisme érasmien et théologiens louvanistes* Louvain/Gembloux 1956
Evans, G.R. *The Language and Logic of the Bible: The Road to Reformation* Cambridge 1985
Fantazzi, C. (ed) *Juan Luis Vives: In Pseudodialecticos* Leiden 1979
Farge, J.K. *Orthodoxy and Reform in Early Reformation France* Leiden 1985
Flitner, A. *Erasmus im Urteil seiner Nachwelt* Tübingen 1952
Froude, J.A. *Life and Letters of Erasmus* London 1897
Fuhrmann, M. *Die antike Rhetorik* München/Zürich 1987
Fumaroli, M. *L'âge de l'éloquence: Rhétorique et 'res literaria' de la Renaissance au seuil de l'époque classique* Geneva 1980
Gadamer, H.G. *Truth and Method* New York 1975
Gebhardt, G. *Die Stellung des Erasmus von Rotterdam zur Römischen Kirche* Marburg 1966
Gleason, J.B. *John Colet* Berkeley 1989
Godin, A. *Erasme lecteur d'Origène* Geneva 1982
– 'The *Enchiridion militis Christiani*: Modes of an Origenian Appropriation' *Erasmus of Rotterdam Society Yearbook* 2 (1982) 47–79
– 'La Bible et la "philosophie chrétienne"' in *Les temps de réformes et la Bible* ed G. Bedouelle and B. Roussel eds, Paris 1989, 563–86

Gogan, B. 'The Ecclesiology of Erasmus of Rotterdam: A Genetic Account' *The Heythrop Journal* 21 (1981) 393–411
Grundwald, M. *Der 'Ecclesiastes' des Erasmus von Rotterdam, Reform der Predigt durch Erneuerung des Predigers* diss Innsbruck 1969
Guarneschelli, J. S. *Erasmus' Concept of the Church, 1499–1524* diss Yale 1966
Guerlac, R. *Juan Vives Against the Pseudodialecticians: A Humanist Attack on Medieval Logic* Dort 1979
Hager, F.P. 'Natur' *Historisches Wörterbuch der Philosophie* 6, 421–41
Halkin, L.E. 'La pieté d'Erasme,' *Revue d'Histoire Ecclésiastique* 74 (1984) 671–708
– *Erasme parmi nous* Paris 1987
Heer, F. *Die dritte Kraft, Der europäische Humanismus in den Fronten des konfessionellen Zeitalters* Frankfurt 1959
Hentze, W. *Kirche und kirchliche Einheit bei Desiderius Erasmus von Rotterdam* Paderborn 1974
Hoffmann, M. *Erkenntnis und Verwirklichung der wahren Theologie nach Erasmus von Rotterdam* Tübingen 1972
– 'Erasmus and Religious Toleration' *Erasmus of Rotterdam Society Yearbook* 2 (1982) 80–106
– 'Erasmus on Church and Ministry' *Erasmus of Rotterdam Society Yearbook* 6 (1986) 1–30
– 'Faith and Piety in Erasmus's Thought' *The Sixteenth Century Journal* 20:2 (1989) 241–58
– 'Erasmus on Free Will: An Issue Revisited' *Erasmus of Rotterdam Society Yearbook* 10 (1990) 101–21
– 'Erasmus on Language and Interpretation' *Moreana* 28:106–7 (July 1991) 1–20
Holborn, H. *On the Eve of the Reformation: Letters of Obscure Men* New York 1964
Holeczek, H. *Humanistische Bibelphilologie als Reformproblem bei Erasmus von Rotterdam, Thomas More und William Tyndale* Leiden 1975
– *Erasmus Deutsch* Stuttgart 1983
Hügli A. and Theissmann, U. 'Invention, Erfindung, Entdeckung' *Historisches Wörterbuch der Philosophie* 4, 544–52
Huizinga, J. *Erasmus* Haarlem 1924; tr F. Hopkin *Erasmus of Rotterdam* New York/London 1924; repr 1952; repr *Erasmus and the Age of Reformation* New York 1957
– *Homo ludens, Vom Ursprung der Kultur im Spiel* Hamburg 1956
Joachimson, P. *'Loci communes*: Eine Untersuchung zur Geistesgeschichte des Humanismus und der Reformation' *Luther-Jahrbuch* 8 (1926) 27–97
Jonge, H.J. de. '*Novum Testamentum a nobis versum*: The Essence of

Erasmus' Edition of the New Testament' *Journal of Theological Studies* 35 (1984) 394-413

Ijsseling, S. *Rhetoric and Philosophy in Conflict: An Historical Survey* The Hague 1976

Jonkers, E.J. 'Aequitas' *Reallexikon für Antike und Christentum* 1, 141-4

Jüngel, E. 'Quae supra nos, nihil ad nos. Eine Kurzformel der Lehre vom verborgenen Gott, im Anschluß an Luthers Lehre interpretiert' *Evangelische Theologie* 32:3 (1972) 197-240

Kaegi, W. 'Erasmus im achtzehnten Jahrhundert' in *Gedenkschrift zum 400. Todestage des Erasmus von Rotterdam* Basel 1936, 205-27

Kaufman, P.I. *Augustinian Piety and Catholic Reform: Augustine, Colet, and Erasmus* Macon 1982

Kennedy, G.A. *The Art of Persuasion in Greece* Princeton 1963
- *The Art of Rhetoric in the Roman World* Princeton 1972
- *Classical Rhetoric and its Christian and Secular Tradition from Ancient to Modern Times* Chapel Hill 1980

Kisch, G. *Erasmus und die Jurisprudenz seiner Zeit* Basel 1960
- *Erasmus Stellung zu den Juden und Judentum* Tübingen 1969

Kleinhans, R.G. *Erasmus' Doctrine of Preaching: A Study of 'Ecclesiastes sive de ratione concionandi'* diss Princeton 1968
- '"Ecclesiastes sive de ratione concionandi"' in *Essays on the Works of Erasmus* ed R.L. DeMolen, New Haven/London 1978

Klinkenberg, H.M. 'Artes liberales' in *Historisches Wörterbuch der Philosophie* 1, 531-5

Koerber, E. v. *Die Staatstheorie des Erasmus von Rotterdam* Berlin 1967

Köhler, W. *Erasmus, ein Lebensbild in Auszügen aus seinen Werken* Berlin 1917

Kohls, E.W. *Die Theologie des Erasmus* 2 vols Basel 1966

Krüger, F. *Humanistische Evangelienauslegung, Desiderius Erasmus von Rotterdam als Ausleger der Evangelien in seinen Paraphrasen* Tübingen 1986

La Fontaine, M. J. *A Critical Translation of Philip Melanchthon's 'Elementorum rhetorices librio duo'* diss Michigan 1968

Lausberg, H. *Handbuch der literarischen Rhetorik. Eine Grundlegung der Literaturwissenschaft* München 1960
- *Elemente der literarischen Rhetorik* München 1963

Lindhardt, J. *Rhetor, Poeta, Historicus, Studien über die rhetorische Erkenntnis und Lebensanschauung im italienischen Renaissancehumanismus* Leiden 1976

Lorch, M. 'Lorenzo Valla' in *Renaissance Humanism: Foundations, Forms, and Legacy* 1 ed A. Rabil, 332-49

Lortz, J. *Die Reformation in Deutschland* 2 vols Freiburg 1940
- 'Erasmus kirchengeschichtlich' in *Aus Theologie und Philosophie, Festschrift F. Tillmann* Düsseldorf 1950, 271-86

Lubac, H. de. *Exégèse médiévale: Les quatre sens de l'Ecriture* Paris 1964
McConica, J.K. *English Humanists and Reformation Politics* Oxford 1965
- 'Erasmus and the Grammar of Consent' in *Scrinium Erasmianum* 2 77-99
McCullough, C.D. 'The Concept of Law in the Thought of Erasmus' *Erasmus of Rotterdam Society Yearbook* 1 (1981) 89-112
McSorley, H.J. *Luther: Right Or Wrong? An ecumenical-theological Study of Luther's Major Work, The Bondage of the Will* München 1967
Mansfield, B. 'Erasmus in the Nineteenth Century, the Liberal Tradition' *Studies in the Renaissance* 15 (1968) 195-219
- *Phoenix of His Age: Interpretations of Erasmus c. 1550-1750* Toronto 1979
- 'Erasmus in the Age of Revolution' in *Erasmus of Rotterdam: The Man and the Scholar* ed J. Sperna Weiland and W.Th.M. Frijhoff, Leiden 1988, 228-39
- *Interpretations of Erasmus c 1750-1920: Man On His Own* Toronto 1992
Marcel, R. 'L'*Enchiridion militis Christiani*: Sa genèse et sa doctrine, son succès et ses vicissitudes' in *Colloquia Erasmiana Turonensia* 2 613-46
Marc'hadour, G. '*Omnium horarum homo*: A Man For all Seasons' *Erasmus of Rotterdam Society Yearbook* 1 (1981) 141-7
Margolin, J.C. *Recherches Erasmiennes* Geneva 1969
- *Guerre et paix dans la pensée d'Erasme* Paris 1973
- *Erasme: Le Prix des mots et de l'homme* London 1986
- 'Huizinga et les recherches erasmiennes' in ibid *Erasme dans son miroir et dans son sillage* London 1987, 258-74
- 'La Religion d'Erasme et l'Allemagne des Lumières' in ibid *Erasme dans son miroir et dans son sillage* London 1987, 197-230
Markish, S. *Erasmus and the Jews* Chicago/London 1986
Meyer, H. 'Schriftsinn, mehrfacher' *Historisches Wörterbuch der Philosophie* 8, 1431-39
Monfasani, J. 'Humanism and Rhetoric' in *Renaissance Humanism: Foundations, Forms, and Legacy* 3 ed A. Rabil, 171-235
O'Donnell, A.M. 'Rhetoric and Style in Erasmus' *Enchiridion militis Christiani*' *Studies in Philology* 77 (1980) 26-49
Oelrich, K.H. *Der späte Erasmus und die Reformation* Münster 1961
O'Malley, J.W. *Praise and Blame in Renaissance Rome: Rhetoric, Doctrine, and Reform in the Sacred Orators of the Papal Court, c 1450-1521* Durham 1979
- 'Erasmus and the History of Sacred Rhetoric' *Erasmus of Rotterdam Society Yearbook* 5 (1985) 1-29
- 'Grammar and Rhetoric in the *Pietas* of Erasmus' *The Journal of Medieval and Renaissance Studies* 18 (1988) 81-98
Padberg, R. *Personaler Humanismus* Paderborn 1964

- *Erasmus von Rotterdam: Seine Spiritualität, Grundlage seines Reformprogramms* Paderborn 1979
Parker, T.H.L. *Calvin's New Testament Commentaries* London 1971
Pattison, M. 'Erasmus' *Encyclopedia Britannica* 9th ed, 8, 512–18
Payne, J.B. 'Toward the Hermeneutics of Erasmus' *Scrinium Erasmianum* 2 13–49
- *Erasmus: His Theology of the Sacraments* Richmond 1970
- 'Erasmus and Lefèvre d'Etaples as Interpreters of Paul' *Archiv für Reformationsgeschichte* 65 (1974) 54–83
Percival, W.K. 'Renaissance Grammar' in *Renaissance Humanism: Foundations, Forms, and Legacy* 3 ed A. Rabil, 67–83
Pesch, O.H. (ed) *Humanismus und Reformation: Martin Luther und Erasmus von Rotterdam in den Konflikten ihrer Zeit* München/Zürich 1985
Phillips, M.M. *Erasmus and the Northern Renaissance* London 1949, rev ed Woodbridge 1981
- 'Visages d'Erasme' in *Colloque Erasmien de Liège* 17–29
- 'Erasmus on the Tongue' *Erasmus of Rotterdam Society Yearbook* 1 (1981) 113–25
Pohlenz, M. *Stoa und die Stoiker* Zürich/Stuttgart 1964
Pollet, J.V. 'Origine et structure du *De Sarcienda Ecclesiae Concordia* (1533) d'Erasme' in *Scrinium Erasmianum* 2 183–95
Post, R.R. *The Modern Devotion: Confrontation with Reformation and Humanism* Leiden 1968
Rabil, A. *Erasmus and the New Testament: The Mind of a Christian Humanist* San Antonio 1972
- 'Erasmus's Paraphrases on the New Testament' in *Essays on the Works of Erasmus* ed R.L. DeMolen, New Haven/London 1978, 145–61
- (ed) *Renaissance Humanism: Foundations, Forms, and Legacy* 3 vols, Philadelphia 1988
- 'Cicero and Erasmus' Moral Philosophy' *Erasmus of Rotterdam Society Yearbook* 8 (1988) 70–90
Reedjik, C. *Tandem bona causa triumphat. Zur Geschichte des Gesamtwerkes des Erasmus von Rotterdam* Basel/Stuttgart 1980
Renaudet, A. *Erasme, sa pensée religieuse et son action d'après sa correspondance (1518–1521)* Paris 1926
- *Etudes Erasmiennes (1521–1529)* Paris 1939
Ritter, G. *Die geschichtliche Bedeutung des deutschen Humanismus* Darmstadt 1963
Rummel, E. *Erasmus as a Tranlator of the Classics* Toronto 1985
- *Erasmus' "Annotations" on the New Testament: From Philologist to Theologian* Toronto 1986
- 'God and Solecism: Erasmus as a Literary Critic of the Bible' *Erasmus of Rotterdam Society Yearbook* 7 (1987) 54–72

- *Erasmus and His Catholic Critics* 2 vols, Nieuwkoop 1989
- 'Et cum theologo bella poeta gerit: The Conflict between Humanists and Scholastics Revisited' *The Sixteenth Century Journal* 23:4 (Winter 1992) 713–26

Rupp, G. and Watson, P. (eds) *Luther and Erasmus: Free Will and Salvation* Philadelphia 1969

Schätti, K. *Erasmus von Rotterdam und die römische Kurie* Basel 1954

Schmidinger, H.M. 'Philosophie, christliche' *Historisches Wörterbuch der Philosophie* 7, 886–9

Schoeck, R.J. *Erasmus Grandescens: The Growth of a Humanist's Mind and Spirituality* Nieuwkoop 1988

Schottenloher, O. *Erasmus im Ringen um die humanistische Bildungsreform: Ein Beitrag zum Verständnis seiner geistigen Entwicklung* Münster 1933
- 'Erasmus, Johann Popenruyter und die Entstehung des *Enchiridion militis Christiani*' *Archiv für Reformationsgeschichte* 45 (1954) 109–16

Schwarz, W. *Principles and Problems of Biblical Translation: Some Reformation Controversies and Their Background* Cambridge 1955

Screech, M.A. *Ecstasy and the Praise of Folly* London 1980

Scrinium Erasmianum ed J. Coppens, 2 vols, Leiden 1969

Seidel-Menchi, S. *Erasmo in Italia 1520–1580* Turin 1987

Seigel, J.E. *Rhetoric and Philosophy in Renaissance Humanism: The Union of Eloquence and Wisdom, Petrarch to Valla* Princeton 1968

Smith, P. *Erasmus: A Study of His Life, Ideals and Place in History* New York/London 1923; repr New York 1962

Sowards, J.K. *Desiderius Erasmus* Boston 1975

Spitz, L.W. *The Religious Renaissance of the German Humanists* Cambridge, Mass 1963
- 'Humanismus/Humanismusforschung' in *Theologische Realenzyklopädie* 15, 639–61

Staats, R. 'Hauptsünden' *Reallexikon für Antike und Christentum* 13, 738

Stanford, W.B. *Ambiguity in Greek Literature* Oxford 1939

Stupperich, R. *Erasmus von Rotterdam und seine Welt* Berlin/New York 1977
- 'Das *Enchiridion militis Christiani* des Erasmus von Rotterdam nach seiner Entstehung, seinem Sinn und Charakter' *Archiv für Reformationsgeschichte* 69 (1978) 5–23
- 'Zur Entstehungsgeschichte der *Ratio seu methodus compendio perveniendi ad veram Theologiam*' *Nederlandsch Archief voor Kerkgeschiedenis* 67 (1987) 110–19

Thompson, C.R. 'Erasmus as Internationalist and Cosmopolitan' *Archiv für Reformationsgeschichte* 46 (1955) 167–95

Torrance, T.F. 'The Hermeneutics of Erasmus' in *Probing the Reformed*

Tradition, Historical Studies in Honor of Edward A. Dowey Jr ed E.A. McKee and B.G. Armstrong, Louisville 1989, 48–76
Tracy, J.D. *Erasmus: The Growth of a Mind* Geneva 1972
– *The Politics of Erasmus: A Pacifist Intellectual and His Political Milieu* Toronto 1978
– 'Against the "Barbarians": The Young Erasmus and His Humanist Contemporaries' *The Sixteenth Century Journal* 11 (1980) 3–22
– 'Humanists Among the Scholastics: Erasmus, More, and Lefèvre d'Etaples on the Humanity of Christ' *Erasmus of Rotterdam Society Yearbook* 5 (1985) 30–51
Trinkaus, C. *In Our Image and Likeness: Humanity and Divinity in Italian Humanist Thought* 2 vols, London 1970
– 'Erasmus, Augustine and the Nominalists' *Archiv für Reformationsgeschichte* 67 (1976) 1–32
– *The Poet as Philosopher: Petrarch and the Formation of Renaissance Consciousness* New Haven 1979
– *The Scope of Renaissance Humanism* Ann Arbor 1983
– 'Italian Humanism and Scholastic Theology' in *Renaissance Humanism: Foundations, Forms, and Legacy* 3 ed A. Rabil, 327–48
Troeltsch, E. 'Protestantisches Christentum und die Kirche in der Neuzeit' in *Die Kultur der Gegenwart I IV.1* ed P. Hinneberg, Leipzig/Berlin 1922, 431–792
Tuynman, P. 'Erasmus: functionele rhetorica bij een christen-ciceroniaan' *Lampas* 9 (1976) 163–96
Varwig, F.R. *Der rhetorische Naturbegriff bei Quintilian* Heidelberg 1970
Vocht, H. de. *History of the Foundation and the Rise of the Collegium Trilingue Lovaniense 1517–1555* 4 vols, Louvain 1951–5
Wagenvoort. H. and Tellenbach G. *'Auctoritas' Reallexikon für Antike und Christentum* 1, 902–9
Walter, J. v. *Das Wesen der Religion nach Erasmus und Luther* Leipzig 1909
Walter, P. *Theologie aus dem Geist der Rhetorik, Zur Schriftauslegung des Erasmus von Rotterdam* Mainz 1991
– 'Philosophie' *Historisches Wörterbuch der Philosophie* 7, 662–7
Waswo, R. *Language and Meaning in the Renaissance* Princeton 1987
Weiss, J. 'Ecclesiastes and Erasmus: The Mirror and the Image' *Archiv für Reformationsgeschichte* 65 (1974) 83–108
Wernle, P. *Die Renaissance des Christentums im 16. Jahrhundert* Tübingen/Leipzig 1904
– *Renaissance und Reformation* Tübingen 1912
Wiedenhofer, S. *Formalstrukturen humanistischer und reformatorischer Theologie bei Philipp Melanchthon* Bern/Frankfurt/München 1976
Winkler, G. *Erasmus von Rotterdam und die Einleitungsschriften zum Neuen Testament* Münster 1974

Witt, R.G. and B.G. Kohl (eds) *The Earthly Republic: Italian Humanists on Government and Society* Pittsburgh 1978
Wollgast, S. *Zur Friedensidee in der Reformationszeit* Berlin 1968
Woodward, W.H. *Desiderius Erasmus Concerning the Aim and Method of Education* New York 1964
Zundel, E. *Clavis Quintilianea, Quintilians 'Institutio oratoria' aufgeschlüsselt nach rhetorischen Begriffen* Darmstadt 1989

Index of Technical Terms

accommodatio 41, 45, 52, 106–12, 113, 116–18, 123–6, 178–9, 181–2, 197–8, 215
acrimonia *sv* vehementia
actio *sv* pronuntiatio
adfectus 12, 47, 51, 81, 106, 116, 118, 164, 186–9, 200–5, 215–16, 260 n91, 269 n54, 278 n32, 286 n187
aequitas naturae *sv* natura
affectus *sv* adfectus
akineta 49, 156, 179
allegoria 10–11, 12, 25–8, 35–7, 52–3, 106–18, 118–26, 126–33, 179, 181, 185–8, 190, 211, 213–15, 223
ambiguitas *sv* obscuritas
amor 48, 202–4
amphibologia 36, 175, 186, 233 n5, 264 n145
amplificatio (copia) 32, 50–1, 62, 75, 141, 145–7, 158, 171, 174, 185, 186, 188, 200, 220, 269 n54
analogia *sv* similitudo
antiquitas *sv* vetustas
aptum (decorum) 12, 67–8, 170, 176–84, 192, 197, 200, 222–3, 279 n44
argumentatio *sv* probatio
ars (artifex) 39, 45–6, 92, 139–41, 142, 171, 176, 185, 193–4, 218, 277 n10
auctor, auctoritas 73, 81, 86, 89, 90, 95, 147, 166, 173, 198, 204, 221, 244 n5, 252 n110

balbultire 107, 123–4, 132–3, 263 n126
benevolentia 49, 177, 205
bonae litterae 78–81, 83–4, 92, 102, 104, 110, 120, 130–1, 135, 212–13

caput *sv* status
caritas 35, 38, 42, 53, 54–5, 57, 111–12, 118, 120, 132, 151–3, 161, 166, 198, 202–3, 208–10, 215, 220–1, 225–7, 260 n91
character orationis *sv* genera elocutionis
chorismos-methexis 100–1, 107, 122, 125
circumstantia *sv* varietas
collatio 24, 37–8, 51, 52, 59, 114–16, 127, 164, 178–81, 187, 190, 195, 196, 215, 222, 260 n84, 279 n50
– visibilium ad invisibilia 27–8, 103, 212

commodum, commoditas 45, 50, 144, 178, 182–4, 205, 222–3
concio 40
consensus 9, 52, 98, 149, 164–6, 173, 174, 182, 221, 270 n69
consilium *sv* prudentia
consuetudo *sv* usus
consummatio *sv* partes operis (divisio)
contraria (dissimilia, pugnantia) 49, 55, 114, 174
conventio 178–9, 181
copia *sv* amplificatio
curiositas (impia) 122, 280 n71

decorum *sv* aptum
delectare *sv* officia in dicendo
detorquere 52, 265 n148
dialectica 3, 6–7, 22–3, 32, 38–9, 67–8, 194–7
dialogismon 196
dispositio (ordo, oikonomia) 11–12, 47, 50, 73, 136–8, 142–8, 155–6, 169–71, 174, 195–6, 211–12, 218, 219, 244 n5, 267 n33
dissimilia *sv* contraria
dissimulatio 33, 123, 199, 263 n122, 281 n84
divisio *sv* partes operis
docere *sv* officia in dicendo
docilitas 45, 198

ellipsis 128, 172, 220, 264 n145
elocutio 12, 50, 56, 136–7, 169–76, 196, 221–7, 277 n10
emphasis 36, 51, 185, 186
enthymema 195, 225, 284 n145
epoché 21, 126
ethos (pathos) 32, 78–9, 121, 144, 189, 201–2, 225
evangelium 43–4, 98, 149–50, 156–62
evidentia 51, 172, 174, 187, 188, 189, 203, 278 n32

exemplum *sv* similitudo
exordium *sv* partes operis (divisio)
expedientia 45, 176, 184, 189–200, 205–6

fabula 32, 82, 142, 149–51, 216–17, 219, 220, 250 n96
festivitas *sv* jucunditas
fictio *sv* similitudo
fides 35, 38, 41, 57–8, 77, 90, 91, 120, 127, 131–2, 152–4, 166, 192, 208–10, 217–18, 226–7
figurae (schemata) 36, 51–2, 171–2, 184–8, 223–4
finis 41, 130, 183, 217, 251 n104
fontes 37, 52, 66, 80, 212, 244 n5
fortitudo 54, 120, 153, 208, 226

genera elocutionis (genus humile, mediocre-moderatum, grande) 52, 143–4, 171, 189–90
genera orationis (causarum) 47, 143–4, 170–1, 218, 224, 248 n55
 – genus forense (judiciale) 47, 143, 170, 201, 224
 – genus suasorium (deliberativum) 47–8, 56, 120, 170, 173, 185, 190, 206, 224, 249 n80
 – genus encomiasticum (laudativum) 47, 51, 190, 224
genus-species (partes) 49, 53, 131, 153, 154, 258 n50
gradus, gradatio 37, 48, 50, 142, 156, 181, 183, 219, 244 n5, 260 n90, 268 n37
gravitas 36, 51, 189

harmonia 11, 34, 109, 120, 148–51, 164–7, 182, 197, 217, 219
homo pro se 16, 126, 233 n5
honestum 12, 48, 80, 200, 205–8, 225–6

humanitas 23, 62–4, 81, 104, 109, 212
hyperbaton 36, 186
hyperbole 36, 128, 172, 185, 186, 220, 264 n145

imago *sv* similitudo
imitatio 31, 46, 73–4, 108, 112, 123, 126, 138–40, 147, 166, 212, 218, 248 n54, 267 n19
incrementum *sv* partes operis (divisio)
ingenium 112, 164
initium *sv* partes operis (divisio)
instauratio 85, 108, 161, 207, 212, 252 n111, 278 n27
inventio 11–12, 47–9, 50, 73, 135–42, 152, 169–70, 212, 218, 247 n52, 266 n15
ironia 36, 185, 186, 281 n84

jucunditas (festivitas, venustas, voluptas) 12, 36, 47, 50, 51, 52, 53, 79, 171, 172, 173, 178, 187–90, 223, 249 n83
judaizare 160, 259 n79
judicium *sv* prudentia
justitia 54–5, 120, 153, 208, 226

lex 12, 54, 98, 156–62, 184, 196, 200, 206–7, 226, 262 n107
lingua 35–6, 46, 61–71, 135–6
littera-spiritus 95–101, 102–3, 118–19, 213–15
loci (topoi) 6, 8, 11, 13, 25, 37–8, 40, 49–50, 51, 54, 56, 58–9, 73, 74, 136, 142, 145–6, 147–8, 150, 151–6, 157, 169, 180–1, 186, 196, 211–12, 217–18, 247 n52, 266 n6

mediocritas (moderatio) 12, 36, 57, 66, 70, 127, 128, 133, 143–4, 153, 160–1, 163, 172, 174, 182–4, 196, 200, 208, 216, 219, 226, 264 n135, 277 n22, 280 n71
– oblivio mediocritatis 41, 160, 196
memoria 38, 47, 50, 56, 122, 136–7, 141, 170, 243 n91, 276 n8
metamorphosis 110, 113
metaphora 51–2, 72, 116, 183, 185, 186–7, 223
methexis *sv* chorismos
methodus *sv* via
moderatio *sv* mediocritas
modus (modulatio) 39, 50, 144, 178, 182–4, 222–3
movere *sv* officia in dicendo

natura 10, 46, 65–6, 85, 89, 92–3, 109, 119–21, 139–41, 142, 161–2, 193–4, 201–2, 206–7, 216, 225–6
– aequitas naturae 12, 37, 89, 120–1, 127, 130, 149, 151, 206–7, 215–16, 261 n104, 262 n107
necessitas, necessaria 53, 207, 226, 287 n215
neoterici (recentiores; *see also* dialectica) 18–19, 22–3, 38–9, 68, 80, 122

oblivio mediocritatis *sv* mediocritas
obscuritas (ambiguitas) 53, 174–5, 222, 261 n97
occasio *sv* opportunitas
officia in dicendo 39, 47, 56, 141, 144, 170–1, 190, 201, 224
– docere (probare) 41–5, 47, 74, 78–9, 132, 190–1, 209, 248 n55
– delectare (conciliare) 47, 69, 74, 78–9, 121, 132, 172, 189–90, 209, 248 n55, 249 nn80, 83
– flectere (movere) 47, 74, 78–9, 132, 172, 189–90, 201, 209, 248 n55, 249 n83
omnia omnibus 34, 108, 144, 215
opinio 194–5, 225

302 Index of Technical Terms

opportunitas (occasio, tempus) 37, 154, 198–200, 225, 285 n170
orbis 34, 37, 83, 127, 130, 142–3, 148–50, 153–4, 166, 216, 219
ordo *sv* dispositio
ornatus 178, 184–91, 223, 279 n44

parabola *sv* similitudo
partes operis 39, 47, 170
- exordium 47
- narratio 47
- divisio 47, 50, 143, 144, 170, 220, 276 n9; exordium (initium), incrementum (progressus), summa (comsummatio, perfectio) 11, 50, 137, 142–5, 152, 162, 217, 219, 250 n96, 260 n90, 268 n52
- confirmatio 47, 170
- confutatio 47, 170
- conclusio 47, 50, 170, 201
pathos *sv* ethos
perfectio *sv* partes operis (divisio)
perspicuitas 50, 51, 171–4, 176, 188, 189, 222
perturbatio *sv* turba
philosophia Christi (Christiana) 20, 26, 29, 31, 41, 45, 57, 77, 84, 87, 99, 121, 148, 216–17, 255 n9
pietas 20, 31, 41, 45, 50, 67, 86, 88, 91, 127, 132, 162, 174, 202–3, 207, 225, 260 n91
praeposterum judicium *sv* prudentia
probabilitas 24, 49, 172, 173, 188, 189, 195
probatio (argumentatio, propositio) 32, 163, 173, 190–1, 195
progressus *sv* partes operis (divisio)
progymnasmata 91, 258 n57
pronuntiatio (actio) 47, 50, 56, 136–7, 169–70, 184, 243 n91

propositio *sv* probatio
prudentia 40–1, 47, 54, 57, 92, 153, 154, 177, 188, 191–200, 201, 205, 208, 214, 224–5, 226, 259 n70, 261 n104, 277 n22, 282 nn126, 134
- judicium 7, 22, 40–1, 47, 52, 54, 57, 92, 188, 193–7, 208, 224–5, 226, 283 n139; praeposterum judicium 41, 44, 160–1, 196–7, 204, 225, 274 n124
- consilium 41, 47, 54, 57, 188, 193–8, 224–5, 283 n139
pugnantia *sv* contraria
puritas 38, 40–1, 42, 67, 68, 85, 89–92, 150, 173–4, 195, 221, 278 n27

rapere 30, 47, 201, 241 n72, 260 n91
ratio 23, 50, 173, 181, 194–5, 199–200, 208, 221, 225, 272 n100
- ratiocinatio 51, 52, 145, 173, 195–6, 225
resipiscentia 244 n8
rusticitas 132–3

sacrae litterae 29, 81–9, 99–101, 102, 104, 130–1, 213–14
sapientia 28, 33, 40, 92, 195
schemata *sv* figurae
scientia 40, 195, 225
scopus 10, 13, 28, 33, 38, 48, 56, 84, 89, 95, 122–3, 125, 131, 148, 150, 156, 158, 164, 181, 211–12, 213, 216, 220, 251 n104
sensus 37, 52–3, 101–6, 136, 188, 214
- historicus 11, 37, 52–3, 88–9, 101–6, 128–9, 131, 136, 147, 154, 157, 188, 214
- tropologicus 11, 37, 52–3, 88–9, 92, 101–6, 121, 130–2, 136, 147, 154, 157, 188, 214

Index of Technical Terms 303

– allegoricus 11, 37, 52–3, 88–9, 92, 101–6, 121, 126–33, 136, 147, 154, 157, 188, 214
– anagogicus 37, 52–3, 101, 103–4, 188, 214
sententia 40, 47, 51, 187
sermo (verbum) 40, 76, 81–3, 89, 176
similia similibus 11, 90, 107–8, 116, 128, 144, 202, 215
similitudo (analogia, exemplum, fictio, imago, parabola) 33, 35, 49, 51–2, 75, 112–18, 119, 186–7, 189–90, 263 n122, 275 n143
simplicitas 32, 33, 57, 90, 150, 154, 184, 192, 216
simulatio 263 n122
species *sv* genus
spes 54, 151, 153, 203, 205, 208–9, 217, 226
spoliatio Aegyptiorum 27
status (caput) 32, 48, 162–3, 244 n5, 251 n104
summa *sv* partes operis (divisio)
supercilium 41, 160, 196, 274 n124
superstitio 41, 128–9, 159–60, 193, 196, 221, 270 n75, 274 n124
synecdoche 36, 52, 185–6

temperantia 55, 57, 120–1, 143, 153, 184, 200, 208, 226
tempus *sv* opportunitas
topoi *sv* loci
turba (perturbatio) 97, 196, 201, 246 n25, 286 n186

turpia 207, 226, 254 n5
typus 37, 52, 181, 188, 274 n118

usus (consuetudo) 23, 25, 38, 46, 139–40, 173, 207, 218, 221
utilitas 12, 23–4, 48, 69, 104, 127, 130, 145, 183, 200, 205–7, 223, 225

varietas (circumstantia) 11, 33–4, 41, 49, 52, 54, 56, 59, 162–6, 197–8, 202, 206, 214, 217, 219, 244 n5
vehementia (acrimonia) 12, 50, 51, 52, 171–2, 178, 187–90, 223
venustas *sv* jucunditas
verbum *sv* sermo
verbum-res 27, 71–8, 89, 128, 141, 169, 178, 212
vetustas (antiquitas) 52, 173–4, 221
via (methodus) 12, 155–6, 218, 219, 272 n100
vir bonus 91, 177, 245 n17, 279 n46
virtus (vitia) 23, 24–5, 39, 42–3, 44, 48, 54–5, 57, 106, 120–1, 131–2, 152, 170, 176–7, 188, 203–5, 205–10, 216–17, 225–7, 277 n22
voluptas *sv* jucunditas
vulgus 45, 67, 129, 196–7, 246 n25, 286 n186

Erasmus Studies

A series of studies concerned with Erasmus and related subjects

1 *Under Pretext of Praise: Satiric Mode in Erasmus' Fiction*
   Sister Geraldine Thompson

2 *Erasmus on Language and Method in Theology*
   Marjorie O'Rourke Boyle

3 *The Politics of Erasmus: A Pacifist Intellectual and His Political Milieu*
   James D. Tracy

4 *Phoenix of His Age: Interpretations of Erasmus, c 1550–1750*
   Bruce Mansfield

5 *Christening Pagan Mysteries: Erasmus in Pursuit of Wisdom*
   Marjorie O'Rourke Boyle

6 *Renaissance English Translations of Erasmus: A Bibliography to 1700*
   E.J. Devereux

7 *Erasmus as a Translator of the Classics*
   Erika Rummel

8 *Erasmus' Annotations on the New Testament: From Philologist to Theologian*
   Erika Rummel

9 *Humanist Play and Belief: The Seriocomic Art of Desiderius Erasmus*
   Walter M. Gordon

10 *Erasmus: His Life, Works, and Influence*
   Cornelis Augustijn

11 *Interpretations of Erasmus, c 1750–1920: Man on His Own*
   Bruce Mansfield

12 *Rhetoric and Theology: The Hermeneutic of Erasmus*
   Manfred Hoffmann

www.ingramcontent.com/pod-product-compliance
Lightning Source LLC
Chambersburg PA
CBHW020355080526
44584CB00014B/1021